Alexander Hugh Hore

The Church In England

From William III. To Victoria

Alexander Hugh Hore

The Church In England
From William III. To Victoria

ISBN/EAN: 9783741152030

Manufactured in Europe, USA, Canada, Australia, Japa

Cover: Foto ©ninafisch / pixelio.de

Manufactured and distributed by brebook publishing software (www.brebook.com)

Alexander Hugh Hore

The Church In England

THE CHURCH IN ENGLAND

FROM

WILLIAM III. TO VICTORIA.

BY THE

REV. A. H. HORE, M.A.
TRINITY COLLEGE, OXFORD.

VOLUME I.

Parker and Co.
OXFORD, AND 6 SOUTHAMPTON-STREET,
STRAND, LONDON.
M DCCC LXXXVI

PREFACE.

THIS book is offered as a contribution to the cause of Church Defence. It commences with the time when by the Act of Toleration the Nonconformists began to be relieved from the intolerant laws imposed by the State; it ends with the time when they find themselves on a political equality with the Church. It commences with the time when religious Nonconformists thought that there ought to be a National Church, and sought to be comprehended (on their own terms) within its pale; it ends with the time when a small, but compact and somewhat noisy, band of political Dissenters teach that there ought *not* to be a National Church, and strive to compass its destruction.

For two hundred years—the period which this work embraces—successive governments have, with few intermissions, vied with each other in favouring the Dissenters to the prejudice of the Church. Not only has the State freed them from civil disabilities, but it has left them all their old rights, whilst releasing them from their duties; it has relieved them from the payment of Church-rates, it has allowed them to perform their marriages in their own chapels, and to bury their dead in the consecrated burial-grounds of the Church, and it has admitted them, at the Universities, to Fellowships and Headships, which were founded by Churchmen for teaching the religion of the Church of England. And yet at the very time when they have got all that they could reasonably have desired, and more than they had a right to expect, nothing short of the destruction of the Church will satisfy them.

The history of the Church of England is the history of England in a sense which does not apply to any other Institution in the country, and the Church has been for centuries England's strength. During a period of more than twelve hundred years the Church of England has preserved its identity, and during that time England has advanced from a group of small and divided kingdoms into a vast empire, on which the sun never sets, in every quarter of the globe; and love for their country demands from Englishmen a love for their Church. But of late years a society has arisen bearing the specious but misleading title of "The Society for the Liberation of Religion from State Patronage and Control," the members of which, no doubt through unacquaintance with Church History, sow misstatements broadcast over the land, with the view of educating people, who know no better, to their opinions, and inducing them to return members to Parliament who will vote for the Disestablishment and Disendowment, in other words, for the political destruction, of the Church of England.

These Liberationists, as they call themselves, profess to object on principle to established and endowed Churches, unmindful of the fact that Nonconformity is just as much established as the Church[a], and that (as the Church never was) Nonconformity has been endowed by the State[b]. Although numbering in their ranks unbelievers and atheists, they profess to be the friends of religion, and say that established Churches are contrary to Scripture; a strange assertion when God Himself sanctioned the

---

[a] See vol. i. p. 80.   [b] See vol. i. p. 414.

union between the Jewish Church and Jewish Nation. They advocate a voluntary system, but no system is so voluntary as that of the Church of England; its ancient endowments were all the voluntary gifts of Churchmen, and yet these are wholly insufficient unless supplemented by the free-will offerings of the congregations. They profess to be the friends of the people, and try to make them believe that they would be better off if the Church were disestablished; whereas they would be much worse off, for neither the farmer, nor the labourer, nor the working-man, pays at present anything for the ministrations of religion. They profess to be the friends of the poor, yet it is the poor who, more than any other class, would suffer if the Church were disestablished and disendowed; for if the Church, even *with* her endowments, is not able to defray the cost of all that is done and all that requires to be done, but wants more funds to meet the urgent calls which are made upon her, it is clear that, if those endowments were swept away, there would not be the present means of providing for poor districts, and that in order that they may be served as now, other important works must be starved, and schemes of extension crippled or abandoned. And then (to mention one other objection) these Liberationists allege that the Church has failed in her mission, whereas every one knows that the Church was never so active, never so prosperous, never did so great a work as it is doing in the present day.

The historical objections which Liberationists urge against the Church are grounded upon two fallacies. They would have people believe that the State or Parliament established and endowed the Church, and that what the State gave, it has the right to recall. So far from this being true, it would be more correct to say that the Church made the State and Parliament, for the present Church of England is two hundred and thirty years older than the State, and six hundred years older than Parliament; it was the Synods of the English Church which first suggested the idea of a National Parliament; the Canons passed in those Synods were the origin of our Statute-Law, and instead of the State having endowed the Church, Church property is incomparably the oldest form of property which exists [c].

---

[c] See vol. ii. pp. 484 and 485.

But again the Liberationists assert that the State having originally established and endowed one Church—the Roman Catholic—thought fit at the Reformation to disestablish and disendow that Church, to take away its property, and cathedrals, and churches, and to transfer them to a Protestant Church, the existing Church of England. The truth is that there never was a Roman Church (properly or legally so styled) in England; that no new Church was made and endowed at the Reformation, but only that the old Church was, as the word implies, *reformed*. Necessarily, if the old Church had been disestablished, and a new Church established in its place, some Act of Parliament, or some State document of equivalent weight, would show this; but the Liberationists can adduce none, for the reason that such a thing was never done, and consequently no such document exists; though precisely such evidence is producible for the occurrence of just this very proceeding, thrice over, in Scotland, in 1560, 1637, and 1690.

Such misstatements can be disposed of, and disposed of only, by an appeal to history. That such an appeal should be made needs no apology. The Author can urge one, and only one, advantage for the task which he has undertaken, and that is, that he neither holds nor would accept any preferment in the Church; so that he cannot on that account be accused of personal or interested motives. His only desire is that the truth may be known; and if he succeeds in setting before English Churchmen, particularly the more unlearned of their number, the true character and claims of their Church, the object of this book will be attained.

EASTBOURNE,
October, 1886.

CONTENTS.

INTRODUCTION.
THE CAUSES OF THE REVOLUTION.
FLOURISHING state of the Church at the commencement of James II.'s reign.—Why James lost the Throne.—His promises.—How he broke them.—His appointment of Roman Catholics to Church Preferments.—Magdalen College, Oxford.—The High Court of Commission.—First Publication of A Declaration for Liberty of Conscience.—Its Republication.—The Seven Bishops committed to the Tower.—Joy of the Nation on their acquittal.—Flight of James from England.

pp. 1—32

PART I.
THE CHURCH AT ITS HIGHEST POINT OF INFLUENCE.

CHAPTER I.
THE NEW DEFENDER OF THE FAITH.
William III. and Mary II. elected King and Queen.—Character of William.—His dislike to the English Church.—Defender of the Faith.—The Royal Supremacy in England.—Change in the Coronation Oath.—The meaning of the word Protestant.—Severity of the Penal Laws.—William favourable to Toleration.—The Bishops favour Toleration.—Difference between the Nonconformists at the Revolution and in the present day.—Nonconformists when in power violent opponents of Toleration . . . . pp. 35—60

CHAPTER II.
THE BIRTH OF TOLERATION.
Toleration and Comprehension.—The Toleration Act passed.—The House of Commons advise the summoning of Convocation.—Burnet opposed to the plan.—The King summons Convocation.—Commission to revise the Prayer-Book.—Extensive alterations proposed.—Convo-

CONTENTS.

cation.—The Lower House object to the English Church being designated *Protestant*.—Commencement of the disputes between the two Houses.—Failure of the Comprehension Scheme.—Change in the relations between Church and State.—Nonconformity established.
pp. 61—82

CHAPTER III.
THE FIRST GENERATION OF NONJURORS.

Fresh oaths to the new Government.—The Nonjuring Bishops.—The other Nonjurors.—Loss to the Church by their secession.—Archbishop Sancroft.—Bishop Ken.—Queen Anne offers to reinstate Ken.—Ken's refusal.—The 'pious' Robert Nelson . . pp. 83—109

CHAPTER IV.
THE LATITUDINARIAN BISHOPS.

Holland the Birth-place of Latitudinariansim.—Introduced into England by Hales and Chillingworth.—The Cambridge Platonists.—Latitudinarian Theology.—Gilbert Burnet, Bishop of Salisbury. — His writings.—The other Latitudinarian Bishops.—Tillotson Primate.—Dr. Sharp appointed to the See of York.—Death of Tillotson.—Tenison appointed his Successor.—Death of Queen Mary.—Two Commissions for Ecclesiastical Preferments.—Erastian policy of Tenison.—The King's Injunctions . . . . . . pp. 110—138

CHAPTER V.
THE EARLY TRINITARIAN AND THE CONVOCATION CONTROVERSIES.

Spread of Unitarianism and Deism.—Biddle.—Firmin.—The early Trinitarian Controversy. — Dr. Wallis. — Sherlock. — South. — Bingham.—The King's *Directions*.—The Letter to a Convocation Man.—The Convocation Controversy.—Wake.—Atterbury.—Kennet.—Gibson.—Convocation meets.—Disputes between the two Houses.—The Lower House censure Burnet's Exposition of the XXXIX. Articles.
pp. 139—160

CHAPTER VI.
STATE OF THE CHURCH UNDER WILLIAM III.

The seeds of immorality and irreligion sown under the Puritans.—Irreligion at the Revolution as depicted by the Nonjuror Kettlewell.

—Church Revival in William's reign.—The "Religious Societies."—The "Societies for the Reformation of Manners."—Failure of the Societies.—The "Society for Promoting Christian Knowledge."—The "Society for the Propagation of the Gospel."—Religion in the Colonies and America.—Dr. Bray.—George Keith.—The "Associates of Dr. Bray."—Charity Schools.—The Hon. Robert Boyle.—Severe Act passed against the Roman Catholics.—Death of the Duke of Gloucester.—The Crown vested, after the Princess Anne, in the House of Hanover.—Death of James II.—His son recognized by the King of France and the Pope as King.—Imposition of fresh oaths.—Death of the King.
pp. 161—185

CHAPTER VII.

THE HIGH CHURCH REACTION.

Queen Anne.—Her Character.—Dissolution of the Commission for Ecclesiastical Preferments.—Ascendancy of the Tories or Church Party.—Occasional Conformity.—Bill against Occasional Conformity.—The Bill defeated.—Ill-feeling amongst the Clergy.—Unpopularity of the Queen.—Queen Anne's Bounty.—Manœuvre of the Commons to get the Occasional Conformity Bill passed.—Defeat of the "Tackers," and of the Bill.—The "Church in danger."—Act of Union between England and Scotland.—Convocation prorogued.—Sacheverell.—His trial.—The result.—Popularity of the Church . . . pp. 186—214

CHAPTER VIII.

CONVOCATION IN THE REIGN OF QUEEN ANNE.

First Convocation of the Reign.—Small number of Bishops appointed in Queen Anne's Reign.—This accounts for the continued disputes between the two Houses.—Disaffection of the Church party to the Whig Government.—Letter from the Queen censuring the conduct of the Lower House.—Open quarrel between Burnet and the Prolocutor.—Prorogation of Convocation.—"Representation" of the Lower House.—The Queen pronounces it as an invasion of her supremacy.—Sentence of contumacy passed on the Prolocutor.—Convocation after the Sacheverell Riots.—Atterbury chosen Prolocutor.—Case of Whiston.—And of Dr. Clarke.—Atterbury appointed Bishop of Rochester.—Better feeling between the two Houses . . . pp. 215—236

CHAPTER IX.

THE CHURCH AT ITS HEIGHT.

The Occasional Conformity Bill passed.—Great influence of the Church.—Grant for building fifty new Churches.—Care of the Queen in the appointment of Bishops.—Dean Swift.—Dr. George Hooper.—Dr. Beveridge.—Dr. Bull.—Dr. Bull and the Quakers.—Sir Jonathan Trelawney.—Sir William Dawes, Archbishop of York.—The Queen's appointment of Bishops distasteful to the Whig Government.—Compton, Bishop of London.—The Church reaches its highest point since the Reformation.—Influence abroad.—Johann Ernst Grabe.—Daniel Ernst Jablouski.—Intolerant Act passed against Dissenters.—Death of the Queen . . . . pp. 237—266

PART II.
THE CHURCH AT ITS LOWEST POINT OF INFLUENCE.

CHAPTER I.
THE DECLINE OF THE CHURCH.

The decline of the Church throughout the Eighteenth Century.—Growth of Dissent.—Character of George I.—Of George II.—Of Queen Caroline.—Of Frederick, Prince of Wales.—The three Parties in the State.—Character of Sir Robert Walpole.—The promotion of Hoadly.—Evil effects of the suppression of Convocation.—The Bishops in the eighteenth century.—Letter of George III. to Archbishop Cornwallis.—Pluralities held by Bishops.—Many good Clergymen unknown to fame.—The general run of Clergy.—State of the Universities.—The general relaxation of morals.—Objections of the Liberationists, true of the eighteenth century but untrue now.

pp. 269—308

CHAPTER II.
THE SILENCING OF CONVOCATION.

Religion mixed up with Politics.—Feeling of the Universities.—Death of Burnet.—Archbishop Tenison.—Dr. Wake appointed his successor.—Hoadly.—The last Agenda of Convocation.—Its suppression.—The Bangorian Controversy.—The suppression of Convocation a national calamity.—Powers of Convocation abridged by the Act of Submission in the reign of Henry VIII.—The disputes between the two Houses.—Church indebted to the Lower House for having its Prayer-Book unmutilated.—Archbishop Wake.—Attempt for union between the Anglican and Gallican Churches.—Dr. Courayer.

pp. 309—340

CHAPTER III.

THE NONJURING SCHISM.

Hickes and Wagstaff appointed Suffragan Bishops for the Nonjurors.—Hickes in ordaining Bishops in the Province of Canterbury formally in Schism.—Short account of Hickes.—William Law.—Other Nonjurors.—The Nonjuring Bishops and the Patriarchs of the Oriental Church.—Schism in the Nonjuring bodies.—"The Usages."—Jeremy Collier.—The Nonjurors become extinct.—Important place held by them in Anglican Theology . . . . . pp. 341—366

CHAPTER IV.

THE DEISTICAL CONTROVERSY.

The supremacy of Reason established by Chillingworth.—Lord Herbert of Cherbury.—Hobbes the Patriarch of Freethinkers.—An impulse given to Freethinking by Locke.—René Descartes the parent of English Deism.—The principal English Deists of the eighteenth century.—Toland.—Lord Shaftesbury.—Collins.—Woolston.—Tindal. —Morgan.—Chubb.—Lord Bolingbroke.—Conyers Middleton.—Three Phases of English Deism.—Answers to the Deists.—Butler's Analogy.

pp. 367—397

CHAPTER V.

THE GROWTH OF TOLERATION.

The Dissenters urge their claims upon the Hanoverian Government. —Lord Stanhope's Bill.—Passed, after the Clauses for the abolition of the Test and Corporation Acts were withdrawn.—Quakers' Affirmation Bill.—Bishop Atterbury.—His banishment and death in Paris.—The Regium Donum to Dissenters.—Death of George I.—The Indemnity Acts.—Agitation of Dissenters for Repeal of Test and Corporation Acts.—Walpole's Dilemma.—Hoadly raised to the See of Winchester. —Walpole opposes the Repeal of the Test and Corporation Acts.— Quakers' Relief Bill.—Opposition in the country to *establishing* the

Jews.—The Fleet Clergy.—Lord Hardwicke's Marriage Act.—Change in the Calendar.—Death of George II.—Character of George III.—Church "Nullum Tempus" Bill.—Bill in favour of Dissenting Ministers and Schoolmasters.—Relief of the Roman Catholics.—The Gordon Riots . . . . pp. 398—440

CHAPTER VI.

LEADING CHURCHMEN OF THE PERIOD.

Potter, Archbishop of Canterbury.--Succeeded by two Latitudinarian Archbishops, Dr. Herring and Dr. Hutton.—Dr. Gilbert, Archbishop of York.—Secker, Archbishop of Canterbury.—Cornwallis, Archbishop of Canterbury.—Bishop Gibson, of London.—Bishop Sherlock.—Bishop Lowth.—Bishop Butler.—Warburton.—Bishop Hurd.—Bishop Zachary Pearce.--Bishop Horne.—The "Hutchinsonian" system.—Dr. Bentley.--"The good" Bishop Wilson, of Sodor and Man.—Bishop Hildesley . . . . . pp. 441--500

ERRATA IN VOL. I.

Page 1, *line* 11, *for* Revolution *read* Rebellion.
— 114, *line* 7, *for* fitted *read* filled.
— — *line* 20, *for* outward *read* outwardly.
— 118, *line* 23, *for* regarded *read* regarded him.
— 253, *line* 7, *for* scholar *read* preacher.
— 296, *note* ʳ, *for* P. II. *read* Pitt.
— 348, *line* 11, *for* unto *read* to.
— 371, *line* 3, *for* inferiority *read* superiority,
— 414, *line* 18 and *note* ˣ, *for* Domum *read* Donum.
— 492, *line* 18, *for* work *read* Church work.

INTRODUCTION.

The Causes of the Revolution.

NEVER did the Church stand higher in the affections of the nation, than when James II. ascended the throne of England. The character of Charles II. and of his Court had been as profligate as it well could be; but with all Charles's faults, one thing must be said in his favour,—that he never abused his Church Patronage; so that probably the Church never at one time boasted so noble an array of Divines as during his reign. Under these Caroline Divines wonderful strides had been made since the Revolution; the ruins effected by the Commonwealth had been repaired, and the Church was once more, not in name only, but in reality, the Church of the nation. "The Church of England," wrote the Nonjuror Kettlewell of the reign of James II., "was never known to be in a more flourishing condition than at this time."

When James became King of England, few people would have imagined that in less than four years he would be an exile. Never did a King of England begin his reign under better auspices. All animosity against him was buried, and he, whom only a few years before people wished, not only to be excluded from the throne, but proscribed and banished, found himself, in power and in the loyalty of his subjects, equal to any of his predecessors. How was it that so powerful a monarch fell so suddenly, broken "like an overgrown bubble, never to be recovered again [a]?"

"See there a man who has given up three kingdoms for a Mass [b]!" was the derisive language of the Archbishop of Rheims to the courtiers assembled in the residence of James at St. Germains. The Archbishop mistook, if he imagined that James lost the throne of England because he was a Roman Catholic. That James was a Confessor for his Faith, we cannot for a moment admit. He might be called a confessor for his bigotry, or his obstinacy, which amounted to insanity, or his unconstitutional measures; but Confessor for his Faith he certainly was not. James lost the throne of England, not because he was a Roman Catholic himself, but because he tried to force his religion by unlawful means on a reluctant people. It had been known all along that he was a Roman Catholic; it was known when it was proposed by the Exclusion Bill of 1680 to keep him from the throne; it was known when he came to the throne; yet the nation, though it hated Romanism

---

[a] Echard's Hist. of the Revolution.
[b] Voilà un homme qui a quitté trois royaumes pour une Messe.

much, hated Puritanism more, and was willing to be governed by a Roman Catholic, so long as he would keep his hands off the Church.

There is nothing to admire in the character of James at this period of his life. He was not an honest man. He bound himself by oath to defend the Church of England, and when Parliament, relying upon his oath, conferred on him a revenue which made him independent for life, he took the money, but broke his oath. Nor was he a religious man. He was scarcely more moral, although outwardly more decent, than his brother Charles, who used to laugh at him, because he said his mistresses were so ugly that they were inflicted upon him as penances by his Father Confessor. At the very time when he was displaying much zeal for the Church of Rome, he was living in the deepest immorality (in a sin which the Church of Rome equally with that of England condemns) with a woman (Catharine Sedley) whose delight it was to make profane jests against the Church, the clergy, and the doctrines which they preached [c]. "Is it possible," said his wife to him, "that you are ready to sacrifice a Crown for your Faith and cannot discard a mistress for it? Will you, for such a passion, lose the merit of your sacrifices [d]?"

---

[c] Catharine Sedley, afterwards created Countess of Dorchester.

[d] Mackintosh's English Rev. p. 55; Reresby's Memoirs, 356.

Still, bigot as he was, if James II. had only exercised common sense and common honesty he might not only have lived and died King of England, but, as he said himself, he "might have carried the kingdom's reputation yet higher in the world than ever it had been in the times of his ancestors."

The most loyal part of the nation were the clergy, and but for their opposition to the Exclusion Bill, James would long before have been an exile. "The clergy," says Burnet[e], "struck up a higher strain with such zeal for the Duke's succession, as if a Popish king had been a special blessing from Heaven to be much longed for by a Protestant Church." James, with his narrow mind and the stubbornness common to his family, trusted too much to their forbearance, and put upon the Divine Right and passive obedience a meaning which the clergy never meant them to convey. With regard to those doctrines, Church and Realm were at one. Whilst they would resign almost everything to the King, there was one thing which they would not resign, and that was their Church. If James had tampered with the civil freedom of the people, he would have met with but faint resistance; but with regard to the Church the feelings of all classes of the Community, Churchmen as well as Dissenters, admitted of no excessive authority and no encroachment from the Crown. In *civil*

---

[e] Own Times, ii. 501.

matters, *absolute* authority was the rule, but when the nation had to choose between their King and their Church, they threw over the former and clung to the latter [f].

Nothing could have been better than James' promises. As soon as he became King, he promised his Privy Council: "I shall make it my endeavour to preserve the government both in Church and State as it is *now* by law established." And this promise he repeated to his first Parliament on May 19, 1685. Parliament believed him, and unanimously resolved that, "This House doth acquiesce and entirely rely and rest wholly satisfied in his Majesty's gracious word and repeated declaration to support and defend the religion of the Church of England." The people believed him. "We have," they said, "the word of a King, and a word never yet broken." The Church believed him. Sharp [g] said in a sermon, "As to our religion, we have the word of a King, which (with reverence be it spoken) is as sacred as my text [h]." Addresses, and congratulations, and flattery flowed in upon him from all sides. The University of Oxford promised to obey him *without limitations or restrictions;* and when the Clergy of London appended to their address the proviso of "our religion established by law," they were looked upon as ill-bred.

---

[f] Fox's Hist. of James II. [g] Afterwards Archbishop of York.
[h] Life of Calamy, i. 118.

The Coronation Oath taken by James, and used for the last time in his case, was worded thus [1]:—Archbishop: "Sir, will you grant and keep and by your oath confirm to the people of England the laws and customs to them granted by the Kings of England, your lawful and religious predecessors; and, namely the laws, customs, and franchises granted to the Clergy by the glorious King St. Edward, your predecessor, according to the laws of God, the true profession of the Gospel *established in this kingdom*, and agreeing to the prerogatives of the King thereof, and the ancient customs of the Realm?" King: "I grant and promise to keep them." We will now shew how he kept his oath.

The first Sunday after his accession he attended Mass in St. James' Palace, and publicly proclaimed himself a Roman Catholic. Shortly afterwards he went out of his way and caused it to be published that the late King, Charles II., had died in communion with the Church of Rome, with full particulars as to how Father Huddlestone gave him Extreme Unction and the Holy Eucharist. So rash was this act, that even Pope Innocent XI. thought it necessary to remonstrate with him on his intemperate zeal; "he was highly pleased," he wrote, "with his Majesty's zeal for the Catholic religion, but he was afraid his Majesty might push it too far, and instead

---

[1] For the new oath prescribed by the Parliament of 1689, and taken by the Kings and Queens ever since, see next chapter.

of contributing to his own greatness, and to the advancement of the Catholic Church, he might come to do both it and himself the greatest prejudice by attempting that which his Holiness was well assured from long experience could not succeed [k]."

James was crowned on April 23rd, the feast of St. George, the Patron Saint of the Realm. Sancroft, the Archbishop of Canterbury, officiated at the ceremony; Turner, Bishop of Ely, preached the sermon. The King had ordered Sancroft to abridge the service, and Sancroft complied (a piece of culpable weakness of which he afterwards repented); the Holy Communion was omitted, as also the custom of presenting the Sovereign with the English Bible. The King made an offering on the altar; he appeared to join in the Litany, and received the Unction from the English Bishops.

James admitted a Papal Nuncio, one Ferdinando d'Adda, domestic Prelate to the Pope, into England, although the exercise of his office in that capacity was by the law of the land high treason. He allowed four Roman Catholic Priests to be publicly consecrated in the Chapel Royal under the title of Vicars Apostolic, and to exercise Episcopal Functions, whilst Roman Catholic Clergy appeared in their religious dresses at Whitehall and St. James', and made no

---

[k] Puffendorf, quoted Echard, Hist. of England, iii. 731.

scruple to declare that "they hoped in a little time to walk in procession through Cheapside."

The Test Act was particularly obnoxious to James, for he felt that it was passed not only against the Roman Catholics in general, but particularly against himself[1]. He determined, therefore, to repeal the Test Act, if possible by means of Parliament, and if not on his own authority. Accordingly in November, 1685, he announced to Parliament his intention to allow the Roman Catholics to serve in the army without taking the Test. It was undoubtedly a part of the Royal prerogative to remit the sentence or penalty decreed on any person for the violation of the Test Act. It was argued, therefore, that there is no difference in principle between the power of pardoning offenders against a statute, and the power of abrogating the penalties beforehand; that it is a mere detail of administration within the competence of the Sovereign to regulate. But this dispensing power had been recently defined and limited. Charles II., in 1662, and again in 1672, had claimed a similar dispensing power, but Parliament told him plainly

---

[1] The Test Act passed in 1673 made the reception of the Holy Communion at the hands of the Clergy of the Church of England the condition of obtaining or holding any appointment under Government. It was designed against Roman Catholics; but so eager were the Protestant Dissenters against Romanist dissenters that they willingly allowed themselves to be caught in the net, from the meshes of which they afterwards found it difficult to extricate themselves.

that he was exceeding his prerogative, and he had sense enough to withdraw from the false position which he had assumed. But James bent his ear to foolish counsellors. Cartwright, Dean of Durham, declared that the King's promises were free donatives, which ought not to be strictly examined, and which his Majesty should be allowed to interpret in his own manner; and with this advice James was so pleased that he rewarded him with the See of Chester, vacant by the death of the famous Pearson. So the King told Parliament, "I will deal plainly with you; after having had the benefit of their services in such a time of need and danger [m], I will neither expose them to disgrace nor myself to the want of them if there should be another rebellion to make them necessary to me." He declared that he would consider any man his enemy who should oppose the repeal of the Test Act, and when Parliament told him he was acting contrary to the law, he took the law into his own hands, and suspended the Act on his own authority. In vain Compton, Bishop of London, protested in his own name and in that of his brethren against this high-handed proceeding, as a violation of the Constitution; he was removed from his office of Dean of the Chapel Royal [n]. James prorogued Parliament, and never allowed it to re-

---

[m] Referring to Monmouth's rebellion.
[n] Evelyn's Diary, Jan. 1, 1686.

assemble, except to undergo the formalities of successive prorogations º.

At the end of 1686 the King sent Lord Castlemaine as Ambassador Extraordinary to Rome, with instructions "to reconcile the three kingdoms of England, Scotland, and Ireland to the Holy See, from which for more than an age they had revolted by means of the Northern heresy?" The Pope himself was opposed to this rash policy, and whenever the English ambassador appeared before him he received him with marked coolness P, and none of the Cardinals took more notice of him than good manners compelled them. Yet James bore this rebuff with the greatest meekness; the following year he caused the Papal Nuncio d'Adda to receive marks of great pomp and ceremony; not only was he consecrated Archbishop of Amasia in the Royal Chapel of Whitehall, but, amidst an extraordinary concourse of people, he had an interview with their Majesties at Windsor, and dined on Lord Mayor's day in company with the King at Guildhall. Such sights were seen as had not been witnessed in England for more than one hundred and fifty years; "the people with great indignation beheld a representation of the Pope in all his Pontificalibus preceded by a cross-bearer

---

º James treated Parliament much the same as his successors treated Convocation.

P He had always "a fit of coughing at his command." Echard, iii. 810.

and attended by a flock of Priests and Monks in the habits of their respective orders q," whilst their King fell on his knees in the presence of the whole Church to ask his blessing r.

At the end of the same year, or the beginning of 1687, he dismissed his faithful servant and relative, Lawrence Hyde, Lord Rochester, from the Treasury, because, although he would do everything else for him, he would not abandon his Church s.

Little doubt could be entertained as to the purpose on which the King had set his heart. As far, however, as he had as yet gone, he may be said to have been only acting in defence of his own Faith. We now come to other matters which shew that he was bent on the destruction of the Church of England. He claimed the right of appointing Roman Catholic clergy to high preferments in the Church of England. In 1686 he appointed Dr. Parker, who, if not a professed Roman Catholic, as was generally believed, was at any rate an open favourer of Rome, to the

---

q Kennet's Complete History, p. 494.

r Barillon, May, 1687.

s "The King," writes the Roman Catholic historian, Lingard, "complained to Barillon of the obstinacy and insincerity of the Treasurer, and the latter received from the French Envoy a very intelligible hint that the loss of office would result from his adherence to his religious Creed. He was, however, inflexible, and James after a long delay communicated to him, but with considerable embarrassment and many tears, his fixed determination."

Bishopric of Oxford [t]. Obadiah Walker, Master of University College, Oxford, with three of the Fellows and some Undergraduates, seceded from the Church in 1686 and received a dispensation [u], by virtue of which a Roman Catholic Chapel was established and Roman Mass celebrated in the College. Massey, a Roman Catholic, was appointed Dean of Christ Church, and thus became not only the Head of the most important College in the University, but also a high Dignitary in the Church. He refused the oaths of supremacy, but truth compels us to say that Aldrich, the Sub-dean, installed him without remonstrance, and accepted a dispensation in lieu of the oaths required by law [x].

The King next proceeded to attack the Universities, the two great centres of education which the Church of England possessed; and began with Cambridge. In 1687 he sent a mandamus ordering the Vice-Chancellor "to admit Alban Francis, a Bene-

---

[t] Father Petre, James's Confessor, writes: "The Bishop of Oxford has not yet declared himself openly; the great obstacle is his wife, whom he cannot rid himself of, his design being to continue Bishop and only change Communion." It appears, however, that on his death-bed Parker refused to declare himself a Roman Catholic.—Evelyn, i. 605.

[u] For refusing to draw up this warrant, "Mr. Finch, the Solicitor-General, was turned out, and one, Mr. Powis, put in his stead, who did what the other refused."—Reresby, 302.

[x] For more about this excellent Divine, Dean Aldrich, see under chapter on Convocation.

The Causes of the Revolution. 13

dictine monk, to the degree of M.A., without administering any oaths whatever, notwithstanding any law or statute to the contrary;" and the Vice-Chancellor, for refusing to comply with this demand, was brought before the Ecclesiastical Commission which James had revived, and suspended from his office and the Headship of his college.

But a far more important and more memorable invasion of rights took place with regard to Oxford. Magdalen College enjoyed one of the richest foundations in the kingdom. Upon the death of their President, James sent a mandamus to the Fellows to elect as President, "any statutes or customs notwithstanding," one named Farmer, a recent convert to Rome, a man of notoriously profligate character; and when he was forced on that account to withdraw him, he next ordered them to elect Parker, Bishop of Oxford[y]. The Fellows, however, had according to the rules of the College elected one of their own body, Dr. Hough, who was accordingly sworn and admitted as President. In consequence of this the President and all the Fellows, except two who signed the paper tendered to them by the Ecclesiastical Commission[z], were expelled; Bishop Parker became

---

[y] Oxford men may be interested in the fact that a son of Bishop Parker was the founder of the Publishing Firm in Broad-street, Oxford, which is still carried on by his descendants of the same name.

[z] One of these two, Charnock, was executed for High Treason

President, and when he shortly afterwards died, Bonaventure Giffard, a Roman Catholic Bishop *in partibus*, was appointed, and the College turned into a Roman seminary.

In the same year the King granted a dispensation to Edward Sclater, Rector of Esher and Curate of Putney, a recent convert to Rome, enabling him to hold his benefice, although he was personally relieved from all acts incompatible with his new religion [a]. Sclater's convictions, however, do not appear to have troubled him much, for in 1689, after the accession of William III., he returned to the Church of England [b].

Meanwhile, whilst James was endeavouring to propagate the Roman Catholic religion, he did all he could to prevent the Church of England defending itself. He issued an order to the Bishops "prohibiting all the inferior clergy from preaching on controversial points of divinity;" and it was in order to enforce this command that he revived the High Court of Commission [c], of which he appointed the

---

in the conspiracy for which Sir John Friend and Sir William Perkins suffered in 1696.

[a] This dispensation violated sixteen Acts of Parliament from 21 Henry VIII. to 17 Charles II. Mackintosh, 133.

[b] Dr. Horneck, who relates this incident, owns that "the juncture of time tempted him to smile." Mackintosh, *ibid.*

[c] By appointing the High Court of Commission James made a fresh departure which could not be palliated by his prerogative; he directly invaded an Act of Parliament (13 Car. II. 12)

The Causes of the Revolution. 15

infamous Jefferies the President. The other Commissioners appointed were Sancroft, Archbishop of Canterbury, Crewe, Bishop of Durham, Sprat, Bishop of Rochester, Lord Rochester, Lord Sunderland, and Sir Edward Herbert; and when Sancroft, on the plea of business and ill-health, declined to act, Cartwright, a creature of the Court, was substituted in his place [d]. Sharp, Rector of St. Giles' and Dean of Norwich, one of the leading clergy of the day [e], took occasion in a sermon to vindicate the Church of England; James thereupon ordered Compton, Bishop of London, to suspend him; and when Compton replied that it was impossible for him to suspend a clergyman unheard, he was himself brought before the Commission and suspended.

This action of the Commission only increased the defiance of the clergy. Not even the Pope, it was said, ever claimed such a jurisdiction as was asserted by James. Tillotson and Stillingfleet [f], two of the most eminent clergymen of the day, put themselves

---

repealing an Act (17 Car. I.) except as regards the abolition of the High Commission and the prohibition of the *future creation* of any like Court, which it affirmed.

[d] In consequence of this refusal, although his name was not absolutely struck out of the list of Privy Councillors, he was no longer summoned on Council Days: "If," said the King, "he is too sick or busy to go to the Commission, it is a kindness to relieve him from attendance at Council."   [e] See page 5.

[f] The former afterwards intruded Archbishop of Canterbury, the latter Bishop of Worcester.

at the head of the opposition; sermons against superstition were preached from every pulpit. Tracts in defence of the Church were scattered broadcast throughout the land.

We now come to the great crisis in James' history, the last straw which broke the patience of the Church, and drove him from the throne.

At an early period of the proceedings against the Universities, the King, no longer satisfied with granting dispensations for particular cases, determined by one general measure to suspend all Penal Laws and all Tests. Accordingly in April, 1687, he issued "A Declaration for Liberty of Conscience." The Preamble sets forth:—"That he cannot but heartily wish that all his subjects were members of the Catholic Church, yet in his opinion conscience ought not to be constrained;" and then, "By virtue of his Royal Prerogative, he thinks fit to issue forth his Declaration of Indulgence, making no doubt of the concurrence of his two Houses of Parliament, when he shall think it convenient for them to meet." At the same time he declared that "He will protect his Archbishops, Bishops, and Clergy and all other his subjects of the Church of England in the free exercise of their religion as by law established, and in the quiet and full enjoyment of their possessions." He further declared that as it was his will that none of his subjects should be under a disability by reason of Tests and Oaths, "That it was his will and pleasure

The Causes of the Revolution.

that the Oaths of Supremacy and Allegiance and the several Tests and Declarations mentioned in the Acts of Parliament in the 25th and 30th year of his Brother's reign, shall not hereafter be required to be Taken, Declared, or Subscribed by any persons whatsoever who are or shall be employed in any office or place of trust, either civil or military, under him or in his government; and it is his intention from time to time hereafter to grant his Royal Dispensations to all his subjects to be employed, who shall not take the same oaths, or Declare the said Tests or Declarations."

On April 27, 1688, the King republished his Declaration; and this renewed Declaration would have passed off as quietly as the first, had it not been followed on May 4 by the following Order in Council: "At the Court, Whitehall, May 4th,—It is this day ordered by his Majesty in Council that his Majesty's late gracious Declaration bearing date the 27th April last be read at the usual time of Divine Service on the 20th and 27th of this month in all Churches and Chapels within the City of London and Westminster and ten miles thereabout; and upon the 3rd and 10th of June next in all other Churches and Chapels throughout the Kingdom. And it is hereby further ordered that the Right Reverend the Bishops cause the said Declaration to be sent and distributed throughout their several and respective Dioceses to be read accordingly."

Such a violation not only of the rights of the Church but of the laws of the Realm excited universal indignation amongst all classes of the community, Whigs as well as Tories, Dissenters as well as Churchmen. James had for his own purposes chosen a most inopportune time for the Declaration. His intimate friend and ally, Louis XIV. of France, had lately revoked the Edict of Nantes, and a crowd of decrees against the Protestants appeared in rapid succession. In a few months fifty thousand families, and those amongst the most intelligent and industrious of the population, had left France for ever, many of them to seek an asylum in England. The memory of the St. Bartholomew Day of 1572 was revived. One cry of grief and rage rose from the whole of Protestant Europe. Louis had, like James, boasted of toleration, yet he was now avowedly a persecutor of the Reformed Faith. Nothing could have been more disastrous to James; he declared publicly that he disapproved of the treatment of the Huguenots and granted them relief from his privy purse. But his designs were too transparent. Whatever reason James alleged, it was evident to all that his object was to divide the Church against itself, and to turn the Protestant Dissenters against the Church, so that his scheme in behalf of the Roman Catholics might meet with less opposition[g].

---

[g] Reresby, 372.

The Causes of the Revolution. 19

James thought that whilst the great bulk of the clergy would follow their theory of the Divine Right, the Dissenters, whom before he had bitterly persecuted, would be blinded by the prospect of toleration and side with him against the Church. He mistook on both points. It is true that when the Declaration was first published, and before its tendency was fully understood, the Nonconformists had wavered for a time, and about sixty addresses of thanks had been presented to the King [h]. But the more venerable amongst the Dissenters, such as Baxter, and Howe, and Bunyan, from the first remained true to the cause of freedom, and refused an Indulgence which could only be purchased by a violent overthrow of the law. Six Bishops, viz. Parker of Oxford, Cartwright of Chester, Barlow of Lincoln, Crewe of Durham, Wood of Lichfield [i], and Watson of St. David's [k], addressed James in thanks for the Declaration. When, therefore, the Declaration was republished, every eye throughout the kingdom was turned towards the Bishops. Little time was given them for deliberation. Sancroft, Archbishop of Canterbury, a Tory in politics, a man of a naturally quiet and retiring spirit, seeing the Church's danger, hesitated not a moment, but after consulting with some

---

[h] The Dissenters "caught greedily at the bait without discerning the hook in it."—Kennet's Comp. Hist., iii. 489.
[i] Suspended by Sancroft for immorality.
[k] Deprived for simony.

of the Bishops and of the London clergy summoned such Prelates as could arrive on so short a notice, together with some of the leading clergy, to meet him at Lambeth[1]. In compliance with the Archbishop's letter a meeting was held at Lambeth on May 18. Mew, Bishop of Winchester, was too old to undertake so long a journey; the letter to Lloyd, Bishop of Norwich, was stopped by the Postmaster, so that he was prevented from arriving in time; seven Bishops, however, besides the Primate, and several of the leading clergy, were present[m]. They resolved:—"That the point was not whether a Toleration was a lawful or expedient thing; but they judg'd the Matter of the Declaration to be altogether illegal; because a power to dispense, not only in some contingent cases, but was to dispense with all

---

[1] The following is his letter preserved in his own handwriting: "My Lord, This is only in my name and in the name of some of our brethren now here in this place, earnestly to desire you immediately upon the receipt of this letter to come hitherto with what convenience and speed you can, not taking notice to any that you are sent for. Wishing you a prosperous journey and us all a happy meeting, I remain your loving brother."—Gutch's Collectanea Curiosa, i. 329.

[m] These seven Prelates were Compton, Bishop of London, Lloyd, of St. Asaph, Ken, of Bath and Wells, Turner, of Ely, Lake, of Chichester, White, of Peterborough, Trelawney, of Bristol; and the following clergy, Tillotson, Dean of Canterbury, Stillingfleet, Dean of St. Paul's, Patrick, Dean of Peterborough, Tenison, Rector of St. Martin's, Sherlock, Master of the Temple, and Grove, Rector of St. Andrew's, Undershaft.

sorts of laws, in cases contrary to the very end and design of making of them. So that this was not properly a dispensing but a disannulling power, that directly tended to the Total Subversion of government and making that to be an Arbitrary which by the Constitution was a Legal Administration."

They accordingly agreed that the Declaration ought not to be read, and a "humble Petition," drawn up in Sancroft's hand-writing, was signed by him and six of the Bishops (Compton, Bishop of London, being under suspension, did not sign); and as there was no time to be lost (for it was Friday and the King had ordered the Declaration to be read on the following Sunday), at ten o'clock that same night the six Bishops (Sancroft on account of his refusing to act on the Ecclesiastical Commission having been forbidden the Court) obtained an interview with the King in his bed-chamber and presented their Petition. The words of the Petition were :—" That the great averseness found in themselves to their distributing and publishing in all their churches your Majesty's late Declaration for Liberty of Conscience, proceeds neither from any want of duty and obedience to your Majesty (our holy mother, the Church of England, being both in her principles and her constant practice unquestionably loyal, and having to her great honour been more than once publickly acknowledged to be so by your Gracious Majesty), nor yet from any want of tenderness to Dissenters, in relation to whom we are willing to come to such a temper as shall be thought fit, when the matter shall be considered and settled in Parliament and Convocation; but among many other considerations, from this especially, because that Declaration is founded upon such a dispensing power as hath been often declared illegal in Parliament, and particularly in the years 1662 and 1672, and in the beginning of your Majesty's reign, and is a matter of so great moment and consequence to the whole Nation, both in Church and State, that your Petitioners cannot in prudence, honour, or conscience so far make themselves parties to it, as a distribution of it all over the Nation, and the solemn publication of it once and again, even in God's House, and in the time of Divine Service, must amount to in common and reasonable construction." It concluded with the words, "Your Petitioners must, therefore, most humbly and earnestly beseech your Majesty that you will be graciously pleased not to insist upon the distributing and reading your Majesty's said Declaration. And your Petitioners shall ever pray [n]." The King received

---

[n] On two copies of the Petition were the following subscriptions; "Approbo, H. London, May 23, 1688; May 23, W. Norwich: May 21, R. Gloucester; May 26, Seth Sarum; P. Winchester; Tho. Exon, May 29, 1688." Of the remaining Sees, York and Oxford were vacant; six Bishops allowed the Decla-

the Petition with much anger, and called it a standard of rebellion. He told them that "he was their King and they should feel what it was to disobey him." The Bishops remained firm; their answer was, "The will of God be done." That night the Petition was printed (by what means or by whom was unknown) and cried about the streets of London, and soon all England knew that the Bishops had withstood the illegal measures of the King.

The next day was Sunday. The Churches were crowded with people anxious to see what the clergy would do. In London, only four Clergymen read the Declaration, one of whom was Timothy Hall, one of the meanest and most obscure of the City Divines [o], who soon afterwards was promoted to the See of Oxford for his compliance. When Sprat, who with the See of Rochester held the Deanery of Westminster, began to read it, the congregation left the Abbey, and his hands so shook that he could scarcely hold the document. A letter supposed to be the work of Lord Halifax, stating "Reasons against reading the Declaration," was sent to every clergyman in the Kingdom, and powerfully affected the country clergy. "If we read the declaration," it said, "we fall to rise no more. We fall unpitied and despised. We fall amidst the curses of a nation whom our compliance

---

ration; Cartwright, Bishop of Chester, went beyond the rest in voting an address of thanks to the King.

[o] Kennet, iii. 491.

will have ruined ᵖ." Of ten thousand clergy throughout England, only some two hundred read it, and the greater part of the congregations walked out of Church ᵠ. On the following Sunday the opposition was even more general.

The King became alarmed. But his evil genius, Jefferies, stood in his path, and by his advice on May 27 a summons was dispatched to the Archbishop and the six other Bishops to appear before his Majesty on June 8 to answer for a misdemeanour. About 5 p.m. on the appointed day the seven Prelates arrived at Whitehall, and were told that they would be put upon their trial in Westminster Hall, for the Petition, and were required to enter into recognizances. This, however, as Peers of Parliament, they refused, and were committed to the Tower as "seditious libellers of his Majesty and his government." They were conveyed to the Tower by water, that being considered the quietest and safest route, and never perhaps was such a scene witnessed on the Thames as during their passage to and from the Tower. "Of the immense concourse of people,"

ᵖ Macaulay's Hist., ii. 355.

ᵠ Crewe, Bishop of Durham, who was one of the Ecclesiastical Commissioners, is said to have suspended nearly two hundred of his clergy for refusing to read it. Samuel Wesley, father of John and Charles, who was at that time a Curate in London, is reported to have preached from Daniel iii. 18, "Be it known unto thee, O king, that we will not serve thy gods, nor worship the golden image which thou hast set up."

wrote the Papal Nuncio, "who received them on the banks of the river, the majority in their immediate neighbourhood were on their knees; the Archbishop laid his hands upon such as he could reach, exhorting them to continue stedfast in the faith; they cried aloud that all should kneel, while tears flowed from the eyes of many." Even the soldiers who kept guard at the Tower, writes Reresby[r], drank very often their healths, and when the Lieutenant of the Tower, Sir E. Hales, ordered them to desist, they refused to obey.

Immediately on their arrival at the Tower, they attended Evensong in the Chapel, and the words of the Second Lesson must have seemed singularly adapted to their case: "In all things approving ourselves as the ministers of God, in much patience, in afflictions, in distresses, in stripes, in imprisonments." Their trial, to which they were accompanied by half the Peers of England[s], took place in Westminster Hall on June 29. The jury were packed, the judges were mere tools of the Crown, one being a Roman Catholic; but judges and jury were both overawed by the indignation of the people at large[t]. Of the judges two pronounced the Petition a libel, whilst the other two held that the King had no such dispensing power as he claimed. The jury were locked up all night. Not a candle was allowed them where-

---

[r] Reresby, 390.   [s] Mackintosh, 266.
[t] Green, Hist. ii. 24.

with to light their pipes, and when in the morning
water was brought them for washing, so consumed
were they with thirst, that they eagerly lapped up
the whole[u]. At first nine of them were in favour
of, and three against, the Bishops. This minority
dwindled down to one: Arnold, the King's brewer,
felt himself in a pitiful dilemma; if he found them
not guilty, he would no longer brew for the King,
if he found them *guilty*, he would brew for no one
else. It was six o'clock in the morning before he
yielded.

The Court reassembled at ten. Sir Roger Langley,
the foreman of the jury, immediately pronounced the
verdict of Acquittal. The verdict was everywhere
received with the wildest enthusiasm. In a moment
ten thousand people who crowded the great Hall
replied with a shout which made the old oaken roof
crack[x]; in yet another moment the innumerable
multitudes outside raised a cheer which was heard
at Temple Bar. The boats which crowded the
Thames gave an answering cheer. "The universal
joy," writes Mrs. Prowse, the daughter of Dr. Hooper,
Rector of Lambeth, whose guest Bishop Ken was,
"was so great as to be heard at many miles distance,
and the shout given at Westminster Hall at their
deliverance to have almost the same effect at Lambeth upon the windows as the discharge of a cannon

---

[u] Macaulay, ii. 385.   [x] Memoirs of Mrs. Prowse.

gives." She tells us that Bishop Ken travelled to Lambeth in the Archbishop's coach; that they travelled "over London Bridge and Southwark, which took several hours, as the concourse of people was innumerable the whole way, hanging upon the coach, and insisting upon being blessed by those two Prelates."

The King had on that morning gone to visit the camp on Hounslow Heath. The news spread like lightning to the garrison, and the shouts of joy from the soldiers first conveyed the unwelcome tidings to the King. He asked what the cheering meant, and was told that it was nothing but the soldiers shouting upon the acquittal of the Bishops. "And do you call that nothing?" he said, "but so much the worse for them." But that shout told him more than he liked to confess; he knew that he stood alone in the kingdom, the Peerage, the Gentry, the Bishops, the Clergy, the Universities, he knew that he had alienated all, that all stood aloof from him; and now the very soldiers which he had himself raised forsook him.

At night the whole of London was one blaze of light; bonfires were lighted in every street, around which were assembled crowds drinking health to the Bishops and confusion to the Papists; rows of seven candles, the middle one higher than the rest to represent the Archbishop, lighted up every window, and not till the Sunday dawned and the Church bell summoned the early worshippers to its services, did the crowds disperse or the fires languish. Never before did the Church stand higher in the estimation of the people, whether Churchmen or Dissenters; it was to the Church the State was indebted for the termination of that struggle which had continued for nearly a hundred years, the struggle between the Crown and the people; it was the Church that had won the victory for Church and State; the Bishops were represented as the saviours of the liberties of the people, and were compared (somewhat irreverently it must be confessed) to the Seven Golden Candlesticks and to the Seven Stars at Christ's right hand.

But whilst these important events were occurring, on June 10 (that is two days after the Bishops were committed to the Tower) another event of the greatest importance had taken place, and all London was thrown into excitement by the intelligence that the Queen had given birth to a son and heir to the throne.

On the very day that the Bishops were acquitted, an invitation signed in cypher by seven of the leading men in England, one of whom was Compton, Bishop of London[y], was dispatched into Holland

---

[y] These were Shrewsbury, Devonshire, Danby, Lumley, Russell, Sydney, and Compton. With regard to this, Compton undoubtedly was guilty of equivocation to James, which must

calling on the Prince of Orange, the nephew and son-in-law of James, to come over with an army strong enough to justify their rising in arms.

Still unwarned by the popular feeling, the King followed on his mad course. In vain the most devoted Roman Catholics implored him to give way, for now he had brought matters to such a pass that to give way meant nothing short of the reversal of every action of his reign. His temper was only spurred to a more dogged obstinacy. "I will lose all or win all," he said to the Spanish Ambassador. He dismissed the two judges who had favoured the acquittal of the Bishops. He ordered the Archdeacons throughout England to report the clergy who had refused to read the Declaration. The Archdeacons made common cause with the Bishops, and only one sent in a report. Sprat, Bishop of Rochester, unwilling any longer to share its odium, resigned his place on the Ecclesiastial Commission. James sent a mandate to Oxford to elect the odious Jefferies as Chancellor of the University; but the University had foreseen the danger, and had already elected the young Duke of Ormond just before the King's messenger arrived. And he nominated Timothy Hall, who had no recommendation whatever, beyond his having read the Declaration, to the See of Oxford.

---

always be a stain on his character. Echard says, iii. 879, "Several of the Bishops wrote invitations."

Not until warned by the King of France[1] of the danger to be apprehended from the Prince of Orange did James become sensible of his position. He then saw that his only hope lay in the Church of England, and he determined to call to his assistance those very Bishops whom he had used so ill[a]. The Bishops after more than one interview, gave him the best advice in their power[b]. He thanked them, and he followed their advice just so far as he felt inclined, and no further, and thought thus to regain the affections of the people. He removed the suspension of the Bishop of London; he dissolved the Ecclesiastical Commission; he reinstated the Church of England magistrates whom he had deprived of office, and he ordered the Bishop of Winchester to restore the President and Fellows of Magdalen; and by his request the Archbishop drew up some collects to be used in the churches during the threatened danger.

---

[1] The correspondence between Louis XIV. and Barillon, the French Ambassador in England, shews that it was the object of Louis, a man of sounder intellect, but not less bigoted, than James, to assist the latter in introducing the Roman Catholic Religion into England.

[a] Reresby says that when he resolved on flight, he at one time thought of going to the Bishops of Canterbury or Winchester.

[b] One part of their advice was that he would permit them to use such arguments as might induce him to return to the Church.

The Causes of the Revolution.

But it was too late. On November 5 William of Orange landed at Torbay, and attended by Gilbert Burnet, his chaplain [c], marched on Exeter. There, as Burnet tells us [d], "both the clergy and magistrates were very fearful and very backward." Lamplugh, the Bishop, fled in terror to London [e], and was rewarded by James with the long vacant Archbishopric of York. The Dean followed the Bishop's example, and William took up his residence at the Deanery. He attended service in the Cathedral, and sat on the Bishop's throne; a solemn Te Deum was sung, from which, however, the Canons absented themselves, and when Burnet began to read the Declaration which the Prince had set forth, even the choristers left the Cathedral. Burnet, however, was not the man to be frightened, and when the reading was ended, he exclaimed "God save the Prince of Orange," making no mention of James.

Every day now added to the misfortunes of the unhappy King. One by one his friends deserted him. His son-in-law, the Prince of Denmark, forsook him, a loss which did not trouble him much; but soon, as a crown of sorrows, his favourite daughter Anne left him, and under the escort of her former

---

[c] Burnet, the "champion in ordinary of the Revolution," as he has been called, "ready to enter the lists against all comers."—Ralph, iii. 3.

[d] Own Times, iii. 531.

[e] Or "to testify his loyalty." Echard, iii. 911.

tutor, Compton, Bishop of London, fled to Nottingham[f]. On December 23, James, after a previous unsuccessful attempt, succeeded, through the connivance of William, in escaping from England never to return, and on the same day that James left it William entered London[g].

---

[f] On this occasion Compton is said, to the great scandal of the Church, to have recurred to the soldier's life which he had formerly led, and to have worn a purple cloak, and top-boots with pistols hanging before him, and a sword drawn at his side. Ever afterwards he bore the nickname of "Jack Boots."

[g] The people, however, soon began to have doubts as to the future. Thus Lord Clarendon writes in his Journal, "It is not to be imagined what a damp there was over all sorts of men throughout the town." And on December 25, the Bishop of Worcester writes to the Archbishop, "May it please your Lordship, and I am sure it will, his majesty will be here to-morrow."—Tanner MSS.

PART I.

THE CHURCH AT ITS HIGHEST POINT OF INFLUENCE.

CHAPTER I.

THE NEW DEFENDER OF THE FAITH.

A CONVENTION, in lieu of a regular Parliament, met on January 22, 1689. The first thing to be done was to settle the new form of government. On one point both Houses were agreed; they were resolved not to recall James, but to entrust the provisional government to the Prince of Orange; here, however, their unanimity ceased. In the Lower House, the members of which were mostly Whigs, a resolution was soon arrived at,—that the King had violated the fundamental laws, and thus broken the original contract between King and people, and that "having withdrawn himself out of the kingdom, the throne is vacant." The House likewise unanimously voted its thanks to the clergy and Church of England for the stand it had made against Popery, for its refusal to read the King's Declaration, and its opposition to the Ecclesiastical Commission. But the first resolution of the Commons was warmly debated in the House of Lords, in which House the majority were Tories. The opinion of Archbishop Sancroft was that whilst James remained nominally King, the administration of the kingdom should be conferred on a Regent; such also was the opinion of the clergy generally[a]. How such a plan could have worked it is impossible to imagine; there would have been two kings existing together in the country; the one with the name, the other with the power of King: the one always trying to regain what he had lost, the other to hold what he had acquired. Still if that course had been adopted, the oath of allegiance which had been already taken to James would have continued in force, and the clergy might conscientiously have performed their duties under a Regent. Unfortunately Sancroft and several Bishops were absent during the debates in the House of Lords; the perseverance of the Lower House forced the Lords to yield; forty-nine peers voted for the Regency, and fifty-one against it; of the Bishops twelve voted for it, and only two, Compton and Trelawney, against it; whilst on the question as to whether the throne was vacant the Contents were sixty-two, the Non-contents forty-seven.

William, however, had in the meantime settled for himself the question as to the new form of government, and it must be admitted that from first to last he had played his part with consummate skill. He first of all in the Declaration which he published before he came to England, asserted that he came over, in his zeal for the Protestant religion, to me-

---

[a] "The Bishops," writes Evelyn in his Diary, 1689, "were all for a Regency."

diate between King and people, and that when those objects were accomplished he would return to his own country. He next connived at James' escape, for he knew that as long as James remained in England, Whigs and Tories alike would vote for a Regency. And now when James had fled, and the kingdom was at his mercy, he threw off all disguise and flatly refused the Regency; he would be satisfied with nothing short of the *name* as well as the *power* of King. If this were not granted him, he would return at once to Holland, and the government would thus be thrown open to James; a thing which all parties in the kingdom deprecated.

The firmness of William settled the question. The chief parties being now agreed, the Commons drew up, and the Lords assented to, a Declaration of Rights setting forth the grievances which the nation had suffered under James, determining the disputes which had lately taken place between King and people, defining and circumscribing for the future the power of the Royal Prerogative. Having thus vindicated the principles of the Constitution, the two Houses resolved that William and Mary should be King and Queen during their joint lives, and the life of the survivor, the exercise of the Royal Power being in the Prince alone during his life; after their decease the Crown was settled on the children of the Princess, and in default of such on the Princess Anne and her posterity. A Bill was passed by which the Convention was turned into a regular Parliament, and a clause was inserted which enacted that no person should after the first of March sit or vote in either House of Parliament without taking the oaths to the new King and Queen.

The Revolution was thus accomplished, and a new era to Church no less than State commenced. "To the English Nation," Mr. Hallam says, "the reign of William III. was the Nadir of its prosperity." But how did the Revolution affect the Church of England? For the State its ancient rights and liberties were asserted and the principles of the constitution vindicated; but little thought was bestowed upon the Church which had brought about this beneficial change; the King still remained Defender of the Faith; he still retained the distribution of the higher posts in the Church, as well as a large proportion of the lower preferments. We must now enquire what qualifications the King had for the new position with regard to the Church which he was called upon to fill.

William of Orange, son of William of Orange and Mary, daughter of Charles I. of England, was born at the Hague in 1650, and in 1678 married, when she was only sixteen years of age, his cousin the Princess Mary, daughter of the Duke of York, afterwards King James II.

An alien by birth, William never at any time bore any love to England; and when he became its King

The New Defender of the Faith.   39

he disliked it still more, and was offended because he did not meet with the same abject obedience here to which he was accustomed in Holland. It is even doubtful whether he would ever have accepted the throne but that he regarded this country as a powerful ally against France, with whom he was always at war [b], and by whom he was nearly always beaten. "I wish I were ten thousand miles from England, and that I had never been King of it," he said to the Duke of Hamilton [c]. One form of government was to him as distasteful as the other, the only difference he knew between Whigs and Tories was that the "former would cut his throat in the morning, the latter in the afternoon [d]." So in his dislike to England and the English, he always kept his Dutch followers around him; he would allow them to dine with him at his own table, whilst Marlborough and Godolphin were left to stand unnoticed.

Unfitted by birth, by education, by taste, to understand the English character, he was still more unfitted to form a proper estimate of the Church of England, or to be the Defender of its Faith.

In Holland there were two sorts of Protestants, the Arminians and the Calvinists. By birth William was a Presbyterian, by education and taste he was

---

[b] It was said the soil of Flanders was "literally deluged with English blood."
[c] Ralph's Hist. of England.   [d] Ibid., ii. 8.

a Calvinist, the doctrine of absolute decrees and predestination was the key-note of his religion, although, it must be stated in his favour, unlike the Calvinistic body generally, he was opposed to intolerance and religious persecution.

It is scarcely possible to imagine two forms of Christianity more opposed than the religion in which he was educated, and the religion of the Church of England. A Dutch Presbyterian, he was opposed to Episcopacy, and to the doctrines which it involved; he had no reverence for antiquity, no taste for Church music, no love of ritual; on the contrary, he had a rooted antipathy to the most ordinary points of ritual, such as the surplice and the sign of the Cross in Baptism. He brought his Dutch irreverence with him to England[e]; he could, it is true, conform to the English services, and even, as Burnet tells us, preferred them to the Dutch; but when first he came to England, he used to wear his hat during the whole of the service, afterwards he consented to take it off during the Prayers, and to wear it only during the Sermon; and when he attended service in Canterbury Cathedral, he took his seat on the Archbishop's throne, the Dean attending him as his Clerk of the Closet.

---

[e] When the English services were particularly slovenly, Queen Mary compared them to the Dutch; in March, 1693, she wrote to Dean Hooper that she was reminded of "a Dutch church, for the people stood on the Communion Table to look at her."

The New Defender of the Faith. 41

To the English Church he bore a bitter antipathy. In 1677 Dr. Hooper [f] was appointed Chaplain and Almoner to the Princess Mary; at the Hague he proposed to her a course of study; by his advice she read Eusebius and Hooker, which, when William saw her doing, we are told he "uttered an ominous growl." He would not even allow Hooper a Chapel for the Church Services, so Hooper was obliged to fit up a Chapel in the Princess's dining-room, she contenting herself with dining for the future in a small dark room. In this room Hooper erected an Altar; but this arrangement was not to the Prince's liking, and "he kicked at it with his foot [g]." He at last compelled her to attend the Dutch services, whereupon Hooper being thus thwarted, found it necessary to resign the appointment. He was succeeded in 1679 by the holy Ken; but William disliked Ken even more than he had disliked Hooper, and he was obliged to leave the Hague, bearing with him the hatred of William, which, as we shall see later on [h], so materially affected his after life and the history of the Church. Such was William at the Hague. Soon after he became King of England, owing to the opposition which he met with from the Archbishop and some of the leading Bishops, he became thoroughly estranged from the English Church; the

---

[f] Afterwards Bishop.   [g] Mrs. Prowse's Memoirs.
[h] Chapter in the Nonjurors.

disaffection of the Clergy inclined him to the Dissenters, whom he regarded as better affected to his person and title; and the favours which he shewed to the Dissenters set Churchmen, and especially Tory Churchmen, against him.

Nor was William's character such as to ingratiate him with the Church. Burnet, who is always inclined to look favourably on his faults, is obliged to confess that "he had no vice *save one* in which he was very cautious and secret." What that vice was, he has left us no difficulty in discerning. The Princess was always described as a person of a particularly sweet and gentle disposition. Yet Hooper dwells on the cruel treatment which she suffered from William first at the Hague, and afterwards in England; he says that "he often found her in tears after she came to England, and in Holland it was daily so." Ken said the same; "Dr. Ken was with me," wrote the Hon Henry Sidney[i], "he is horribly dissatisfied with the Prince of Orange. He thinks he is not kind to his wife, and is determined to speak to him about it, even if he kicks him out of doors." The same complaint was made five years later by Dr. Cavell, who succeeded Ken in the Chaplaincy; in allusion to William's conduct to her, he says "the Princess's heart is ready to break[k]."

---

[i] Diary, March 21, 1680.
[k] It is, however, just to state that towards the end of Mary's

The New Defender of the Faith. 43

In one word, in no relation of life, except as a soldier and an administrator, can William be regarded as an estimable character. But besides his moral disqualifications, his cold and forbidding manner, arising no doubt partly from illness and physical suffering, made him universally disliked in England, so that at the time of his death it is doubtful whether a single Englishman felt a personal attachment to him [1].

To the Catholic and Apostolic Church of England William III., a Dutch Presbyterian, was now elected by the State to be the "Defender of the Faith," and "supreme governour over all persons in all causes, ecclesiastical as well as civil [m]." The principle of the Royal Supremacy is of no modern date, but is anterior to the English monarchy, and even coeval with Christianity itself [n]." In this country we must seek for its commencement in the Saxon Heptarchy; from the Conquest to the Reformation the King was regarded as the Vicar of God, and an oath was taken

---

life William's conduct, probably owing to Burnet's intervention, improved.

[1] Stanhope's Hist. of England.

[m] The title of "Defender of the Faith" was first conferred on Henry VIII. by the Pope for a book which he had written against Luther ("Assertio Septem Sacramentorum, adversus Martinum Lutherum).

[n] It may be said to be even anterior to it, for we read in Isaiah xlix. 23 of the Jewish Church that 'Kings have become her nursing-fathers and Queens her nursing-mothers.'

by him to observe the laws of King Edward [o]. At the Reformation Henry VIII. only reclaimed the title which had been for centuries usurped by the Popes of Rome; he required the Clergy to acknowledge him as "Sole Protector and Supreme Head of the Church;" but this title, even when modified by the words "after God [p]," the Convocation refused to concede to him, and only agreed to it "as far as is permitted by the law of Christ [q]." The assertion of the title in England was a defensive protest on the part of the Church of England, originally against the Church of Rome, and afterwards against modern usurpation [r]. The Act of Supremacy of Henry VIII. was repealed by 1 & 2 Phil. and Mary, cap. 8, sec. 6; Queen Mary, however, not only assumed the title

---

[o] "Rex qui Vicarius Summi Regis est, ad hoc est Constitutus, ut regnum terrenum et populum Domini, et super omnia Sanctam veneretur Ecclesiam Ejus, et regat, et ab injuriosis defendat, et maleficos ab eâ evellat, et distruat et penitus disperdat."

[p] Post Deum.

[q] "Ecclesia et cleri Anglicani singularem protectorem et unicum supremum Dominum, et *quantum per Christi legem licet* etiam supremum caput, ipsius majestatem recognoscimus."

[r] "Originally against appeals from the Crown to the Pope, and afterwards against the Puritans of all denominations; against the Presbyterians, who claimed for their Consistories absolute jurisdiction over Princes with power to excommunicate them; and against the Independents, who exempted their congregations from all spiritual jurisdiction under them." See Bp. Sanderson on Episcopacy; Article xxxvii.; Canon xxxvi.; and Hooker, viii. 2, 3.

of "Supreme Head" in the earlier part of her reign, but all her proceedings in matters ecclesiastical throughout her reign were based on the authority annexed to that title, although she had nominally laid it aside[s]. Queen Elizabeth repudiated the title of Head of the Church, which has not been borne by any monarch since her time; and received that title which has been used ever since, of "Supreme Governour over all persons in all causes ecclesiastical as well as civil[t]."

And in this principle of the Royal Supremacy, as defined by the Formularies of the Church, there is nothing so unreasonable or inconsistent with the rule of the primitive Church as is often supposed. Thus the XXXVII. Article declares that the Church gives to Sovereigns "that only prerogative which she sees to have been given always to all godly persons in Holy Scripture by God Himself;" and in the second Canon of 1604 she states that "the King's Majesty hath the same authority as *godly* Kings had among the Jews, and Christian Emperors in the Christian Church." Neither in the Jewish

---

[s] Having proclaimed on August 18, 1553, that no one should preach without a licence from the Crown, she issued the actual licences in a form beginning, "Mary by the grace of God, on earth *Supreme Head* of the Church of England" (Collier, Records, lxviii.). See also Cardwell's Docum. Ann. i. 109, for the Injunctions which in March, 1554, she exactly on the Edwardian model issued to the clergy.

[t] Canon xxxvi.

Church nor under the Emperors was the title and authority supposed to be given to one of a different faith, or to one who would use his power to the detriment of the Church of which he was appointed to be the Defender. It is in this respect, by according to a King of an alien faith temporal supremacy in the Church, that the Revolution inaugurated an era lasting to our own times, so disastrous to the Church of England.

We must here notice one change which was introduced at the Revolution by Parliament, viz. the change of the form of oath in the Coronation Service[u]. The new Coronation oath, which has been taken by the Monarchs of England from that time to this, is in the following words:—Archbishop: "Will you to the utmost of your power maintain the laws of God, the true profession of the Gospel, and the *Protestant* Reformed religion established by law? And will you maintain and preserve inviolably the settlement of the United Church of England and Ireland, and the doctrine, worship, discipline, and government thereof as by law established within England and Ireland and the territories thereunto belonging? And will you preserve unto the Bishops and Clergy of England and Ireland and to the Churches there committed to their charges, all such

---

[u] The oath previously taken is given in the Introductory chapter.

The New Defender of the Faith. 47

rights and privileges as by law do or shall appertain to them or any of them?"

With regard to this new oath, it may be as well to observe in passing, that it is the only formulary of the Church of England in which the word *Protestant*[1] is used. Through the various changes through which the Prayer-Book has passed, from the first Prayer-Book of King Edward VI. till the last review in 1661, our Reformers have never once used the word; it is excluded alike from the Prayer-Book, the Articles, the Homilies, and the Canons. The name Protestant was first given to those German Reformers who in 1529 *protested* against the condemnation of Luther by the Diet of Spires. Since then it has been applied on the Continent to the Lutherans as distinguished from the Calvinist and Zwinglian Communities which are styled "Reformed." It was applied to those who held the doctrine of Consubstantiation, and on that ground is inapplicable to the English Church. It is a negative term, dwelling on the differences, rather than the word Catholic, on the agreements of Christians; it concedes the title of Catholic to Roman Catholics, and is an obstacle to the union of Christendom. The reason why Parliament (not the Church) intro-

---

[1] The Coronation oath is, however, a purely civil and political formula; it forms no part of the Prayer-Book, the last review of which was made in 1661, and therefore does not come under the Act of Uniformity.

duced at the Revolution the word into the Coronation Service is clear; James II. had wrested the meaning of the former oath, and made it subservient to his Romanizing views, and Parliament in consequence thought it necessary to introduce a word which could not possibly bear a Romish signification.

It was evident when William came to the throne, that some relaxation would be made in those Penal Laws which affected Protestant Dissenters. Up to the time of the Revolution the Penal Laws bore very hardly upon Dissenters, both Roman Catholic and Protestant, and so far as a more tolerant spirit was introduced, the Church was benefitted by the Revolution. Religious intolerance and Statutes imposed by the State to restrain liberty of conscience always have been and always must be a failure, and detrimenal to the Church; at the best they can produce only a hollow uniformity and a superficial oneness, whilst discontent and heartburning are festering beneath, only awaiting their time for coming to the surface[y].

Before he came to the throne, William had expressed his willingness that the Penal Laws should be repealed, provided that those "laws remain still in force by which Roman Catholics are shut out of public employments, civil or military." And in his speech to the Houses of Parliament on March 16,

---

[y] "Religionis non est religionem cogere." Tertullian ad Scapulam.

1689, he expressed a similar desire; "I hope you are sensible there is a necessity of some law to settle the oaths to be taken by all persons to be admitted to such places. I recommend it to your care to make a speedy provision for it, and as I doubt not it will be sufficient against all Papists, so I hope you will leave room for the admission of all Protestants who are able and willing to serve."

This was William's idea of Toleration. He placed, no doubt from ignorance, the Church of England on a level with the Protestant Churches of the Continent, and thought that an amalgamation between the Church and the Protestant Dissenters could be easily and profitably effected. He was very bitter against the Roman Catholics, and only in a less degree against the Church; but his Churchmanship was based on political rather than on religious grounds. In everything William made his religion subservient to his political purposes. He was tolerant of Dissenters, not so much because he was one himself, or from any conscientious preference for Dissenters, but much in the same way as he preferred, on the whole, Whigs to Tories, because he thought the former would be the more useful to him of the two. He would have been equally willing to favour the Roman Catholics as to favour the Protestant Dissenters (indeed at one time he expressed his willingness to do so), if it had suited his purposes.

We shall be the better able to appreciate the sincerity of William's convictions, if we compare his conduct with regard to the Churches of England and Scotland respectively. In England he was willing to retain Episcopacy, because he could find such Latitudinarian Bishops as Tillotson and Burnet to support his views. In Scotland he abolished Episcopacy, although he was quite willing to continue it in that country also if it had suited his interests. The Duke of Hamilton said "he had it in special charge from King William that nothing should be done to the prejudice of Episcopacy in Scotland in case the Bishops could by any means be brought to befriend his interests, and prayed us most pathetically for our own sake to follow the example of the Church of England [z]." To this suggestion, however, the Scottish Bishops (who were at that time fourteen in number), and by far the greater number of the clergy, refused to bind themselves; so Episcopacy was abolished in Scotland; the clergy were ejected, and Presbyterians appointed to their livings. "Episcopacy was abolished and Presbytery established upon the inclinations of the people, though not a third part at that time was Presbyterian, and some say not a fourth [a]."

---

[z] Letter preserved in Bishop Keith's "Catalogue of the Scottish Bishops."

[a] Life of Kettlewell. In the life of Sage it is said, "It was certain that not one of three parts of the common people were

The Church may be thankful to the Revolution that it inaugurated an era of toleration in religion, but even on that ground it is possible to give William more credit than he deserves. Already, before the Revolution, a spirit of civil and religious freedom had been gaining ground in the Church of England. Fear of Rome during the reign of James had effaced the recollections of the Protectorate, and the intolerance of the Puritans; and the question, not only of the toleration of Dissenters, but also of their comprehension within the Church, had been inaugurated by the Bishops, and was one of the leading questions of the day.

Sancroft, the Primate, had become as strong an advocate in the cause of concession to Dissenters as King William himself. He saw the injustice entailed upon them by the Penal Laws and the necessity of remedying it. We have several instances of this in Sancroft's history. The memorable Petition of the Seven Bishops, which was drawn up in his handwriting, declared, that there was no want of "due tenderness to Dissenters, in relation to whom they were willing to come to such a temper as should be thought fit, when that matter should be considered and settled in Parliament and Convocation." Immediately after his trial, he issued articles to the

---

then for the Presbytery, and not one in ten among the gentlemen or people of education."

Bishops of his Province, in which he enjoined the clergy to have "a very tender regard to our brethren the Protestant Dissenters;" he advised that they should exhort them "to join with us in daily fervent prayer to the God of peace, for an universal blessed union of all reformed Churches both at home and abroad against our common enemies." At the very time the Bishops were resisting James' Declaration, Sancroft, in concert with Patrick [b], Sharp [c], Wake [d] More [e], and others of the clergy, was actually engaged in a project, not only for Toleration but for Comprehension also. "That wise Prelate," said Wake (at the time Bishop of Lincoln), "foreseeing such a Revolution as that which soon after occurred, began to consider how utterly unprepared they had been at the Restoration of Charles II., to settle many things to the advantage of the Church, and what a happy opportunity had been lost for want of care for its more perfect establishment [f]." In further confirmation of this, we have evidence from Bishop Patrick [g]: "On the 14th January I went in the afternoon to the Dean of St. Paul's (Tillotson's) house, where I met the Bishop of St. Asaph, the Dean of Canterbury

---

[b] Afterwards Bishop of Chichester and of Ely.
[c] Afterwards Archbishop of York.
[d] Afterwards Bishop of Lincoln and Archbishop of Canterbury.
[e] Afterwards Bishop of Norwich and of Ely.
[f] Wake's Speech at Sacheverell's Trial.
[g] History of his own Life.

(Dr. Sharp), the Dean of Norwich (Dr. Fairfax), and Dr. Tenison, to consult about such concessions as might bring Dissenters to our Communion; for which the Bishop of St. Asaph told us he had the Archbishop of Canterbury's leave. We agreed that a Bill should be prepared to be offered to the Bishops, and we drew up the matter of it in ten or eleven heads." And consistently with this plan, before the 1st March (the day appointed for taking the new oaths to William and Mary) arrived, the last act of the Nonjuring Bishops was to move that two Bills might be introduced into Parliament, the one for Toleration the other for Comprehension [h].

The cause of Comprehension was frustrated rather than advanced by the Revolution, and the cause of the failure is to be found in the difference between the characters of Archbishop Sancroft and Gilbert Burnet, Bishop of Salisbury, the latter of whom was William's chief adviser in the plan. Sancroft was a staunch Churchman, and understood the temper of the times better than Burnet did; he knew how far the Church could go without touching any essential point of doctrine or of ritual. He understood how that concessions, except in indifferent matters, although they might gain over some opponents for a time, could patch up only a hollow truce and bring

---

[h] Burnet, O. T. iii. 8, sneers at this action of the Bishops as an artifice and a show of moderation.

in the end additional insecurity. He wished therefore to devise such a plan as might be approved by Convocation and Parliament; to improve, if possible, our discipline; to review and enlarge our Prayer-Book by omitting some few ceremonies, which might be found indifferent in their nature and also indifferent in their usage[i]; which might thus remove the scruples of Dissenters and pave the way for their admission into the Church.

Gilbert Burnet was no Churchman at all, or at best an ultra-Protestant Gallio, who cared little whether he was a Churchman or Dissenter: a Scotchman and a Dissenter by birth, he had lost his way and found himself by accident in the Church of England. It was the action of Burnet and of other Bishops like-minded with himself, which ruined the cause of the Dissenters. Sancroft was entirely opposed to the plan of Burnet[k]. It was the Erastian policy of the Latitudinarians (who were soon about to become a power in the Church), who by trying too much overreached themselves and shewed themselves in their true colours, that opened the eyes of Church-

---

[i] Wake's Speech.

[k] "Maugre the defection of some of her Bishops, from the malice and rage of Presbyterians, and Anabaptists, and other wild sectaries, who with united force are labouring hard to ruin her (the Church) under the spurious and popular, but most scandalous and unjustifiable pretensions of Comprehension and Toleration."—Letter of Sancroft to Compton in Tanner MSS.

men, so that the plan of comprehension, so strenuously favoured by the King, failed, and has never since from that time to this been attempted. The Dissenters would naturally desire Toleration and to be freed from the operation of the Penal Laws: but the question naturally arises, Why should they wish to be comprehended in the Church? The very fact of their being Dissenters would seem to imply an unwillingness on their part to be Churchmen. In order to answer the question, it must be observed that there was a marked difference between the Dissenters of two hundred years ago, and those of our own times. The Nonconformists of the Revolution, the lineal descendants of the Puritans of the Commonwealth, held that there *ought to be* a National Church, and regarded separation from it as a sin; whereas Dissenters in the present day consider separation to be no sin at all; that there ought to be no National Church, and do all in their power to weaken and to destroy it. At the former period the Dissenters never considered themselves to be separatists, but Nonconformists in communion with the Church, differing from it only on certain forms and points of discipline, which they desired, indeed, to be reformed, but which, even in their unreformed state, they did not consider to be so unchristian as to necessitate or to justify separation from the Church. And the higher the Church stood the more desirous were they for a closer union with it.

Another important question—a question which perhaps may be important to Church Reformers of our own times—arises. Supposing that the Church's doctrine and ritual had been lowered, as King William wished, would it not have produced discord rather than peace amongst the Dissenters themselves? Is it possible (to omit the many sects into which Dissent was broken up) that the four principal sects, the Presbyterians, Independents, Baptists, and Quakers, would have agreed either with the Church or amongst themselves?

A question still more important to the Church arises; How would the Church have been affected if it had admitted the Dissenters to terms of equality?

Fortunately we have history to guide us and to enable us to estimate the consequences of yielding too much to Dissenters. The Dissenters in opposition are very different from Dissenters in power. Once, at the time of the Rebellion, they had their way; they professed to take up arms for "liberty of conscience;" they succeeded, and their intolerance was fanatical[1]. Never was there a period of less religious freedom and toleration than under the Presbyterians at the time of the Commonwealth[m].

---

[1] "New Presbyter," to use Milton's words, was but "Old Priest writ large."

[m] "The Presbyterian Church wherever it had coercive power proved quite as intolerant, and to the majority of the people less

Authority over religion was usurped and exercised in their Provincial Assemblies, and the Commonwealth passed, for punishing what they called heresies, an Ordinance than which no decree of any Council, no Bull of any Pope, was more dogmatical or more authoritative; few, if any, more cruel [n]. "The imposition on the Nation of the Solemn League and Covenant," writes the Dissenting author above referred to [o], "was a more odious infraction of religious liberty than the imposition of the whole of the Prayer-Book and the Thirty-nine Articles, for it was enforced on laymen as well as on the clergy." And we must add one point more, viz. that the Puritans of the Commonwealth were not only persecutors, but in their advocacy of a state-established religion, they had no objection to tithes and Church-rates, to which Nonconformists in the present day profess so strong antipathy.

The Dissenters who, when in opposition, were the advocates, were, when in power, the most violent opponents of Toleration. The Presbyterians protested against Toleration to the Westminster Assembly [p]: "We cannot dissemble how we detest and abhor the much endeavoured Toleration;" it was denounced

---

pleasant than the Episcopalian had been."—Skeats' "History of the Free Churches." This is from a Dissenter.

[n] Toulmin's History, ii.
[o] Skeats, p. 51.
[p] December 18, 1645.

by them as the "grand design of the Devil;" "the most ready compendium and sure way to destroy all religion, all the devils in hell and their instruments being at work to promote it [q]." Cromwell, himself an Independent, guaranteed freedom in religion to all except Papists and *Prelatists*. The Triers and Commissioners for rejecting ignorant and scandalous ministers treated every Episcopally ordained clergyman with marked injustice; it is computed that they ejected from their Livings not fewer than seven thousand clergymen, besides curates, masters of hospitals and schoolmasters; and as the great majority of these were married men, it is probable that full thirty thousand people were turned out into the world to get their living as they could, or to starve [r]. Those eleven years of Puritan ascendancy must still have *lived* in the minds of many people surviving at the time of the Revolution; many must have remembered the days when ordination at the hands of the sequestered Bishops, the attendance at the services of the Church, and even the use of the Prayer-Book, were exposed to the greatest peril [s]. Is it possible that men who hated Episcopacy, who hated the

---

[q] Gangræna, i. 58.
[r] Walker's Sufferings of the Clergy.
[s] Evelyn tells us that after Christmas, 1655, "the Church was reduced to a chamber or a Conventicle;" that when "we went up to receive the Sacrament, the miscreants held their muskets at us, as if they would shoot us at the Altar."

The New Defender of the Faith. 59

Prayer-Book, which they designated as "the Mass in English," "Porridge," and by other such like terms of opprobrium, would have been contented with the concessions that even the most Latitudinarian Churchmen could have afforded them¹? Here again history answers the question. What happened under the Commonwealth did actually happen again in Scotland a few years after toleration was conceded under William to the Dissenters in England. As Toleration had been granted to the Presbyterians in England it does not appear an extravagant demand that the Presbyterians would grant a like Toleration to the Episcopalians in Scotland. But when in 1703 a Bill to that effect was offered to the Scottish Parliament, the General Assembly was scandalized, and published a protestation; "they were persuaded that to enact a Toleration for those of the Episcopal way (which God in His mercy avert!) would be to establish iniquity by law;" and so an Act was passed by which it was declared High Treason to "endeavour any alteration in it;" i.e. in the government of the Church.

It is unpleasant to rake up the memorial of past misdeeds, but it is of the first importance at the present time that such points of history should be borne

---

¹ The question of the ejection of the intruders on St. Bartholomew's day, whether or how it could have been avoided, does not come within the scope of this work.

in mind, and it is useful to reflect that what happened once may, in a mitigated degree, happen again. When we duly consider those historical facts which have been related, and how intolerant and prone to persecution the Nonconformists when in power were in times gone by; when we remember that there were no stronger advocates for a state-religion, or more willing recipients of tithes and Church rates than the Puritans of the Commonwealth, we think that many of the objections brought by the Liberationists at the present day against the Church must vanish into thin air, and that the people of England will think twice before, to please the whims of Liberationists, they consent to disestablish, disendow, or in any way to weaken a Church which for centuries has been the cause of so much peace and so many blessings to the community at large.

CHAPTER II.

THE BIRTH OF TOLERATION.

A SCHEME for the Toleration and Comprehension of Dissenters in the Church, found an advocate in the Earl of Nottingham, at that time Secretary of State. Of all the ministers of William, Nottingham, from the purity of his moral character and his devoted attachment to the Church, was the most acceptable to Churchmen. He understood the desirability of conciliating Dissenters, and was thoroughly in favour of toleration; he was also not unwilling to make some modifications in the discipline and ritual of the Church, with the view of admitting into the Church the more moderate Dissenters, and favoured some compromise in the Test Act. With this view he brought forward a Bill in the House of Lords for "uniting their Majesties' Protestant subjects," and a few days afterwards he brought forward another Bill for "exempting their Majesties' Protestant subjects, dissenting from the Church of England, from the penalties of certain laws;" the former is better known as a Bill for Comprehension, the latter as the Bill for Toleration [a].

---

[a] Burnet, whom William had already made Bishop of Salisbury, says, O. T. iii. 11, "I happened to come into the House

The Comprehension Bill was supported in the House of Lords by Compton, Bishop of London—who, on the retirement of Sancroft from public business, was virtually Primate—and Burnet [b], and although the clauses relating to the Test Act were rejected, the Bill passed the House of Lords on April 8, 1689. On the 18th of the same month the Bill for Toleration also passed the House of Lords, and both Bills went down together to the House of Commons, there to meet with a very different fate. The Toleration Bill had an easy passage through the Commons, and soon became law. Far otherwise was it with the Comprehension Bill [c]. The members of that House, Whigs as well as Tories, were opposed to the King's scheme for comprehending Dissenters; it was too much to expect from Englishmen that they would alter the constitution of their Church to suit the views of a King who was a Presbyterian; it was evident to them that he only thought about obliging the Dissenters without

---

of Lords when two great debates were managed with much heat in it. The one was about the Toleration, and the other was about imposing oaths on the clergy. And I was engaged in my first coming there to bear a large share in both."

[b] "I professed myself zealous for it," wrote Burnet.

[c] "The Church party was far more numerous in Parliament."—Dalrymple's Memoirs, ii. Lord Macaulay says, without, however, adducing any authority, "Nothing is more certain than that two-thirds of the members were either Low Churchmen, or no Churchmen at all."

caring what became of the Church; and it is to the House of Commons that the Church owes its salvation at that momentous crisis. The question of the admission of Dissenters into the Church was one on which the Church had a right to be consulted, and the constitutional organ of the Church was Convocation. With the Convention Parliament, by which William and Mary had been called to the throne, the Convocation did not assemble; perhaps the King had never heard of Convocation, at any rate Burnet was not the man to speak to him in its favour. But now, says Burnet[d], the members of the House of Commons "were much offended with the Bill of Comprehension as containing matters relating to the Church in which the representative body of the clergy had not been so much as advised with;" they refused so much as to discuss the Bill, and were of opinion that Convocation should be summoned, according to ancient usage, in time of Parliament. To this plan the House of Lords assented; and a joint address was adopted by the two Houses praying the King that "according to the ancient practice and usage of the kingdom in time of Parliament," his Majesty would be graciously pleased to issue forth his writs as conveniently as might be for calling a Convocation of the Clergy of this kingdom to be advised with in all Ecclesiastical matters.

---

[d] O. T. iii. 15.

Burnet was opposed to this plan, which he said would be the ruin of the Comprehension scheme; and he was right. The King, however, consulted Tillotson, at that time Dean of St. Paul's. Tillotson, although not less Latitudinarian, was less headstrong than Burnet; he told the King how that its enemies often represented the Church as a Parliamentary Church; he knew that if Convocation were not consulted Churchmen would be disgusted; moreover he had hopes that Convocation would vote for even greater changes than those proposed [e].

The King determined to follow Tillotson's advice, and to summon Convocation with the next Session of Parliament, but in the meantime he determined to appoint a Commission to prepare matters to be submitted to its consideration. Accordingly on September 13, the Commission was issued to ten Bishops and twenty Priests. "Great care," says Burnet, "was taken to name these so impartially that no exception could lie against any of them..... They had before them all the exceptions that either the Puritans before the war, or the Nonconformists since the Restoration, had made to any part of the Church Service.... Matters were well considered and calmly debated; and all was digested into an entire correction of everything that seemed liable to any just objection [f]."

---

[e] Birch's Life of Tillotson.   [f] O. T. iii. 41.

The Birth of Toleration.

The Commission seems, as Burnet says, to have been appointed with fairness. Double the number of Priests to that of Bishops was very properly placed on it. As the Crown appoints the Bishops the independence of the Church might otherwise have been placed in jeopardy; in the Catholic Church the second Order of the Clergy is invested with authority nearly equal to the Episcopal, and more especially is this the case with regard to the Anglican branch of it, where no Canon can be made without the concurrence of the Lower House of Convocation [g].

As soon as the Commission was appointed, Tillotson drew up a paper of "Concessions which he thought would probably be made by the Church of England for the Union of Protestants [h]."

---

[g] The Prelates appointed were Lamplugh, Archbishop of York, Compton, Bishop of London, Mew, of Winchester, Lloyd, of St. Asaph, Sprat, of Rochester, Smith, of Carlisle, Trelawney, of Exeter, Burnet, of Salisbury, Humphreys, of Bangor, and Stratford, of Chester. The other clergy were Stillingfleet, Patrick, Tillotson, Tenison, Meggott, Sharp, Kidder, Aldrich, Jane, Hall, Beaumont, Montague, Goodman, Beveridge, Batteley, Alston, Scott, Fowler, Grove, Williams.

[h] It comprised the following heads:—(1) Ceremonies to be left indifferent; (2) To review the Liturgy and remove all ground of exception; to leave out Apocryphal Lessons, and correct the translation of the Psalms: (3) Ministers only to subscribe one general declaration of submission to the doctrine, discipline, and worship of the Church of England, and to promise to teach and practise accordingly; (4) to make a new body of Canons; (5) To regulate the Ecclesiastical Courts; (6) That those who have been ordained in any of the foreign reformed

So far all went well. An outcry, however, was soon raised against the legality of the Commission, and against anything at all being prepared before the meeting of Convocation. Sprat, who had had considerable experience on James's Ecclesiastical Commission, at nce raised the question and withdrew, and his example was soon followed by Mew, Bishop of Winchester, as well as Jane and Aldrich. But whatever good might otherwise have come from the Commission was prevented by the leading part which the Latitudinarians who were placed on it at once assumed. The chief place was taken by Patrick, Burnet, Stillingfleet, Tillotson, Tenison, and Kidder, all Latitudinarians. New Collects were drawn up by Patrick; great force was, it is said, added to them by Burnet; they were next examined by Stillingfleet, and a last touch was given by Tillotson. Dr. Kidder made a new version of the Psalms. Objections having been made to certain parts of the Prayer-Book; to the Calendar which prescribed the Apocryphal Lessons, and to the Athanasian Creed, Tenison cut out all expressions to which, rightly or wrongly, objections had been made, and proposed others.

The document containing the proposed alterations,

Churches be not required to be re-ordained here, to render them capable of preferment in this Church; (7) But none to be capable of Ecclesiastical preferment that shall be ordained in England otherwise than by Bishops.—Procter on Book of Common Prayer, p. 145, n.

The Birth of Toleration. 67

which were 598 in number, was left in charge of Tenison, afterwards Archbishop of Canterbury, by whom it was not allowed to be made public, and was long supposed to be lost. In 1727, however, it fell into the hands of Gibson, Bishop of London, who placed it in the Lambeth Library [i].

The most important of the changes proposed by the Commissioners were the following :—Chanting in Cathedrals to be laid aside; the Apocryphal Lessons, and such lessons out of the Old Testament as were *too natural*, to be thrown out; all Legendary Saints' Days, and such as are not strictly referred to in the Service Book, to be omitted from the Calendar. If any clergyman objected to the use of the surplice the Bishop should dispense with his using it, and if he shall think fit, "appoint a Curate to officiate in a surplice." The use of the Cross and Godparents in Holy Baptism to be optional; the Lenten Fast to be explained in a Rubric as consisting only in extraordinary acts of devotion, not in distinction of meats; permission to be allowed for the Absolution to be pronounced by Deacons, and the word Priest to be changed into Minister, and Sunday to Lord's Day; the *Gloria Patri* to be said only once at the end of the Psalms for the day; the Absolution in the Visitation of the Sick to be altered to "Upon thy true

---

[i] It is now accessible in the form of a Blue Book, viz. "A Return to an Address of the House of Commons March 14, 1854, and ordered by the House to be printed, June 2, 1854."

faith and repentance, by His authority committed to me I pronounce thee absolved;" the Commination Service to be altered; all titles of the King and Queen, such as 'most religious and gracious,' to be omitted; additional suffrages to be inserted in the Litany; the Prayer beginning "O God, whose nature and property," to be thrown out as "full of strange and impertinent expressions, and not in the original, but foisted in since;" a most extensive revision was made of the Collects, scarcely one of which remained unchanged; being thought too short an almost entirely new body was drawn up by Patrick; lest the rejection of the Athanasian Creed should be by unreasonable persons imputed to Socinianism, it was proposed that a Rubric should be appended to it, declaring the condemning clauses to apply only to those who deny the substance of the Christian Religion in general.

Such a scheme was nothing short of an attempt to Presbyterianize the Church. It was said that "the Church was to be pulled down and Presbytery to be set up[k]." The greatest issues were at stake; everything now depended upon the Lower House of Convocation. "Great canvassings," Burnet tells us, "were everywhere in the election of Convocation men, a thing not known in former times." It was nothing short of a battle between the Latitudinarian Bishops and the other Clergy.

---

[k] O. T., iii. 144.

The Birth of Toleration. 69

Convocation met on November 20, 1689. Beveridge preached the Latin sermon from the text 1 Cor. xi. 16, "If any man seem to be contentious, we have no such custom, neither the Churches of God;" in his sermon he advocated a moderate reform, but not a change in such laws as were fundamental or affected the vitality of the Church. The House then proceeded to the election of a Prolocutor. There were two candidates, Tillotson, the Latitudinarian candidate, who was proposed by Sharp, and Jane, Regius Professor of Divinity at Oxford and Dean of Gloucester, who had refused to serve on the Commission, and was proposed on the other side. Jane was elected by a majority of nearly two to one. In the customary Latin oration, the new Prolocutor "extolled the excellence of the English Church over other Churches, and implied that it wanted no amendment[1]," and concluded with the old Declaration of the English Barons, "Nolumus Leges Angliæ mutari [m]," and Compton, the President, concluded his speech in words exhorting them to unanimity. Convocation was then prorogued by the President on the ground that the Royal Commis-

---

[1] Kennet's Complete Hist., iii. 552.

[m] These were the words which Compton, who now, in the absence of the Archbishop, was President of the Convocation, had inscribed on his banner when he conducted the Princess Anne from London.

sion, under which they acted, was defective through the loss of the Great Seal [n], till December 4.

When on that day both Houses assembled in Henry VIIth's chapel, the King, through the Earl of Nottingham, sent to them a message which concluded in these words: "His Majesty expects that the things that shall be proposed shall be calmly and impartially considered by you, and assures you that he will offer nothing to you but what shall be for the honor, peace, and advantage both of the *Protestant religion in general and particularly of the Church of England.*" This was somewhat like begging the question. Where did the Dutch King of England gain such intimate acquaintance with the Church of England? or who were the counsellors who told him what would be to its advantage? Surely it must have been those very Latitudinarians who bore so important a part on the Commission, and who brought the Church to the very brink of ruin. However, the Bishops speedily agreed in an address of thanks for the Royal Message, to which they requested the concurrence of the Lower House. But the Lower House did not regard the matter in the same light as the Bishops [o]. They entertained scruples with regard to the address. They first

---

[n] Which James, in his flight from England, was supposed to have thrown into the Thames.

[o] It was with difficulty that the Lower House could be prevailed upon to consent to an address at all. One of its mem-

claimed their right to present a separate address to
the King, and when this was overruled, they refused
to agree to any address in which the English Church
was placed on a level with the Protestant Communities of the Continent. A conference was in
consequence resorted to between the two Houses,
which was chiefly conducted by Burnet on the one
side and by Jane on the other. Burnet insisted that
the Church of England was only distinguished from
other Protestant sects by the Hierarchy and by its
revenues, and that to designate the Church as the
Church of England, instead of as the *Protestant
Church,* was equivocal, because, if Popery were ever
restored, the Church would still remain the Church
of England. Jane, on the other hand, insisted that
the Anglican Church was distinguished from the
Protestant Churches by its doctrines, as found in the
Articles, the Liturgy, and the Homilies, as well as
by its Hierarchy, and that the term Protestant was
very equivocal, because it included Socinians, Anabaptists, and Quakers. A compromise between the
two Houses was at last effected; an address was
agreed upon to the King, thanking his Majesty for
his concern for the Church of England, " whereby we
doubt not the interests of the Protestant religion in
all other Protestant Churches, which is dear to us,
will be better secured under the influence of your

---

bers proposed that the Nonjurors should sit with them.—Kennet's Comp. Hist., iii. 555.

Majesty's government and protection." The King fully understood the force of the alterations, and was displeased, but returned a gracious answer: "My Lord, I take the address very kindly from your Convocations; you may depend upon it that all I have promised, and all I can do for the service of the Church of England, I will do; I give you the assurance that I will improve all occasions and opportunities for its service."

It was plain that the Lower House of Convocation was far from pleased with the action of the Commissioners. They thought the Nonconformists had obtained all they needed from the Act of Toleration; there were also other considerations that appeared to warn them against unnecessary changes. The Nonjurors[p] had, on account of the sanctity they attached to an oath, been suspended from their Bishoprics and Preferments, and were in the eyes of nearly the whole Church of England objects of the deepest respect and sympathy. The preference of the King for Dissent and his designs on the Church were unmistakeable. He had abolished Episcopacy in Scotland, and the Bishops in that country had been branded as Papists and treated with the greatest severity. These things opened the eyes of Churchmen, they believed the King wished to Presbyterianise England as he had Scotland; and so evident

---

[p] See next chapter.

was the temper of the Lower House that the scheme of the Commissioners was not even submitted to them. The Upper House had lost in the Nonjuring Bishops some of its most learned and influential members, and with those Nonjurors the Lower House felt sympathy. The two Houses were brought into antagonism; it was the Lower House that saved the Church. Burnet himself admits this. He attributes the refusal of the Lower House to make alterations to the Providence of God; they prevented a schism compared to which the separation of the Nonjurors was a trifle, which would have rent the Church in twain and carried a large majority of the Clergy with it; "the Jacobite clergy," he says [q], "who were then under suspension were designing to make a schism in the Church, whensoever they should be turned out and their places filled up with others .... and if we had made alterations in the Prayer-Book, they would have pretended they still stuck to the ancient Church of England in opposition to those who were altering it and setting up new models."

But this difference between the two Houses was a great and lasting misfortune to the Church. At this early period arose the contest between High and Low Church (names which came into vogue in this reign); between the Upper and Lower Houses of Convocation, which ended in the final suppression

---

[q] O. T., iii. 45.

of Convocation [r]. Tillotson, when he became Archbishop, saw, from his point of view, the mistakes he had made in advising the King to summon Convocation, and determined to have nothing to do with it as long as he was Archbishop, and Convocation was prorogued from time to time, and by successive prorogations was discontinued for more than ten years. "Then," says Burnet, "seeing they were in no disposition to enter upon business, they were kept from doing mischief for a course of ten years [s]."

One point in this comprehension controversy must not be omitted, viz. that even the Dissenters

---

[r] "By this disagreement between the two Houses of Convocation on the business of the Royal Commission was laid the foundation of the differences that afterwards rose to so great a height, subsisted through many years, and broke out on different occasions to the injury of religion and contempt of the clergy."—O. T., iii. 45.

[s] Various Tracts for and against the proposed Comprehension were published. Dr. Sherlock published a Pamphlet entitled "Address to a Friend concerning some Queries about the New Commission," &c., denying that there was any need for any alteration in the Prayer-Book; this was answered by Dr. Tenison, although anonymously, for the other party; then appeared "Vox Cleri," supposed to have been written by a Prebendary of Exeter, which objected to the clergy being used as "Ecclesiastical tinkers, who, undertaking to mend one hole, do usually make two or three." Against this appeared "An Answer to Vox Cleri," shewing the expediency of the proposed alterations; "Vox Populi, or The Sense of the Sober Laity of the Church of England;" "Vox regis et regni, or a Protest against Vox Cleri," &c.

themselves were opposed to it. The Dissenters set it up for a maxim, that it was fit to keep up a strong faction both in Church and State, and that it was not agreeable to that, to suffer so great a body as the Presbyterians to be made more easy or more inclinable to unite with the Church[t]. And this must always be an important point to be duly weighed by those who advocate Disestablishment. Would it not produce discord rather than peace even amongst themselves?

And supposing that Convocation had yielded the points which the Commissioners proposed, could it have produced anything like a lasting peace to the Church? When once a beginning was made, and when once the formularies and doctrines of that Church which Christ and his Apostles founded had been altered, is it probable that the spirit of innovation would have stopped there? New grounds of dissatisfaction would have arisen; new objections would have been raised; for experience teaches us that alterations which would satisfy one generation, in the progress of the human man towards enquiry, would by no means satisfy the requirements of a more advanced, or, as people claim, a more enlightened state of society. Why should not a further advance be advocated, and the principle, which had already received many supporters, be adopted, the

---

[t] Burnet, O. T., iii. 15.

Creeds be removed from the Prayer-Book, and Socinianism inculcated? From such a prospect the Lower House of Convocation saved the Church. Thanks to them, the Prayer-Book remained unmutilated. The most the Latitudinarians could do, and this they did do, was to effect a laxity in ceremonial and discipline. Disappointed with regard to the proposed changes in the Prayer-Book, they were not likely to adhere to rubrics and ceremonies which they fervently wished to abolish, nor to enforce their observance upon others. Indifference on the part of the Bishops produced after a time indifference amongst the clergy; and the clergy, who at first strove manfully against Latitudinarianism, in time became themselves indifferent, and ceased to observe the Rubrics and orders of the Church, when they found that in the eyes of their Diocesans they were more honoured in the breach than in the observance. No further important attempt to alter the Prayer-Book was made until 1859, when three out of the four State services were expunged from it, viz. those for November 5, January 30, and May 29, that only for the Accession of the Sovereign being retained. Those services, however, formed no part of the Book put forth by the joint authority of Convocation, Parliament and the Queen, and therefore no part of the Act of Uniformity. It must be added that the one State service which is retained, viz. that for the Accession of the

The Birth of Toleration. 77

Sovereign, has the least authority of all; and is actually illegal, for it rests only on an Order in Council which is beyond the power of the Crown to issue, as the last Act of Uniformity limits Royal interference with the Prayer-Book to changing the names and style of the members of the Royal Family.

We now return to the Toleration Act, and will briefly sum up what that Act (the Magna Charta of Dissent, as it has been called) did, and what it did not do, for Dissenters. It allowed the public worship of all Protestant Dissenters who would take the oaths of allegiance and supremacy, and subscribe a Declaration against Transubstantiation; but it did not relieve them from the Test and Corporation Acts[u]. But by Section V. of that Act they were not allowed to hold their meetings with "their doors locked, barred, or bolted[v];" nor by Sec. VI. were they exempted from paying tithes or other parochial duties to the Church or Minister; nor from any prosecution in any Ecclesiastical Courts, or else-

---

[u] These were not repealed until 1828, but from the beginning of the reign of George II. Acts of Indemnity were passed nearly every year freeing Dissenters from the operation of these Acts.

[v] This shews that the *law* regulates the services of the Dissenters quite as much as those of the Church. Under subsequent Acts of Parliament the Dissenters are protected from disturbance during their services, as also in their endowments; their Trust deeds are enrolled in the Court of Chancery; under Acts of Parliament their ministers solemnize marriages, and perform funerals.

where, for the same. By Sec. VIII. no Dissenting Teacher or Preacher, who made the prescribed declaration, and took the oaths of allegiance at the general or quarter sessions, and also subscribed the XXXIX. Articles, with the exception of the XXXIVth., XXXVth., and XXXVIth., and the commencement of the XXVIth. Articles[x], was liable to penalties under the Act of Uniformity, or the Conventicle, or the Five Miles Act passed in the reign of Charles II[y]. By Sec. XIII. Quakers[z] were allowed to make a declaration of fidelity to William and Mary, and to subscribe a profession of their belief in the Trinity and in the inspiration of the Scriptures of the Old and New Testaments. Sec. XVII. provides that the benefits of the Act shall not extend "to any Papist or Popish recusant whatsoever, or any person who shall deny in his preaching or writing the doctrine of the Blessed Trinity as it is declared in the Articles of Religion. By Sec. XIX. no Dissenting congregation was permitted to assemble until the place of meeting was certified before the Bishop of the Diocese, or the Archdeacon, or a Justice of the Peace, and registered in the Bishop's or Archdeacon's

---

[x] "The Church hath power to decree rites and Ceremonies and authority in Controversies of Faith."

[y] By Sec. IX. the names of those who subscribed were to be registered, "for which sixpence shall be paid to the Clerk of the Peace and no more."

[z] Referred to as "Certain persons ... who scruple the taking of any oath."

The Birth of Toleration.

Court, and recorded at the General or Quarter Sessions."

Such were the principal provisions in the Act of Toleration. The pre-Revolution system of persecuting Dissenters, which ought never to have commenced, passed away. But with that Act an entirely new epoch commenced for the Church. Up to that time Church and State had been (agreeably to Hooker's theory [a]) one body under different aspects. The Church was the Church of the State and the Church of the people, and no person could be a member of one without being at the same time a member of the other. Nonconformity was as much an offence against the State as it was against the Church. The Toleration Act was the first public recognition of the right of public worship outside the pale of the Established Church. But that Act completely altered the terms of the alliance between Church and State. From the moment the State protected and legalized Dissent, the Church of England (or as it is commonly called the Established Church) ceased to be the National Church in the sense that it was before. The theory of an Established Church is that it is the duty of the State to promote truth and to suppress error. The Revolution did one of two things; it either disestablished the Church, or it established Dissent alongside of it; there is

---

[a] Eccles. Pol., bk. viii.

at present in England either none, or there are a hundred equally established religions. If we allow that the Church of England is established by law, we have it on the highest authority that Dissent also was established at the Revolution. A few years after the Act of Toleration was passed Sir Humphrey Edwin, Lord Mayor of London in 1697, carried the Corporation Regalia with him to a Dissenting Meeting-house, and defended himself on the ground that the Act of Parliament "*established* their religion as much as the religion of Churchmen." In 1767, Lord Mansfield, in delivering a judgment in the House of Lords, said, " The Toleration Act renders that which was illegal before *now* legal. The Dissenting way of worship is permitted and allowed by this Act. It is not only exempted from punishment, but rendered innocent and lawful. *It is established*, it is under the protection, and not merely the connivance of the law." Mr. Speaker Onslow, commenting upon this judgment, remarked that the Dissenters were as truly *established* as the Church of England. Such was the opinion of Lawyers, and Statesmen, and Nonconformists themselves in the last century [b].

But the Church should at least have been allowed

---

[b] The meaning of established is "legibus stabilita," and every Church which can appeal to legal protection is a Church *established by law*.

The Birth of Toleration.   81

the same liberty as was granted to Dissenters. So far from this being the case, the Church alone continued to be considered as "Established;" whilst all the advantages which might be imagined to be derived from that position were taken away, and all the disadvantages left. For Dissenters the basis of religious equality was laid, and the way opened for future exemptions and enlargements. The Church on the contrary was placed, and has ever since remained, on an unfavourable footing in relation to Dissent. It has been debarred from the privileges which are allowed to Dissenters; and the Church alone, of all Communions, has been forbidden by the State to have or to use a conscience. It is prevented under the penalties of *Præmunire* from exercising a voice in the election of its own Bishops. Its Bishops are not allowed, under pain of civil terrors, to enforce discipline upon their clergy; the Church is obliged to tolerate errors in the sects, but not allowed to correct them in its own body; obliged to admit to Communion Dissenters, and unfit persons, who had to "qualify" for civil appointments under the Test Act; forbidden from regulating its own business in its Synods, and from determining the meaning of its formularies; a duty which laymen and even Dissenters are thought more competent to perform [c].

---

[c] The Nonconformists at the time of the Revolution numbered only about 10,000 persons, or one-hundredth part of the

inhabitants of England and Wales. But during William's reign they took out licences for no fewer than two thousand four hundred places of worship.—Skeats' Hist. of the Free Churches, 151. Burnet, however, in his speech against the Occasional Conformity Bill said that since the Act of Toleration the numbers of Dissenters were "abated by a moderate computation a fourth part if not a third."

CHAPTER III.

THE FIRST GENERATION OF NONJURORS.

THE first of March, 1689, was the day appointed for taking the oaths to William and Mary. When that day arrived Sancroft and several Bishops absented themselves from the House of Lords, and only eight spiritual Peers took the oaths[a]. An act of Parliament was consequently passed rendering the oaths compulsory, not only on all who should afterwards hold, but on all who already held, any public office[b]. The question was warmly debated in the House of Lords, Whether those who had already held Ecclesiastical offices could be required to take the new oath under pain of deprivation? It was contended that

---

[a] These were the Archbishop of York (Lamplugh), the Bishops of London (Compton), Lincoln (Barlow), Bristol (Trelawney), Winchester (Mew), Rochester (Spratt), Llandaff (Beaw) and St. Asaph (Lloyd), and their example was soon followed by the Bishops of Carlisle (Smith), and St. David's (Watson).—Kennet's Comp. Hist., iii. 552.

[b] Evelyn writes, March 29, 1689: "The Archbishop and *four* other Bishops refusing to come to Parliament, it was deliberated whether they should incur *Præmunire;* but it was thought fit to let this fall and be connived at for fear of the people, to whom these Prelates were very dear for the opposition they had given to Popery."

Parliament had not the power to sever the tie which bound the successors of the Apostles to their Sees; "What God had joined together, man could not put asunder^c." It was, however, eventually determined that all ecclesiastical persons must take the oaths by August 1 in that year, under penalty of six months' suspension, to be followed, if the oaths were not taken by the First of February, by deprivation^d.

A few weeks before the first of February, 1690 (the day fixed for the deprivation of those who refused to take the oaths), arrived, a supposed plot against the Government was discovered, in which Lord Preston, Mr. Ashton, and several others were implicated, and two letters in the handwriting of Turner, Bishop of Ely (one of the seven Bishops who were committed to the Tower), were found addressed to Lord Preston^e. In these letters the writer spoke of "the sentiment of my elder brother" and "the rest of the family," and Burnet, who could spy out an

---

^c Macaulay's Hist. of England, iii. 100.

^d The oath, however, was altered; it was not to be taken to "the rightful and lawful king," but "I, A. B., do solemnly promise to bear true allegiance to their Majesties, King William and Queen Mary." From this says Burnet, O. T., ii. 579, began the notion of a king "*de facto* but not *de jure.*"

^e "There was a pretended discovery of a pretended plot of the Jacobites or Nonjurors, whereupon some of them were imprisoned, and Dr. Turner being suspected to be in the same pretended plot" withdrew and absconded.—Wood's Athenæ Oxon.

The first generation of Nonjurors. 85

opponent through a stone wall, makes out to his own satisfaction that the writer must needs be Turner, Bishop of Ely, the "elder brother" Sancroft, and "the rest of the family" the other Nonjuring Prelates. The charge, whether founded or unfounded, was the very thing needed to inflame the public mind, and to deprive Sancroft and the other Bishops of the sympathy which their courage and sufferings had obtained for them. Burnet tells us that this discovery determined the King to fill up the Sees of the Nonjurors at once, "which perhaps, but for that event, might have been hung up for another year."

When the first of February arrived, three of the Bishops who had not taken the oaths were dead, viz. Thomas of Worcester, Cartwright of Chester, and Lake of Chichester. Six Prelates, viz. Sancroft, Archbishop of Canterbury, Ken, Bishop of Bath and Wells, Turner of Ely, Frampton of Gloucester, Lloyd of Norwich, and White of Peterborough, together with about four hundred of the Clergy, refused to take the oaths and were deprived [f].

Of the seven Bishops committed to the Tower by James, all except Lloyd, Bishop of St. Asaph, and Sir Jonathan Trelawney, translated to the See of Exeter, were amongst the Nonjuring Bishops [g]. It was

---

[f] A fairly full list of the Nonjuring clergy will be found in the Life of Kettlewell, App. VI.

[g] Thomas, Bishop of Worcester, and Lake, Bishop of Chichester, had, as we have seen, died before the day of depriva-

consequently said of these two Bishops that whereas the other five were fine gold, these two were only Prince's metal [h]. They, however, soon got their reward under William. Lloyd was appointed Almoner to the King (a somewhat sinecure appointment in William's reign it was said to be); in 1692 he was translated to Lichfield and Coventry, and in 1709 to Worcester [i].

Sir Jonathan Trelawney, a Cornish Baronet (although at a later period he seems to have amended his ways, and is known as the patron and friend of Atterbury), was not at one time a very creditable Bishop. He had an inveterate habit of swearing, which he excused on the ground that he did not swear as a Bishop, but as a Baronet. A letter of his to the Lord Chancellor Rochester is extant, which does him little credit; it was in these words: "My Lord, Give me leave to throw myself at your Lordship's feet, humbly imploring your patronage if not for the Bishopric of Peterborough, at least for Chichester, if the Bishop of Exeter cannot be prevailed upon to accept that now vacant See.... If Peterborough and Chichester shall both be refused me, I shall not deny Bristol. But

---

tion, but their places were taken by two other Nonjurors, Lloyd, Bishop of Norwich, and Frampton, Bishop of Gloucester.

[h] In allusion to the Mint which was at that time kept in the Tower.

[i] Lloyd died in 1717, aged 90. He was early in Queen Anne's reign deprived of the office of Almoner, on a charge of a breach of Privilege brought against him by Sir John Pakington, M.P.

I hope the King (James) will have some tender compassion on his *slave*. J. Trelawney." The slave got neither Peterborough nor Chichester, but only Bristol [j], and he never forgave James; we may question whether it was not enmity to the King rather than zeal for the Church which prompted him in his opposition and sent him to the Tower [k].

Of the early Nonjurors (for we shall have to speak afterwards of a later generation [l]) the most conspicuous amongst the Prelates were Sancroft, Archbishop of Canterbury, and Ken, Bishop of Bath and Wells; whilst amongst the Second Order of the Clergy we must notice the following:—William Sherlock (1641—1707), Master of the Temple [m]; Charles Leslie (1650—1722), Chancellor of the Diocese of Clogher [n]; George Hickes (1642—1715), Dean of Worcester [o]; John Kettlewell (1653—1695), Vicar

---

[j] The See of Bristol was then, and till quite recent times, worth only £700 yearly.

[k] In 1689 he was translated to the coveted See of Exeter, and in 1707 (under Queen Anne) to Winchester.

[l] See chapter headed "The Nonjuring Schism."

[m] He afterwards took the oaths and was made Dean of St. Paul's.

[n] Of whom Dr. Johnson said, he was the only Nonjuror who could *reason*. Being obliged to leave the kingdom in 1713, he retired to the Pretender's Court, but died in his own country in 1722.

[o] Afterwards a Nonjuring Bishop; brother of a Nonconformist Minister, who was executed for the part he took in Monmouth's Rebellion.

of Coleshill, Warwickshire, of whom Ken said, "He certainly was as saint-like a man as ever I knew ᵖ;" Nathaniel Spinkes (1653—1727)ᵍ; and Jeremy Collier, the Historian ʳ. Conspicuous amongst the Laity were Henry Dodwell (1641—1711) ˢ, and "the Pious" Robert Nelson, Author of the "Companion of the Fasts and Festivals of the Church." The whole number of the Nonjurors did not much exceed four hundred, and surprise is sometimes expressed on the one hand that there were so few Nonjurors (for some twenty-nine thirtieths of the clergy took the oaths), and on the other that there were any Nonjurors at all ᵗ.

But the position in which the Clergy were placed was so novel, that they scarcely knew how to act. The great mass of the Clergy agreed in the opinions of the Nonjurors, but when the day, looked forward to with anxiety by all, arrived, from different reasons and motives they took the oaths. Many regarded the oaths as a matter of political rather than of

---

ᵖ He graduated at St. Edmund's Hall, Oxford, and was by the interest of Hickes, elected Fellow of Lincoln. He published in 1681 the "Measures of Christian Obedience."

ᵍ Afterwards a Nonjuring Bishop, of whom it was remarked, "happy would it have been for a Diocese, had he been legally appointed to it."

ʳ Afterwards a Nonjuring Bishop.

ˢ Educated at and Fellow of Trinity College, Dublin; Camden Professor at Oxford in 1688.

ᵗ Lord Macaulay uses a two-edged sword against them. In one place he sneers at the idea of there being any, in another at there being so few Nonjurors.

ecclesiastical importance. Whiston tells us that many members of Cambridge University took them with a doubting, if not an accusing, conscience [u]. Many took the oaths at first but recanted afterwards [v]. Many again were no doubt influenced by the Latitudinarian Bishop, whom the King had set over them, and retained their livings with discontented feelings. Some took the oaths as the lesser of two evils. "We did dreadfully apprehend," wrote a Dignitary of the Church, "that if we did not take the oaths, the whole Church might have been overturned at once, and Presbytery or something like it set up in the Church [w]."

All must admire the courage of an Archbishop, and Bishops, and others of the Clergy, who could resign their sees, their benefices, their all, in many cases to face with their families starvation, rather than do what they thought wrong. But however much we may admire the courage and self-denial of these good men, room for doubt is left whether this unhappy secession, doubly lamentable because it was political rather than religious, did not arise from an over-sensitive conscientiousness.

[u] For such persons the Nonjurors had little compassion, and spoke of them contemptuously as "a pack of jolly swearers."—Toulmin's Hist. of Dissenters.

[v] See Kettlewell's Life for the form of recantation used. One clergyman, Mr. Pinchbeck, who made his recantation publicly in church, was tried at the Lincoln Assizes, and condemned to stand in the Pillory and to pay a fine of £200.

[w] *Querela Temporum*, or Danger of the Church of England.

To say the least, the imposition of the new oaths, which was unusual and unnecessary, was an uncalled for hardship inflicted on the Clergy. It was to Sancroft and the Bishops that William was indebted for his Crown. Here was an Archbishop of whom the Church at any period might have been proud; a man, naturally of a timid and retiring position, but bold as a lion in opposing evil. This was not the first time he had suffered for conscience' sake. He had given up his Fellowship at Cambridge rather than take the Engagement under the Commonwealth; he had gone to prison rather than bow the knee to Romanism; and now he gave up all, rather than take, what he considered to be, an unlawful oath. William cared nothing for the Church of England. Had he done so, he would have known how to value such a man. That the King did not place much importance upon the oaths is evident, for he offered to excuse them altogether, if only the Nonconformists might be freed from the operation of the Test Act. The Test, however, was in those days regarded as the bulwark of the Church; his offer was rejected, and he took his revenge on the Church.

Still, although the King was wrong, it does not necessarily follow that the Nonjurors were right. William was *de facto* king, and the oaths were so altered as to recognise nothing more than an acknowledgment of his *de facto* right. He was acknowledged as lawful king by the crowned heads of

Christendom, and the oath was in no respect contradictory to the law of God or of the Church. The question, therefore, arises whether it was not their duty to stand by, rather than forsake, the Church in her hour of need. Stillingfleet, Bishop of Worcester, probably the most learned Bishop of the day, was strongly opposed to the course taken by the Nonjurors. "Nothing," he said, "was required of them contrary to Scripture, Fathers, or Councils, or Articles of the Church." And again he says, "As to the public offices of the Church with regard to their Majesties, I can find no one instance in the Greek or Latin Church, where these were scrupled to be used with respect to those who were in actual possession of the throne by the Providence of God and consent of the people[x]."

But still we must look at the matter in the light in which it presented itself to the Nonjurors themselves. Probably few of them would accept Stillingfleet, who was somewhat of a Latitudinarian, as an authority. We ourselves, living at the end of the nineteenth century, can scarcely realize the feelings of those Bishops and Clergy who lived at the end of the seventeenth. We must enquire a little more closely into the question. Ever since the Reformation the doctrines of non-resistance and passive obedience had been "the distinguishing character of the Church

---

[x] Miscellaneous Discourses.

of England, if not the true test of Christianity y." At the Restoration they assumed, and up to the Revolution, notwithstanding the strain which was put upon them by James, they maintained, an almost paramount importance. Lake, Bishop of Chichester, one of the Seven Bishops, declared shortly before his death, "I took this to be the distinguishing mark of the Church . . . . . and in consequence have incurred suspension from the exercise of my office, and deprivation ᶻ." Thomas, Bishop of Worcester, who also was one of the Seven Bishops, only three days before his death averred, in still stronger language, "If my heart do not deceive me, I think I could suffer at the stake rather than take the oath."

On the whole, when we find on one side such names as Sancroft, and Ken, and Kettlewell, and Robert Nelson, and on the other, Bull, and Beveridge, and the saintly Bishop Wilson ᵃ, all hasty judgment

---

ʸ They were taught in the "Institution of a Christian Man," published in 1537, as afterwards in the Homilies and Canons, and were declared by the University of Oxford in her Decrees of 1622, 1647, and 1683.—Blunt's Dict., Art. "Nonjurors."

ᶻ Kettlewell's Life.

ᵃ Wilson was ordained Priest by Stratford, who took Cartwright's See of Chester. He was also consecrated Bishop by Archbishop Sharp, Bishops Stratford and More, the latter of whom had succeeded the Nonjuror Lloyd. Indeed Bishop Wilson is said to have been a favourer of the principles of the Revolution, and to have had a personal regard for King William.—Keble's Life of Wilson, i. 78.

The first Generation of Nonjurors. 93

must be suspended, and we must be contented to leave the question undecided. But as to their own position, the Nonjuring Bishops entertained no doubts. They felt that if they took the oaths, their whole afterlife would be a lie. In vain Parliament altered the form of the oaths; in vain Queen Mary offered that, if only they would continue to perform their duties—to ordain, to institute, and to confirm, she would endeavour that a Bill should be introduced into Parliament to excuse them from the oaths. They thought this could not diminish their faith, so long as they were obliged, in the services of the Church, to pray for King William and Queen Mary.

To the Nonjurors no pension was given by the government, and they were turned out on the world to live as best they could [b], and there can be no doubt that some even of the Nonjuring Bishops were reduced to great want. Some few, like Sancroft, had a small pittance of their own; some became tutors in the families of noblemen and gentry [c]; some few found friends, as Ken did, in Lord Weymouth at Longleat; and there was a settlement at Shottisbrooke in Berkshire, of which White Kennet (of whom we shall hear more further on) was Rector, and where the residence of a hospitable county gentleman, Mr.

---

[b] The only mitigation was power given to the King to allow to a number not exceeding twelve of the Clergy a sum not exceeding the third part of their Livings.

[c] As Law, in the family of the Historian Gibbon.

Francis Cherry, became an asylum always open to the deprived Clergy, a home for learning and distress[d]. Many tried to keep themselves and their families from starvation by their writings, and many men of talent, who were too poor to buy books, lived at Oxford for the sake of the libraries, which drew from John Wesley the remark that "Oxford was paved with the skulls of Nonjurors." For the relief of the Nonjurors a fund was started by Kettlewell in January, 1695, the management of which was entrusted to Spinkes, but the death of Kettlewell shortly afterwards prevented his taking part in the distribution. It might have been hoped that such a charitable object could not possibly have given offence to the government, yet Ken was summoned before the Privy Council for taking part in it.

The loss that the secession of the Nonjurors entailed upon the Church could not easily be repaired, for their numbers comprised not only some of the most holy and most learned men in the Church, but men of the soundest Church principles, and the men most fitted to counteract the Latitudinarianism of William's Bishops. The greatest loss were Archbishop Sancroft and Ken, Bishop of Bath and Wells, of whose lives we must give some fuller account.

---

[d] So devoted was Mr. Cherry to the Jacobite cause that in the hunting-field he would frequently venture his own neck at a dangerous leap in the hope that William might be induced to follow and break his neck.

The first Generation of Nonjurors. 95

William Sancroft (1617—1693), born at Fresingfield in Suffolk, educated at Emmanuel College, Cambridge, was elected a Fellow of his College in 1642, but in 1649 was deprived of his Fellowship by the Puritans for refusing to take the Covenant and the Engagement[e]. Being driven from the University, he devoted much of his time to literature[f], but in 1659 he went abroad, where he was able not only to support himself but others also, and amongst them Cosin, who also had been deprived of his preferments by the Puritans. Having returned with Cosin to England at the Restoration, Cosin, when he was consecrated, in 1660, Bishop of Durham, shewed his gratitude by making him his chaplain, conferring on him a golden Prebend at Durham, and the Living of Houghton-le-Spring, one of the richest benefices in England; and it was probably by the recommendation of Cosin, who bore the most important part in the work, that he was actively employed in the last revision of the Prayer-Book in 1662, and when the work was ended was appointed supervisor of the Press. His rise was now rapid. In 1662 he

---

[e] A contrast: Sancroft was deprived of his Fellowship for being a Churchman, Tillotson, his successor as Archbishop, was elected to a Fellowship for not being a Churchman.

[f] He is supposed to be the author of "Fur Prædestinatus," which was written in Latin with the object of exposing ultra-Calvinism, and a work entitled "Modern Policies taken from Machiavel, Borgia, and other choice Authors."

became Master of Emmanuel; then Dean of York; and in 1664 Dean of St. Paul's [g].

In 1666 the greater part of old St. Paul's was destroyed in the fire of London. For some years previous to the fire the Cathedral had been in a very ruinous state, and funds had been raised for its restoration; the funds, however, together with the revenues of the Dean and Chapter, were seized under the Commonwealth, and the Cathedral turned into a barrack for the soldiers. After the fire, Sancroft still clung to the hope of being able to restore the Cathedral, but was dissuaded by the advice of Wren, who, since he built the Sheldonian Theatre at Oxford in 1669, enjoyed the reputation of being the first Architect of the day, and was chosen Architect of the new Cathedral, the first stone of which was laid in 1675. In 1668 Sancroft became Archdeacon of Canterbury, and in 1678, much against his will, he was, through the recommendation of the Duke of York, elected to succeed Sheldon as Archbishop of Canterbury [h]. His lot was now cast in times scarcely less difficult than those of Laud, but, though he cannot always be acquitted of timidity and vacillation, attributable to the

---

[g] Milman's Annals of St. Paul's.

[h] "The King was under some difficulty to find a proper person, but at last, by the recommendation of his brother, the Duke of York, he resolved upon Sancroft as a person of great prudence and moderation."—Kennet's Complete History.

The first Generation of Nonjurors. 97

gentleness of his character, he shewed, on more than one occasion, that he would not deviate a hair's breadth from the path of duty. Thus in 1686 he refused to act, although he thought it necessary to excuse himself on the ground of his great age, on James's illegal Commission, for which he was forbidden the Court. And when Queen Mary, soon after her arrival in England, asked of him his blessing, he told her she must first ask the blessing of her Father whom she had wronged, "for mine otherwise would not be registered in Heaven."

We now come to the great events in his life, which have already been recorded in these pages: his opposition to the illegal measures of James, and his imprisonment in the Tower; his refusal to take, during the lifetime of James, fresh oaths of allegiance to William and Mary, and his consequent deprivation. The sentence of deprivation against him was not immediately enforced. The See of Canterbury was not at that time a bed of roses, and it was some time before Tillotson could be prevailed upon to become Sancroft's successor; in consequence of the King's absence in Flanders the *congé d'élire* was not issued till May 1, 1691, and Tillotson was not consecrated before the 31st of that month. Sancroft, who never recognised the authority by which he was deprived, refused to quit the Palace until compelled to do so by a process of ejectment; on June 23, however, he left, a poorer man than he entered it, and retired for

H

a time to a private house in Palgrave Court [i], which, after remaining there for six weeks, he left, to spend the remainder of his life at Fresingfield. At Fresingfield he, on Feb. 9, 1692, executed a deed by which he delegated his archiepiscopal duties to Lloyd, Bishop of Norwich, in whose diocese Fresingfield was situated, and by whom the Nonjuring Scheme was continued [k]. At Fresingfield, Sancroft lived his simple life in conscious rectitude, cultivating his garden with his own hands. A plain and humble life was nothing new to him. Mr. Needham, his Chaplain, describes the life he had led in his Palace at Lambeth: "He was the most pious, humble, good Christian I ever knew in all my life. His hours for Chapel were 6 in the morning, 12 before dinner, 3 in the afternoon, and 9 at night . . . His usual diet, when it was not fast day, was two small dishes of coffee and a pipe of tobacco for breakfast; at noon chicken or mutton; at night a glass of mum [l] and a bit of bread, if anything?" If such was his mode of living in a Palace, he would not need much luxury in his cottage at

---

[i] Here he was visited by the Earl of Aylesbury. The deprived Prelate himself opened the door, and the Earl, who had often visited him in his Palace, was so moved with the change of circumstances, that he burst into tears. Sancroft, however, remarked: "O, my Lord, rather rejoice with me, for now I live again."—Granger, iv. 281.

[k] See Part II. chap. iii.

[l] i.e. ale brewed from wheat.

Fresingfield. So he lived out his life comfortably on £50 a year, and was buried amongst his ancestors in the churchyard at Fresingfield in a spot selected by himself.

Thomas Ken (1637—1711), the author of the well-known Morning and Evening hymns, was born at Berkhampstead, and after being educated at Winchester, where he formed his life-long acquaintance with Francis Turner, afterwards the Nonjuring Bishop of Ely, he became a member of Hart Hall, Oxford, until he succeeded to a vacancy at New College. The University was at that time under the dominion of the Puritans, Cromwell being Chancellor, Dr. Owen, the Independent, Dean of Christ Church and Vice-Chancellor, and Marshall, who was not a Wykehamist, had been obtruded as Warden of New College by the Parliamentary party. At Oxford Ken formed a friendship with two men who, in his after life, were intimately associated with him, Thomas Thynne, afterwards Lord Weymouth, and George Hooper. In 1660 he was ordained, and in 1666 was presented by Lord Maynard to a small Living in Essex, but in the same year he returned as Fellow to Winchester, to which See Bishop Morley had lately been translated from Worcester; and at Winchester he found the pious Izaak Walton an inmate of the Bishop's Palace. Izaak Walton, the Author of "The Complete Angler," was a layman who led a holy and religious life in a time of much darkness and corruption; and under his hospitable roof on the banks of the Dove, Morley, who had been ejected from his Canonry at Christ Church during the troublous times of the Commonwealth, found a home. This kindness Morley, when he became Bishop of Winchester, returned by giving Izaak a home, and we can picture to ourselves the family circle—Morley, Izaak Walton ("honest Izaak," as people called him), and Ken. Izaak had taken, as his second wife, Ken's sister Anne (Kenna as he called her), which was a strong recommendation to the Bishop in Ken's favour. Bishop Morley made Ken his Chaplain, and gave him first the Living of Brightstone in the Isle of Wight, and then that of East Woodhay, and he made him a Prebendary of Winchester. In 1674 Ken published a Manual of Prayers for the use of the scholars of Winchester College, in the later editions of which appeared the well-known Morning and Evening hymns, as well as the less-known hymn for Midnight. In 1675, in company with young Izaak Walton, the only son of "Piscator," Ken visited Rome, and as that was the year of the Jubilee, it must have been to him a journey of great interest; he returned to England the same year, "if it were possible," he said, "more confirmed in the purity of the Protestant religion than he was before." In 1679 he went to the Hague as Chaplain to the Princess of Orange, in succession to Dr. Hooper; both Hooper and Ken having been his Chaplains, it is probable they were

The first Generation of Nonjurors.   101

recommended to her by Bishop Morley, who had been Confessor to her mother, the Duchess of York[m]. The Prince of Orange hated both Hooper and Ken, but Ken even more than Hooper, and for the following reason[n]. When William came to England to solicit in marriage the hand of the Princess Mary, he was accompanied by his uncle, Count Zulestein, who abused the affections of Jane Wroth, one of the Maids of Honour, and but for Ken, Jane would probably have been an outcast from society. Ken, however, remonstrated with the Count, and prevailed upon him to marry her[o], which the Count did in the presence of the Princess. This brought upon Ken the anger of William. King Charles II., who knew the circumstances, so highly approved of Ken's conduct, that in 1680 he appointed him as his Chaplain[p]. In 1683 Ken went to Tangier as Chaplain under the command of Lord Dartmouth, and on his return he

---

[m] Burnet says, "He, Morley, told me that she had practised secret confession to him from the time she had been twelve years old."—Bowles' Life of Ken, ii. 41.

[n] Mrs. Prowse writes in her memoranda that Hooper soon disagreed with the Prince, and then Ken was recommended, as being more conciliatory, but "he agreed worse."

[o] The Count afterwards became Lord Rochford, and by her he had four sons and four daughters.

[p] Boswell relates an observation of Dr. Johnson respecting Charles II. : "he was licentious in his practice, but he always had a reverence for what was good. He knew his people and reverenced merit. The Church was at no time better served than in his reign."

resumed his residence as Prebendary at Winchester. In the summer of that year Charles visited Winchester to inspect the palace which he was building in that city. During the visits which he used to pay to Winchester he was generally in the habit of stopping at the Deanery; but on the present occasion, not finding sufficient accommodation there for his suite, he demanded of Ken the use of his Prebendal House for Nell Gwynne. " Not for his kingdom," was the only reply which Ken gave him [q]. And here we must notice a good trait in Charles's character; instead of being offended with Ken, he said to one of his courtiers, " Odds fish, man! although I am not good myself, I can respect those that are [r]." The See of Bath and Wells soon afterwards became vacant through the translation of Dr. Mew, on the death of Bishop Morley, to Winchester, and Charles appointed to the See Ken, " the little fellow," as he called him, " who refused to give poor Nelly a lodging [s]."

Of all the Prelates, Charles liked Ken most; before the end of the month Ken was called upon to attend

---

[q] The Dean, Dr. Meggott, was more compliant. He had a small room built for her off the drawing-room, known afterwards as "Nell Gwynne," and here she lodged whilst Charles was at the Deanery.—Bowles' Life of Ken, ii. 56. The room was taken down by Dean Reynell.

[r] Strickland's Lives of the Seven Bishops.

[s] The cringing Dean was passed over and died Dean of Winchester in 1692.

Charles's deathbed. Here, Burnet tells us that "Ken spoke with great elevation of thought and expression, like a man inspired;" and although he failed to persuade Charles to receive the Holy Eucharist from the English Bishops, it was Ken who interdicted the Duchess of Portsmouth from the dying chamber, and prevailed upon Charles to ask forgiveness from his deeply-injured wife.

Wherever good was to be done or evil prevented, there Ken found work to do. After Monmouth's defeat at Sedgemoor, although the punishment for concealing fugitives was death, Ken's Palace, which was within a day's journey of the battlefield, was thrown open to them as a refuge, and Ken prayed with and doled out charity to them at his Palace gates. King James knew what Ken did, and yet he was the very person whom the king thought most fitted to prepare Monmouth for his death, and so Ken stood by the scaffold of the son with the same pious earnestness with which he had attended the deathbed of the father. And when the General, Lord Feversham, was using great cruelty to the prisoners whom he had taken after the battle, Ken rushed into the midst, and stopped the military executions, exclaiming, "My Lord, this is murder in law. These poor wretches, now that the battle is over, must be tried before they can be put to death."

Every Sunday at Wells twelve poor men and

women dined with him in his hall; and so general and extensive was his liberality, that when he was obliged to retire from his See he quitted it a poor man. At the Revolution he could not himself take the oaths to the new King and Queen; but this did not prevent him from persuading those who could do so with a clear conscience to take them; to his friend Dr. Hooper he said, "I am satisfied that you take them with as clear and well-resolved conscience as I refuse them;" he thought little of his own deprivation, and congratulated himself on being "eased of a great load," and "having nothing to do but to think of eternity." After he was deprived, he found a home at Longleat, the seat of his old college friend, Lord Weymouth, a nobleman worthy of being the entertainer of such a guest [u]. The sale of his goods was effected for £700; this small sum was all he possessed, and this he handed over to Lord Weymouth, receiving from him an annuity of £80.

He was succeeded in the See of Bath and Wells by Dr. Kidder, Dean of Peterborough. Dr. Kidder was, together with his wife, killed in his bed in the Palace of Wells by the fall of a stack of chimneys during the great storm of 1703, and the See of Bath and Wells was then offered to Ken's friend, Hooper, who that same year had been consecrated to the See

---

[u] To use Ken's words, "he conducted his life by the divine maxims recorded by St. Paul."—Life, by a Layman.

of St. Asaph. Hooper excused himself for refusing it, "as he could by no means eat the bread of so old a friend as Bishop Ken had been to him," and entreated Queen Anne to restore Ken. The Queen joyfully followed his advice, and offered Ken his old See. Ken received the offer "with great acknowledgment," and "desired Hooper to return his most grateful thanks to the Queen for her gracious remembrance of him; but that he could not return into the business of the world again, but would ever beseech God to accumulate the blessings of both upon her." He pressed Hooper to accept the See; "he charged him as he would answer at the Great Day, to take the charge of his flock[x]." Such a request it was impossible for Hooper to refuse; he accepted the See, but only on condition that he should be allowed to hold the Chantership of Exeter Cathedral *in commendam*, and to devote the income, £200 a year, to Ken: and when Bishop Trelawney objected to this arrangement, the Queen paid the £200 a year to him from her own purse.

The only time Ken is known to have officiated publicly after his deprivation, was at the funeral of Kettlewell at All Hallows, Barking, on which occasion he officiated in his episcopal robes, and afterwards took part in the Evensong at the church.

Once, and once only, was he disturbed by the

---

[x] Mrs. Prowse's MSS.

government, and that was with regard to the charity inaugurated by Kettlewell for the relief of the starving families of the Nonjurors. On April 28, 1696, he was ordered to appear before the Privy Council, on which occasion he presented himself in his episcopal dress. Being accused of "usurping episcopal functions" his reply was, "My Lords, I never knew that *begging* was a part of Episcopal jurisdiction:" perhaps the soft answer turned away wrath; at any rate it was decisive; thenceforward he was allowed to perform his humble duties unmolested.

After his deprivation he lived on at Longleat (with a few intermissions) for twenty years; "there he wrote hymns, and sang them to his viol, and prayed and died [y]." On March 19, 1711, this holy Confessor, the last survivor of the Nonjuring Bishops, died in his 74th year, and having arrayed himself for his burial with his own hands in the shroud which he had for many years carried about with him, he was by his own request buried in the churchyard of Frome-Selwood [z].

We cannot dismiss this early generation of Nonjurors without saying a few words on a Nonjuring

---

[y] Life, by a Layman.

[z] In his will he declared, "I die in the Holy Catholic and Apostolic Faith professed by the whole Church before the disunion of East and West, more particularly I die in the Communion of the Church of England, as it stands distinguished from all Papal and Puritan innovations, and as it adheres to the doctrines of the Cross."

Layman, who in many respects bore a close resemblance to Bishop Ken—the "pious" Robert Nelson.

Robert Nelson (1656—1715), the son of an opulent merchant, having received his earliest education at St. Paul's School, afterwards became a pupil of the famous George Bull, to whose teaching and influence must no doubt to a large degree be attributed Nelson's regard for primitive antiquity and Church authority. In 1682 he married Lady Theophila Lucy, a lady much older than himself, who not long afterwards, during the Romanizing movement which at that time took place in England, and under the influence of Bossuet, Bishop of Meaux, was induced to join the Roman Catholic Church.

One of the noblest traits in Nelson's character was that, although he could not take the oaths himself, he lived on the closest terms of friendship with Jurors and Nonjurors alike; he was the intimate friend of Kettlewell, and, after Kettlewell's death, of Hickes, and yet he co-operated with the juring members of the Church in all good works. He was the intimate friend of Archbishop Tillotson, with whom he commenced a correspondence as early as 1680. It was Tillotson whose advice he asked as to whether he could continue a member of the Church of England, when he could not join in the prayers for William and Mary. The answer was, "I think it is plain that no man can join in prayers in which there is any petition which he is verily persuaded is sinful.

I cannot endure a trick, much less in religion [a]." So Nelson joined the Nonjurors, and it is not known that any further correspondence took place between Nelson and Tillotson; but to the last he remained the firm friend of the Archbishop, at whose deathbed he watched through the last nights of his life, and who died in his arms on November 23, 1694.

There was scarcely any good work of the day with which Nelson was not more or less associated. He was the Patron and Advocate of the Religious Societies and of the Societies for the Reformation of Manners. He was one of the original members, and frequently the Chairman, of the Society for Promoting Christian Knowledge; a constant attendant at the meetings of the sister society, the Society for the Propagation of the Gospel; the supporter of the charitable designs of Dr. Bray; he interested himself in the establishment of Queen Anne's Bounty; he was one of the Commissioners for building fifty new churches; he took a lively interest in the Corporation of the Sons of the Clergy, and in the attempts that were made for the establishment of workhouses. He foresaw the necessity of those agencies, many of which, though delayed through more than a hundred years of torpor, have been supplied in these later days, such as Theological Colleges for the Clergy; Training-schools for Masters and Mistresses

---

[a] Birch's Tillotson, p. 259.

of Charity Schools; schools for blackguard boys, corresponding to the "ragged schools" of our day; Penitentiaries; Foundlings; plans for Religious Retreats; and the appointment of Bishops for the American Plantations [b].

---

[b] Secretan's Life of Nelson, p. 91.

CHAPTER IV.

THE LATITUDINARIAN BISHOPS.

AS much has already been said, and more will necessarily be said in the history of the eighteenth century, on the subject of Latitudinarianism, we may, perhaps, be pardoned for making a few preliminary remarks on the history of that way of thinking, which was now about to exercise so strong an influence on the Church of England.

Latitudinarianism, or Indifferentism, owed its origin to William's own country, Holland. Arminius (Jakob Harmensen) who was born in Holland in 1560, and who, though at first his devoted adherent, became afterwards the opponent of Calvin, devised a plan which he intended to embrace all Christians except Roman Catholics. His plan was first digested into a regular system by his pupil Episcopius, who was born in Amsterdam in 1583; and as the next step to Indifferentism is Rationalism, we learn that the followers of Arminius "went still further, and bringing the greatest part of the doctrines of Christianity before the Tribunal of Reason, they modified them considerably and reduced them to an excessive degree of simplicity[a]." Such opinions are always favourable to Socinianism; so we are told of Episcopius that though "himself no Socinian, he very indiscreetly concurred with the Socinians of his time in maintaining that the opinion of the mere Humanity of Christ had prevailed very generally in the first ages, and was never deemed heretical by the Fathers of the orthodox persuasion, at least not in such degree as to exclude them from the Communion of the Church[b]."

The system of Latitudinarianism was first introduced into England by Hales and Chillingworth. Their mantle fell on a body of Divines known as the Cambridge Platonists who lived at the time of the Restoration, of whom the principal were Dr. Cudworth, Henry More, Bishop Williams, Whichcote, and Worthington. This school received a great impetus at the Revolution from King William's Bishops, and, except during the short interval of Queen Anne's reign, held its own through the eighteenth century, and considerably affected the condition and the destiny of the Church to the times in which we ourselves live.

Burnet, Bishop of Salisbury, himself the most prominent of the Latitudinarians, thus describes the party: "They declared against superstition on the one hand and enthusiasm on the other. They loved

---

[a] Mosheim, v. 457.
[b] Horsley's Tracts in Controversy with Priestley.

the constitution of the Church and the Liturgy, and could well live under them, but they did not think it unlawful to live under any other form. They wished that things might be carried on with more moderation. And they continued to keep a good correspondence with those who differed from them in opinion, and allowed a great freedom in philosophy and divinity, from whence they were called 'men of Latitude.' And upon this, men of narrow thoughts and fiercer temper fastened upon them the name of *Latitudinarians*. They read Episcopius much," and were regarded by their enemies as Socinians[c].

How perilous this system was is evident. The school was anti-dogmatic, and without any fixed system of theology. The negation of all objective truth entirely destroyed the doctrine of the indwelling in the Church of the Holy Ghost, as well as that of the authority of the Church. This led to the rejection of the Church's teaching and the Church's doctrine, of the importance of Catholic teaching in the interpretation of faith; it taught the sufficiency of Scripture as interpreted by each man's private judgment; that, whatever sect people belonged to, they might find in it salvation, so long as they framed their lives according to the law and the light of nature[d]. It reversed the Apostolic rule, and taught that men

---

[c] O. T., i. 263.
[d] This is the doctrine condemned in Article XVIII.

The Latitudinarian Bishops.

may live by sight and not by faith. It inculcated a religion of common sense; a person need only believe what he understands; as though the Bible were given for men to pick out just as much as they liked and reject the rest, or as if common sense (supposing people to possess it) were enough to guide men into all truth. So when people were free to choose only what they liked, and to reject all that they could not understand, soon men began to discard prophecies and miracles and all that was supernatural; or they tried to explain them away; to attribute matters above them to an illusion of the senses, or to some unknown natural phenomena; and when that was impossible, to deny altogether the truth of the Scripture narrative. And by carrying out this principle a little further, they learnt to treat the divine Nature of our Lord as a myth, and to denounce the Trinity in Unity as a corruption[e].

The question naturally arises,—How did William find amongst the Anglican Clergy the men of Latitudinarian and Low Church views whom he appointed to Bishoprics? and how did the Bishops find ready to their hands the tools which enabled them to carry out their Latitudinarian views? The answer is to be found in the state of the Church at the Restoration; the source of the Broad Church and Low Church element in the Church of England were those con-

[e] Church and World, 2nd Series, 491.

forming Puritans who on "Black Bartholomew" (as the day is commemorated in the Puritan Calendar) accepted the terms of the Act of Uniformity in order to retain their benefices, but who did not honestly conform to its conditions. The places of the eight thousand Clergy whom Cromwell had expelled had been fitted up by men of the Puritan faction, mostly Presbyterians, with a few Independents and Baptists, and a sprinkling of various kinds of enthusiasts. Since the overthrow of the Church no Clergyman had been ordained for the Church; the majority of the eight thousand expelled Clergy were dead; it follows, therefore, that, even if the intruding Nonconformists had resigned in a body, the requisite number of orthodox Clergy could not have been found to fill the Livings. But so far from this being the case, only about 1600 or 1700 on St. Bartholomew's Day, 1662, refused Conformity; the rest remained on as a dead weight to the Church, conforming outward, but opposed in their heart, and, as much as possible in their practice, to its doctrine and discipline.

Let us hear what South says of this School:—" It was a saying of a judicious Prelate, 'That of all sorts of enemies which the Church had, there was none so deadly, so pernicious, and likely to prove so fatal to it as the conforming Puritan—a great truth and ratified. He is one who lives by the Altar and turns his back on it; one who catches at the prefer-

The Latitudinarian Bishops.

ment of the Church, but hates the discipline and order of it; one who practises conformity as Papists take oaths and tests, that is, with an inward abhorrence of what he does for the present, and a resolution to act quite contrary when occasion serves.' Otherwise what means the service of the Church so imperfectly and by halves read over? What makes them mince and mangle that in their practice which they could swallow whole in their subscriptions? Why are the public prayers curtailed and left out —prayers enjoined with authority—only to make the more room for a long crude harangue before the sermon? Such persons seem to conform only that they may despise the Church's injunctions under the Church's wing, and continue authority within the protection of the laws."

We will listen again to what South says in another sermon :—" Then it will follow that in the same Diocese, and sometimes in the very same town, some shall use the surplice and some shall not; and each have their parties persecuting one another. Some in the same church and at the same time shall receive the Sacrament *kneeling*, some *standing*, and others possibly *sitting*. Some shall use the Cross in Baptism, and others shall not only not use it themselves, but also shall inveigh and preach against those who do. . . . The Liturgy so read and mangled in the reading, as if they were ashamed of it. These, and the like vile passages, have made some schismatics, and confirmed others; and in a word, have made so many *Nonconformists* to the Church, by their conforming to their Minister f."

The first Bishop appointed by William was his Chaplain, Burnet, who was, on the death of Dr. Seth Ward, appointed to the See of Salisbury g. Gilbert Burnet (1643—1715), who was born in Edinburgh of a Presbyterian family on his mother's side, and educated at Marischal College, Aberdeen, having first applied himself to the study of the Law, soon turned his thoughts to Divinity, his early education in which was entrusted to the most eminent Scottish Divines. In 1663 he came to England, and paid a six months' visit to the two Universities. At Cambridge he made the acquaintance of Dr. Cudworth and Dr. More, and arriving soon afterwards in London he was thrown into the society of Whichcot, Wilkins, Tillotson, Stillingfleet, and Patrick. After being ordained by the Bishop of Edinburgh, he held a Living in Scotland, and in 1669 he became Professor of Divinity in the University of Glasgow. In 1673 he settled in London, and became one of the Royal Chaplains, and in 1675 was appointed Preacher at the Rolls. In 1679 he published the first volume of his *History of the Reformation*, for which work he

---

f See Ch. Quar. Rev., July, 1877.

g Dr. Seth Ward recovered for the See of Salisbury the Chancellorship of the Garter, which had been in lay hands for more than 150 years.—Echard, iii. 9.12.

The Latitudinarian Bishops. 117

received the thanks of both Houses of Parliament, and two years afterwards he published the second volume [h]. In the reign of Charles II. Burnet was a man of considerable importance, and attempts were made to detach him from the Liberal party; he was offered the Bishopric of Chichester, and it is supposed other Sees also, "provided he would come into his interest." He refused the bribe, and shortly afterwards found occasion to expostulate with the King on the errors of his life and of his government. " I set before him," he says, " his past life and the effects it had upon the Nation, with the judgments of God that lay on him. I pressed him earnestly to change his whole course of life. . . . The King read it (the document) twice and then threw it into the fire." In 1684, under James II., he was removed from the Preachership of the Rolls on account of a sermon which he preached there on November 5 (for whatever his faults were, he was never afraid to do and to say what he thought right [i]). Having thus incurred the wrath of King James, he retired to the Continent, and after making a tour in France, Italy, Switzerland, and Germany, he, at the invitation of

---

[h] The third volume was not published till 1715.

[i] What the character of the sermon was may be gathered from his Epitaph in the chancel of Clerkenwell church: " In templo Rotulorum Londini dum nimis acriter (ut iis qui rerum tum potiebantur visum est) Ecclesiæ Romanæ malas artes insectatur, ab officio submotus est."

the Prince and Princess of Orange, took up his abode in Holland: he was, however, demanded by James and outlawed. But when William determined to come to England, he found Burnet indispensable. Burnet entirely threw in his lot with William; it was he who drew up, or rather abridged and translated, William's Declaration, and who, after his arrival in England, advocated his cause from the pulpit.

Burnet, therefore, had strong claims upon the King, and he was the first Bishop whom William appointed. This, for the King's purpose, was the worst thing he could have done. To have a King who was a Presbyterian set over the Church was bad enough, but by the appointment of Burnet, William plainly shewed his hostility to the Church. Swift describes Burnet as a man "of generosity and good nature, but who was party-mad, and *saw Popery under every bush.*" He was an extreme Latitudinarian, and his very name was odious to Churchmen. He would communicate with the Churches of Holland and Geneva, and dispense with the surplice, with the sign of the Cross in Baptism, and with subscription to the Articles[j]. Sancroft the Archbishop regarded as a Presbyterian in disguise, and a disgrace to the Church; "he would not even see me," says Burnet[k], and determined to

---

[j] In the debates on the Occasional Conformity Bill, he confessed himself to have been an occasional Nonconformist, "but at the same time I continued my Communion with our Church."   [k] O. T., iii. 10.

The Latitudinarian Bishops. 119

brave the penalties of Præmunire rather than consecrate him [1]. In vain Lloyd, Bishop of St. Asaph, a common friend of both of them; in vain the Earl of Nottingham, who of all members of the government was most popular with the Church, endeavoured to persuade Sancroft. At the last moment he hit upon an expedient which seemed at the time to satisfy his conscience, and issued a commission empowering any three of his suffragans, with the Bishop of London, to act for him [m].

Though a man of considerable learning [n], Burnet had no tact, and he soon vented his obnoxious sentiments [o]. Before he went into his Diocese he issued a Pastoral Letter, in which he intimated, in no vague terms, that William had gained the throne of England *by conquest;* "the success of a just war gives a lawful

---

[1] "If an Archbishop or Bishop refuse to consecrate the person elected within twenty days after such election is signified to him, he shall incur the pains and penalties of a Præmunire." 25 Hen. VIII. 20.

[m] That Sancroft was afterwards sensible of the evasion is evident from the fact that he caused the document to be abstracted from the Diocesan Registry, which could not be recovered till after his death, and then only under threat of legal proceedings.

[n] Bossuet spoke of him as the most formidable of all the champions of the Reformation.

[o] At his consecration his opposition to Church customs shewed itself by his wearing Cambric, instead of lawn, sleeves, from which the nickname of *Cambric sleeves* afterwards attached to him.

title to that which is acquired in the progress of it." This letter was condemned in 1692 by both Houses of Parliament, and ordered to be burnt by the public hangman, and again was brought against him when, in 1699, he was appointed Tutor to the young Duke of Gloucester.

But whatever his faults, it is only just to say that Burnet was an active and laborious Bishop; he was essentially a working Bishop, and, much to his credit, befriended the Nonjurors, although he had with them but little sympathy [p]. Besides the works alluded to above he wrote several books, of which we may mention the *Pastoral Care*, published in 1692, in which he pointed out and enforced the duties of the Clergy: and the *Exposition of the Thirty-nine Articles of the Church of England* in 1699, a work which was in 1701 condemned by the Lower House of Convocation. After his death, was published, in two volumes, the *History of his Own Times*, the first volume appearing in 1724, and the second in 1734; a work which, though frequently quoted in these pages, cannot generally be recommended as a safe guide, but in writing which his best friends must acknowledge that he was partial, vain, credulous, and careless [q]. The work has been facetiously called

---

[p] To an ejected Vicar of his Diocese, who had been a Prebendary of the Cathedral, Burnet, out of his own pocket, paid the yearly income during his life.—Salisbury Dioc. Hist., p. 508.

[q] Edinburgh Review, LXI. 280.

"The Bishop's Story-book." In his notes on this book Lord Dartmouth writes: "I wrote in the first volume that I did not believe the Bishop designedly published anything he believed to be false; therefore think myself to be obliged to write in this, that I am fully satisfied that he published many things which he knew to be so[r]!"

The same year (1689) in which Burnet was made a Bishop, five other Episcopal appointments were made by William, viz. those of Humfrey Humphries to Bangor; Nicholas Stratford, Dean of St. Asaph, to Chester; Edward Stillingfleet, Dean of St. Paul's, to Worcester; Simon Patrick, Dean of Peterborough, to Chichester; and Gilbert Ironside to Bristol. "The King," says Burnet[s], "named six Bishops within six months. And the Persons promoted to those Sees were generally men of those principles," i. e. Latitudinarians.

On April 10, 1690, died the notorious Timothy Hall, whom James, for the sole reason that he was

---

[r] Burnet married three wives with considerable fortunes, but it must be mentioned to his credit that he saved little from his Bishopric, and only left to his family the money derived from them, and he added to his charities the whole stipend which he received as Tutor to the Duke of Gloucester. "Dr. Burnet was extravagantly fond of tobacco and writing; to enjoy both at the same time he perforated the broad brim of his large hat, and putting his long pipe through it, puffed and wrote, and wrote and puffed again."—Nich. Lit. An., i. 283.

[s] O. T., iii. 39.

one of the four London Clergymen who read his Declaration, had appointed to the See of Oxford. An excellent appointment was now made to that See; the claims of Dr. Hough, President of Magdalen, who with the other Fellows of the College had been expelled by James, could not, on political grounds, be overlooked, so he was appointed to the vacant See, holding the Presidency of Magdalen *in commendam* [t].

But now the task was imposed upon the King of filling up the Sees of the Nonjurors, and this he found by no means an easy one. The greater bulk of the leading Clergy considered these Bishops to have been uncanonically deprived, and were unwilling to occupy Sees which they did not believe to be lawfully vacant; a circumstance which no doubt added fuel to William's wrath against the orthodox Clergy. Thus Sharp refused the See of Norwich, vacant by the deprivation of Lloyd, thereby greatly offending the King; Beveridge refused Ken's See of Bath and Wells, and thus lost all hope of preferment in William's reign [u].

But eventually Clergymen were found to accept the Nonjuring Sees. Tillotson, Dean of St. Paul's,

---

[t] In 1692 he was translated to Lichfield and Coventry, and on the death of Tenison he was offered, but from modesty declined, the Primacy, but in the following year he accepted the See of Worcester.

[u] It was not till 1704, in the reign of Anne and when he was 68 years old, that he was appointed to St. Asaph.

succeeded Sancroft as Archbishop of Canterbury. In 1689 Tillotson exchanged the Deanery of Canterbury for that of St. Paul's, and on kissing hands for the latter appointment he was considerably surprised and somewhat alarmed by the King's announcement that he would soon be required to fill the highest post in the Church; and in due time he was chosen to fill Sancroft's place[x]. Extreme Latitudinarian as he was, he must have felt some compunction, he must have felt that Sancroft was not canonically deprived, that he himself would be a usurper, and his own private letters shew that it was with extreme reluctance that he accepted the Primacy.

However, Tillotson did accept the Primacy. Patrick, Bishop of Chichester, was translated to Ely in the place of Turner, he himself being succeeded at Chichester by Dr. Grove[y]. Dr. More[z] was appointed to Norwich in the place of Lloyd; Dr. Cumberland[a] to Peterborough, in the place of White; Dr. Fowler

---

[x] Six Bishops assisted at his consecration, but Compton was not one of them; probably Compton was disappointed at being thus passed over.

[y] Dr. Grove was one of the London Clergy who were instrumental in drawing up the Bishops' Petition to James.

[z] Translated to Ely 1707, d. 1714.

[a] The learned Author of the *De Legibus Naturæ*. His learning was not more conspicuous than his charities. It was said that at the end of every year whatever money beyond £25 he possessed he gave to the poor, reserving that sum for his funeral.—Memoirs of R. Cumberland, i. 47.

to Gloucester in the place of Frampton; whilst Ironside, Bishop of Bristol, was translated to Hereford, being succeeded at Bristol by Dr. Hall[h].

Strong efforts were made, but without avail, to retain Ken. The See was, as mentioned before, offered to and refused by Beveridge; it was then accepted, although reluctantly, by Kidder, Dean of Peterborough. Kidder afterwards repented of the step he had taken; he himself said, "Of this I am sure, that since I have considered things better, I should not have done it, were it to do again. I did not consult my ease; I have often repented of accepting it, and looked upon it as a great infelicity[c]. Kidder had been a Dissenter and a Republican under the Commonwealth but conformed at the Restoration. He was a learned Hebrew and Arabic scholar, but, like most of William's Bishops, he was a Latitudinarian, and his appointment to his See caused Ken the greatest sorrow.

One very excellent appointment William made, by Tillotson's recommendation, viz. that of Dr. Sharp, in succession to Dr. Lamplugh, to the Archbishopric of York.

Church appointments rained thickly upon William.

---

[b] Of all William's Bishops Hall may be considered the most decided Puritan, of whom Calamy says, "he brought the Theology of the Westminster Assembly out of the Church Catechism."—Stoughton's Revolution, p. 386.

[c] Bowles' Life of Ken, 214.

About the same time Dr. Tenison was, on the recommendation of Tillotson, appointed to the See of Lincoln [d]. Sherlock, Master of the Temple, who was at first a Nonjuror, but afterwards took the oath, was appointed Dean of St. Paul's; Dr. Comber, in the place of Dr. Grenville, who refused to take the oath, Dean of Durham; Mr. Talbot [e], in the place of Hickes the Nonjuror, Dean of Worcester; and Dr. Woodward Dean of Sarum. Shortly afterwards Dr. Hooper was, during the absence of William from England, and greatly to his anger when he heard of it, appointed by Queen Mary to the Deanery of Canterbury, and Dr. Freeman became Dean of Peterborough.

The Archbishopric of Canterbury was, as already stated, conferred on Tillotson, that of York on Sharp. The two new Primates were men of a very different stamp and type of Churchmanship. Tillotson was a thorough Latitudinarian, Sharp a thorough Catholic. Tillotson, a man of naturally quiet and retiring habits, had no qualifications whatever for his new position, he was no Theologian, had no previous experience as a Bishop, was almost as unpopular as Burnet was with the Clergy, and his appointment to the Primacy could not fail to be most injurious to the Church.

John Tillotson (1630—1694), the son of a clothier

---

[d] Soon afterwards Tenison was offered, but refused, the Archbishopric of Dublin.
[e] Father of Lord Chancellor Talbot.

near Halifax, was, like many of those who became Latitudinarians, by birth and early education a Puritan ; he graduated at Clare Hall, Cambridge, where his Tutor also was a Puritan; in 1650 he became a Fellow of Clare Hall, and at that time was a Presbyterian; he continued to hold careless and philosophical views about the doctrine and discipline of the Church, yet shortly after the Restoration he did not scruple to receive orders from Dr. Sydserf, Bishop of Galloway, nor did he hesitate to conform according to the Act of Uniformity in 1662. Although at no time of his life a denier of, he certainly was never more than a semi-believer in, the doctrines of the Church ; he never at any time shook off the Puritanical principles which by birth, in childhood, by education, and by taste, he had imbibed ; he married a niece of Oliver Cromwell, and his personal sympathies were always with those who held the Puritans', rather than the Church's Creed. He was, what is called by some people, a large-hearted man, the intimate friend of Churchmen and Dissenters alike ; of Firmin the Socinian, Howe the Nonconformist, and Penn the Quaker, on the one hand ; of Archbishop Sharp, Dean Comber, Bishop Barrow, and Robert Nelson on the other. But this large-heartedness was carried too far considering he was an Archbishop, whose duty it was to discountenance rather than encourage heresy and schism. It was no doubt his misfortune to be made Archbishop, and it is more than probable that the effects of opposition which he met with materially shortened his life. We can understand why the King offered him the Archbishopric, but it is difficult to understand why Tillotson accepted it. Wherever he could he acted as a Dissenter rather than a Churchman. It was his custom to administer the Holy Eucharist to persons sitting, instead of kneeling; he would walk about the Church, administering first to those who were in their pews, and then to those kneeling at the rails, he himself not going within, but standing outside the rails [f]. He was accused of being an Atheist, a Deist, an Arian, a Socinian; the charge was untrue; he frequently protested that he was not a Socinian. Still that the charge should be made shews what people thought of him; "See," said a courtier, speaking of him to the King, "See Mr. Hobbes in the Pulpit;" of the Athanasian Creed he said, "The account is no wise satisfactory; I wish we were well rid of it." That in his private life he was an estimable man we may well believe; there is no reason to doubt the character given him by Burnet [g], that he was kind and benevolent, as also that he was sincerely religious, without affectation, bigotry, or superstition. Burnet, whilst preaching his funeral sermon, was so overcome that he burst

---

[f] Lathbury's Nonjurors, 156.
[g] O. T., iii. 186.

into tears, and the King said of him, "I have lost the best friend I ever had, and the best man I ever knew." He was considered the first Preacher of the day, and although his style would in the present day be considered too diffuse, and marked with a want of animation, yet the warm praise of Addison, and of the leading critics of the day, prove that his style was at that time held in high admiration [h].

A very different man from Tillotson was Sharp, the new Archbishop of York. It is somewhat difficult to account for the reason of William's appointing such a man, who was not only no Latitudinarian, but as nearly a model Bishop as could be, and the very opposite to his general appointments. John Sharp (1644—1714) had been a man of considerable mark in the previous reign. At an early age he rose to distinction in the Church. He became Archdeacon of Berks when he was only twenty-eight years of age; in 1675 he was made a Prebendary of Norwich, in 1681 Dean of Norwich, and (although he refused to accept any of the ejected Nonjurors' Sees) he in 1689 accepted from William the Deanery of Canterbury, and in 1691 the Archbishopric of York. With the Deanery of Norwich he held also the Rectory of St. Giles-in-the-Fields, in which latter capacity he, in 1686, preached in his Parish Church

---

[h] After his death his Sermons were purchased by the Booksellers at 2,500 guineas, whilst Dryden only received £1,300 for his translation of Virgil.

the sermon for which Compton got into trouble with James, and was suspended by the Ecclesiastical Commission [i]. The illegality of this Court, next to the imprisonment of the seven Bishops, was the chief cause of James's dethronement, and perhaps for this reason Sharp seemed to William to deserve his gratitude. But then the question arises, Why did not William, instead of promoting Sharp promote Compton, who had really suffered under that Court, and had so many claims upon the government [k]?

During her life-time, Queen Mary is supposed to have had the management of the Church appointments, but whether the Queen or William appointed there is little doubt that Tillotson, and in a lesser degree Burnet, had a voice in the matter. Sharp, dissimilar as he was from him, was the intimate friend of Tillotson, and it was Tillotson who recommended Sharp for the See of York. Sharp was one of the few who are beloved by every one. To be a High Churchman and yet to be praised by Burnet speaks volumes for him. He was a man who said and did what he thought right, without troubling himself about what people thought of him, and who lived

---

[i] See introductory chapter.

[k] The reason why Sharp was not punished together with Compton seems to be that even Jefferies admired Sharp and "advised him to get out of the way." This would account for Sharp's visit to Jefferies when the latter was a prisoner in the Tower.—Life of Sharp by his Son, i. 97.

down all opposition. "Those who were called Tories," writes his son[1], "or the High-Church party, claimed him as theirs, for he was observed more generally to favour their principles—go more along with them than those of the other side," and though he admired our Communion Office, yet "he preferred that in King Edward's first Service-Book," and he thought there was one blot in the Reformation Establishment "in regard to discipline which has never effectually been provided for[m]." He was one of the first Preachers of the day[n]; he had been a model Parish Priest, nor does there seem to have been one relation of life in which he did not excel. It was he who in Queen Anne's reign became the most influential Bishop at Court; he was the Queen's spiritual adviser; it was he whom Lord Nottingham consulted as to the Church appointments, and whom the Church, therefore, has to thank, if in her reign the tide of Latitudinarianism was stemmed, and the influence of the Church revived.

We will sum up Archbishop Sharp's character in words selected from one of his own sermons[o], in which he unintentionally gives an exact character of himself: "He lives as he believes, is ready to endure anything for religious principles, is honest God-ward, an Israelite indeed, in whom is no guile; and with respect to men, is just in all his dealings, never takes advan-

---

[1] Life, i. 256.   [m] Ibid., i. 355.   [n] Burnet, iii. 104.
[o] On the "upright man," from Psalm cxii. 4.

tage of credulity, nor abuses confidence reposed in him, hates all mean compliance, and dares to speak his mind, is a man of great simplicity and plainness, open and free. You may always know where to have him, for his words and thoughts always go together;—above all things hates a trick; so free is both his heart and actions from all imposture, that he cares not if all the world were privy to them. With the wisdom of the serpent he joins the innocency and simplicity of the dove; he is not steered by the mind of popular applause but the sense of duty; therefore he is of great courage and resolution; nothing can frighten him from his duty, for he fears none but God. You may as soon draw the sun from his line, as him from the steady and strict paths of righteousness[p]."

Tillotson did not long survive his appointment to the Archbishopric of Canterbury. He died on March 23, 1694, at the age of sixty-four years, having held the Primacy for little more than two and a-half years, surviving Archbishop Sancroft little more than two years. On the death of Tillotson the Queen wished Stillingfleet, Bishop of Worcester, to succeed to the Primacy. Stillingfleet was a Latitudinarian, but not

---

[p] Overton's Life in the English Church. Mr. Overton says Sharp was not an *extreme* Churchman. It is a pity he did not give us his definition of this word; we have it on the best authority that he was in favour of King Edward VI.th's First Prayer-Book, and no (so-called) *extreme* man in the present wants to go, either in doctrine or ritual, beyond that.

equally so with most of William's Bishops. Edward Stillingfleet (1635—1699), who graduated at St. John's College, Cambridge, of which he became a Fellow, published in 1659, and therefore when he was only twenty-four years of age, an Irenicum, in which he made large overtures to Dissenters. Amongst other things, he proposed that the Sign of the Cross in Baptism should be omitted; that the surplice might be taken away; that Dissenters should be required to subscribe only 36 of the Articles; that the Apocryphal Lessons should be changed for others, and that the Rubrics should be corrected [q]. It is true that Stillingfleet afterwards apologised for this work on the ground of his youth and want of consideration. Still Bishop Kennet reckons him with Tillotson, Patrick, and Reynolds, as one of the Bishops who favoured the Presbyterians, but who did not "hesitate to conform for the sake of unity and brotherly love." However this might be, he was not Latitudinarian enough for William, and Burnet tells us that the Whig government opposed his appointment because "both his notions and his temper were too high [r]. Dr. Hall, Bishop of Bristol,

---

[q] Long's Vox Cleri, 6.

[r] Of Stillingfleet's numerous works, two especially must be mentioned as bearing upon Church History. In 1662 he published the "Origines Sacræ," which Sanderson, his Bishop, could scarcely believe possible to have been written by a man only 27 years of age. In 1685 he published his "Origines Britan-

seems also (but on what grounds it is difficult to understand) to have been recommended for the Primacy [8]; but eventually Tenison, Bishop of Lincoln, a Latitudinarian scarcely less pronounced than Tillotson or Burnet, became Archbishop of Canterbury.

A few days after Christmas, 1695, between the death of Tillotson and the consecration of Tenison, Queen Mary died of smallpox. Tenison attended her on her death and preached her funeral sermon, in which he eulogised her as eminently devout, thereby drawing down upon himself a severe letter from Ken for not having said a word as to her having repented for her ingratitude towards her father.

Queen Mary, though the King is said to have left the Church appointments in her hands, must frequently have subjected her own judgment to that of Tillotson. No doubt the Low Church notions which she received from her husband were considerably strengthened by the influence which Burnet and Tillotson excercised over her. Yet though doubtless Mary had no High Church tendencies, and the example of her father, for whom she showed but little reverence, might possibly have driven her into an opposite

---

nicæ," a work of profound research, although the ground had been somewhat prepared for him by Archbishop Usher in his work "De Ecclesiarum Britannicarum primordiis."

[8] Kennet says he was "recommended by a great party of men who had an opinion of his piety and moderation."

extreme of religion; yet it can scarcely be imagined that, after the teaching of Hooper and Ken, both of whom she held in high esteem, she could possibly have approved of the Latitudinarian Bishops with whom her husband swamped the Church. At any rate she incurred his wrath on one occasion by appointing Hooper to the Deanery of Canterbury; and it certainly was a bold step for her to take; for although Hooper was a man worthy of her choice [t], William had put his veto on Hooper's promotion [u].

But on the death of Mary, William adopted a plan which is much desired at the present day; when the *Congé d'élire* is an unmeaning form; when the appointment of Bishops has passed from the Crown to the Prime Minister, who need not be a Churchman, whose office depends upon a Majority in Parliament not necessarily Churchmen, and who, therefore, may be swayed by mere Political considerations. He appointed two Commissions consisting of six persons to dispense the Patronage of the Crown. On the first Commission, appointed in 1695, were placed Tenison, Archbishop of Canterbury, Sharp, Archbishop of York,

---

[t] The famous Busby said of Hooper, that "he was the best scholar, the finest gentleman, and would make the best Bishop that ever was educated at Westminster School."—Wood's Athen. Oxon.

[u] William said to him bluntly at the Hague, "Well, Dr. Hooper, you will never be a Bishop;" and on another occasion that if ever he had anything to do with England, Dr. Hooper should be Dr. Hooper still.—Mrs. Prowse's MSS.

Lloyd, Bishop of Lichfield and Coventry, Burnet, Bishop of Sarum, Patrick, Bishop of Ely, and Stillingfleet, Bishop of Worcester; and on the second Commission, which was appointed upon the death of Stillingfleet, More, Bishop of Norwich, was nominated in his place. Of these Commissioners, three (of whom the Archbishop of Canterbury, or if the vacancy was in the Province of York, the Archbishop of that Province, was to be one) were to recommend to the King for Bishoprics and other preferments in the gift of the Crown, one or more persons "as you in your wisdom shall think most fit to be appointed by us to any such vacant preferments, to the end that the name of such person or persons may be presented to us by one of our Principal Secretaries of State, that our Royal pleasure may be further known thereof." Nor might the Principal Secretaries of State recommend to the King any person for preferment, without first having communicated his name to, and received the approval of, the Commissioners. No doubt by these Commissions William meant to act fairly, but his mind was too biassed to admit of his doing so. The Bishops whom he named on the Commission were mostly Latitudinarians, and for the remainder, as during the previous years of his reign, Church preferment was the reward, not of the most deserving, but of Whig and Latitudinarian, Clergy. That this plan was regarded as a party one is plain; for when the Tories came into power in 1701, the Ministers frequently urged the King, although unsuccessfully, to dissolve the Commission; and one of the first Acts of the Government in Queen Anne's reign was to dissolve it. Thus in Queen Anne's reign ended a system, which, if it had been fairly worked, might have saved the Church from the dark days of apathy and deadness which were soon about to overwhelm her.

Tenison, the new Archbishop, valued the Church from its political rather than its spiritual side. Being called to a station which he had not the abilities to fill properly; being too Erastian to avail himself of the Church's machinery, and hating Convocation quite as much as Tillotson had ever hated it, he advised the King not to summon Convocation, but to govern the Church by Royal Injunctions. It appears that Tillotson, shortly before his death, had drawn up, and Tenison soon after his promotion to Canterbury prevailed upon the King to issue, these Injunctions to the Archbishops to be communicated by them to their Clergy[x]. The Injunctions recommend amongst other matters to the Bishops:—Care in conferring Orders, that the 34th and 35th Canons be observed; That Candidates for Ordination should

---

[x] The Preamble of these Injunctions states: "William Rex. Most Reverend Father in God. We ... have upon mature consideration with you and other our Bishops by virtue of our Royal and supreme authority, thought fit with the advice of our Privy Council, to ordain and publish the following Injunctions."

signify to the Bishop of the Diocese their names fourteen days before, and should appear by the Thursday in the Ember Weeks for examination; That the Bishops should satisfy themselves that the Candidates have a sufficient title, and brought a certificate of their age; That Bishops reside in their dioceses, and the Clergy in their cures; That the Bishops restrain pluralities, and look well to the lives of their Clergy, and oblige them to have public prayers in their Churches not only on holydays, but as often as may be, and to celebrate the Holy Communion frequently; That they promote proper observance of the Lord's Day, frequent visitations of the sick and catechizing; That the Bishops hold Confirmations not only at their Triennial Visitations but at other seasons also; That no commutation of penance be made but by the express order and directions of the Bishop; And that no licence of marriage be granted without the oaths of two sufficient witnesses being taken, and proper security given for performing the conditions of the licence according to the 102 and 103 Canons.

The Injunctions, dated February 15, 1695, were unexceptionable enough in themselves; but why could not the Archbishop and Bishops arrange such simple matters for themselves without the interference of the King? It certainly seems ludicrous that an Anglicised Dutchman, who was in his heart a Calvinist and a Presbyterian, should be requested by an Archbishop of Canterbury to teach the Bishops their duty.

In the same month in which these *Injunctions* were issued, certain *Directions* were also published for the "preserving Unity in the Church and the purity of the Christian faith concerning the Holy Trinity;" but these Directions will be more fitly described in the relation of the Controversy which called them forth.

Church and State seemed now to be playing into each other's hands. In former times Bishops had held the highest offices of State; but since the days of Juxon, at that time Bishop of London, who in 1635 was appointed Lord Treasurer, no Ecclesiastic had held any high civil appointment. William, however, placed such confidence in Tenison, that when he was about to leave the kingdom in 1695 he revived the custom, and appointed him one of the Lords Justices for the Administration of Public Affairs during his absence.

CHAPTER V.

THE EARLY TRINITARIAN AND THE CONVOCATION CONTROVERSIES.

SOON after the passing of the Act of Toleration a wave of scepticism and infidelity broke over the land. When the mind became unfettered by authority, and as soon as the spirit, fostered by Latitudinarians, got abroad, of every one forming his own judgment on points of doctrine, then a Rationalizing spirit sprang up, and the Church was challenged to prove the very elements of religion and the fundamentals of the Christian Faith. And this Rationalizing spirit manifested itself in two ways: firstly, in the denial of the Divine Nature of our Saviour, which developed itself into Unitarianism; and secondly, in the denial of a revealed (as distinct from natural) religion, and consequently of the truth and authority of the Bible, which acquired the name of Deism. Under one or both of these heads may be placed the various controversies which agitated the Church during the last quarter of the seventeenth and throughout a great part of the eighteenth centuries.

During the latter part of the seventeenth century the peace of the Church was disturbed by a recurrence of the heresies which troubled the Church in the Nicene Age. Anti-Trinitarian and Arian doctrines came once more in vogue. John Biddle (1615—1662), the founder of the Society which, from his name, were called Bidellians, may be considered as the Father of Socinianism in England. Biddle died in prison in 1662, but the spread of his heresy was owing to the republication in 1691 of his Tracts, and the zealous support which they received from his disciple, Thomas Firmin (1632—1697). Firmin was a rich linendraper in Leadenhall Street, who devoted his immense wealth to works of charity, but he was an Arian[a], and spent his money freely in propagating his opinion and in distributing publications in denial of our Lord's Divinity. "Profane wits," writes Burnet[b], "were much delighted with this; all mysteries in religion came to be talked about as the controversies of Priests; Priestcraft grew to a word in fashion, under cover of which the enemies of religion vented their impieties[c]."

The men who at this early stage of the heresy advocated anti-Trinitarian opinions in England were not generally men of intellectual eminence; but a

---

[a] He was, says Burnet, "called a Socinian but was really an Arian."

[b] O. T., iii. 292.

[c] And yet this same author says that "Archbishop Tillotson and some of the Bishops had lived in great friendship with Mr. Firmin."

case occurred at Oxford which, owing to a curious point of law which arose out of it, requires a passing notice. In 1690 Dr. Bury, Rector of Exeter College, was deprived by the Visitor, Dr. Trelawney, for publishing a work entitled "The Naked Truth," which contained heterodox doctrine on the Trinity. The King's Bench reversed the Bishop's decision, on the ground that the Visitor's jurisdiction could not exclude the Common Law. The Lord Chief Justice decided, in opposition to this judgment, that "by the Common Law the office of Visitor is to judge according to the Statutes of the College, to expel and deprive upon just occasions, and to hear all appeals *of course*; and that from him, and him only, the party grieved ought to have redress; the Founder having reposed in him so entire a confidence that he will administer justice impartially; and his determinations are final, and examinable in no court whatever." In this opinion the House of Lords concurred, and to this leading case all subsequent judgments have been conformable [d].

Unhappily Controversy begets Controversy, and now *Churchmen*, with the best possible intentions, but the most unfortunate results, set themselves to explain the doctrine of the Trinity (a doctrine necessarily mysterious) by hypothesis rather than proof,

---

[d] Blackstone's Comm., i. 18. Lord Mansfield declared that "the Jurisdiction of a Visitor is summary and without appeal from it."

and were so led on into the dark recesses of metaphysical speculation as to overstep the boundaries of scriptural and historical testimony; the enemies of the Church were only too glad to follow them, and the controversy was thus carried on with such acrimony as to lead the Archbishop to think that the interposition of the King was necessary.

In 1690 Dr. Wallis (1616—1703), a better Mathematician than Theologian, who having graduated at Cambridge, was in 1649 appointed Savilian Professor of Geometry at Oxford, published a Pamphlet entitled "The Doctrine of the Ever-blessed Trinity explained in a Letter to a Friend." He endeavoured to explain the greatest of all mysteries by Mathematical terms, and compared the Trinity in Unity to the length, breadth, and height of a Cube, the three equal sides of one substance. This absurd definition would have been supposed, but for the character and piety of the writer, to have been adopted by him for the purpose of bringing the doctrine into contempt; such, however, was not the case, but the work called forth many writers, and was the fruitful source of attacks on the Trinity.

In 1693 Dr. William Sherlock, Dean of St. Paul's, who in the previous reign had gained a high reputation by his writings against Romanism, wrote against a Socinian work lately published [e], "A Vindication

---

[e] "A brief History of the Unitarians, called also Socinians, in a letter to a Friend."

of the Doctrine of the Ever-blessed Trinity," with the intention of showing that there was nothing in the doctrine opposed to right reason. It is possible that Dr. Sherlock's character may have had something to do with causing the very bitter controversy which followed between him and Dr. South. Dr. Sherlock was probably the most unpopular Clergyman of the day. He had in 1684 published "The Case of Resistance of the Supreme Powers," &c., in which he advocated "the Divine Right of Kings;" he at first refused to take the oaths to William and Mary, and was deprived; but after the Battle of Boyne (in consequence, he said, of reading Overall's Convocation Book) he conformed, and was made Dean of St. Paul's. Sancroft, soon after the Revolution, had re-published Bishop Overall's [f] Book; a book which, although containing some passages (which doubtless Sancroft overlooked) asserting the rights of a *de facto* government, clearly advocated the doctrine of Non-Resistance. Sancroft published the book for one purpose, and Sherlock used it for exactly the opposite purpose, and took the oaths on the ground which he deduced from that book, that the Church recognised a *de facto* government. In defence of his conduct he published his "Case of Allegiance due to Sovereign Powers stated," in which

---

[f] Bishop Overall (1559—1619) was appointed to the Bishopric of Lichfield and Coventry in 1614, and translated to Norwich in 1618.

he says, "Stick I did, and could find no help for it, and there I should have stuck to this day had I not been relieved by Bishop Overall's Convocation Book." It is probable that Sherlock sought for a colourable reason for returning to the Church and found it in Overall's book; but his having returned just as the Battle of Boyne seemed to render William's throne secure, subjected him to much unpopularity and ridicule [g].

Dr. Sherlock's work on the Trinity certainly laid him open to attack, for in it he had described the Tri-Unity as Three distinct Minds or Spirits " having self-consciousness and mutual consciousness." South (1633—1716), Canon of Christ Church and Public Orator at Oxford, at once rushed into the fray, and in an anonymous work (which, however, was soon known to be his) unmercifully attacked Sherlock's book, and exposed with cutting sarcasm the theory of mutual consciousness as savouring of Tritheism [h]. But now South represented the Three Persons in the Godhead as modes, properties, and affections of the

---

[g] A satire of the time attributes his return to Sherlock's wife:—
"In the meantime I want my coach and four;
The neighbouring wives already slight me too,
Justle me to the wall, and take the upper pew."

[h] Burnet describes South's Book as written "not without learning, but without any measure of Christian charity and without any regard to the dignity of the subject or the decencies of his profession."

Divine Substance, thus setting aside their Personal distinction; and Sherlock in his turn accused him of Sabellianism.

Both combatants were doubtless in intention orthodox, and each indignantly denied the imputations of the other; but the controversy was a most unfortunate one as unsettling men's minds, and bringing the Church into disrepute. One doctrine seemed to preserve the Trinity whilst it lost the Unity; the other to preserve the Unity but to lose the Trinity; and the Unitarians declared their readiness to assent to the Prayer-Book and Articles, if that was the kind of Trinity which the Church held[i].

On October 28, 1695, Joseph Bingham (1668—1723), Fellow of University College, Oxford, in a Sermon preached at St. Mary's, on the Text "There are Three that bear record in Heaven," appealed to tradition, as Sherlock had to reason, in support of Sherlock's view. In his Sermon Bingham asserted that "there are Three infinite, distinct Minds or Spirits, and Three individual Substances." For this teaching he was condemned by the Hebdomadal Board as preaching Tritheism and Arianism, and although it was said at the time that in their condemnation of Bingham the Board had also condemned the Nicene doctrine, yet he was forced to resign his Fellowship and to leave Oxford[k]. Thus

---

[i] Toulmin's Hist. of Dissenters, p. 178.

[k] A protest was entered that "what the Heads of Oxford had

was one of its most learned sons driven from the University; the Church, however, received its consolation from the fact that in his retirement he published his famous work, the "Origines Ecclesiasticæ, the Antiquities of the Christian Church," which has supplied a great void in Ecclesiastical Literature[1].

The contest between Sherlock and South was carried on with such bitter acrimony, that though Stillingfleet, Bishop of Worcester, brought the weight of his influence to bear upon it in the Preface of the "Vindication of the Trinity," the King was induced by Tenison to interfere, with a view to stopping the strife, and the King issued the *Directions* alluded to at the end of the last chapter. These Directions required the Clergy (1) Not to preach any other doctrine concerning the blessed Trinity than is contained in the Scriptures and is agreeable to the Creeds and the Thirty-nine Articles; (2) Carefully to avoid all new terms and to confine themselves to such explications as have commonly been used in the Church; (3) That *they* especially do observe the 53rd Canon, which forbids public opposition between Preachers,

---

condemned as heretical and impious was the very Catholic Faith; that the decree was a censure of the Nicene Faith and of the Faith of the Church of England as heresy, and exposed both to the scorn and triumph of the Socinians."

[1] The first volume was published in 1708, and the remainder of the work in 1722.

and to abstain from bitter invectives and scurrilous language; and (4) these Directions were to be observed by those who write on the doctrine. And with regard to the Laity it was also enjoined: "For your assistance we will charge our Judges and all other our Civil officers, to do their duty therein in executing the laws against all such persons as shall herein give occasion of scandal, discord, or disturbance in our Church and Kingdom."

But the mischief was already done. This unhappy controversy was seized upon not only by Anti-Trinitarians, but by the ungodly and the enemies of all religion; the Press teemed with offensive invectives; the Church was represented as being divided into two parties, the Tritheists and Nominalists, or real and nominal Trinitarians, the former the followers of Sherlock, the latter of South; and it was asserted that the Church of England countenanced no other doctrine.

But whilst these disputes were rending the Church asunder, and the Archbishop had thought fit to advise the King to exercise his Royal authority, men's minds naturally turned to Convocation, as the constitutional mode for settling religious disputes. Tenison was by no means fonder of Convocation than his predecessor had been; like Tillotson he preferred the Erastian policy of governing the Church through the civil power; and he, whose duty it was to see that Convocation legislated for the Church, determined (to use his own words) to defer it "till the Clergy were in a better temper," and advised the King not to permit Convocation to meet for business. The history of Convocation, therefore, for ten years was little more than a series of writs and prorogations without any business being transacted. At last the Clergy grew weary of Tenison's policy; they were disgusted with Royal Injunctions being issued to teach Bishops their duty, and by Royal Directions to settle disputes about the Trinity; they complained, with reason, of the constant prorogations of Convocation as a violation of the Constitution, and animadverted on the conduct of the Bishops generally, and of the Archbishop in particular.

Whilst such a feeling existed amongst the Clergy, there appeared in 1697 a "Letter to a Convocation Man concerning the Rights, Powers, and Privileges of Convocation [m]," which not only asserted the right of Convocation to meet with every Parliament, but that to confer, debate, and resolve without the King's licence, is at Common law the undoubted right of Convocation." This, therefore, was the point on which the Convocation Controversy which ensued hinged :—Whether or not Convocation was restrained by the Act of Submission from proceeding to business without the Royal Licence. The Letter was

---

[m] This letter is attributed in the Somers Tracts, published in 1751, to Sir Bartholomew Shower, who had been Recorder of London in the reign of James II.; by others it is attributed to Dr. Binkes, Vicar of Leamington, afterwards, in 1703, appointed Dean of Lichfield.

answered in the same year by Wake, Rector of St. James's, Westminster, a man already known to the Theological world from his controversy with Bossuet and his translation of the writings of the Ecclesiastical Fathers, in a Treatise entitled "The Authority of Christian Princes over their Ecclesiastical Synods asserted, with particular respect to the Clergy of the Realm and Church of England." In this work he maintained that Christian Princes always had the right to call Synods and to regulate their proceedings, and he claimed this same right for the sovereign of England, appealing to the Act of Submission as a proof that the Clergy cannot transact business without the Royal Licence. During the same year Mr. Wright, a Lawyer, wrote on the same side as Wake, in "A Letter to a Member of Parliament occasioned by a Letter to a Convocation Man." On the other side Mr. Hill, in "Municipium Ecclesiasticum," accused Wake of betraying the rights of the Church, a work which Wake answered in 1698 in "An Appeal to all true Members of the Church of England on behalf of the King's Ecclesiastical Supremacy."

Such was the state of the Controversy when in 1700 a more formidable antagonist to Wake appeared in the person of Atterbury[a], a Student of Christ

---

[a] "The pert gentleman from Christ Church," as Archdeacon Nicholson, afterwards Bishop of Carlisle, called him.

Church, Oxford, already known to the literary world from the part he had taken in the dispute between Boyle and Bentley as to the genuineness of the Epistles of Phalaris. Atterbury, in his work, "The Rights, Powers, and Privileges of an English Convocation stated and indicated, in answer to a later work of Dr. Wake's," &c., attacked Wake with great severity. He maintained that the Clergy were first summoned to Parliament by the "Præmonentes" clause in the Bishops' Writ in the reign of Edward I.; then that being heavily taxed, they resisted the summons, whereupon the Provincial Writ was addressed to the Archbishop to compel their attendance. Not that the clause "præmonentes" became useless and insignificant, for still the Bishops who executed the royal writs upon the Clergy of the Diocese "transmitted it to those of the Lower Clergy concerned, and they still made their returns to it." The Clergy, therefore, still had the same right to meet in Convocation as the Laity had to meet in Parliament, and the Act of Submission did not prevent the Clergy from making Canons, but only from promulgating and expressing them without the King's approval. "It has so happened," says Atterbury, "that upon the calling of a new Parliament, the Writ for the Province of York has been dropped — through forgetfulness no doubt;—however, for the same reason it may so happen again, when another Parliament is called, that the Province of Canterbury may be forgotten too." Lord Chief Justice Holt and Archbishop Tenison were desirous that Atterbury's work should be censured, but Atterbury's time for persecution had not yet arrived [o]. All his opponents admitted that Atterbury conducted his case with learning and ability. Wake, writing in May, 1700, says, "The world is full of Mr. Atterbury's book. ... In this all agree that it was writ with a hearty good-will, and may be a pattern for charity and good breeding [p]." But, he said, "He only wanted one thing—the truth—on his side." At this point of the Controversy probably both of the chief antagonists were wrong; if Atterbury went too far in one direction, Wake went equally far in the other. Even such a moderate man as Nicholson, who became afterwards one of Atterbury's strongest opponents, is forced thus to write to Wake: "The Church you say has no inherent right of assembling synods. How will this agree with the Convocation being essential to our Constitution and when (manifestly needful) the Church has a right to its sitting [q]?" At this point of the Controversy the Convocation of 1700 met for the despatch of business, but for the sake of conciseness we will follow on the Controversy to its end.

---

[o] For this work Atterbury received the degree of D.D. from the University of Oxford, and afterwards the thanks of the Lower House of Convocation.

[p] This opinion, however, Wake soon altered.

[q] Nicholson's Correspondence, i. 66; Lathbury's Convocation, 346.

During the year 1700 Atterbury reprinted his work, and corrected some mistakes into which it was evident that he had fallen. White Kennet now became one of Atterbury's ablest opponents in a work, "Ecclesiastical Synods and Parliamentary Convocations in the Church of England historically stated and justly vindicated from the Misrepresentations of Mr. Atterbury," published in 1701. Atterbury was also opposed by Dr. Humphrey Hody[r]. Gibson, afterwards Bishop of Lincoln and of London, supported Wake, and Hooper, afterwards Bishop, first of St. Asaph and then of Bath and Wells, supported Atterbury, and numerous other pamphlets were published. But a work surpassing all, and which ended and decided the Controversy, was, in 1703, published by Wake, who two years previously had been appointed to the Deanery of Exeter; a work which is in the present day the text-book as to the law of Convocations, entitled "The State of the Church and Clergy of England, in their Councils, Synods, Convocations, Conventions, and other public Assemblies, historically deduced, from the Conversion of the Saxons to the present time," and if only that it called forth this work, the Church has reason to be thankful that the Convocation Controversy took place.

The truth was really on Wake's side, although, as was said at the time, the *appearance* of truth was on

---

[r] "A History of English Councils and Convocations and of the Clergy's sitting in Parliament," 1701.

Atterbury's. At any rate victory practically rested with Atterbury, for whilst the Controversy was still going on, so great was the excitement caused, and so great the public favour bestowed on Atterbury's work, that a widespread indignation was felt at the long suppression of Convocation, and the Tory government which succeeded to power in 1700 accepted office on the condition that Convocation should be allowed to meet and to deliberate.

Accordingly, after a suspension of more than ten years, Convocation was allowed to meet for business on February 10, 1701, Dr. Haley, Dean of Chichester, preaching the Latin Sermon, and Dr. Hooper, Dean of Canterbury, in consequence of the illness of Dr. Jane, being chosen Prolocutor[s]. In this Convocation began those continuous disputes between the Upper and Lower Houses, which lasted through sixteen years, and eventually ended in the suppression of Convocation.

It had been the custom for the Archbishop to sign a schedule by which the Upper House was immediately adjourned, and which being sent to the Prolocutor, the Lower was thereby prorogued also. But Archbishop Tenison had shown himself to be the persistent enemy of Convocation; the Lower House,

---

[s] The fact that Hooper was the intimate friend of Ken is sufficient to disprove what Burnet says of him, that "though a man of learning and good conduct, he was reserved, crafty, and ambitious."—O. T., iii. 391.

therefore, could put no confidence in him, and felt that he had thus the power to prorogue them at any moment, and to break off their debates [t], and they resolved to dispute his right [u]. When, therefore, at the second Session, on February 25, the Archbishop's Schedule was brought down to them, the Lower House insisted on their right to adjourn themselves, through their Prolocutor, and continuing to sit, eventually adjourned, to meet again, not (as appointed in the Archbishop's Schedule) in the Jerusalem Chamber, but in Henry VII.th's Chapel. With regard to this proceeding, the Archbishop at the Session of February 28 sent for the Prolocutor, and demanded of him: (1.) "Whether the Lower House did sit after they were prorogued on the 25th?" (2.) "Whether they did meet this morning without attending in this place, to which they were prorogued?" To these questions he demanded a written reply. The Pro-

---

[t] Even so moderate a member of the Lower House as Dr. Prideaux acknowledged that "As the Bishops generally break up very early to attend the Service of the House of Lords in Parliament, and then send down the schedule of adjournment to the Lower House, if on the receipt of the schedule the Lower House must immediately break up also, what time could they have to despatch the business before them?"

[u] The position taken up by the Upper House as declared by them in the Session of June 6, 1701, was that Convocation was only one body, meeting at first in one place, of which the Archbishop was the Head; and that though the debates are carried on in different houses, both houses are continued and prorogued by one instrument.

locutor answered that the Lower House was preparing something on the subject to submit to the Upper House.

But in order to leave no doubt as to the place for the next meeting, the words were inserted in the Archbishop's Schedule of prorogation, "hunc locum vulgo vocatum Jerusalem Chamber," the previous form having been merely "hunc locum." To this alteration the Lower House consented *salvo jure*, and at the next session, on March 6, the Prolocutor having first met the Bishops in the Jerusalem Chamber, the Lower House sent to the Bishops a Paper, in which they asserted their rights to adjourn themselves; for which they cited precedents. "A copious answer," says Burnet[x], "was returned by the Bishops; but on March 31 the Lower House sent a message to the Upper, to the effect that they considered the answer unsatisfactory. The Archbishop told them that he expected a written answer to the questions of February 28; the Prolocutor in reply said that their answer would occupy twenty sheets; upon which the Archbishop announced that "he did not confine them to length and breadth, but expected their answer in *writing*." The Lower House refused to give a written answer, and demanded a free Conference. This the Bishops refused as unprecedented[y].

---

[x] O. T., iii. 392.

[y] This, however, does not seem to be strictly accurate. In 1661, during their consideration of the Prayer-Book, the Lower

The Lower House determined in consequence to take no further notice of the Archbishop's adjournment, and though they observed the rule of adjourning on the day named in the Archbishop's Schedule, yet they did so as their own act, and adjourned themselves through their own Prolocutor, in order that Committees of the whole House might sit, to intermediate days[1].

In the meantime (March 20) the Prolocutor laid before the Upper House certain resolutions which their House had passed in condemnation of a book which had been submitted to them by the Vice-Chancellor of Oxford, and which was at that time creating much alarm, "Toland's Christianity not mysterious[a]." A Committee of Bishops which was appointed to examine the book reported that the book was of dangerous tendency, but, following a precedent which had been set in 1689, they determined to take Counsel's opinion as to the powers of Convocation. Counsel were divided, but Sir Edward Nor-

House asked for a Conference: "Dec. 12. Dominus Prolocutor cum assensu, ut asserebatur, totiûs Domus inferioris ad Præsidentem et domum superiorem missus est ad petend' se cum tribus vel duobus aliis è Domo Inferiori admitti ad conferend' cum dominis Episcopis in Domo suâ seden."

[1] O. T., iii. 392.

[a] Burnet says that they drew their propositions from this work with so little care, that they passed over the weak passages and selected such as were capable of a good sense.— O. T., iii. 392.

they, afterwards Attorney-General, gave it as his opinion that Convocation could not censure books without the Royal Licence, under the Penalty of Præmunire. Convocation was then prorogued to May 8; the Lower House, however, with its Prolocutor, continued to sit for some time; on May 8 the Lower House met the somewhat lame excuse as to the absence of the Royal Licence, by saying that the Archbishop might, if he had liked, have obtained the Royal Licence without consulting the Lawyers.

The Bishops, who had hitherto shown themselves as unconciliatory as the Lower House, now (May 8) took a laudable step with a view to reconciliation. They appointed a Committee of five, to meet an equal number of the Lower House, to consult on these points of dispute; this proposal, however, the majority of the Lower House refused; and when the Archbishop's schedule of prorogation to May 18 was brought down, the Prolocutor, without making any intimation of it to the Clergy, himself adjourned the House to the next day.

On May 30 the Lower House presented to the Archbishop a *Representation of their sense upon the Bishop of Sarum's Exposition of the XXXIX. Articles*, as introducing a latitude such as the Articles were framed to avoid; as being contrary to their meaning and to the received doctrines of the Church, dangerous to the Church of England, and derogating from the honour of the Reformation. On June 6 the Archbishop told the Prolocutor that the Upper House would have adhered to their resolution of receiving nothing from the Lower until their irregularity in refusing to meet the Committee of the Upper House was set right, had not the Bishop of Sarum himself requested them to receive the Representation. The Bishops replied to the Representation that the Lower House had no right to examine books without first consulting with the Upper House ; that they had no right to censure any books ; that their action in censuring a book in general terms without specifying the particulars complained of, was defamatory and scandalous ; and that the Bishop of Sarum, by his excellent history of the Reformation, approved of by both Houses of Parliament, and by his other writings, had done good service to the Church and justly deserved the thanks of the House [b].

In the new Convocation which met at the commencement of 1702, Dr. Sherlock, Dean of St. Paul's, having preached the Latin Sermon, the Lower House marked their feeling against the Bishop of Sarum by electing as Prolocutor, by 37 to 30 votes, Dr. Wood-

---

[b] In those disputes between the two Houses there were three Bishops, Compton, of London, Sprat, of Rochester, and Trelawney, of Exeter, who countenanced the proceedings of the Lower House ; whilst in the latter there was a considerable minority, amongst whom were Beveridge, and Bull, and Sherlock, who, on more than one occasion, addressed the Bishops against the course taken by their brethren.

ward, Dean of Sarum, who was at that time under prosecution by his Diocesan, his opponent being Dr. Beveridge, the candidate of the Whigs, and in this case, it must be confessed, the moderate party. In this Convocation the breach between the two Houses became widened. Hitherto it had been entered on the minutes of the Lower House that Convocation had met on the days and at the hours appointed by the Archbishop; but on January 28 a motion was proposed and carried enabling the Prolocutor to adjourn, or to continue the meetings of the Lower House in his own name [c]. The Lower House, however, was divided against itself, till a plan was discovered by Beveridge, by whose advice a Committee was formed to compose the matter; and a kind of accommodation was for the time patched up [d].

On February 12, the Prolocutor having been seized with illness, deputed Aldrich, Dean of Christ Church, to act in his place; it was acknowledged on all sides that a deputy ought to be appointed, but a new difficulty arose, as to whose right it was to appoint. On the 13th of February, however, the Prolocutor died;

---

[c] Instead of the usual form *Prolocutor intimavit hanc Convocationem esse continuatam*, the form now used was *Dominus Prolocutor continuavit et prorogavit quoad hanc domum*.

[d] It consisted on one side of Drs. Hooper, Jane, Aldrich, Binkes, Wynne, and Mr. Needham, and on the other of Drs. Beveridge, Hayley, Willis, Kennet, Prideaux, and Mr. Lloyd.

and the King dying on the following 8th of March, the Convocation virtually expired, although the Lower House claimed the same right as Parliament of sitting into the next reign.

CHAPTER VI.

STATE OF THE CHURCH UNDER WILLIAM III.

AFTER the restoration of Charles II., such a general licentiousness and infidelity pervaded the country, and so lowered the standard of morals, as to threaten the very existence of society. For twelve dreary years the nation had tolerated a gloomy Puritanism, which not only rendered religion ridiculous, but sowed the seeds of the decay of morals which followed after the Restoration. The era of Puritanism was marked, beyond that spirit of persecution which was inherent in it, by two characteristics, its gloominess and its hypocrisy. Not only were innocent amusements of all kinds proscribed; not only was the Sunday rendered as gloomy as a Pharisaical Sabbath, and Christmas-day, which from time immemorial had been observed as a season of joy and domestic affection, converted into a Fast; but one of the first resolutions of the Barebones Parliament was that no person should be admitted into the public service until the House was satisfied as to his real holiness. The consequence was that the sincere, although mistaken, Puritans soon found themselves lost in a multitude not only of men of the world, but of the worst sort of men, who saw that their only road to favour lay in an outward profession of religion. When no man could rise to eminence without having upon him the conventional signs of godliness—the sad-coloured dress, the sour look, the lank hair, the nasal whine—the religious tenets of the party were adopted by the most notorious libertines, who lived in the constant practice of fraud, rapacity, and secret debauchery [a]. When the Restoration was effected, and the restraints of Puritanism were removed, the rebound was sudden and dangerous; Religion, in the minds of many people, was associated with gloominess and hypocrisy, and so people, whilst they shook off whatever was good, adhered to the bad part which had brought disgrace upon the Puritan name. They determined that, whatever they were, they would not be, and in truth they were not, hypocrites and dissemblers.

The example of a good and moral king would have done much to counteract the evil. Charles II., a man by nature addicted to frivolous amusements, had been a prisoner in the hands of the austere Puritans, whose restraints he hated, and whose absurdities he ridiculed. Without belief in human virtue, he thought that every one could be brought to minister to his pleasures; and unfortunately the life which the King and the Court led, at a time

---

[a] Macaulay's England, i. 167.

when the Palace became the resort of gamblers and other profligate people, only added fuel to the flame which was ready to be kindled; and a state of things, rendered attractive by the good nature of the " merry monarch," even worse than had existed under the Puritans ensued. So that under Charles II. the ground was prepared, and the seeds of immorality and irreligion, if not then sown, were watered, which were soon to bring forth an abundant crop, and to lead to a chronic indifference to religion, beginning with the upper and communicating itself to the lower classes of the community.

As early as 1663 Dr. Barrow preached in Westminster Abbey a sermon, in which he said: " That was an age not less degenerate than corrupt in manners, when all wisdom and virtue and religion were almost in all places grown ridiculous ... when innocence was reputed a mere defect of wit and weakness of judgment." Passing over the short reign of James, we come to the time of the Revolution. We cannot of course accept as entirely unprejudiced the authority of even so good a man as the Nonjuror Kettlewell, but neither can his testimony, if somewhat overdrawn, be lightly discarded. In the written history of his life a sad picture is drawn of the state of religion at the Revolution. A change for the worse, he tells us, had set in soon after the accession of William and Mary. Amongst the Clergy there was a considerable number who were painful and exemplary in discharging the great care committed to them, but there were too many supinely negligent. There were a number of the Clergy very poor, and also very weak, and of small understanding, who were consequently under strong temptations to bad compliances and to follow a majority, and were easily imposed upon. The public prayers of the Church, which had been so much frequented when King James sat upon the throne, began more to be neglected everywhere. The Communion, which was ministered every Lord's Day in several of the parish churches in and about London and Westminster, as also upon the Festivals of the Church, was now much unfrequented in comparison of what it had been, and in cathedral churches was still worse, so that the alms collected at the Communion did little more than defray the expenses of the Bread and Wine[b]. It was observed that several dignitaries of the Church, and they some of the most zealous for bringing about the Revolution as in behalf of the Church which was in danger, neglected now their residence (how short soever that was) enjoined by the Statutes, and that many of the inferior Clergy were notoriously guilty of non-residence. It was complained that there were numerous faults in their morals, that they gave not

---

[b] Patrick writing of about the same time lamented "Scarce a handful of people appearing in many Churches, when the Play-Houses were crowded every day with numerous spectators."—Works, viii. 451.

due attendance to their offices, and that some of the dignified Clergy had cures more than one apiece, which was inconsistent with that duty which they did owe to the mother Church, and against the Ecclesiastical Canons. Nay, it was publicly represented by the hearty friends of what was then commonly called the Constitution, that others belonging to the Church were often seen in ale-houses and taverns, and to be in a great disorder through their intemperance[c]. That not a few of them were newsmongers and busy-bodies. That those Presbyters whom the Bishops ought to consult with were generally absent from the church, and the Archdeacons which were to be their eyes, were in the ends of the earth. That they had indeed their deputies, who did little more than dine, call over names, and take their money[d]. That some in the country had two cures, and resided on neither. That the catechizing of children

---

[c] This, however, does not agree with the general account given by cotemporary writers. The Clergy, though remiss in their duties, are generally described as leading moral lives. Samuel Wesley, the father of John and Charles, says in the *Athenian Oracle*, that in all his acquaintance he only knew three or four clergymen who disgraced their office.

[d] In the Lambeth Archives there is a letter from the Rector speaking of the irreligion of the people and the desecration of the Church. "They played cards on the Communion Table, and when they met to choose churchwardens, sat with their hats on smoking and drinking, the Clerk gravely saying, with a pipe in his mouth, that such had been the practice for the last sixty years."—Stoughton's Revolution, 324.

and servants was now very much disused, and even by those who vaunted not a little of their zeal to the Church. That there was not that care that there ought to be in instructing the youth and preparing them for the Holy Sacrament of Christ's Body and Blood. And that, lastly, the preparing of children for Confirmation was extremely neglected, the bare saying some words by rote being as much as was generally done and sometimes more.

The shock of an earthquake in the autumn of 1692 brought the people to their senses, and there was for a time a great show of piety and virtue: but it was only for a time; the nation soon again became corrupted in principle, and Burnet, writing of the same year [e], tells us that "a disbelief of revealed religion and a profane mocking of the Christian Faith and the mysteries of it became avowed and scandalous. The nation was falling under such a general corruption both as to morals and principles, and that was so much spread among all sorts of people, that it gave us great apprehensions of heavy judgments from Heaven."

Such was the state of Society as described by eye-witnesses at the time of the Revolution; still the Church continued to make good progress. The reign of James II. gave a check to the advance which it was making at the time of his accession: but the firmness

---

[e] O. T., iii. 139.

State of the Church under William III. 167

and resolution of the Church led to his overthrow before he had time to materially affect its position. William and his Latitudinarian Bishops did their best to weaken it, but the Church, so far from losing ground, not only maintained its doctrine and discipline unimpaired, but put forth new life; so that probably at no time since the Reformation did it exhibit greater signs of energy and vigour than during the latter years of King William's reign. And during the last decade of the seventeenth century one of the most remarkable and most permanent of the many revivals which have taken place in the Church of England occurred.

With a view to counteracting the prevailing evils of the times people began to unite in Associations, under the name of "Societies for the Reformation of Manners:" but before speaking of these Societies we must give some account of the "Religious Societies" in the reign of Charles II., of which those later Societies were the offshoot. Similar Societies had been many years before established in Paris, but were unknown in England until they were, between 1670—1680, established in London by the name of "Religious Societies," under the guidance of Dr. Horneck, Preacher at the Savoy Chapel, Mr. Smythies, Lecturer at St. Michael's, Cornhill, and Dr. Beveridge, with a view to counteracting the Atheistical and Socinian Clubs which existed, and of promoting personal piety among their members on the principles of the

Church of England[f]. Certain rules were drawn up for the guidance of these Religious Societies, by which the members bound themselves to pray many times a day; to receive the Holy Eucharist at least once a month; to examine themselves every night; to fast and to mortify the flesh; to read pious books, and especially the Bible; and generally to promote piety amongst themselves and the other members of the Societies. The Religious Societies so increased their finances by collections that they were enabled to remunerate the services of Clergymen to read prayers in the churches; they procured the preaching of sermons every Sunday evening in some of the largest churches in London, "to confirm Communicants in their holy vows;" they employed themselves in giving alms to the poor, in sending poor children to school, in helping poor scholars at the Universities, and in releasing debtors from prison. They assisted in establishing nearly one hundred charity-schools in London and many in the country; they contributed to Dr. Bray's Mission Schemes, and by degrees these Societies became so widely diffused that in 1710, when

---

[f] Anthony Horneck (1641—1696) was born at Bacharach on the Rhine, and, coming to England at the age of nineteen, graduated at Queen's College, Oxford, of which he afterwards became Chaplain, as well as Vicar of All Saints, Oxford. In 1671 he was elected Preacher at the Savoy Chapel; in 1693 Prebendary of Westminster, and the next year a Prebendary of Wells by Bishop Kidder, and dying in 1696 was buried in Westminster Abbey.

Robert Nelson was one of their most zealous supporters, no fewer than fifty-two had been founded in London and Westminster, and were to be found in almost every large town of England and Ireland. "These aids to devotion . . . extended to so many different places as to include every hour of the day. On every Lord's Day there were constant Sacraments in many churches. Greater numbers appeared at Prayers and Sacraments, and greater appearance of devotion was diffused throughout the city than had been known in the memory of man [g]."

The fundamental principle of these "Religious Societies" was attachment to the Church of England, and the great success that attended them led, at the Revolution, to the formation of other Societies, not confined like the former to the Church, but including both Dissenters and Churchmen, under the name of "Societies for the Reformation of Manners."

In 1691 (the year before the Societies were founded) Queen Mary, acting under the advice of Stillingfleet, Bishop of Worcester, addressed a letter to the Magistrates of Middlesex, exhorting them to execute the laws which were still in force, but which by a "long continued neglect and connivance of the Magistrates and Officers concerned" had fallen into abeyance, especially when the magistrates themselves were guilty of the offences against which those laws were directed.

---

[g] Toulmin's Hist. of Dissenters, p. 416.

On January 21 in the following year the King issued a Proclamation for the execution of the existing laws. The Proclamation set forth: "Being thereunto moved by the pious address of our Archbishops and Bishops, we have thought fit, by the advice of our Privy Council, to issue this our Royal Proclamation; and to declare our Princely intention and resolution to discountenance all manner of vice and sensuality in all persons from the highest to the lowest degree in our Realm. And we do hereby for that purpose straitly require, charge, and command, all singular our Judges, Mayors, Sheriffs, Justices of the Peace, and all other our officers ecclesiastical and civil in their respective stations, to execute the laws against blasphemy, profane swearing and cursing, drunkenness, lewdness, and profanation of the Lord's Day, or any other dissolute, immoral, or disorderly practices, as they will answer it to Almighty God, and upon pain of our highest displeasure. And for the more effectual providing herein we do hereby direct and command our Judges of Assizes and Justices of Peace to give a strict charge at their respective Assizes and Sessions, for the due prosecution and punishment of all persons that shall presume to offend in any of the kinds aforesaid; and also of all persons that, contrary to their duty, shall be remiss or negligent in putting the said laws in execution."

It was in order to carry out this Royal Proclamation that these "Societies for the Reformation of

State of the Church under William III.

Manners" were formed, differing from the "Religious Societies," not only by their including Dissenters as well as Churchmen, but also in their object, which was not so much the promotion of personal piety amongst themselves, as the carrying out the laws which existed against profanity and vice. In order to promote their object, a central body, composed of persons of eminence, Members of Parliament, Magistrates, and other gentlemen, subscribed to a fund for putting the law into motion against swearing, drunkenness, and profanation of the Lord's Day. A second body, composed of about fifty tradesmen and others, had the task assigned to it of suppressing immorality in the streets. A third undertook the obnoxious task of public prosecutors, of inspecting disorderly houses, taking up drunkards, lewd persons, profaners of the Lord's Day, and swearers, and carrying them before the Magistrates. By these means the Sunday markets were stopped; no "tippling" was allowed on Sunday; hundreds of dissolute houses were closed; thousands of lewd persons were imprisoned, fined, and whipped; whilst many persons were, at their own request, transported to America, to gain an honest livelihood in the Plantations.

The Societies for the Reformation of Manners were supported from the first by Archbishops Tillotson and Tenison, the latter of whom issued a letter to the Bishops of his Province, requesting them to instruct their Clergy in the matter. Many of the

Bishops, as, for instance, Bishops Fowler, Stillingfleet, Kidder, Trelawney, Patrick, and Burnet, thought well of these Societies, as also did the "pious" Robert Nelson [h]. Others, on the other hand, as Sharp, Archbishop of York, and Nicholson, Archdeacon and afterwards Bishop of Carlisle, thought that the good might have been done more effectually on the lines of the Church, and doubted whether the Societies might not come under the Conventicles which are forbidden by the 12th and 73rd Canons. Archbishop Sharp wrote to Nicholson that he thought the interchange of pulpits with Dissenters was opposed to the principles of our Church, and that if the Clergy devoted themselves to the reading of prayers on Wednesdays and Fridays and on Holydays, and every day in populous places, in monthly Communions and Celebrations, this would "more contribute to the promoting a Reformation than the informing against criminals."

These Societies ended, as might have been expected, in failure, for Englishmen do not like the office of a secret or even of an open informer. Vice may be punished, but is not likely to be eradicated, by magistrates; it may be made to assume a more decent exterior, although the disease is festering beneath. It was easy enough to hale before the magistrates a poor man who was found drunk in

---

[h] Woodward's Rise and Progress of the Religious Societies; Secretan's Life of Nelson.

the streets, but the rich could get off with impunity. And worst of all, the magistrates themselves were at fault; they were not only remiss but themselves guilty, and did all they could to discourage the work of the Societies.

But a far greater result than any which we have yet mentioned arose from these Societies: the same spirit in the Church which led to their being founded led also to the foundation of the Society for Promoting Christian Knowledge, and the Society for the Propagation of the Gospel, for which the Church is mainly indebted to the indefatigable labours of Dr. Bray.

Dr. Thomas Bray (1656—1730), a man of rare energy and devotion, was, about 1696, appointed by Dr. Compton, Bishop of London, as his Commissary in Maryland. For three years and a half after accepting the appointment he remained in London, where he occupied himself in making preparations for his mission, in procuring suitable missionaries, and in forming libraries. Seeing the necessity of co-operation for his new task, he rested not night or day till he had laid the foundation of those Societies which from that time to this have proved an incalculable benefit to the Church.

On March 8, 1698, five gentlemen belonging to the two Societies, the Religious Societies and the Societies for the Reformation of Manners—Lord Guildford, Sir Humphrey Mackworth, Serjeant Hook, Colonel Maynard, and Dr. Bray—met together (the place of meeting is unknown, but probably it was Serjeant Hook's chambers in Gray's Inn) and formed that Society, which, at first assuming the name of the "Society for *Propagating* Christian Knowledge," ten years afterwards exchanged it for that of the "Society for *Promoting* Christian Knowledge." The objects of the Society were (1) the Education of the Poor; (2) the care of the Colonies; (3) the printing and circulating books of sound Christian Doctrine. Dr. Bray was requested to lay before the Society "his scheme for promoting Religion in the Colonies, and his accounts of benefactions and disbursements towards the same."

Up to that time little or nothing had been done by the Church to advance the cause of religion in the Colonies, and the Church's system was almost unknown in America. In the charter granted in 1806 by James I. to Virginia, reference is made to "the preaching of the true Word and observance of the due service of God according to the rites and ceremonies of the Church of England;" but the labourers in the vineyard were few, and when they were removed by death, the strifes that hampered England at the great rebellion in Charles I.'s reign turned men's thoughts from the wants of her distant children to her own sorer wants at home. At the Restoration, a Corporation, of which Mr. Boyle was President, was founded under the title of "the Society for the

Propagation of the Gospel in New England and the parts adjacent," but its revenues never exceeded £600 a year, and one church, called the "King's Chapel," commenced in Boston in 1679 at the instigation of Compton, Bishop of London, and by the direction of Charles II., was the only church which existed in all the settlements of New England [i].

One of the first objects of the new Society was to relieve the spiritual destitution of our Plantations, an object which was greatly promoted by the self-denying labours of Dr. Bray. Abandoning the prospect of high preferment in this country, he left England in December, 1699, and at his own expense, and selling his goods to enable him to do so, reached Maryland in the following March. Whilst in America Dr. Bray saw the spiritual want which existed amongst the rapidly-growing Colonies, and the great need that there was for a larger supply of Clergy; and on his return to England, to maintain the cause which he had undertaken, he induced the Society to approve of Libraries in North America for the use of the Clergy. The extra work thus entailed on the Society was more than it could properly perform; and it was found necessary to throw off an offshoot.

---

[i] Except a garrison chapel at New York which came into the possession of the governor when that Colony, or rather the Colony of New Amsterdam as it was then called, was ceded by the Dutch at the treaty of Breda in 1667.

Dr. Bray therefore proposed to form a separate Society for Propagating the Gospel in our foreign Plantations, and in May, 1701, through the instrumentality of Tenison and Compton, he succeeded in obtaining a royal Charter for a new Society under the name of the "Society for the Propagation of the Gospel in Foreign Parts." The work was not begun a moment too soon, for the Church in America was languishing for want of Church teachers, and the country was overrun with Sects. The Charter mentions the insufficient maintenance or the total absence of Ministers of the Church in the Plantations, Colonies, and Factories beyond the Seas, so that the population "seemed to be abandoned to Atheism and Infidelity;" and "divers Romish Priests and Jesuits are the more encouraged to draw them over to Popish superstition and Idolatry;" and the new Corporation was charged with the "receiving, managing, and disposing of charity given for the maintenance of an orthodox Clergy, and for making such provision as may be necessary for the Propagation of the Gospel in those parts."

The object of the Society, it will be observed, was at first much more limited than it is at the present day, not carrying, as it does now, religion to the heathen world, but confining itself to mission-work in the English settlements. For the first thirteen years of its existence the income of the Society did not exceed £1,000. Nevertheless a staff of Clergymen was soon sent, with a small but competent income, into the New World; Dr. Bray did all he could, and through him many Libraries were established, and practical and devotional books dispersed throughout the Colonies. We must notice especially the work of one Missioner, George Keith. He went out as a Quaker, but became converted to the Church and took Holy Orders, after which he was indefatigable in the work of the Church. Between 1702 and 1705 he travelled through all the *governments of England* between North Carolina and New England, preaching twice on Sundays and on weekdays; disputing with the Quakers, and establishing the Church. With his own hand he baptized two hundred "Quakers or Quakerly-affected" converts, besides "divers other Dissenters in Pennsylvania, West and East Jersey, and New York." But what was wanted in America was the Church's system and the establishment of an Episcopate; and what the results would have been had Dr. Bray been appointed a Bishop in Maryland it is impossible to calculate; but unhappily this was neglected. In 1712 a resolution was passed by the Society for the sending out Bishops, but the enthusiasm which prevailed when the work was started died away in the darkness of the eighteenth century, and, as we shall see afterwards, no Bishop was consecrated for America until after the Declaration of Independence.

But we must not yet bid adieu to the venerable

name of Dr. Bray. Whilst engaged in the work of providing Libraries for the Colonies, he learnt to feel of what great advantage Parochial and other Libraries would also be for the Clergy of England and Wales. His plan, in which he received the hearty co-operation of Dr. Wilson, of Sodor and Man[k], seems to have been to revive the ancient office of Rural Deans with the jurisdiction pertaining to their several Deaneries, and he designed those Libraries for the use of the Parochial Clergy belonging to each Deanery, and as places where the Clergy of the Deanery might meet together for instruction and for conference. In 1709 an Act of Parliament was passed for the preservation of these Libraries, and a body of Trustees was formed under the title of the "Associates of Dr. Bray;" and so indefatigable was his zeal, that before his death he had the satisfaction of seeing no fewer than sixty-seven Parochial Libraries established for the local Clergy, and eighty-three Libraries in central localities for loan amongst the neighbouring Clergy. In addition to these, more than fifty Libraries were sent out to North America, the West Indies, and to a factory in Bengal, and to Cape Corso Castle on the African Coast[l].

---

[k] "By ye encouragement and assistance of my worthy Friend D^r. Tho. Bray, I began this year a foundation of Par. Libr. in this Diocese, wch by the good blessing of God upon His servant, I have been improving ever since with books both practical and devotional."—Keble's Life of Bp. Wilson.

[l] Secretan's Life of Nelson, p. 140.

One of the original objects of the S.P.C.K. was the establishment of charity-schools, and at its first meeting the question of erecting schools for the poor in and about London was taken into consideration. In this manner charity-schools were established entirely by the Church and for the Church. The standard of education for boys was, in those early days of elementary education, confined to Reading, Writing, and the grounds of Arithmetic, such studies as might fit them for service or apprenticeship; whilst for girls it was thought sufficient if they were taught to read, to knit, to sew, and to make their own clothes. The schoolmaster was required to be "one that frequents the Holy Communion, and who is approved by the minister before he is licensed by the Ordinary." He was to instruct the children in, and to explain the principles of, the Christian Religion as laid down in the Church Catechism, and was afterwards to inform them more largely of their duty by the help of the "Whole Duty of Man." He was to be diligent to correct the beginnings of vice, more especially lying, swearing, taking God's name in vain, and profaning the Lord's Day. He was to teach them to pray at home in the morning and at night, to say grace before and after meals, to take the children every Lord's Day and on Holydays to church, and to teach them to behave reverently there; whilst means were taken that the children should not be lost sight of when they went out into the world.

So rapidly did these charity-schools, commencing with such humble endeavours, increase, that when the first Assembly, which is now held annually at St. Paul's, took place in 1704 in St. Andrew's Church, Holborn, as many as fifty-four schools, numbering 2,131 children, had been founded, whilst by 1712 one hundred and seventeen schools were set up in London and Westminster, comprising 5,000 children; more than 4,000 children were clothed as well as fed, and 2,000 were placed as apprentices, whilst in the same period more than 500 schools were established in England and Wales; and the work extended to the Colonies.

As one sign of life in the Church during William's reign, we may mention the foundation of the Boyle Lectures. The Hon. Robert Boyle, seventh son of the first Earl of Cork, dying on December 30, 1691, bequeathed by his will £50 a year for a course of eight Lectures, to be preached annually by "some divine or preaching Minister," in defence of the Christian Religion against Atheists, Deists, Pagans, Jews, and Mahomedans [m]. Burnet tells us [n] that Mr. Boyle "was a very devout Christian, humble and modest almost to a fault, of a most spotless and exemplary life in all respects." Burnet also preached his funeral sermon, in which he said he had been

---

[m] Of these Lectures the Deist Collins remarked, "Nobody doubted the existence of a Deity till the Boyle Lectures endeavoured to prove it."   [n] O. T., iii. 270.

in the habit of devoting no less than a thousand pounds every year to works of charity, and especially to the propagation of Christianity, and this work he wished to be continued after his death.

It is difficult to exaggerate the perils to which the Church was exposed during the reign of William III.; but weakened though it was by the secessions of some of its ablest Bishops, and hampered by the action of the government which appointed to the vacant Sees men of Latitudinarian principles, who were indifferent to its doctrines and discipline, the Church if it did not advance, certainly did not go backwards. Doubtless William bore no goodwill to a Church so different from that to which he had been accustomed when in his own country; but his religion was political, and founded on his own interest rather than on conviction; he felt that the Church was strong in the affections of the Nation, and he allowed Convocation to meet, and as long as the State allowed the Church her Convocation (that is to say, allowed the Church the same rights which it accords to Dissenters), the Church was able to maintain its own alike against foes and, still worse, treacherous allies.

We must now notice the last events affecting the Church in King William's reign. In the Declaration which he published before he came to England he had promised to extend to all his subjects freedom from persecution, "to cover and secure all those who would live peaceably under the government from all persecutions on account of their religion." After the peace of Ryswick in 1697, a great swarm of Roman Catholic Priests, who had fled from the country at the Revolution, returned to England, and were living peaceably and unmolested by the government; exaggerated stories were spread concerning them, and on account of the toleration afforded them, the absurd rumour got abroad that the King was a Papist in disguise. On no other apparent ground a most cruel Act of Parliament was passed against the Roman Catholics in 1700: banishing Roman Catholic Priests from England, and offering a reward of £100 to such persons who should discover and convict a Roman Catholic Priest in the performance of his duties. It enacted that all, even suspected, Roman Catholics who should inherit an estate before eighteen years of age should, on attaining that age, take the oaths of Allegiance and Supremacy and the Test, in default of which they were incapable of purchasing, inheriting, or holding any estate; and their estates were to devolve upon their next of kin being Protestants. They were even prohibited from sending their children abroad to be educated in their own faith. The Bill fortunately was drafted in such vague terms as to render it difficult of enforcement, so that the Law became little more than a dead letter [o].

---

[o] But in 1706, and again in 1711, Proclamations were published for enforcing the Penal Laws against them. Again, after

State of the Church under William III. 183

In 1700 the young Duke of Gloucester, the only surviving child of the nineteen children whom Anne had borne, died in the eleventh year of his age, and the Jacobites exulted that the succession of the Pretender was all but secured. But unpopular though William was, there was no party in the kingdom of any consequence that had a desire that the whole work of the Revolution should be undone, and a Roman Catholic King be placed upon the throne, so that when a new Bill of Succession was submitted to Parliament not a single voice was raised on behalf of James or of his son. The Duchess of Savoy, granddaughter of Charles I., was, by the ordinary rule of inheritance, next after the Princess Anne in succession to the throne; but she was a Roman Catholic, so her claims were set aside. By the new Act of Settlement it was resolved that whoever afterwards should come to the throne should be in communion with the Church of England as by Law established, and the Crown was vested in Sophia, widow of the late, and mother of the actual, Elector of Hanover, and the heirs of her body being Protestants.

On September 17, 1701, James II. died at St. Ger-

---

the Rebellion of 1715, Parliament thought to strengthen the Protestant interest by enforcing the laws (1 George I. c. 55). In 1722 the estates of Roman Catholics and Nonjurors were subjected to a tax which was not charged upon other property (9 George I. c. 55), and after the Rebellion of 1745 a reward of £100 was offered for the discovery of Jesuits and Popish priests, and calling upon the magistrates to enforce the law.

mains. During the later years of his life he had given up all idea of wordly grandeur; he subjected himself to severe penance and mortification, and frequently visited the poor monks of La Trappe. To the last he conjured his son to prefer religion to every worldly advantage, to be faithful to his Church, and to renounce all thoughts of the Crown, if it involved a change of Faith.

The greatest indignation was felt throughout the country when it became known that his son was recognised by the King of France and also by the Pope as King of England under the title of James III. William summoned Parliament with all possible speed, and implored them to lay aside all party spirit and divisions on the matter. "Let there be no other distinction heard among us for the future but of those who are for the Protestant Religion and the present establishment, and of those who mean a Popish Prince and French Government." Parliament accordingly passed two Acts, the one for Attainting the pretending Prince; holding any communication with him was declared to be High Treason. The second Bill, for abjuring him, was introduced under the specious title of "An Act for the further security of his Majesty's person, and the succession of the Crown in the Protestant line;" but here the unanimity which had marked the passing of the first Act ceased. The Bill not only required an oath for abjuring James and his descendants, but also recog-

State of the Church under William III. 185

nised William and his successors, not only as *de facto* but as *rightful and lawful King*. Warm debates arose as to whether the oath should be imposed or voluntary; at length the imposition of the oath was carried by a majority of one in the House of Commons. The Bill was strenuously opposed in the House of Lords, and when it passed on February 24, 1702, ten Lords entered a protest against it as an unnecessary and severe imposition.

The Bill was still pending when, on February 20, the King was thrown from his horse. After the accident he was in so weak a state that he could not write his name, but was only able to affix a stamp, prepared for the purpose, to the Bill of Abjuration, and died on the eighth of March, 1702.

CHAPTER VII.

THE HIGH CHURCH REACTION.

THE reign of Queen Anne, who succeeded to the throne on the death of William, forms an interregnum between the Presbyterian-Calvinist who preceded, and the *Lutheran* Defender of the Faith who succeeded, her. She was a devout, if a somewhat narrow-minded, daughter of the Church. She had married in 1683 a Lutheran, Prince George of Denmark, who had a seat in the House of Lords as Duke of Cumberland. He is described as "being very fat, loving news, his bottle, and his wife," qualities good, bad, and indifferent; he was created Generalissimo of the Forces and High Admiral; but in religious matters he was a nonentity.

The new Queen was said indeed to be the stupidest person in the kingdom except her husband; " She was ignorant of everything except what the Parsons taught her," wrote the Duchess of Marlborough; but she had two qualifications which suited well a Defender of the Faith,—she was religious and a Churchwoman. Although a daughter of James II., and notwithstanding that attempts had been made to draw her over to the Church of Rome, she was untainted by Romanism on the one hand, as she was uninfluenced by the Latitudinarianism of William's Bishops on the other[a]. She received, we are told (as a mark, we may suppose, of advanced Churchmanship of the time), the Holy Communion once a month, and she rebuked her Chaplain at Windsor for administering the Sacrament to her before the Clergy. The Duchess of Marlborough, a woman whom Swift describes as showing her wit "by the usual mode of the times, in arguing against religion, and endeavouring to prove the doctrines of Christianity impossible," had at one time in all other matters a complete ascendancy over her, but failed to taint her with the prevailing scepticism of the day. Nothing could deflect her from her religion, and she chose as her spiritual adviser Dr. Sharp, Archbishop of York, who preached the Coronation Sermon on April 23, 1702.

No scandalous voice was ever raised against her character, as to which even Lord Chesterfield was obliged to bear a grudging testimony: "Queen Anne has always been devout, chaste, and formal, in short a prude. Her Drawing-rooms were more respectable than agreeable, and had more the air of solemn places of worship than the gaiety of a Court."

---

[a] In April, 1688, she wrote to her sister Mary, "I abhor the principles of the Church of Rome as much as it is possible for any to do, and I as much value the doctrine of the Church of England."

Anne dismissed William's Parliament before the expiration of the six months during which it was allowed by law to sit into the new reign, and the words which she spoke on that occasion were the key-note of the Church policy which she afterwards pursued: "My own principles must always keep me entirely firm to the Church of England, and will incline me to countenance those who have the truest zeal to support it." And at the opening of the new Parliament, in which the last elections were entirely revised, and double the number of Tories (that is, the friends of the Church) were returned, she said, "I am resolved to defend the Church as by law established, and to protect you in the full enjoyment of your rights and liberties [b]."

The first act of her reign in connection with the Church was to dissolve William's Commission for Ecclesiastical Preferments, an act which showed that she was alive to the danger with which the ascendancy of the Latitudinarian Bishops, of whom that Commission principally consisted, was fraught to the Church.

The Tories, or Church Party, being restored to

---

[b] The influence of the Tory majority was at once shown when Sir John Pakington complained of the Whig Bishop, Lloyd, of Worcester, having tried to prevent his election. The Commons voted his conduct to be malicious and unchristian, and advised the Queen to remove him from the office of Sub-Almoner, which (notwithstanding a protest from the House of Lords) the Queen did.

The High Church Reaction. 189

power[e], their first endeavour was to prevent the evasion of the Test Act by "occasional Conformity." The Test Act of 1673, although directed in the first instance against Roman Catholics, applied equally to Protestant Dissenters, and required all persons who held any office, civil or military, to receive the Holy Communion from the Clergy of the Church of England. But whilst effective against Roman Catholics, it was entirely useless as far as Protestant Dissenters were concerned, amongst whom a miserable system existed: for whilst adhering to their sect and attending its services, in which they were protected by the Toleration Act, they *qualified* for office, as the expression went, by *occasional Conformity*, that is, by receiving the Holy Communion once a year. The ceremony by which they did this was thoroughly recognised. During the early part of the service the Dissenters remained outside the Church, perhaps in some neighbouring house, or sometimes in the nearest

---

[e] It is necessary to state that to the frequent mention of Whigs and Tories no political signification is attached. The Tories at that time were the friends of the Church, the Whigs its opponents, or at any rate equally the friends of Nonconformity. Lord Stanhope says that in Queen Anne's reign the relative meaning of Whig and Tory "was not only different, but opposite, to that which they bore at the accession of William IV.... The same person who would have been a Whig in 1712 would have been a Tory in 1830:" and in this opinion Lord Macaulay, although he at first disagreed, afterwards concurred.

tavern, till the Communion Office was commenced, when some one appointed for that purpose would call out, "Those who want to be *qualified* will step this way;" they then entered the Church, received the Holy Communion, and became qualified to obtain or to continue to hold an office; thus making, as the poet Cowper expressed it,—

> "The Symbols of Atoning Grace
> An office key, a picklock to a place."

It is difficult to imagine a greater scandal to religion than this degradation of the highest Ordinance of the Church into a piece of State machinery. It is, however, necessary to state that there were two kinds of Occasional Conformists. One class thought that it was their *duty* to hold occasional Communion with the Church, and that if they did not do so they would be guilty of schism. This of course was a very different case from those who held occasional Communion with the Church for the mercenary motive of retaining their places and salary. It was hard enough for the Clergy to be compelled to receive such voluntary schismatics even of the better class to Communion. But it was an intolerable hardship that they were obliged to receive not only Dissenters but also men of questionable character, who came to Church simply because they were obliged to come. It was hard upon the Clergy that whilst the Dissenters were allowed to act inconsistently in order to obtain the benefits of the law, they themselves, by acting consistently and repelling them, should incur the penalties of the law[d].

The persons who availed themselves of this practice being Dissenters were generally Whigs, and therefore the opponents of the Government and of the High Church party. The obvious remedy would have been to get rid of the Test Act, but the High Churchmanship of those days, which was little better than an Ecclesiastical Toryism, was in favour of the Test. The zeal of the Tories was political rather than religious, and they determined to attack the practice of occasional Conformity. On November 14, 1702, Mr. Bromley, Mr. St. John[e], and Mr. Annesley, Members for the two Universities, brought a Bill into the House of Commons for preventing occasional Conformity. In the preamble, all persecution for conscience' sake was condemned; the Bill proposed that all those who had received Holy Communion as

---

[d] De Foe, known to all as the author of Robinson Crusoe, himself a Dissenter, published in 1697 "An Enquiry into the Occasional Nonconformity of Dissenters in cases of Preferment," and inveighed strongly against the practice. He maintained that if a man could conscientiously communicate in the Church, he was guilty of schism if he forsook the Church. He would ask such a man, "How can you take it as a civil act in one place and a religious act in another; is not this playing bo-peep with God Almighty?" The Nonconformist Howe published a Pamphlet against De Foe's "Enquiry."

[e] Afterwards Lord Bolingbroke.

a qualification for office, and afterwards frequented any meeting-house where more than five people attended, should pay a fine of one hundred pounds, and five pounds for every day they continued in their employments after having attended such a meeting. They were to be rendered incapable of holding any other employment till after one year's Conformity, and if they relapsed, the penalty and the period of probation were to be doubled. The promoters of the Bill argued that an established religion and a national Church were absolutely necessary for the well-being of the State; that the most effectual way to preserve this national Church was the maintenance of the civil power in the hands of those who expressed regard for the Church in their principles and practice; that Parliament, by the Corporation and Test Acts, never imagined that a set of men would rise up whose consciences would be too tender to obey the laws, but hardened enough to break them; that this Bill did not intrench upon the Act of Toleration or deprive the Dissenters of any rights, or add anything to the legal rights of the Church of England; that the toleration was intended only for the case of tender consciences, and not to give license to occasional Conformity; that if a man's conscience allows him to conform occasionally, then his separation is a schism, which in itself was sinful; and that as the last reign began with an Act in favour of Dissenters, so the Commons were desirous that the commencement of the present reign should be marked by an Act in favour of the Church.

The Bill passed the Lower House by a considerable majority. The Queen exerted all her influence to get it passed in the House of Lords, and sent her husband down to vote for it, which was certainly rather hard upon him, for he was himself an Occasional Conformist, and although he generally attended his Lutheran Chapel, was obliged, like other Dissenters, to receive the Holy Communion for the civil offices which he held[f].

But in the House of Lords, which was to a considerable extent a House of William's creation, and in which his Bishops bore a preponderating influence, the Bill was warmly opposed, and was sent back to the Commons with considerable alterations, which the latter refused to accept. In vain a free conference between the two Houses was held; the Lords persisted in their amendments, the Commons persisted in rejecting them; so the Bill was lost, and both Houses published their proceedings as an appeal to the Nation.

In the same Session another Bill of considerable importance, in favour of the Jacobites, was introduced into the House of Commons, allowing another year's grace to those who had not yet taken the Oath of

---

[f] On one of the occasions when he was sent down to vote he remarked to Lord Wharton, an opponent of the Bill, "My heart is vid you."—Tindal, iii. 452.

Abjuration. The House of Lords, which was less favourable than the House of Commons to the Jacobites, added to the Bill three clauses: the first, allowing those persons who should take the oaths within the prescribed period to return to their benefices and employments, unless they were already legally filled up; the second, making it High Treason to attempt to defeat the Protestant succession to the throne; the third, extending the oath of Abjuration to Ireland. The Commons, although at first they made some objections, eventually agreed to the Lords' Amendments, and the Bill, which in its amended form was a severe blow to the Jacobites, passed into law.

But there was evidently a very bitter feeling existing between the two Houses of Parliament, so the Queen at the end of February, 1703, ended the Session with some abruptness. At the closing of the Parliament she took the opportunity of expressing her attachment to the Church, and said that "upon all occasions of promotion to any Ecclesiastical Dignity she would have a just regard for those who were eminent and remarkable for their piety, learning, and constant zeal for the Church."

When Parliament met again in October, the Queen in her speech exhorted the two Houses to avoid all heats and divisions which might give encouragement to the common enemies of the Church and State. The Tories, however, were so intent on passing a Bill to prevent Occasional Conformity, that they deter-

The High Church Reaction. 195

mined at once to bring the matter again before Parliament. In the new draft, however, the penalties were lowered and some of the harshest clauses mitigated. The number of persons that constituted a Conventicle was now increased to twelve, instead of five, besides the family, and the fine was lowered from one hundred to fifty pounds. But now a stronger feeling against the Bill than had existed on the previous occasion prevailed amongst the Commons, and the House was pretty equally divided on the subject; the debates for and against it were maintained with equal spirit and ability, the supporters of the Bill declaring that the Church was in danger, and that this Bill was required for its security; eventually it passed and was sent to the House of Lords, to be handled there even more severely than in the Commons. Lord Godolphin and the Duke of Marlborough thought the Bill unseasonable; the Queen herself was now opposed to it, and did not send down her Nonconformist husband to vote for it; many peers who voted for it on the former occasion now absented themselves; the Bishops were divided, nine voting for and fourteen voting against the Bill. Burnet, who confessed that he had himself been an Occasional Conformist, spoke against it; and although Godolphin and Marlborough reluctantly voted for it, it was thrown out by seventy-one against fifty-nine votes. The Clergy were disgusted, and the Queen herself fell under their displeasure.

At this time, when Lords and Commons, animated by opposite principles, were seizing every opportunity of thwarting each other, the Queen performed a noble act of munificence to the Church, which was agreeable to both parties. The Anniversary of her Birthday falling, in 1704, on a Sunday, on the next day (February 7) Sir Henry Hedges, the Secretary of State, brought a message from the Queen to the House of Commons, that "having taken into her serious consideration the mean and insufficient maintenance belonging to the Clergy in divers parts of the kingdom, to give them some ease, she had been pleased to remit the arrears of the tenths to the poor Clergy, and for the augmentation of their maintenance would make a grant of her whole revenue arising out of the first-fruits and tenths [g], as far as it should become free from incumbrances, to be applied to this purpose," and she desired that an Act of Parliament might be passed to sanction the transfer [h]. Bishop Burnet claims for himself (and perhaps he had a voice in the matter) the merit of procuring this grant, and says that in the previous reign he had so frequently advocated the cause,

---

[g] The tenths amounted to nearly £11,000 annually, and the first-fruits to about £5,000.

[h] The revenues arising from the first-fruits and tenths having been anticipated by various grants for many years, were not available until long afterwards. Only 300 Livings had been benefitted by the bounty in 1720.—Chamberlayne's Past State of Great Britain, p. 202.

The High Church Reaction.

that Queen Mary determined, had she lived, to apply the revenue arising from those sources to the augmentation of small Livings. The tax had been originally imposed upon the Clergy by the Pope for the support of the Crusades, but, although frequently objected to by Parliament, and termed in one Act [1] a "horrible mischief and a damnable custom," continued long after the Crusades ended, to the time of the Reformation. Under Henry VIII. the Annates Act was, at the request of Convocation, passed, and payments to the Pope abolished, but no relief to the Clergy was effected, for the money only went from the Pope into the pockets of the plunderers of the Church. Queen Mary remitted, but Elizabeth again imposed, and even tried to increase, the tax, and by Charles II. it was devoted to his female favourites and their natural children. This act of the Queen was, therefore, a restoration to the Church of what it had been sacrilegiously plundered, but it stands out notwithstanding an honourable memorial to her who was styled the *good* Queen Anne.

On receiving the Queen's Message, a Bill was passed enabling her to alienate from the Crown this branch of the revenue, and to create by charter a Corporation, which has ever since been known by the title of "the governours of the Bounty of Queen

---

[1] 6 Henry IV.

Anne for the augmentation of the maintenance of the poor Clergy," and a clause was added to the Bill repealing so much of the Statute of Mortmain as to enable people to bequeath money by deed or will to the augmentation of Benefices [k]. Such was the origin of Queen Anne's Bounty.

In December of this year, 1704, the Occasional Conformity Bill was again brought forward, and rapidly passed through its different stages in the House of Commons. But this time the Commons tried a manœuvre for getting it through the Lords; Mr. Bromley, who brought it in, moved that it might be "tacked" on to a Land-tax Bill which was to be brought forward with the certainty of being passed that Session; and so sent to the House of Lords. The Land-tax Bill, being a money Bill, the Lords were obliged either to accept or reject it, in either case without alteration, and the Commons ventured to think that the Upper House was sure to pass it [l]. To this proposal, however, Harley and St. John and the other Tory Leaders in the House of Commons were themselves opposed, and the *Tackers* were defeated by 251 to 134 votes, the Bill being sent without the *Tack*

---

[k] This clause gave rise to great debates in the House of Lords : "It seems not reasonable," some of them said, "to open the door to practices upon dying men." The Bishops, however, supported it.

[l] From this manœuvre the Advocates of the Tack and the ultra-Tories received the nickname of "Tackers."

to the House of Lords. In that House, where the Queen herself was present at the second reading, it was opposed by the Ministers; on this occasion Godolphin and Marlborough voted against it, and it was defeated by 71 against 50 votes. Seven years elapsed before another attempt was made to pass it.

But great discontent now existed amongst the Clergy. A feeling of mistrust in the Queen had got abroad; she seemed to them to be wavering in her Churchmanship, and to be going over to the Whigs. The Bishops were unpopular, Dissent was increasing, and a belief was entertained that "the Church was in danger." A violent pamphlet was published by Dr. Drake, entitled "The Memorial of the Church of England," in which he maintained that the Church was sick with "hectic fever," which, if not cured in time, would destroy its very being; Dissent was increasing and alienating the Queen's affections, whilst the Bishops were traitors who, under the specious title of moderation, preached indifference to the interests of the Church. Such was the purport of the "Memorial."

Whilst such a temper prevailed in the Church, and especially amongst the Clergy, Parliament was dissolved on April 5, 1705; and the elections to the new Parliament were carried on with such bitterness of feeling as has rarely been equalled at elections in England. The Clergy instilled into the people what Burnet calls "tragical apprehensions" that in consequence of the rejection of the Occasional Conformity Bill the Church was in danger [m]. But whilst the Tories were divided into Tackers and Non-Tackers, the Whigs were everywhere united, and so triumphed. The new Parliament opened in October, 1705. The Queen, acting under her Whig advisers, complained of malicious insinuations which were made about the Church's danger; she affirmed that persons who fomented such statements were enemies to her and to her kingdom; she declared that she would always affectionately support the Church of England, as by law established; and she expressed surprise that "any one of my subjects can really entertain a doubt of my affection for the Church, or so much as suspect that it will not be my chief care to support it, and leave it secure after me [n]."

The Queen's protest, however, had no effect in producing a change of opinion, so it was thought advisable that a day should be appointed on which the question as to whether the Church was or was not in danger should be debated in Parliament. The question was accordingly submitted to Parliament on December 6, the Queen herself being present in

---

[m] At Epworth, during the election, Samuel Wesley, the High Church Rector, and father of John Wesley, was abused as "rascal and scoundrel," whilst "drumming, shouting, and firing of pistols went on under his very windows."—Tyerman's Life and Times of Samuel Wesley.

[n] Parliamentary History, vi. 452.

the House of Lords; Lord Rochester affirmed that there was danger to the Church; that whilst Presbyterianism had been established in Scotland, no toleration in that country had been afforded to the Episcopal Church; that the heir to the throne of England was not a member of the Church, and that the Occasional Conformity Bill, whilst it had been carried in the House of Commons, had been rejected in the Lords. Compton, Bishop of London, alleged that the Church was in danger from the irreligion and the licentiousness of the Press. He complained of a vile book published by Hickeringill, a Clergyman in his Diocese, whom he had endeavoured in vain to punish; and of a sermon preached by Hoadly (a name with which we shall soon become familiar), in which "rebellion was countenanced and resistance to the higher powers encouraged." Burnet, Bishop of Sarum, then said that Compton was the last person who ought to complain of that sermon, for how could he himself defend his having appeared in arms at Nottingham[o]? He declared that profaneness was on the decrease, and that this decrease was mainly owing to the Society for the Reformation of Manners, and the Society for Promoting Christian Knowledge, which had done much good by erecting libraries in country parishes, by sending able Clergy to the Plantations, and by establishing charity-schools. The

---

[o] This was in allusion to his having escorted the Princess Anne just before the Revolution to Nottingham.

Archbishop of York represented that there was danger to the Church from the increase of Dissenters and the many Academies which they had instituted. In answering the Archbishop, Lord Wharton complained of the schools and seminaries held by the Nonjurors, in one of which the sons of a noble Lord in that House had been educated. This sarcasm was evidently aimed at the Archbishop of York; he replied that his sons had indeed been taught by Mr. Ellis, a sober and virtuous man, but that when he refused to take the oath of abjuration, they were immediately withdrawn from his care. Patrick, Bishop of Ely, complained of the violent spirit displayed in the Universities against Dissenters, and of the undutiful behaviour of the Clergy towards their Bishops, in which he was seconded by Hough, Bishop of Lichfield and Coventry. Hooper, Bishop of Bath and Wells, complained of the invidious distinctions implied in the terms "High" and "Low" Church [p].

Other Lords spoke on either one or the other side, and when the debate was finished, and the question was put whether or not the Church was in danger, it was decided by 60 to 30 votes that the Church was

---

[p] Atterbury, at this time Archdeacon of Totnes, complained in his Charge of the title of "High Church" being given to his party: "The men who take pleasure in traducing their brethren 'under the invidious title of High Churchmen.' What they mean by that term I cannot tell."

not in danger. The House resolved that "the Church of England, as by law established, which was rescued from the extremest danger by King William III. of glorious memory, is now, by God's blessing, under the happy reign of her Majesty, in a most safe and flourishing condition; and that whosoever goes about to suggest or insinuate that the Church is in danger under her Majesty's administration is an enemy to the Queen, the Church, and the Kingdom." The next day the Commons, by 212 against 160 votes, concurred in this resolution, and joined the Lords in an address to the Queen; the Queen issued a Royal Proclamation, offering a reward for the discovery of the author of the "Memorial of the Church of England," which was a "malicious and seditious libel," and for apprehending the printer. She then prorogued Parliament till May 21 following.

A Protestant fever seems now and then to have come over the country during Queen Anne's reign. On April 4, 1706, the Privy Council sent a circular to the Archbishop of Canterbury, stating that her Majesty, having become acquainted with several instances of "the very great boldness and presumption of the Romish Priests and Papists in this Kingdom," directed the Clergy to make a return of the number of Papists and reputed Papists in their parishes. This was followed on April 11 by a Proclamation for putting in force the laws against persons endeavouring to pervert her Majesty's subjects to the Roman religion ^q. On March 15, 1711, another Proclamation was issued, ordering all Papists to remove from the cities of London and Westminster. And at the end of Queen Anne's reign we read ^r that at the Assizes at Chelmsford a Popish Priest, named Hanmer, was accused of saying Mass according to the Roman rite in the county of Essex, to which he pleaded "Not Guilty," and was called upon to find sureties to appear at the next Assizes.

That such vigorous measures should be resorted to by Parliament and the Queen only shows the popularity of the Church, and the widespread fear of any cause liable to endanger it. This fear was increased by the Union in 1707 between England and Scotland. Before the Lords began to discuss the articles of Union, a Bill, at the instance of the Archbishop of Canterbury, providing for the security of the Church of England as a fundamental part of the treaty, passed both Houses of Parliament without opposition, and received the Royal assent ^s. A feel-

---

^q The Acts to be put in force were one of 23 Elizabeth, "An Act to retain the Queen's subjects in their allegiance," and another 3 James I., "An Act for the discovering and repressing Popish Recusants."

^r The Flying Post, July 17, 1714.

^s On May 1 a thanksgiving service was held in St. Paul's, when Dr. Talbot, Bishop of Oxford, preached the sermon. Dr. Talbot had strongly advocated the Union in the House of Lords; the University of Oxford was, however, of a different mind, and, whilst congratulations flowed in to the government from other parts of the country, was silent.

ing of alarm existed in England as to the influence which might be exercised by the addition of fifteen Presbyterian Peers to the Upper, and forty-five Presbyterian members to the Lower House of Parliament. And there certainly was danger to the Church, when the Union was between two nations, in one of which Presbyterianism, in the other Prelacy, was held in abhorrence. Bishop Hooper in the House of Lords, and Sir John Pakington in the House of Commons, drew attention to this anomaly; the latter stated that "the Church of England being established *jure divino*, and the Sects pretending that the Kirk was also *jure divino*, he could not tell how the two nations that clashed in so essential a point could unite, and therefore he thought it very proper to consult Convocation upon this critical point." It was a point above all others on which Convocation ought to have been called upon to deliberate, for it materially affected the relations between the Church and the State. From the moment the Act of Union came into operation Hooker's view of Church and State was no longer tenable; the English Parliament ceased to be in theory the laity of the Church of England by representation, and Presbyterians thenceforward could and did vote in Parliament on all questions affecting the Church[t]. Convocation, however, was not con-

---

[t] The following extract from a letter of Edmund Burke may throw some light upon the Act of Union: "The Act of the 5th

sulted, but was arbitrarily prorogued by the Queen until the Act of Union had passed.

But notwithstanding opposition, the High Church party went on steadily increasing, and the country showed every disposition to side with the Church. The successive prorogations of Convocation; the admission of Presbyterians into Parliament; the evasion of the Test Act by Occasional Conformity, called up again and again the cry of the "Church in danger ;" the Queen, who had offended the Whigs by the excellent Church appointments which she made, veered round once more to her old Tory predilections; serious symptoms of Jacobitism began to manifest themselves; when an event occurred, insignificant enough in itself, but which, being thoroughly mismanaged by the government, threw the whole country into a blaze, caused the overthrow

---

of Anne made in prospect of the Union is entitled 'An Act for securing the Church of England as by law established.' It meant to guard the Church implicitly against any other mode of Protestant religion which might creep in by means of the Union. It proves beyond all doubt that the Legislature did not mean to guard the Church in one part only, and to leave it defenceless and exposed upon every other. The Church in that Act is declared to be 'fundamental and essential for ever in the constitution of the United Kingdom, so far as England is concerned.' All this shows that the religion which the King is bound to maintain has a positive part in it as well as a negative." From this it is evident that the ecclesiastical conduct of a King or Queen of England is regulated by statute as well as by moral and religious duty.

of the ministry, and raised the Church higher in popular estimation than ever.

Henry Sacheverell, grandson of an Independent Minister, and son of a Low Church Incumbent at Marlborough, was born in that town in 1672, and although he is represented as not distinguished for ability or learning, he became a Demy and, in due course, Fellow of Magdalen College, Oxford [u]. Swift[x] says he was a man whom the eminent writers of his own party never mentioned without contempt. In 1705 he was appointed by popular election Preacher of St. Saviour's, Southwark, where he preached to crowded congregations his favourite doctrines of Divine Right and Passive Obedience, in opposition to the Reverend Benjamin Hoadly, Rector of St. Peter-le-Poer in the City, who carried the opposite doctrines to an equal extreme.

The language which he was accustomed to use in the pulpit was certainly most objectionable. He had already gained some bad fame from a sermon which he preached in 1702, in which he charged the Dissenting Academies as "fountains of lewdness," from

---

[u] Nevertheless he does not appear to have been so contemptible as he has been represented. He was elected Demy in company with Addison, Boulter, afterwards Bishop of Bristol and Archbishop of Armagh, and Smallbroke; his Latin Verses appear in the *Musæ Anglicanæ*, and Addison dedicated to him his "Farewell to the Muses."

[x] Works, vi. 250.

which were "spawned all descriptions of heterodox, lewd, and Atheistical Books," and he described their supporters as "worse monsters than Jews, Mahomedans, Socinians, or Papists." As a reply to his sermon De Foe, a prominent Dissenter, wrote a very bitter satire, entitled "The shortest way with Dissenters." It was written anonymously, and was at first supposed to be the work of a High Churchman, written in favour of the Church, with a view to the extermination of Dissenters. But when the name of the author leaked out, and it was found that it was a satire on the Church written by a Dissenter, De Foe was committed to Newgate, sentenced to pay a fine of two hundred marks, and to be imprisoned during the Queen's pleasure: and the pamphlet was ordered to be burnt by the common hangman. But we must turn to that event in his life which has immortalized the name of Sacheverell.

Having taken his D.D. degree in 1708, Sacheverell the next year preached two sermons, the first on August 15, before the Judges at Derby, on "The Communication of Sin," in which he spoke of the dangers arising to the Church from the betrayal of its rights and interests; the second on November 5, before the Lord Mayor, entitled "Perils from false Brethren," in which he attacked the Revolution and the Act of Toleration, and hinted at Burnet and Hoadly as the false brethren, and not obscurely, under his well-known nickname of Volpone, at the

Lord Treasurer Godolphin. This Sermon, with a dedication to the Lord Mayor, he printed, and in a short time no fewer than 40,000 copies of it were sold. The best thing would have been to leave him alone; the Whig Ministry, however, in spite of the warnings of Somers and Marlborough, adopted the worst possible course, and impeached him before the House of Lords of high crimes and misdemeanours, February 27, 1710, being appointed for the trial in Westminster Hall. No State Trial since that of the Seven Bishops caused so great excitement. The whole paraphernalia of the judicature was put in motion : the Attorney and Solicitor-General were employed for the prosecution, and the Queen, who had at first condemned the Sermon[y], finding that the Clergy (except, of course, the Whig Bishops), headed by Atterbury and the community at large, were in his favour, took the side of the accused, and on several occasions attended the trial, the mob thronging around her sedan chair with shouts of "God bless your Majesty and the Church ; we hope your Majesty is for Dr. Sacheverell[z]." On the second day of the

---

[y] "It is a bad sermon and he well deserves to be punished for it."

[z] Prayers were asked in the Queen's Chapel for Henry Sacheverell under persecution : (The Danger of Looking Back, p. 11). White Kennet, an opponent of Sacheverell, was "often pointed at in the streets and affronted in the Aisles of the Church, for refusing to pray for one under persecution."— Kennet's Life, 102.

trial riots occurred in London. The mob, with the shout of "High Church and Sacheverell," attacked and burnt the chapel of Mr. Burgess, a celebrated Dissenting Minister in Lincoln's Inn Fields, and made a large bonfire in the square of the pulpit, pews, cushions, and Bibles. Other Dissenting chapels were treated in a similar manner; an Episcopal church, because it had no steeple, was mistaken for a Dissenting chapel and narrowly escaped, and Bishop Burnet's house was in imminent danger [a].

The case against Sacheverell was opened by the Attorney-General. The charges submitted to the House of Lords were four in number: (1) that he had preached against the Revolution; (2) against the Act of Toleration; (3) that he had asserted that the Church was in danger; and (4) that the present government were false brethren and traitors to the Church. Sacheverell was well defended, and he himself concluded his defence in so able a speech that it was supposed to be too good to be his own composition, and was generally attributed to Atterbury [b].

---

[a] A brochure of the times thus alludes to the burning of Mr. Burgess' chapel:—
"Invidious Whigs, since you have made your boast,
That you a Church of England Priest would roast,
Blame not the mob for having a desire
With Presbyterian tubs to light the fire."

[b] He read, says Burnet, "with much bold heat and spirit, which, however, was so different and superior to his ordinary state

The Lords adjourned to consider their judgment. Dr. Hooper, Bishop of Bath and Wells, allowed the necessity of resistance in certain cases, but thought that the Revolution should not be boasted of, nor made a precedent, and that there was a justification for preaching non-resistance at that time when resistance was justified. Burnet upheld the doctrine of resistance from the Book of Maccabees. Sharp, Archbishop of York, the most influential of all the Bishops, condemned the sermon, but did not consider Sacheverell guilty of a misdemeanour. On the next day Wake, Bishop of Lincoln, brought to light many interesting facts in connection with Archbishop Sancroft's scheme of Comprehension, and accused Sacheverell of having falsely represented the Comprehension Scheme. Trimnell, Bishop of Norwich, spoke of Sacheverell's insolence in charging Archbishop Grindal with favouring the discipline of Geneva. Burnet, speaking a second time, accused Sacheverell of attacking the Queen herself, and of attributing the nickname of Volpone to the Lord Treasurer.

Ultimately, after a trial extending over three weeks, during which Burnet says it so engrossed men's minds that all other business was suspended, the House of Lords resolved that the charges against Sacheverell were established, and 69 against 52 Peers

---

that it was clearly seen not to be his own composition, but was generally attributed to Atterbury."

found him guilty of high crimes and misdemeanours[c]; seven Bishops voting against him and five in his favour.

But now arose the difficulty—What should they do with him? Eventually it was decided (but only by a majority of six) that he should be suspended for three years, although a motion that during that time he should be incapable of accepting any Church preferment was lost by one vote. The Sermon was condemned to be burnt by the common hangman; a decree passed by the Convocation of Oxford in 1663, which asserted the absolute authority and indefensible right of Princes, being condemned to be burnt at the same time. Sacheverell's rival, Hoadly, was recommended to the Queen by the House of Commons for Church preferment for having done good service in justifying the principles of the late happy Revolution. The Queen returned a civil answer, but Hoadly remained unrewarded during her reign.

The mildness of the sentence passed on him was equivalent to a victory to Sacheverell. He was now the hero of the day. Such enthusiasm as had not been shown since the acquittal of the Bishops followed him everywhere. He was debarred indeed from preaching, but crowds flocked to the church to hear him read prayers; such zeal for him, especially amongst ladies, prevailed, that he was sent for in all

---

[c] Thirty-four Peers entered a Protest against this decision.

directions to baptize their children, and to be named after him was considered a high privilege. When in June he set out from London to take possession of a good Living in Wales, the journey resembled a festal procession; and soon afterwards the Queen herself appointed him to the valuable Living of St. Andrew's, Holborn.

But the matter was far from ending thus. The Tories regarded the trial as a victory to themselves. Harley, soon to be created Earl of Oxford, and St. John, soon to become Viscount Bolingbroke, seized the moment of excitement caused by the Sacheverell riots, and having gained the ear of the Queen induced her to dissolve Parliament [d].

Now began the war of the Elections. Handbills were posted everywhere by the High Church party declaring that the Church was in danger [e]. Caricatures were freely used on both sides. By the Whigs Sacheverell was represented in the act of writing his famous sermon, with the Pope on one

---

[d] "You had a sermon to condemn," wrote Bolingbroke, "and a Parson to roast (for I think that was the decent language of the time), and to carry out the allegory, you roasted him at so fierce a fire that you burned yourselves."—Dedication to Sir R. Walpole of the Dissertation on Parties.

[e] The following inscription on a placard was used at the Middlesex election:—
    "Join, Churchmen, join, no longer separate,
    Lest you repent it when it is too late;
    Low Church is no Church."

side and the Devil on the other (these being the false brethren); whilst the Tories retaliated by leaving Sacheverell out of the picture and substituting Hoadly in his place. But the cry of the "Church in danger" drowned all other voices, and it is not too much to say that it was through Sacheverell, and the fear that the Church was really in danger under the Whig government, that the Whigs sustained a crushing defeat[f]. The Queen dismissed her Whig Counsellors, and in their place appointed a Tory Ministry, with Harley and St. John at its head, and the new government appointed Sacheverell to preach the Sermon on the anniversary of the Restoration, for which he received the thanks of Parliament.

---

[f] Burnet attributes this to the influence of the Clergy; a useful lesson to the Clergy of the present day if they would learn their power.

CHAPTER VIII.

CONVOCATION IN THE REIGN OF QUEEN ANNE.

WE must now notice the proceedings in Convocation under Queen Anne.

The first Convocation of her reign met, together with Parliament, in October, 1702, Aldrich, Dean of Christ Church, being chosen Prolocutor of the Lower House. At its opening a contest respecting the address usually made to the throne arose between the two Houses. At last an address was agreed on, to which the Queen replied that "their concurrence in the dutiful address was a good presage of their union in all other matters, which was desirable for her service and the good of the Church."

Whilst noticing the bad feeling which continued to exist between the two Houses of Convocation all through this reign, it is important to bear in mind the cause to which such an unfortunate result is attributable. It is, we imagine, attributable to the fact that during Queen Anne's reign a comparatively small number of Bishoprics—only seventeen in twelve years—fell vacant; thus William's Episcopate still dominated, and carried on its Latitudinarian traditions, whilst the Latitudinarian Tenison continued Archbishop (1695—1716) through the whole reign.

The agreement between the two Houses on which the Queen remarked was of short duration. The Bishops were willing to make concessions as to the right of prorogations, and they stated that, with a view to terminating their differences, they had appointed a Committee of seven Bishops to arrange matters with a deputation from the Lower House. They offered that the Lower House might, in the intervals of the Sessions, appoint Committees to propose matters for deliberation, and that the Archbishop should so order the prorogations as to suit the convenience of the Lower House. Unfortunately to this reasonable proposal the Lower House objected, as still infringing their independence, and they proposed to refer the matter for the Queen's decision; the Bishops replied that the rights of the Church were a trust committed to their charge which they could not make a matter of reference, and they added that their enemies, and especially the Papists, would rejoice to see Convocation pleading their rights before a Committee of Privy Council.

This reply of the Bishops seemed to the Clergy to impugn their Churchmanship, and to charge them with favouring Presbyterianism; so they determined to draw up a Declaration, which must have astonished some of the Latitudinarian Bishops, to the effect that they held Episcopacy to be an Apostolical and Divine Institution; and this they sent to the Upper House, inviting the concurrence of the Bishops in order that it might become the standing rule of the Church. "But," says Burnet[a], "the Bishops saw into their designs, and sent them for answer that they acquiesced in the declaration already made on that head in the book of Ordinations.... and they did not think it safe either for them or the Clergy to go further in that matter without a royal Licence." They commended the zeal of the Lower House for Episcopacy, and expressed a hope that they would continue to act in accordance with it for the future; a hope which was not destined to be realised.

In the meantime (whilst the Bishops had the Declaration under their consideration) the Lower House drew up and presented to the Queen a petition, in which, after stating that they had offered to submit the whole matter of their differences to her Majesty, a proposal which the Bishops had declined, they asked her to take the matter into her consideration; the Queen promised to send them an answer as quickly as possible, but no answer came.

The hostility between the two Houses now became fixed and embittered. The whole kingdom was made to share in the strife, and the dissensions between the High Church and Low Church parties

---

[a] O. T., iii. 483.

—by which they were now familiarly known—divided with the war on the Continent the interest and animosity of the nation [b].

In the Convocation which met, together with Parliament, in the autumn of 1703, the Lower House, with the evident intention of reflecting upon the Bishops, drew up a representation of abuses that existed in the Consistorial Courts, but, says Burnet [c], they "took care not to mention those great ones of which many amongst themselves were eminently guilty, such as Pluralities, Non-residence, the neglect of their Cures, and the irregularities of the lives of the Clergy which were too visible."

In the Autumn Session of 1704, the Lower House of Convocation, of which Dr. Binkes, Dean of Lichfield, was chosen Prolocutor, met with very discontented feelings. The Occasional Conformity Bill had been again rejected. Tory Churchmen were being gradually replaced in the government of the country by Whig statesmen; the Marlborough party was carrying all before it, and there was reason for fearing that the Queen herself was becoming alienated from the Church party. On December 1 the Lower House presented to the Bishops a Paper complaining of the hardship of being compelled to administer the Holy Communion to notorious schismatics in order to keep them in office. In February, 1705, they

---

[b] Cardwell's Synod., ii. 710. [c] O. T., iv. 57.

complained of the encroachment of Dissenting Ministers on the rights of the Church, and of a late Charge of Bishop Burnet to the Clergy of his diocese, in which he spoke of the Lower House as enemies to the Bishops, to the Queen, and to the Nation; and the Prolocutor, on February 14, placed a Paper on the table of the Upper House, asking the Bishops "to interpose their authority to obtain for them some speedy and sufficient reparation." The Archbishop asked him whether the Lower House had, since the day of Prorogation, held any intermediate Sessions. The Prolocutor allowed that they had done so. Thereupon the Archbishop told him that "it was very irregular to hold intermediate Sessions as being a violation of the President's right, and contrary to the constant custom of Convocation." To this the Lower House strongly objected; they respectfully declined to obey, if the Archbishop's admonition was a paternal act, and protested against it as void and null in law, if intended as a judicial act. The Archbishop had, at the same time, defended Burnet, and threatened them that if in the next Convocation they did not show a more dutiful disposition, he might be called upon to exercise his authority. On March 15 he declared Convocation to be prorogued.

Convocation met with the new Parliament on October 25, 1705, Dr. Stanhope preaching the Latin Sermon, and Dr. Binkes being again chosen Prolocutor. The two Houses occupied themselves in discussing the same question which engaged the Houses of Parliament, as to whether or not the Church was in danger. The Upper House agreed in an address to the Queen censuring those who had raised the cry of the " Church in danger," and expressing their satisfaction with the state of things which existed under her Majesty's government. The Lower House, on the ground that it would be easier to draw up a new one than to make amendments in it, refused to concur in the Bishops' address[d]; they acknowledged that the Church could be in no danger from her Majesty, but they avoided saying that it was not in danger from others [e], and it was agreed that a separate address should be prepared. This plan was rejected by the Bishops; they insisted that the Lower House must either concur in the address, or assign their reasons for disagreeing to it. The Lower House maintained that they had an unquestionable right, without assigning their reasons, of dissenting from the Upper House, and that their Lordships' demand was contrary to the known method of proceeding in the two Houses. To this the Bishops replied that Convocation was not an assembly consisting of two bodies, but that the Presbyters were the Council of the Bishops. The Lower House, however, adhered to their opinion, and without dis-

---

[d] Bowyer's Life of Queen Anne, 225.
[e] Atterbury's Correspondence, iii. 273.

Convocation in the Reign of Queen Anne. 221

puting any more about the matter, constituted themselves a separate House; they made no further reference to the Bishops, but prorogued themselves, and thus all communication between the two Houses ceased. The Lower House continued to hold its intermediate Sessions, notwithstanding a protest made by Kennet and 51 out of 145 members of their House, against the irregularity of its proceedings.

The Convocation was prorogued to February 1, 1706. On February 25 an unexpected blow fell upon the Lower House. On that day a letter from the Queen, probably written by the Archbishop, was addressed to Convocation, censuring the conduct of the Lower House towards the Bishops, and expressing her determination to uphold her supremacy, and the due subordination of the Presbyters to the Bishops, which is a fundamental part of it. After this letter had been read by the Bishop of Norwich, who acted as Commissary to the Archbishop,—and just when he was producing a new document,—Atterbury, not liking the look of things, plucked the Prolocutor by the sleeve, and suggested their retirement, for, he said, "this is no place for us." Burnet in a moment sprang to his feet, and exclaimed with excited gestures, "This is the greatest piece of insolence I ever knew, to refuse to hear the Queen's orders! Mr. Prolocutor, go at your peril!" The Prolocutor was in a strait between two, Burnet and Atterbury, and whilst he hesitated what to do, the Commissary proceeded to read the prorogation; but before it was concluded the Lower House rushed to the door, determined not to hear the words of prorogation: they returned to their own House, and by way of asserting their rights, held a sitting, although they did not venture to pass any vote [f].

In a letter addressed to the Bishops on February 19, 1706, the Lower House reminded their Lordships of a previous letter to them which still remained unanswered; they complained of the immorality of the stage, and of the insults heaped upon the Clergy, and stated that a congregation of Unitarians met publicly in London, in which the preacher denied the Divinity of our Lord's Nature [g]. But their chief complaint was against a sermon which had been preached by Hoadly before the Lord Mayor: "They do earnestly desire your Lordships that some synodical action may be taken of the dishonour done to the Church by a sermon preached by Mr. Benjamin Hoadly at St. Lawrence, Jury, September 29, M DCCV., containing positions contrary to the doctrine of the Church expressed in the first and second parts of the Homily against disobedience and wilful rebellion." They also censured the "lewd and profane writings of Hickeringill, Rector of St. Mary's,

---

[f] It must be mentioned that Burnet in relating this incident, O. T., iv. 145, does not mention his own disgraceful share in it.

[g] The preacher alluded to was Mr. Emlyn.

Colchester," but they at the same time commended Wall's "History of Infant Baptism [h]."

The union between England and Scotland, though completed in 1706, was not finally settled by Act of Parliament till 1707. A report was circulated to the effect that the Lower House intended to address the Commons against the measure [i]; and in order to prevent this step being taken, the Queen, on the 12th February, ordered the Archbishop to prorogue Convocation for three weeks, before the expiration of which time the Act, by which the two kingdoms were united under the common title of Great Britain, had passed.

This arbitrary prorogation of Convocation was certainly a very high-handed proceeding on the part of the Government. When, therefore, Convocation met again on March 19 the Lower House voted a "Representation" to the Upper House, which declared that "ever since the submission of the Clergy in the time of Henry VIII., for a space of 173 years, no such Prorogation had been ordered during the sitting of Parliament." This "Representation" was laid before the Queen; on April 2 the Archbishop

---

[h] The work particularly censured was "Priestcraft, its Character and Consequences."

[i] The Lower House had appointed Committees to consider the subject, and it was given out that they intended to make application to the House of Commons against the Union.—Burnet, O. T., iv. 184.

informed the Lower House that search had been made, and that it was found that seven or eight similar prorogations had been made during the sitting of Parliament. On April 8 the Queen sent to the Archbishop a letter, evidently written by himself, reflecting on the "Representation" as an invasion of her supremacy. She referred to her letter of February 25, 1706; she had indeed hoped that that letter would have been a sufficient warning; she had shown much tenderness to the Clergy, but if anything of the same nature occurred again, it would be necessary "to use such means for punishing offences of this nature as are warranted by law."

This letter the Archbishop was commanded to communicate to Convocation, and on April 18 the Lower House was summoned to hear it. But lo! the Prolocutor was absent—it was said that he had gone into the country. The Archbishop proceeded to pass sentence of contumacy upon him, but reserved the declaration of the penalty till April 30. The Lower House voted that the sentence was unlawful, and tried to persuade the Prolocutor to stand his ground; the Prolocutor, however, thought differently, and submitted, and the sentence was removed.

No other business was transacted in this Convocation; the members of the Lower House were too refractory to allow of anything being done, and Convocation was dissolved together with the Parliament.

Convocation was again convened with the new Parliament of 1708, but it was prorogued by royal writ from November to February, even before the customary sermon had been preached. When February came no business was transacted, and it was prorogued from time to time during this whole Session of Parliament[j].

We come now to the year 1710, the year of the Sacheverell riots. Convocation met on November 25, when Atterbury, the champion of the High Church, was chosen by a large majority Prolocutor over Kennet, the candidate of the Low Church party. Her Majesty's Licence was brought to them by Lord Dartmouth, and an address to the Queen, in which both Houses concurred, was presented on January 26, 1711. The Queen sent a letter to the Archbishop containing certain subjects for discussion. These were—(1) the drawing up a Representation with regard to the late excessive growth of infidelity, heresy, and profaneness; (2) the regulating the proceedings in excommunications and reforming the abuses of Commutation-money; (3) the preparing a form for the visitation of prisoners, and particularly condemned prisoners, and admitting converts into the Church; (4) establishing Rural Deans, and making them more useful; (5) giving exact accounts of glebes, tithes, and other possessions be-

---

[j] Lathbury, 406.

longing to Livings; and (6) regulating Licences for marriage.

The Licence summoning Convocation was (probably through Atterbury's influence with the new government) issued without the Archbishop being, as was usually the case, nominated as President, or even being left to choose his commissaries in case of ill health, the Bishops of London and Bath and Wells being mentioned by name for that office [k], to which afterwards were added the names of Trelawney, Bishop of Winchester, Atterbury's great friend, Robinson, Bishop of Bristol, and Bull, of St. David's.

Committees were formed and proceeded to consider the subjects presented to them by the Queen. Atterbury drew up a representation of the condition of the Church, reflecting severely on the low state of religion ever since the Revolution; the draft was carried in the Lower House, but rejected by the Bishops; and the other matters submitted to them by the Queen not receiving the sanction of both Houses, no business was done, and the matter dropped [l].

---

[k] The Archbishop was laid up by gout, and this was evidently done to prevent him nominating Burnet to act in his place.

[l] The House of Commons having taken into consideration the want of churches in London, the thanks of the Lower House of Convocation were presented to them by the Prolocutor, who, by the request of the Commons, gave in a scheme for the new

But now, as Burnet says, "an incident happened which diverted their thoughts to another matter." High as the Church stood in the affection of the nation, the results of Latitudinarian teaching began to manifest themselves. Sherlock and South had been, if at all, unintentionally unorthodox with regard to the Trinity; they were sound in the doctrine, but fell into error in trying to expound it. But now two clergymen, both of whom had been Boyle Lecturers, were not only notorious Professors of Arianism, but tried to engraft their opinions on the doctrines of the Church.

The first of these two clergymen who engaged the attention of Convocation was Whiston, a man whom Burnet describes [m] as partly Apollinarian, partly Arian. William Whiston (1667—1747), educated at Clare Hall, Cambridge, was in 1698 appointed Chaplain to Dr. More, Bishop of Norwich, and in 1701 assistant to Sir Isaac Newton whom he afterwards succeeded, as Lucasian Professor at Cambridge; in 1707 he was Boyle Lecturer, and up to that time he was orthodox [n]. But in 1708 he pub-

---

churches which led to the erection of the churches referred to in the next chapter.

[m] O. T., iv. 324.

[n] In 1696 he had published a "New Theory of the Earth," in which he showed that the Creation of the world in six days, the Universal Deluge, and the general Conflagration, as laid down in Scripture, are agreeable to reason and philosophy

lished an Essay on the Apostolical Constitutions, which the Vice-Chancellor would not allow to be printed at the University Press; he had got a craze in his head after reading the history of the first two centuries of the Church, that the Eusebian, or what are called the Arian doctrines, were the received doctrines of those ages; that the Athanasian Creed was unscriptural, and that the Apostolical Constitutions were "the most sacred of the Canonical books of the New Testament." In 1709 he published a volume of Essays, in which he maintained that " our Blessed Saviour had several Brothers and Sisters *properly so called*," i.e. the children of His reputed Father Joseph, and His true Mother the Virgin Mary. In 1710 he was deprived of his Fellowship and expelled the University on account of his heretical opinions.

In the same year appeared the work which gave him the greatest notoriety: "An Historical Preface of Primitive Christianity Revived, with an Appendix," giving an account of his expulsion from Cambridge; and this work he dedicated to Convocation. He openly maintained that the Arian doctrine of the Trinity is the right one; that when the Scriptures speak of One God they mean the Father only; that the Son was created, but before the world, and that the Son and the Holy Ghost were inferior and subject to the Father[o].

---

[o] Whiston appears scarcely to have been sane. When Prince Eugene visited London in 1712, Whiston presented him with

The Lower House of Convocation took this work into their consideration, and represented to the Bishops that "A book hath during this Session of Convocation been published and dispersed through several parts of the Province, entitled, 'An Historical Preface of Primitive Christianity Revived, by William Whiston, M.A.,' a book which in their opinion was 'directly opposite to the fundamental Articles of the Christian Religion.'" As the case appeared to them to be involved in difficulties, the Upper House presented an address to her Majesty, alleging that Whiston had advanced damnable and blasphemous positions against the Trinity, expressly "contradicting the two fundamental Articles of the Nicene Creed, and defaming the whole Athanasian Creed," but as they had doubts as to how far Convocation could act in the matter, they besought her Majesty to submit the case to the consideration of the Judges.

Accordingly the judges were consulted. Of the twelve judges eight (amongst whom were the Attorney-General (Northey) and the Solicitor-General (Raymond)) gave it as their opinion that Convocation had a juris-

---

a copy of an Essay which he had written on the Revelation of St. John, in which he stated his belief that the Prince had "by his glorious victory over the Turks" accomplished a passage in the Revelation. The Prince made him a present of fifteen guineas, remarking, however, that he *did not know he had the honour of being known to St. John.*—Nicholls, Lit. An., i. 499.

diction in cases of heresy, and that an appeal lay from Convocation to the Crown; whilst the remaining four were of opinion that ever since the Statute of Appeals in the time of Henry VIII. Convocation had no jurisdiction in such cases, but that the Ecclesiastical Courts, from which an appeal lay to the Crown, was the proper tribunal before which they should be decided.

Her Majesty's Council adopted the views of the Majority, and the Queen wrote to the Archbishop that "there being no doubt to be made of our Jurisdiction," she expected them to proceed in the matter. The book was therefore proceeded with. Certain propositions were extracted by the Bishops and censured as Arian; the Lower House, except with regard to one proposition, concurred with the Upper; so that, in this case at least, the two houses were in agreement; and the condemnation of the book proceeded from the whole Convocation. Convocation declared that the condemned passages "do contain assertions false and heretical, injurious to our Saviour and the Holy Spirit, repugnant to the Holy Scriptures, and contrariant to the decrees of the two first General Councils, and to the Liturgy and Articles of our Church." The judgment was presented to the Queen for confirmation; but when on various occasions application was made for its return, excuses were urged that it could not be found; so, notwithstanding that the work was condemned by Convocation, Whiston escaped under shelter of the Crown, and still persisted in his heretical opinions [p].

In the Convocation which met in December, 1712, a matter of considerable interest engaged the attention of both Houses. The invalidity of Lay Baptism had of late been asserted, notably by the Nonjuror Dodwell. "The Bishops," says Burnet, "thought it necessary to put a stop to this new and extravagant doctrine." Accordingly the Archbishop of Canterbury summoned a meeting of Bishops to Lambeth Palace on Easter Tuesday, 1712, when a Declaration was agreed to against the irregularity of Lay Baptism, but stating that, according to the practice of the Primitive Church, no baptism in or by water, in the Name of the Father, the Son, and the Holy Ghost, ought to be repeated. This declaration Sharp, Archbishop of York, although at first he agreed to it, refused to sign, on the ground that it would encourage irregular Baptism; in which opinion he was supported by Sir W. Dawes, Bishop of Chester, Blackhall, of Exeter, and Bisse, of St. David's [q]. The Archbishop (Tenison) determined to submit the question to Convocation. Accordingly the declaration of the Bishops was brought before the Upper House and agreed to. The Lower House, however, would not even take the declaration into consideration, but laid

---

[p] Whiston continued outwardly a member of the Church till 1747, when he joined the Baptists.
[q] Life of Abp. Sharp, by his Son.

it aside, thinking that it would encourage those who struck at the dignity of the Priesthood [r].

A new Parliament, and with it a new Convocation, met in February, 1714, and Atterbury having become, through his appointment as Bishop of Rochester, a member of the Upper House, Dr. Stanhope was elected Prolocutor; and Convocation, after presenting a joint address to the Queen, was on March 17 authorized to proceed to business, a similar list of subjects which had been submitted to the last Convocation being again recommended for their consideration. A more important matter, however, engaged their attention in the case of Dr. Clarke, to whom we have referred above as together with Whiston troubling the Church with his heresy at this time.

Samuel Clarke (1675—1729), having graduated at Caius College, Cambridge, was on his Ordination appointed as his Chaplain (in succession to Whiston) by Dr. More, Bishop of Norwich. In his Reflections upon a book called "Amyntor" he had defended the writings of the Apostolical Fathers, and in 1704, and again in the following year, had preached the Boyle Lectures, which he afterwards published in two volumes, entitled "Discourses concerning the Being and Attributes of God, the obligations of Natural Religion, and the truth and certainty of the Christian

---

[r] Burnet, O. T. Waterland, who opposed Lay Baptism, yet admitted that the Church had not determined either way.

Religion." Up to this time he was orthodox in his opinions, but about 1706, when he was Rector of St. Benet, Paul's Wharf, London, he began to hold heretical opinions on the Trinity, and to suspect that the doctrine of the Athanasian Creed was not that of the Primitive Church. In 1709 he became Rector of St. James's, Piccadilly, and took his D.D. degree at Cambridge, although his friend Whiston tried to dissuade him from signing the XXXIX. Articles, and by way of explaining the sense in which he subscribed, he published, in 1712, his "Scripture Doctrine of the Trinity." "This," says Dr. Van Mildert[s], "was the commencement of a new era in polemics." Clarke differed from Whiston, inasmuch as he disclaimed the character of an Anti-Trinitarian; so far from considering himself an Anti-Trinitarian, he endeavoured to prove the doctrine of the Trinity, in the sense in which he himself held it, to be the doctrine of Scripture and of the Church of England. But his starting-point was the Latitudinarian principle, that "every person may reasonably agree to such forms whenever he can *in any sense at all* reconcile them with Scripture." Whiston blames him for his disingenuous conduct in signing the Articles in an Arian sense; and the question of "Arian subscription" now became a matter of warm controversy between several distinguished writers[t]. No sooner was his

---

[s] Life of Waterland, p. 44.
[t] It will enable us to understand the position of Clarke and

work published than it was attacked as a revival of Arianism[u], and the weight of public opinion was against him. But in 1713 he proceeded from theory to practice. He assumed the right of altering and omitting at his pleasure passages of the Prayer-Book, and in order to avoid the reading of the Proper Preface in the Communion Office, he, on Trinity Sunday, omitted the Holy Eucharist altogether, to the great pain of his congregation, and was in consequence removed from the post which he held of Chaplain in Ordinary to the Queen.

In June the Lower House of Convocation complained to the Bishops that Clarke's book was at variance with the catholic doctrine of the Church of England, and when the Bishops requested them to specify the objectionable passages in writing, they presented to them a Paper of extracts from the work. At this period of the proceedings Dr. Clarke drew up a qualifying paper concerning his faith, in which a dif-

---

his followers, if we bear in mind that the advocates of Arian subscription held that the XXXIX. Articles are Calvinistic, and that they had as good ground to subscribe to them in an Anti-Trinitarian sense as others had to sign them in an Arminian sense.

[u] His chief opponents were Dr. Wells, Robert Nelson, Dr. Knight, Dr. Edwards, Mr. Welchman (the author of an illustration of the Thirty-nine Articles), Mr. Edward Potter, and Mr. Mayo; whilst Clarke's cause was espoused by Dr. Whitby, Dr. Sykes, and Mr. John Jackson. — Van Mildert's Life of Waterland.

ferent view was maintained from that contained in the extracts, and presented it to the Upper House; he also undertook not to preach again on the subject, nor to publish any further books on the Trinity. In this declaration he stated that the 3rd and 4th Petitions in the Litany had never been omitted by him in his church; nor had he ever omitted the Athanasian Creed at the 11 o'clock service, but only at early prayers, for the sake of shortness; and that the omission complained of had been made by his curate and not by his appointment. But soon afterwards he sent a second explanation to the Bishop of London, to the effect that his first declaration did not differ from the views which he had maintained in his book, and that it must not be taken as a retractation of anything which he had written.

The Upper House expressed themselves satisfied with these explanations, and informed the Lower House that they "do think fit to proceed no further upon the extract laid before us by the Lower House." The Lower House, however, resolved on July 7 that he had made no retractation at all, "nor doth give such satisfaction for the great scandal occasioned by the said books, as ought to put a stop to any further satisfaction and censure thereof[x]."

---

[x] Smalridge (1668—1719), consecrated Bishop of Bristol in 1714, stood Clarke's friend, as he had before been Whiston's friend. But he himself is said not to have been favourable to

" Thus ended," says Whiston, "this unhappy affair; unhappy to his best friends, and above all unhappy in relation to the opinions the unbelievers were hereupon willing to entertain of him, as if he had prevaricated all along in his former writings for Christianity[y]."

On July 8 Convocation was prorogued by the Bishop of London, acting as President, who did "in the name of the Upper House and by their direction, give the thanks of their Lordships to the Lower House for the great pains and diligence in despatching so many of the heads of business recommended by her Majesty to the Convocation." The Church had put forth its strength; Convocation was not thwarted by the Government; a feeling of greater unanimity between the two Houses began to manifest itself. Such was the state of things when, on August 1, 1714, Queen Anne died.

---

the Athanasian Creed, and an eye-witness asserted that he did not repeat it when it was said in Bristol Cathedral. It is not in Smalridge's favour that the Princess of Wales (afterwards Queen Caroline) was his Patroness.

[y] Whiston's Memoirs of Dr. Clarke.

CHAPTER IX.

THE CHURCH AT ITS HEIGHT.

WE must now resume the thread, which we broke off in the last chapter, of the proceedings in Parliament.

The Tories, restored to power after the Sacheverell riots, having a large majority in the House of Commons, seized the favourable opportunity for again bringing forward their thrice-rejected, but not on that account less fondly cherished, Occasional Conformity Bill. Lord Nottingham formed a Coalition with the Whigs of the House of Commons on a compromise, by which they on their side agreed (not greatly to their credit) to sacrifice their former principles, so a Bill against Occasional Conformity, with a few slight modifications from the former Bills to suit his new allies, was introduced by Lord Nottingham in the House of Lords, and being carried there without a division, passed the Commons with enthusiasm and became Law in 1711. It enacted that "all persons in places of profit and trust, and all the Common Council-men in Corporations who shall be at any meeting for Divine Worship, where there are above ten persons more than the family, in which the Common Prayer was not used, and where the Queen and the Princess Sophia were not prayed for, should, upon conviction, forfeit their place of trust or profit . . . and such persons were to continue incapable of any employment till they should depose that for a whole year together they had been at no Conventicle."

The Church was now the most powerful element in the State, and the new government had discernment enough to appreciate its importance, and to see that by favouring the Church it could draw the people to its side. London was rapidly growing in population, but with the increase of house-building there was no increase of Church accommodation, whilst eighty churches had been destroyed in the fire of London. An address from the Upper House of Convocation stating the want of Churches was presented to the Queen by the Archbishop of Canterbury, whilst Dr. Atterbury, the Prolocutor, waited upon the Speaker with a similar address from the Lower House. The Queen sent a message to the Commons, calling their attention to the spiritual destitution of the Metropolis, and warmly recommending "so good and pious a work." The Commons showed equal zeal: "Neither the long expensive war," they said, "in which we are engaged, nor the pressure of heavy debts under which we labour, shall hinder us from granting to your Majesty whatever is necessary to accomplish so good a design." The Commons appointed a Committee to consider "what Churches are wanting in London and Westminster and the Suburbs thereof." The Lower House of Convocation expressed their pleasure at finding their intentions thus anticipated by the House of Commons, and returned their unanimous thanks for such an instance of affectionate regard for the welfare of the Established Church. To this the Commons replied, "that this House will in all matters relating to religion and the welfare of the Established Church have a particular regard to such applications as shall at any time be made to them by the Clergy in Convocation assembled, according to the ancient usage, together with the Parliament." On March 10, Convocation, through its Prolocutor, Atterbury, presented a Report specifying twenty-seven of the largest parishes which, with a population of 512,924, had only twenty-eight churches and eighteen tabernacles. On April 6, the Commons' Committee made the calculation that, allowing one fifth of the above population to consist of Dissenters and French Protestants, 240,500 Church people remained unprovided for, for whom, computing 4,750 souls for each church, fifty new churches were required; and they stated in an address to the Queen that the want of churches greatly contributed to the miseries and irreligion of the day. In the same Sesson an Act of Parliament was passed for raising the sum of £350,000 for building fifty new churches by a duty of one shilling on every chaldron of coals unloaded in the Port of London for three years[a].

During Queen Anne's reign the work of building the new churches made considerable progress; but after the Hanoverian succession, and the return of the Whigs to office, the Church was no longer courted for political purposes, and Convocation, which would have taken care that the work was properly executed, was suppressed. Through mismanagement and lukewarmness the funds were miserably squandered; only a few churches, and those very extravagantly, were built, and the opportunity, as far as Parliament was concerned, was lost for ever[b].

There can be no question that the type of Bishops appointed during her reign conduced mainly to the efficiency of the Church under Queen Anne. That the Queen felt the responsibility of the trust committed to her is certain; as also that she did not appoint Bishops on mere political grounds, a thing

---

[a] Amongst the Commissioners was Robert Nelson, who suggested that Ground Landlords should be compelled when they build a certain number of houses to erect a church for the new inhabitants (Secretan's Life of Nelson, 145)—a suggestion very useful for the present day.

[b] Maitland, writing in 1756, says: "Hitherto there are only ten of the said churches built upon the new foundations." These were Greenwich, at a cost of £18,269; Deptford, £19,637; St. John's, Westminster, £29,277; St. Mary-le-Strand, £16,341; Spitalfields, £19,418; St. Ann's, Limehouse, £19,679; Ratcliffe Highway, £18,557; Bloomsbury, £9,793; St. Mary, Woolnoth, £8,605; and St. Luke, Old Street.

which cannot be said of her predecessors, or for those that succeeded her during the next hundred years.

A notable instance of the Queen's care in selecting Bishops occurs in the case of Dean Swift, a man who, from the indelicate tone of some of his writings and the flippancy of others, was entirely unsuited for the highest Church preferments. Jonathan Swift (1667—1745), afterwards Dean of St. Patrick's, was educated at Trinity College, Dublin, but at that time he presented none of those marks of genius which characterized his after life. He was prevented, as he himself expresses it, by dulness and insufficiency from taking his B.A. degree, and he afterwards obtained it in a manner little to his credit—"speciali gratiâ [c]." But though we are told that he was looked upon by the Scholars of his college as a blockhead [d], yet at the age of nineteen he composed, although he did not publish it until 1704, his famous "Tale of a Tub." Swift was originally a Whig, but we read that he was forced to become a Tory on account of the Low Church principles at that time advocated by the Whig party [e]. His object in writing the "Tale

---

[c] Sheridan's Life of Swift, p. 3. The cause of his being refused his degree was his ignorance of Logic, at that time a principal object of learning at the Universities.—Scott's Memoirs of Swift.

[d] Sheridan's Life, p. 5.

[e] He joined the Tories in 1710, probably because he had not received such preferment as he thought his due from the Whigs.

of a Tub" was to show the excellency of the Church of England over Romanism on the one hand and Presbyterianism on the other; but it was written in a tone of light ridicule unfitted for such a subject, so that the Clergy, and especially Archbishop Sharp, were scandalized with it. About 1708 there was a scheme on foot to appoint Swift Bishop of Virginia, with power to ordain Priests and Deacons, and with a general jurisdiction over all the Clergy in the American Colonies; this scheme, however, fell to the ground. On the death of Dr. Humfrey Humphries he was recommended to the Queen for the thus vacant See of Hereford [f]; the opposition of Dr. Sharp was, however, too powerful for the united influence of Ministers; he exhorted the Queen "to be sure that the man she was going to make a Bishop was a Christian [g];" he represented the "Tale of a Tub" as a ridicule upon religion in general, and the writer of it little better than an infidel, who had disgraced his sacred Order by profligate levity, and sapped the foundation of revealed Religion; a scoffer, in short, altogether undeserving of Church Preferment [h].

---

[f] It was said that Swift had an enemy at Court in the person of the Duchess of Somerset, whom he had accused of having connived at the murder of her husband and "of having red hair."

[g] Sheridan's Life, 83.

[h] Scott's Memoirs, p. 165. But Dr. King, in Anecdotes of his own Time, p. 60, says that Lord Bolingbroke told him that the Queen denied the truth of this story to him, and Bolingbroke

Swift's subsequent preferment to a Bishopric was always refused by the Queen; nobody, he writes in his journal, "will do anything for me, so the Bishops may die as fast or as slow as they please;" so he had to be contented with the Deanery of St. Patrick's, to which he was appointed in 1713, and which he held till his death in 1745.

The first Bishop whom the Queen appointed was Nicholson (1655—1727), Archdeacon of Carlisle, to the Bishopric of Carlisle in 1702. Nicholson, together with Archbishop Sharp, was a strong opponent of the Society for the Reformation of Manners, but up to the time of his appointment to the Bishopric he was chiefly known through his " English Historical Library," a work which was severely handled by Atterbury, so that there is but small cause for wonder that when Atterbury was appointed to the Deanery of Carlisle there was little cordiality between the Bishop and the Dean [i].

In 1704 Dr. George Hooper (1640—1727), the intimate friend of Ken, was translated from St. Asaph, to which he had been appointed in the previous year, to the See of Bath and Wells. Dr. Kidder, who had

---

added that it was invented by Walpole to deceive Swift, and as a reason for keeping him out of a Bishopric.

See under Atterbury, Part II. chap. i. In 1715 Dr. Nicholson was appointed Lord High Almoner to George I. ; in 1718 he was translated to the See of Londonderry, and in 1727, although he died before he took possession, to the Archbishopric of Cashel.

been intruded into Ken's See, was killed in his Palace at Wells by the fall of a stack of chimneys during the great storm that swept over England on the night of November 26, 1703. The storm is said to have been the most severe that ever visited this country [k]. In several churches the spires were broken off the steeples, and the roof rolled up like a scroll of parchment. The chapel of King's College, Cambridge, lost many of its pinnacles, and some of its painted windows were dashed in [l]. Hooper was now offered the thus vacated See [m], but he was most unwilling to accept it, and begged to be excused, and it was only on the urgent request of Ken that he at last consented.

The See of St. Asaph, vacant by the translation of Dr. Hooper, was conferred upon Dr. Beveridge, Archdeacon of Colchester. William Beveridge (1637—1708) was eminent not only as a scholar, an author, and a preacher, but also for the piety of his life, which is portrayed in the best known of his numerous works, his "Private Thoughts on Religion," a work which, though written when he was only twenty-three years of age, was not published

---

[k] "The only tempest which in our latitude has equalled the rage of a tropical hurricane.... No other tempest was ever in this country the occasional of a National Fast."—Macaulay's Essay on Addison.

[l] Stanhope's Queen Anne, i. 119.

[m] He afterwards refused the See of London on the death of Compton in 1713, and the Archbishopric of York on the death of Sharp in 1714.

till after his death, but which has been often reprinted, and translated into French and German. Having graduated at St. John's College, Cambridge, Beveridge was soon after his ordination appointed by Archbishop Sheldon to the Vicarage of Ealing, where he wrote his great work, the *Pandectæ Canonum* [n]," a collection of the Apostolical Canons, and the Canons of the Early Councils of the Church, a work which drew towards him much attention both at home and abroad, and as in it he attributed to the Apostolical Canons an earlier date (viz. at the end of the second or the beginning of the third century) than is usually assigned to them, involved him in some controversy[o]. In 1672 he was instituted to the Rectory of St. Peter's, Cornhill, where he exercised his ministry for many years with great success, especially over the young men in the city, who thronged the Communions at his church, and formed themselves into Religious Societies under his guidance. In 1673 he was appointed to a Prebend in St. Paul's; in 1681 he became Archdeacon of Colchester, and in 1684 a Canon of Canterbury Cathedral, and for many years took a prominent part with Dr. Horneck

---

[n] Συνοδικόν, sive Pandectæ Canonum SS. Apostolorum et Conciliorum ab Ecclesiâ Græcâ receptorum," &c.

[o] Besides this work, he published amongst others An Explanation of the Church Catechism; a Defence of Sternhold and Hopkins' Version of the Psalms, and an Exposition of the XXXIX. Articles, which was not published till after his death.

in forming and directing the Religious Societies which existed in and about London p.

At the Revolution his conscience allowed him to take the oaths to William and Mary, and being too considerable a Divine to be overlooked he was made a Royal Chaplain, and was offered the See of Bath and Wells. This offer, however, he refused, for he felt that Ken had been uncanonically deprived; and the refusal of the See so offended the King, that he received no other offer of preferment during William's reign, and it was not till 1704, in the reign of Anne, and when he was 67 years of age, that he was appointed to the See of St. Asaph.

The See of St. David's had been vacant ever since 1699, when Dr. Watson, who had been appointed to that See by James II., was sentenced to deprivation for Simony. James II. seemed to try how much he could damage the Church by his Episcopal appointments. In 1687 he appointed Dr. Watson to the See of St. David's. Rumour said that Watson paid a considerable sum of money for the appointment, and that, by way of recouping himself, he sold the Church Preferments in his gift. His case was heard by the Archbishop of Canterbury and his Suffragans, and he was found guilty and deprived. Burnet, who was one of the Judges, says of Watson, "he was one of the worst men I

---

p See chap. vi.

ever knew in Holy Orders," and proposed that he should be excommunicated. Watson, pleading his privilege as a Peer, appealed to the House of Lords; the Lords, however, in consequence of his deprivation, refused to consider him as a Peer, but, owing to the difficulties which his case presented, they expressed a hope that the King would not fill up his vacant See. Watson then appealed to the Court of Delegates, by whom the Archbishop's sentence was confirmed; yet he contrived to elude the sentence till 1705 [q].

To succeed Watson Dr. Bull, the famous author of the "Defence of the Nicene Creed," was appointed. Dr. George Bull, although one of the greatest Divines of whom the Church at any time of its history could boast, had been passed over by successive governments and left to the obscurity of a country parish till he had attained the age of seventy-one years. George Bull (1634—1710), educated at Exeter College, Oxford, and ordained during the Commonwealth Deacon and Priest on the same day by Dr. Skinner, Bishop of Oxford, held first a small Living near Bristol, and afterwards, in 1659, was presented to the Living of Suddington, near Cirencester. In

---

[q] About the same time as Watson, another Welsh Bishop, Dr. Edward Jones, appointed Bishop of Cloyne 1683, and translated to St. Asaph 1692, was tried under presumption, but not on so strong evidence as Watson, of Simony, and dying in 1703 was succeeded by Hooper.

1678 he was preferred to a Stall in Gloucester Cathedral, in 1685 he became Rector of Avening, and in the following year Archbishop Sancroft appointed him to the Archdeaconry of Llandaff, which the Archbishop had received as his option. In 1669 he published his first great work, the *Harmonia Apostolica*, the object of which was to show that good works are necessary as the fruits of faith, and that there was no difference between the teaching of St. Paul and St. James on that subject except such as was due to the different circumstances and times in which they wrote. For thirty years Dr. Bull was the stedfast champion of the Trinity and of our Lord's Divinity against the assailants of those doctrines at home and abroad. His great work, the "*Defence* of the Nicene Faith," which he finished in 1680 (a work written in Latin, and therefore accessible to the learned men on the Continent), was principally directed against Petavius, a Jesuit, Zwicker, a Socinian, and Sandius, an Anti-Trinitarian, who lived in Holland. It is scarcely credible to us in the present day that this work, which extended his fame as a scholar and a divine far beyond his own country, was nearly lost to the world because no bookseller would undertake its publication, and Bull himself was unwilling to risk any expense. Fortunately for the Church he gave the manuscript to Dr. Jane, Regius Professor of Divinity at Oxford; by him it was recommended to Dr. Fell, Bishop of

The Church at its Height. 249

Oxford, who published it in 1685 at his own expense. In 1694 appeared Dr. Bull's next great work, "The Judgment of the Catholic Church of the first three Centuries on the necessity of believing that our Lord Jesus Christ is very God [r]." The work had immediate reference to the lax opinions of Episcopius, and was intended to show that the Nicene Fathers held the belief of our Lord's true Divinity to be one of the indispensable terms of Catholic Communion. Its publication was well-timed, for it was just when the Church was endangered by the controversy between Sherlock and South, and other disputants of a less orthodox character. Robert Nelson presented the book to the famous Bossuet, Bishop of Meaux, through whom the thanks of the Clergy of France assembled in Convocation at St. Germains were returned to the author. Bossuet, in his letter to Robert Nelson, asked what Bull meant by the Catholic Church? Dr. Bull's answer appeared in 1707, under the title of "The Corruptions of the Church of Rome, in relation to Ecclesiastical Government, the Rule of Faith, and Form of Divine Worship; in answer to the Bishop of Meaux's Queries."

His last great work published during his lifetime, entitled "Primitive and Apostolical Tradition [s]," in

---

[r] "Judicium Ecclesiæ Catholicæ trium priorum sæculorum de necessitate credendi quod Dominus noster Jesus Christus sit verus Deus."

[s] The full title was "Primitiva Apostolica traditio dogmatis

continuation of the same subject, was written, as its title implies, against the extravagant assertion of Zwicker and his followers in England, that the doctrines of our Lord's Divinity, Pre-existence, and Incarnation were entirely the inventions of some of the early heretics[t].

As anything connected with this great and learned Divine must be interesting, we will briefly relate one or two anecdotes of his life as a Parish Priest, recorded by his Biographer, Robert Nelson.

At the time that he held his Living near Bristol, the use of the Prayer-Book was prohibited by the Government, and people were in the habit of railing at it as a *lifeless form*. Bull consequently learnt the Church Prayers and the whole of the Baptismal Service by heart, and when, after the baptism of his child, a father who greatly objected to printed forms, thanked him for his beautiful *extempore* prayers, Bull showed him the very same prayers in the Prayer-Book; after this the father and all the family always attended the Services and the Communion of the Church[u].

---

in Ecclesiâ Catholicâ recepti de Jesu Christi, Salvatoris nostri, divinitate, assertâ atque evidenter demonstratâ contra Danielum Zuikerum Borussum ejusque nuperos in Angliâ Sectatores."

[t] Amongst his posthumous works there is a "Discourse on the Doctrine of the Catholic Church for the first Three Ages of Christianity concerning the Trinity in opposition to Sabellianism and Tritheism," and "A Vindication of the Church of England."   [u] Nelson's Life of Bull, p. 47.

His chief opponents in his parishes seem to have been Quakers. On one occasion, when Bull was preaching, a Quaker cried out to him, "George, come down, thou art a false Prophet and a hireling." On another occasion, a Quaker preacher, who was a violent opponent of Bull, tried to convict him of not preaching the Gospel. "George," he said, "as for human learning, I set no value upon it; but if thou wilt talk Scripture, have at thee." "Come on then, friend," said Bull, and opened the Bible at the Book of Proverbs. "Seest thou, friend," Bull said, "Solomon saith in one place, 'Answer a fool according to his folly;' and in another place, 'Answer *not* a fool according to his folly;' how dost thou reconcile these two texts of Scripture?" "Why," said the Quaker, "Solomon don't say so." "Aye, but he doth," said Bull, and showed him the passages. "Why, then, Solomon's a fool," said the Quaker. And so the controversy ended[1].

Dr. Bull was presented to a Bishopric too late in life to render, as a Bishop, much service to the Church. He most reluctantly, and only under strong pressure from the Bishops, accepted a See; he was in his 71st year, and after his appointment he was too weak to make his triennial visitation, and was obliged to appoint a Commission to visit in his place and to read the Charge written by him.

---

[1] Nelson's Life of Bull, p. 68.

In the same year that Dr. Bull was appointed to St. David's, Wake became Bishop of Lincoln[y]. These and other episcopal appointments made by Queen Anne were excellent, but the number of Bishops appointed by her in the first three years of her reign was small in comparison to the fifteen Bishops whom William appointed in two years: whilst in the whole twelve years of her reign she only appointed seventeen Bishops.

In 1707 Sir Jonathan Trelawney was translated, through the interest of the Lord Treasurer, from Exeter to Winchester. This appointment, says Burnet[z], "gave great disgust to many, he being considerable for nothing but his birth and his interest in Cornwall." The Queen, therefore, determined thenceforward to take the appointment of the Bishops into her own hands. So, notwithstanding that the Whigs were in power, she in 1708 appointed Offspring Blackall, who was a strong advocate for the Divine right of kings, and who had at one time joined the ranks of the Nonjurors, to succeed Trelawney at Exeter. Blackall had done good service as an active parish priest, and had been Boyle Lecturer in 1700. Sir William Dawes, Archbishop of York, declared of him that "in his whole conversation he never met with a more perfect pattern of

---

[y] For Wake, Archbishop of Canterbury, 1716, see Part II. chapter ii.

[z] O. T., iv. 208.

a true Christian life than in him." As to his preaching he says that "he universally acquired the reputation of being one of the best preachers of his time."

In the same year the Queen appointed Sir William Dawes, a Tory and a High Churchman, who had the reputation of being the best scholar of the day, to the See of Chester. William Dawes (1671—1724) was in 1687 elected a Scholar, and subsequently became Fellow, of St. John's College, Oxford; but soon afterwards, having succeeded to his father's title, he left Oxford and entered himself at St. Catharine's Hall, Cambridge, of which he became, in 1696, Master. The Queen wished to appoint Dawes to the See of Lincoln in 1705, but some passages in a sermon which he preached before the Queen were thought objectionable by certain members of the government, who persuaded her to appoint Wake instead. Of these two Bishops, Blackall and Dawes, Burnet says: "They were in themselves men of value and worth, but their notions were all on the other side; they had submitted to the government, but they, at least Blackall, seemed to condemn the Revolution and all that had been pursuant of it."

The appointment of such Tory and High Church Bishops was anything but acceptable to the government, and Godolphin and Marlborough thought it necessary to remonstrate with the Queen for appointing Bishops on her sole authority. The Queen defended herself: "I feel myself obliged to fill the Bishops' Bench with those who will be a credit to the Church, and not always take the recommendation of the 29" (the Whig Junto). Still she was, in order to appease the government, obliged to make certain concessions; so on the death of Patrick, Bishop of Ely, in 1707, she appointed to the See Dr. More, who had been intruded into the See of Norwich on the deprivation of the Nonjuror, Dr. Lloyd; and Dr. Trimnell, a Whig, who had formerly been Tutor to Lord Sunderland, Marlborough's son-in-law, was appointed to the See of Norwich.

Through the influence of the Duke of Marlborough, Dr. Potter was appointed to succeed Dr. Jane as Canon of Christ Church, and Regius Professor of Divinity. Potter, although a Whig, was a High Churchman, a combination at that time unusual, and which the Queen did not at first understand. She therefore advocated the appointment of Dr. Smalridge in preference to Potter[a]; the Duke of Marlborough, however, persisted and gained his point: "The consequence is," he wrote, "that if Dr. Potter has not the Professor's place, I will never more meddle with anything that may concern Oxford[b]."

---

[a] Smalridge afterwards became a Canon of Christ Church, and succeeded Atterbury both in the Deanery of Carlisle and that of Christ Church, and was in 1714 appointed by Anne to the See of Carlisle.   [b] Stanhope's Queen Anne, ii. 32.

In 1713 Compton, Bishop of London, died, after having held the See of London, to which he was translated from Oxford, for thirty-eight years, and under four monarchs. It is a difficult matter to form a just estimate of Compton's character. Henry Compton (1632—1713), the youngest son of the Earl of Northampton, entered, in 1649, as a nobleman at Queen's College, Oxford. At the Restoration he became a Cornet in the Horse Guards, but soon quitting the military life he went to Cambridge, and when he was about thirty years of age took Holy Orders. In 1667 he became Master of St. Cross, near Winchester; in 1669 a Canon of Christ Church; in 1674 he was appointed to the See of Oxford; in the following year to that of London; and to him Charles II. entrusted the religious education of the two Princesses, Mary and Anne, afterwards Queens of England.

Of all the Bishops Compton was the first to resist the illegal proceedings of James. He voted for the Exclusion Bill, and was in consequence deprived of the office of Dean of the Chapel, and his name was erased from the list of Privy Councillors. He withstood James's Ecclesiastical Commission, and refused to suspend Sharp[c], and was suspended from his Episcopal Functions. He alone of the Bishops signed the letter inviting William to come over to

---

[c] See Introductory Chapter.

England. On the entry of William into London, Compton, at the head of the London Clergy, and followed by a hundred Nonconformist Ministers, went to meet and welcome him. He, in the absence of Sancroft, was *virtually* Archbishop, and crowned the new King and Queen. He supported William's Comprehension Scheme. He had been the Preceptor to the Queen. He certainly had strong claims to the Primacy, and yet in William's reign the Primacy was twice vacant, and he was twice passed over; on one occasion the Dean of his own Cathedral being promoted over his head. It certainly seemed hard upon him, and Compton was bitterly disappointed; yet it spoke much in his favour that he never bore an unforgiving spirit, but kept up a friendly intercourse with Lambeth [d].

Compton showed no signs of great learning or great piety, and Evelyn speaks of him as not being a great Preacher; but he also says, "the Bishop had been a soldier, and had also travelled in Italy, and became a most sober, grave, and excellent Prelate[e]."

From his firm resistance to Romanism in James's reign he gained much popularity with the laity, but his Ultra-Protestantism (although in his later years he sided with the more orthodox party in Convocation against the Latitudinarian Bishops) made him unpopular amongst the Clergy. He seems to have

---

[d] Birch's Life of Tillotson, p. 267.   [e] Memoirs, vol. ii.

been a man in whose character there was a strong admixture of good and evil, but in which the good predominated. Sancroft, however, had no high opinion of him. Compton wrote him a letter whilst the Toleration and Comprehension Bills were pending, in which he says that "*though we are under a conquest,* God has given us favour in the eyes of our Rulers." Sancroft returned him a stinging reply, and spoke of his "unworthy compliance under all sorts of governments for these forty years;" "I pray God make you thoroughly and truly sensible of your horrid prevarications, and of the many and great mischiefs you have done the Church of England, and give you grace to make some satisfaction to her for them before you die [f]."

Compton was succeeded in the See of London by Dr. John Robinson, translated from Bristol. What fitness Robinson had for such an important post does not appear. He was a diplomatist rather than a Divine; and in his person there was a return to the old practice of rewarding services to the State by high ecclesiastical preferment. He had held a Canonry, a Deanery, and, since 1710, the See of Bristol; and his sole claim to preferment seems to have rested on the service he had done the State, first as Ambassador at Warsaw, and still more as Plenipotentiary at the Treaty of Utrecht [g].

---

[f] Tanner MSS.
[g] Milman's Annals of St. Paul's, 456.

In the same year in which Compton died Atterbury was appointed to the Bishopric of Rochester, holding with it, as was usual, the Deanery of Westminster.

To the personal character of the Queen and to the Bishops whom she appointed must be attributed the great influence of the Church in her reign. During that period the Church reached the highest point of influence to which it had attained at any time since the Reformation. Of the year 1709 we read[h]: "It is a great ease and comfort to good Christians within these cities of London and Westminster and the suburbs of them that in most churches there be constant prayers morning and evening. These are supported by particular benefactions or by voluntary contributions[i]." In 1714 sixty-five churches could be specified in which there were daily prayers, whilst in most others there were at least prayers on Wednesdays and Fridays. Besides the daily prayers there was frequently weekly Communion[k]. In country parishes prayers were generally said on Wednesdays and Fridays; in London there were services at five and six o'clock in the morning, at which as many

---

[h] Defence of the Church and Clergy of England, p. 40.

[i] Chamberlayne mentions that in King William's time at St. Martin's-in-the-Fields and St. Paul's, Covent Garden, there were Services at 6 a.m., 10 a.m., 3 p.m., and 8 p.m., all of which were well frequented; and there were prayers in the King's Chapel thrice every day.—*Angliæ Notitia*. We may suppose that these were not lessened under Queen Anne.

[k] Pietas Londinensis.

as five hundred people sometimes attended[1]. In all cathedrals there was a weekly celebration of the Holy Communion; in towns where there was not a weekly there was at least a monthly celebration [m].

Nor was there any lack of ceremonial observances. "Whenever he officiated at the Altar," says Robert Nelson [n], Dr. Bull, "agreeably to the directions of the Rubric .... always placed the elements of Bread and Wine upon the Altar himself, after he had received them either from the churchwarden or clerk, or had taken them from some convenient place, where they were laid for that purpose [o]." The people carried their observances to such a height as would astonish people in the present day. "Some would not go to their seats in church till they had kneeled and prayed at the rails of the Communion Table; they would not be content to receive the Sacrament there kneeling, but with prostration, and striking the breast, and kissing of the ground, as if there were an Host to be adored. They began to think the Common Prayer without a sermon (at least after noon) to be the best way of serving God, and churches

---

[1] Quarterly Review, No. 313, p. 16.
[m] Defence of the Church, &c., 45.
[n] Life of Bull, p. 53.
[o] Dr. Bull was charged with being a Romanist; good Churchmen before and since have been; but, says his biographer, " in the day of trial the men of this character will be found the best defenders of the Church of England, and the boldest champions against the corruptions of Rome."

without organs had thinner 'congregations..... Even pictures upon the Altar began to be the books of the vulgar. The meeting-houses of Protestant Dissenters were thought to be more defiled places than Popish Chapels." Whether we approve of such practices or not, it is certain that the people, high and low, loved their Church, and it was the fashion no longer to ridicule it, but to praise and extol it, and to consider dissent from it to be a sin [p].

But if we would fully appreciate the high position which the Church held at this period we must pass from England to Prussia, where a most interesting movement was taking place with a view to the introduction of our Apostolical Orders and Liturgy into that country. At the commencement of the century Frederick the First, King of Prussia, conceived a design for a union between the two different communions in his country, that of the Lutherans and that of the Calvinists, who termed themselves the *Reformed*, in one public form of worship, and his Chaplain, Dr. Jablouski, who, after having made two visits to England, and having spent some time in Oxford, had become a great admirer of our Church,

---

[p] The Freeholder, shortly after Queen Anne's death (March 5, 1717), represents the Landlord of an Inn who never went to church himself but would help a mob in pulling down a meeting-house, and who " swelled his body to a prodigious size and worked up his complexion to a standing crimson by his zeal for the prosperity of the Church."

suggested to him that Anglican Orders and Liturgy might form a proper medium of union. The King accordingly ordered that the English Liturgy should be translated into German by the University of Frankfort-on-Oder, and one copy should be sent to Queen Anne and another to the Archbishop of Canterbury; and a scheme was set on foot, if the King's wishes met with encouragement in England, to introduce the Liturgy into the King's Chapel, the Cathedral, and perhaps other Churches on Advent Sunday, 1706.

There was at that time living in England a Prussian named Johann Ernst Grabe (1666—1711), whose interest and connection with the Church is particularly interesting. Grabe's course of reading led him to the study of the early Fathers, from which he became convinced of the necessity for the celebration of the Sacraments of the Apostolical Succession, which he felt did not exist in the Lutheran Church of his country. He thought of joining the Church of Rome, but first sought an interview with Spener, a Lutheran Divine, who having failed to remove his scruples about Lutheranism recommended him to go to England, where, he said, the Succession was equally preserved as in the Church of Rome. To England accordingly he came, and received Orders in 1700; William III. conferred upon him, and Anne continued, a pension of £100 a year, and in 1706 he received a D.D. Degree from the University of Oxford.

Grabe was a strong advocate for the introduction of Episcopal Orders and the English Liturgy into Prussia. Daniel Ernst Jablouski (1660—1742) Chaplain to the Court at Berlin, warmly promoted the scheme; and M. Bouet, the Prussian Minister in London, wrote to the King of Prussia in 1711, that conformity between the two Churches would be welcomed in England, but that the English Clergy insisted upon Episcopacy, which they regarded as an Apostolical institution, and to have "continued in an uninterrupted succession from the Apostles to the present time," as the basis of any agreement. The plan, however, was defeated by the supineness of Tenison, and the opposition of the Whigs and Nonconformists; the attention of diplomatists was drawn off to other matters, so the attempt to unite the Protestant Communion of Germany in the faith of the Church of England fell to the ground, although Archbishop Sharp did not cease to advocate it, and to correspond with his friends in Prussia till the day of his death [q].

The end of Queen Anne's reign was unfortunately marked by one of those unjustifiable measures against Dissenters which are so injurious to the Church, and which it might have been hoped the Act of Toleration had stopped for ever. On May 12, 1714, Sir William Wyndham brought forward a motion in the House

---

[q] Appendix to Sharp's Life, by his Son.

of Commons for leave to bring in a Bill to suppress the growth of schism, and for the further security of the Established Church. The Bill proposed that "no person in Great Britain should keep a public or private school, or act as Tutor, that has not first subscribed the declaration to conform to the Church of England and obtained a licence from the Diocesan; and that upon failure of doing so the party may be committed to prison without trial; and that no such licence shall be granted before the party produces a certificate of his having received the Sacrament according to the Communion of the Church of England within the last year, and also subscribed the oaths of allegiance and supremacy." The design of the Bill was to prevent Dissenters from teaching in schools or academies. It was opposed in both Houses as a persecuting measure, yet it passed the House of Commons by 237 to 126 votes, and, with certain amendments, the House of Lords also; on June 25 it received the Royal Assent, and was to come into operation on August 1. On that day the Queen died.

The First of August fell on a Sunday. On the preceding day, when it was announced that the Queen was dead, the Funds immediately rose three or four per cent., and when in the afternoon it was ascertained that she was still alive, they went down again. But when the Sunday dawned the Queen was lying between life and death. The story goes that Burnet, Bishop of Sarum, whilst driving in his coach to Court, was much concerned to see the Dissenting minister Bradbury cast down and sorrowful, and asked him why he was so troubled? Burnet learnt the cause, and comforted him with the assurance that the Queen might die at any moment; and as Bradbury was on his way to preach at Fetter Lane Chapel, he promised that as soon as she was dead a messenger should announce the fact by dropping a handkerchief from the gallery of the chapel [r]. On receiving the sign, Bradbury is reported to have offered public thanks to God for the delivery of the nation, and to have invoked a blessing on King George I. and the House of Hanover [s].

The Dissenters made no secret of their joy. Dr. Calamy writes [t]: "God once more appeared for us in the most remarkable and distinguished manner; took away the life of that Princess who had so far been seduced as carelessly to seek our destruction, and introduced King William's legacy, the amiable and illustrious House of Hanover [u]."

---

[r] This meeting, however, must have been very early, for Anne is said to have died at 7 o'clock in the morning.—Knight's England, vi. 1.

[s] It is said that Bradbury took for his text the words, "Go see now this cursed woman, and bury her, for she is a king's daughter." [t] Own Life, ii. 293.

[u] In like manner wrote Dr. Watts :—

"George is his name, that glorious star,
  Ye saw his splendour gleaming far;

The Queen not unnaturally wished her brother to succeed her: there is no doubt that the Tories, even the more moderate of the party, were averse to the Hanoverian succession, and were secretly the friends of the exiled family, whilst the Jacobites and Nonjurors were so favourable to them as scarcely to be free from high-treason. The Pretender, had he been willing to renounce his Faith, would probably have succeeded, but to his lasting honour he refused to change his religion for a throne. But the Whigs were prepared, and the Tories were not, and all danger from the Jacobites was averted by the energy of the Whig nobles; it is indeed related that Atterbury immediately on the death of Anne proposed to proclaim the Pretender at Charing Cross, and to head the procession in his lawn sleeves [x]. Bolingbroke, to whom the proposal is said to have been made, shrunk from so desperate a plan, whereupon the Bishop is reported to have said, "Then is the best cause in Europe lost for want of spirit [y]."

The Electress Sophia, the "unbaptized Lutheran,"

Saw in the East your joy arise,
When Anna sunk in Western skies."

[x] The authority for this rumour was Dr. Lockier, Dean of Peterborough, the personal friend of George I.

[y] The French Agent wrote to Louis XIV. that Bolingbroke said that if the Queen's death had occurred six weeks later, matters would have been in such a state that there would have been no cause of fear for the future. "What a world is this, and how does fortune banter us!" wrote Bolingbroke to Swift.

as people called her, died suddenly only a few weeks before the Queen. Probably had she lived she would not have proved so acceptable to the Nation as the English expected. Before the Act of Settlement was passed she had been a Jacobite, and spoke complacently of the restoration of the Prince of Wales [z]. She was certainly a Protestant, but was very lukewarm in her religion [a]. She, however, died at the age of 84, before the Queen, and so her son, under the title of George I., succeeded to the throne.

---

[z] She wrote what Lord Hardwicke called a "Jacobite Letter," bewailing the hard fate of the poor Prince of Wales, and speaking of his restoration. See Stanhope's Queen Anne, i. 22.

[a] M. de Gourville once asked her of what religion her daughter, at that time seventeen years of age, was. The answer was "She has none at present. We are waiting to know what Prince she is to marry, and whenever that point is determined, she will be duly instructed in the religion of her future husband, whether Protestant or Catholic."—Ibid.

PART II.

*THE CHURCH AT ITS LOWEST POINT
OF INFLUENCE.*

CHAPTER I.

THE DECLINE OF THE CHURCH.

THE thirty years which succeeded the peace of Utrecht (1714) were, says Mr. Hallam [a], "the most prosperous season that England had ever experienced." Far different, however, is the aspect which is presented to the historian of moral and religious progress; he is under the necessity of depicting the same period as one of decay of religion, licentiousness of morals, public corruption, profaneness of language; a day of rebuke and blasphemy [b].

At the end of Queen Anne's reign a period of peace and prosperity to the Church no less than to the State seemed to have set in. In Parliament, the Tories, that is to say the professed friends of the Church, had a large preponderance; both parties, Whigs as well as Tories, recognised the Church's power and vied for her support: each denounced the other as her enemies, the Tories charging the Whigs with Puritanism, the Whigs retaliating with charges of favouring Rome and the Pretender; Romanist

---

[a] Const. Hist., ii. 464.
[b] Mr. Mark Pattison, Essays and Reviews, 254.

and Protestant Dissenters alike had tried their strength against the Church and failed; and the National Church was willingly embraced by all members of the Community [c]. Never was the appearance of hope greater than at the commencement of the eighteenth century, never was the frustration of hope more melancholy as the century advanced; in a few years the great influence of the Church entirely disappeared; its doctrines, and ritual, and discipline, became lowered and neglected; as a natural result arose that decay of religion, the coarseness of manners, the moral degradation and the general ignorance which have rendered the eighteenth century a byeword not only in the history of the Church, but also in that of the Protestant and Romanist Dissenters [d].

The Church is blamed for the low state to which it fell in the eighteenth century; but the truth is the State so paralysed its action as to render the Church powerless. It swamped the Church, sometimes with

---

[c] See Abbey and Overton's English Church.

[d] It is right to observe that the same apathy and abuses which enfeebled the English Church in the eighteenth century prevailed all over Western Europe. Churches, like individuals, have their periods of exhaustion after effort, and the dull unspirituality of the eighteenth century was the inevitable reaction after the volcanic controversies of the sixteenth and seventeenth centuries. The lava was cooling in its course, till the French Revolution at the end of the eighteenth century set up a new action.

The Decline of the Church. 271

Latitudinarian Bishops, nearly always with Bishops chosen on political rather than religious grounds; and it deprived it of its Synodal rights so that it could not defend or improve itself. Gradually the Church succumbed and became listless and indifferent. Bishops resided away from their Dioceses (one Bishop held a See for six years without once entering on it); when Bishops failed in their duties, then the Clergy in time followed their example; Pluralities and consequently non-residence became the rule rather than the exception; Curates took the place of the Rectors and Vicars, receiving for their services a miserable stipend, and often obliged to support their families with the labour of their hands and the sweat of their brow. Churches were kept locked from one end of the week to the other; the daily Service was abandoned; two, or perhaps one Service on Sunday became the rule; Holy Communion was celebrated at most once a month, perhaps four or even three times in the year; Baptisms were often performed in private houses; ritual was lowered, or we might say almost abandoned; and whilst the Church was asleep, Dissent, which, unlike the Church, was left unhampered by the State, assumed vitality; by reason of the rapid growth of our manufacturing population, when there were no churches built for them, and no Clergy to look after them, Dissenters grew rapidly in numbers; so that by the beginning of the nineteenth century they had grown from one twenty-fifth to one fourth of the population; when George IV. became King, Dissent and not the Church was in possession of our large towns; by the time that William IV. succeeded to the throne Dissent had become a power in the State.

An acquaintance with the civil history of the times is necessary in order to enable us to understand how this state of things, unfortunate to Church and State alike, was brought about.

George I. was proclaimed King of England as quietly as if he had been the rightful heir of a long line of ancestors. His accession, as we saw at the end of the last chapter, was hailed with joy by the Dissenters; it was equally acceptable to the Latitudinarians[e]; but by the friends of the Church the accession to the throne of a German who, as far as he was of any religion at all, was a Lutheran, but who for the sake of a throne had changed his religion, was regarded with dismay.

George I. had not one single quality which fitted him to be King of England, scarcely one which marked him out as a gentleman. Nature meant him to be a Nobody; good fortune and Protestantism made him a King. All his surroundings were against him. Short in stature; slovenly in person; un-

---

[e] Thus White Kennet (appointed Bishop of Peterborough in 1718) writes, "I am fixed in the opinion that King George is one of the honestest men, and one of the wisest Princes in the world."—Ellis' Original Letters.

graceful in manners; thoroughly ignorant and illiterate; unable to speak a word of English[f]; he was ill-fitted to enlist the respect of the English people.

There was no single station of life, if we except that of a soldier, in which he did not hold a bad pre-eminence. In 1682 he married, much against her will, and when she was only sixteen years of age, his cousin, Sophia Dorothea, daughter of the Duke of Zell, who was at that time of her life distinguished not only for her beauty but for the qualities of her mind. Shortly after the marriage he began to treat her with much cruelty, and to insult her by introducing his mistresses into her presence; and yet, unfaithful as he was himself, on a vague and unproved suspicion, he caused her to be sent a prisoner to the Castle of Ahlden, where, deprived of the society of her children, and never ceasing to proclaim her innocence, she was left to pine away her wretched life for thirty-two years.

But even then, however light were the suspicions against his wife, some charitable construction might perhaps be put upon his conduct, had he changed his character as he advanced to mature years. But even in his fifty-fifth year, when he came to England, he

---

[f] As Walpole could not speak French, and the King could not speak English, Walpole used to say that the kingdom was governed by bad Latin, which he himself certainly exemplified when he was forced to say to one of the German Courtiers, "Mentiris impudentissime."

T

was grossly immoral and debauched, and the seraglio of ugly German women who accompanied him to feed on the fat of the land, and to enrich themselves as speedily as possible, made him from his first arrival an object of ridicule and contempt[g].

The person whom, next in the world to his wife, he detested most was his son, afterwards George II. For many years he never spoke to him, but transacted business through his son's wife, "cette Diablesse, Madame la Princesse," as he not very politely called her.

It must be allowed that it was hard upon George I. to be called forth from his peaceful principality to govern the unruly kingdom of England, with its endless feuds between Whigs and Tories, and between High Church and Low Church. He was quite satisfied with the quiet life he was leading in his own country, where, to do him justice, he was much beloved by his subjects; and truth compels the unflattering confession that he was in so little hurry to leave his country and to come to England, that though Anne died on August 1 it was not till September 18 that he landed at Greenwich.

But such as he was, the Church of England was obliged to accept him. It did not matter that he

---

[g] The mere mention of two of them, one afterwards created Duchess of Kendal, the other Countess of Darlington, commonly known as the "Maypole" and the "Elephant and Castle," is sufficient.

The Decline of the Church. 275

was an alien by birth, by feeling, by faith, the law of England made him Supreme Ruler on Earth of the Church, Defender of the Faith; to be prayed for in its Churches as "our most religious and gracious king," to appoint its Bishops, to silence its voice, so that no other will but his and the party whom he chose to honour should regulate the affairs of the Church.

It may be as well, whilst we are on the subject of the succession of the House of Hanover, to give an account of some of the principal members of the family, in order that we may understand the position in which the Church was placed, and the natural results which, as effect from cause, followed from it.

Equally undistinguished as his father, both in body and mind, was his son and successor, George II.; scarcely more conspicuous for good qualities, and not less addicted to vice; equally with his father a stranger to this country in feelings and taste, speaking its language only a little better, having no quality except that of bravery (which seems to have been hereditary in the family) to recommend him to the English nation, and caring only for his money and for Hanover.

Of the land of his adoption the second George was wont to speak in language far from complimentary: "I wish with all my heart," he said to his wife[h], "that the Devil may take your Bishops, and

---

[h] Hervey's Memoirs, ii. 100.

the Devil may take your Ministers, and the Devil take the Parliament, and the Devil take the whole Island, provided I can get out of it and go to Hanover [i]." No wonder the feeling was reciprocated in England. "If," said Lord Chesterfield in the House of Lords, "we have a mind effectually to prevent the Pretender from ever obtaining the Crown, we should make him Elector of Hanover, for the people of England will never fetch another king from thence [k]."

That Queen Caroline, the wife of George II., was a wonderful woman, although perhaps not quite so clever as she herself imagined, all will readily allow. Though frequently placed in the humbling position of being obliged to admit her husband's female favourites to her Drawing-rooms, she was still able, by the propriety of her own conduct and by surrounding herself with Divines and men of learning, to throw, to a certain extent, an air of decency and decorum over the Court. But how any pure-minded woman could have lived for thirty years with such a

---

[i] To "go to Hanover" became a favourite expression under the Georges. Even George III. threatened to "go to Hanover" rather than give up the one idea he had in his head, of personal government; and George IV. told the Duke of Wellington that, if the Roman Catholics were emancipated, he would himself "go to Hanover," whilst the Duke might go to another place, which we will not mention, but which had the same initial letter.

[k] Jesse's Court of England, iii. 39.

The Decline of the Church. 277

husband, tolerating and even conniving at his conduct [l], is quite inexplicable; it can only be attributed to the coarseness of the times, and to the fact that she was a woman of the eighteenth century [m]. During his numerous absences from England George II. would write her, as Lord Hervey says, letters of forty or fifty pages detailing his love affairs, which were utterly unfit for a woman's ear; he even told her to consult the Prime Minister, Sir Robert Walpole, on these subjects; and if we may believe Horace Walpole, who, however, is never a safe guide where the Clergy are concerned, Archbishop Blackburne praised her [n] for following the bad advice which Walpole gave [o].

The King admired the talents of his wife, and could do nothing without her, and yet, with his little mind, he was jealous of her, and flattered himself, and tried to make others believe, that "the

---

[l] "She countenanced him on the ground that she was old and he might well love a younger woman."—Herv. Mem.

[m] She even sympathized with the "good Howard," when the latter lost the King's favour, on the ground that she must learn philosophy, for, like herself, she was no longer young.

[n] "Madam," he said, "I have been with your Minister Walpole, and he tells me that you are a wise woman, and do not mind your husband having a mistress."—Walpole's Letters, vi 102.

[o] George II. advised her "Consulter ce grand homme (Walpole) qui a plus d'expérience que vous, ma chére Caroline, dans ces affaires."—Herv. Mem., ii. 128.

Queen never meddled in his business [p]." And here was the great difficulty in the life of this remarkable woman. "The Queen," writes Lord Hervey, "by long studying and long experience of his temper, knew how to instil her own sentiments, whilst she affected to receive his Majesty's." It was bad enough for a clever woman such as she was to be obliged to endure the company of such a man for seven or eight hours every day [q], but to be forced to assume the servile obsequiousness that was necessary, and which was the only way of getting into his narrow intelligence the highest designs of state which she and Walpole devised between them, it was this that showed the tact and cleverness of the woman.

But if there was much to find fault with in the Queen's character, there was at least one noble trait which must not be forgotten. She was a woman of unbounded beneficence; her charities are said to have amounted to nearly one fifth of her income, and after her death the King, to his credit, ordered

---

[p] The country, however, knew better, as the following squib shows :—

"You may strut, dapper George, but 'twill all be in vain,
We know 'tis Queen Caroline, not you, who reign."

[q] So his family thought; when the "good Howard" was leaving him, the Princess Royal, with the delicacy peculiar to the period, said, "I wish with all my heart that he would take somebody else, that Mamma might be relieved from the *ennui* of seeing him always in her room."—Oliphant's George I., p. 140.

her pensions, which amounted to £13,000 a year, to be continued. There was another trait in her favour which deserves to be recorded, and that is, she did not object to be told by the Church her faults when she was wrong. The King when in church and not sleeping (as was often the case), and sometimes snoring, used to occupy himself in talking to the Queen, a habit in which she was at one time only too ready to join him. Whiston had the courage to tell her of this fault. She excused herself on the ground that "the King *would* talk to her." Whiston replied that "a greater King was there to be regarded." Instead of being angry, she said to him, "Pray, Mr. Whiston, tell me another fault." "No, Madam," he replied, "let me see you mend this one before I tell you of another." And she promised amendment [r].

A more miserable family than that of the second George it is almost impossible to imagine. At the head of the family was a father whose notorious vices we have by no means exaggerated. The life of Frederick, Prince of Wales, if it had some redeeming qualities (and they were but few), presents a sad catalogue of vices. Even as a boy he indulged in drinking and gambling [s], and in an utter contempt of truth; and when he grew to manhood, England

---

[r] Bishop Newton's Life, i. 109.
[s] Horace Walpole says he not only gambled but he cheated in gambling.

was startled by the humiliating spectacle of three generations of the Royal Family, grandfather, father, and son, living in sin with their mistresses at one and the same time [t]. Even after his marriage he followed the example set him by his father and grandfather, whilst his wife, following the example of her mother-in-law, found it advisable in the interest of peace, to tolerate his behaviour. One thing must, however, be mentioned in his favour, viz. that he cultivated the society of men of letters, and that though a faithless, he was, in other respects, a kind husband, and, unlike his own father and grandfather, an affectionate father [u].

Such an unloving and unloveable family can scarcely be imagined. An unfaithful husband at the head; the parents deceiving each other and deceiving the son; the son hating the father; the children hating each other; whilst truth was a stranger to them all. The Queen made no secret of her feelings towards the Prince of Wales, and openly cursed the day he was born. "My dear Lord," she said to Lord Hervey [x], "I will give it you under my hand, if you are in any fear of my relapsing, that my dear firstborn is the greatest ass, and the greatest liar, and

---

[t] Jesse's Memoirs of George III., 121.

[u] Horace Walpole tells us that he took the Black Prince for his model, "whom, however, he resembled only in one respect, that of dying before his father."—Memoirs of George III.

[x] Hervey's Memoirs.

the greatest *canaille*, and the greatest beast in the whole world, and I heartily wish he were out of it." And the Princess Caroline, the gentlest of all the family, spoke of him as "that nauseous beast," and "declared that she grudged every hour that he continued to breathe ʸ."

When on September 18, 1714, George I. landed in England, he found the government, as Queen Anne had left it, in the hands of the Tories. It must be mentioned that, at the accession of the House of Hanover, there were three political parties in the State : the Jacobites, or ultra-Tories, who were thoroughly opposed to the House of Hanover, and would favour the return of the Stuarts under any terms ; the Tories, who were also opposed to the Hanoverian family, and inclined to favour the Pretender, but whose first care was loyalty to the Church of England ; and the Whigs, who (whether they themselves were Churchmen or not) were united with the Dissenters, and considered the return of the Stuarts would be dangerous, not only to their liberty but to the Church, which all parties were desirous of upholding.

The Hanoverian family never thought they would long continue to be the rulers of the country[z]; they knew that the Pretender had, on all Tory and Monarchical principles, a legal title to the throne ; the

---

[y] Hervey's Memoirs, ii. 255.   [z] Life of Lord Shelburne.

Jacobites, therefore, were naturally King George's enemies. But in the same class with the Jacobites George I. classed the Tories, and in the same class with the Tories he placed High Churchmen. The Tory party, therefore, which was the party friendly to the Church, were at once excluded from the Royal favour; the King dismissed the Tory government, and threw himself completely into the hands of the Whigs, or the Anti-Church party, to whom he was indebted for the quiet occupation of the throne, and who he believed would be more faithful to him than the Tories.

A more unscrupulous minister than Sir Robert Walpole never presided over a great nation. In 1712 he was expelled from the House of Commons and sent to the Tower for a "high breach of trust and notorious corruption [a]." On the accession of George I. he was restored to favour, and for a quarter of a century, with a break of only four years, he bore almost autocratic sway in England; a jest which was circulated during his premiership, that a Bill was to be introduced into Parliament for expunging the word " not " in the Commandments and transferring it to the Creeds, describes only too faithfully what people thought of the administration of the keeper of the King's conscience [b].

---

[a] This was clearly the result of party animosity, too common in those days.

[b] Lady M. W. Montague.

The Decline of the Church. 283

Robert Walpole (1676—1745) received his education at Eton and King's College, Cambridge; he was at first intended for Holy Orders, and used to say that, if this had been his career, he would have been Archbishop of Canterbury; fortunately for the Church this plan was altered, and in 1701 he entered Parliament. In 1708 he became Secretary at War, and in 1710 Treasurer of the Navy: on the accession of George I. he was made a Privy Councillor; in 1715 he became Chancellor of the Exchequer and First Lord of the Treasury. In 1717 a split took place in the Whig party, and he resigned office; in 1720 the Whigs again became a united party, and Walpole returned to power; when the "South Sea Bubble" burst, and a cry of distress was heard from one end of England to the other, it was felt that Walpole was the only person who could help the people in this national calamity, and he again became Chancellor of the Exchequer, and in 1722 Prime Minister; from that time he ruled the destinies of England till 1742, when he was compelled to resign his office, and was created Earl of Orford.

His father, who was a Norfolk Squire of good family, was noted for his hospitality, which, however, does not appear to have been marked with sobriety; and he took the surest means to instil his own principles into his son. "Come, Robert," he would say to him, "you must drink twice to my once; I cannot admit the son in his sober senses to be witness of the intoxication of his father." The child was father to the man; and in after years the Bacchanalian orgies at Sir Robert Walpole's country seat at Houghton showed how the son had profited from the example of his father; the revels that took place there created such scandal in the neighbourhood that respectable people held aloof from his society, and his kinsman and colleague, Lord Townshend, was obliged, during their continuance, to leave his neighbouring mansion at Rainham. These meetings at Houghton were held twice in every year, one in the spring and the other in the autumn [c], and were attended by a very mixed number of guests. The festivities suited Walpole's tastes only too well [d]. His conversation, we are told, was of the most indelicate nature. Savage, the Poet, who was in the habit of meeting him at his patron's (Lord Tyrconnel), says that the whole range of his mind veered from obscenity to politics, and from politics to obscenity [e].

Walpole thoroughly understood the times in which he lived and the power of money, and he was unscrupulous enough to turn the degeneracy of the times to his own account. Impervious to corruption himself, as was admitted, that he practised corruption on a large scale in order to get members of Parliament to vote on his side is indisputable; doubtless

---

[c] The expense of these meetings was reckoned to be £3,000.
[d] Coxe's Walpole, i. 785.
[e] Jesse's Memoirs, iii. 386.

he was not the first to adopt this plan, but he reduced it to a system, and used it more than any minister had ever done before. "Walpole governed by corruption," says Lord Macaulay [f], "because in his time it was impossible to govern otherwise." The fault, he says, was in the constitution of the legislature, but it is a sad reflexion on the times if it was true, as Lord Macaulay adds, that "he managed the legislature in the only way in which it could be managed."

George I. did not believe in honesty; "all *those* men have their price," Walpole also exclaimed, referring to a special group of politicians mouthing patriotism[g]; the King and minister seemed to understand each other, and when on one occasion Walpole remonstrated with the King on the rapacity of his German followers, the King remarked to him, "I suppose you also are paid for your remonstrances."

It is almost impossible to imagine anything lower or more disgraceful than for a minister to use the Church appointments in his gift as portions for his illegitimate daughters: and yet this is what his own son tells us Walpole did. On December 11, 1752, Horace Walpole writes to Sir Horace Mann: "My father gave him (Keene, afterwards Bishop of Chester) a Living of £700 a year to marry one of his natural daughters," and he adds that Keene "took the Living, and my father dying soon after he dispensed himself from

---

[f] Essay on Horace Walpole's Letters to Sir Horace Mann.
[g] Coxe's Mem. of Walpole, iv 369.

taking the wife." We may accept as true the story about his father on the testimony of the son, but with regard to the Clergy the authority of Horace Walpole cannot be accepted as of any weight at all.

In the reign of George II. Queen Caroline was during her lifetime the chief, and as Walpole always acted on her advice, practically the sole, dispenser of the Patronage of the Crown. So that it is necessary to understand what kind of religion the Queen's was, and on what grounds she appointed the rulers of the Church. Lord Stanhope speaks of her discerning and praiseworthy selection of Bishops; but she would naturally be inclined to those who favoured her own views. It is easy to describe the Queen by negatives. It is easier to say what her religion was not, rather than what it was; it certainly was not Catholic, it was not even approximately orthodox. Caroline[h] was eminently Protestant and Latitudinarian, and she bestowed her favours on philosophical

---

[h] Daughter of the Margraf of Anspach. She was born at a time when Lutheranism, never a lofty and spiritual form of opinion, was at its religious nadir, broken up by the shock of the Thirty Years' war, and spending all its energies on polemical Theology of an abstract kind; dry, marrowless, and unspiritual to the last degree. The chances were enormously against any prince or noble getting any religion at all from the Lutheran pastors of that era. The reaction of Pietism under Spener did not begin till about 1691, and then was regarded by the higher classes in Germany just as Methodism was in England a generation later.

rather than on theological grounds. She might, had she been so disposed, have married the Emperor of Austria, but only on condition of her renouncing her Protestantism; but Burnet tells us "she could not be prevailed upon to purchase a crown at so dear a rate." Horace Walpole says in his Reminiscences, "The Queen's chief stay was Divinity, and she had rather weakened her faith than enlightened it. She was at least not orthodox, and her confidante, Lady Sundon, an absurd and pompous simpleton, swayed her confidence to the less-believing Clergy." This explains the sympathy which she always felt for the Latitudinarians and Rationalizers; but it is not pleasant reading when we reflect that on her devolved the appointment of the Bishops. Her wrong notions on the subject of the Trinity made her an admirer of the Arian, Clarke, and there is little doubt that but for his scruples about subscription, Clarke might have been raised to the Episcopate, and it is said that she even recommended him for the primacy on the death of Wake[1]. The way she promoted Hoadly was disgraceful beyond excuse. George II. admitted that Hoadly did not believe a word of the Bible, and yet he allowed such a man,

---

[1] "I have often heard my father, Sir Robert Walpole, say, that he sat up one night at Kensington Palace with Dr. Clarke till the pages of the backstairs asked if they would have fresh candles, to persuade him to subscribe again."—Horace Walpole's Diary.

after holding three other Sees, to be raised to the Bishopric of Winchester. It may be as well to quote George II.nd's words respecting Hoadly, otherwise this scandalous proceeding would be incredible; they will also enable us to form some idea of the manner in which Bishops were appointed at that time. "My Lord," the King said to Lord Hervey [k], "I am very sorry you choose your friends so ill, but I cannot help saying that if the Bishop of Winchester (Hoadly) is your friend, you have a great *puppy*, and a very dull fellow, and a great *rascal* for your friend. It is a very pretty thing for *such scoundrels* when they are raised to favour so much above their deserts, and very modest in a *canting hypocritical knave* to be crying 'The Kingdom of God is not of this world,' at the same time he, as Christ's Ambassador, receives £6,000 or £7,000 a year. But he is just the same in the Church as he is in the government, and as ready to receive the best pay for preaching the Bible, *though he does not believe a word of it.*" And yet the King who spoke the words was the man who promoted him to the See; and this was the Bishop who more than any other person did harm to the Church in the eighteenth century.

It certainly is a humiliating thought that such people as we have described above should be entrusted with the work of appointing Bishops,

---

[k] Herv. Mem., ii. 41.

The Decline of the Church.

and have it in their power to use the Church as a political machine, to prevent it from managing its own affairs, and from even defending itself. But so it was.

The Court patronage of Hoadly; the desperate worldliness of Walpole; the long continuance of Episcopal appointments when Clergymen of the highest ability, of the soundest learning, and undoubted orthodoxy, were studiously passed over, lowered the tone of the Church, and had a palsying effect which led to a religious apathy and listlessness through Church and State.

The first thing the Hanoverian dynasty did in order to render the Church powerless, was to suppress Convocation, an arbitrary and unconstitutional act, and which, we venture to think, was nothing short of a national calamity. Soon after the accession of George I. the Church's voice was silenced; through the loss of her Convocation the Church lost the power of corporate action, and to that loss more than to any other cause, must be attributed not only the torpor and deadness which came upon the Church, but the low state of morality which pervaded the nation through the eighteenth century.

That the Church should be deprived of the right which was enjoyed by every dissenting sect in the country was in itself a great injustice. Why should the Church alone of the religious communities in the country be deprived, simply because it was the National Church, of the right of managing its own affairs? or how was it possible, at a time when the Church was agitated by the Nonjuring, the Bangorian, the Deistical, and the Trinitarian controversies, that its affairs could be administered without its deliberative Assembly? To its Convocation the English Church is indebted for "our Liturgy, our Articles, our Canons, in truth all the external circumstances of our Church, and the regulation of its internal arrangement[1]." The Church of England can trace back the model of its Convocations to the very earliest ages of its history, and at no previous time had it been deprived of its synodal rights. It is true that, owing to the Latitudinarian appointments which William III. made, a spirit of antagonism had been created between the two Houses, and that unseemly contests had arisen between them; but this was only a temporary accident; a better spirit was commencing at the very time Convocation was suppressed; and there is no doubt that some remedy would have been devised, some reformation effected. During the reign of Anne the Church, as has been already stated, reached its highest point; and that was mainly due to the fact that Convocation met regularly, and vigilantly guarded the orthodoxy of the Church. Amongst its latest agenda we find that many practical questions were discussed, such as at that time were most

---

[1] Joyce's Sacred Synods, p. 74.

The Decline of the Church. 291

needed—the establishment of charity-schools and parochial libraries, the want of missions, and the increase of Church accommodation. By its suppression a strong barrier against the pestilential publications and the general licentiousness which prevailed was thrown down. There is, no doubt, some ground for fearing lest, under such Bishops as the majority of those on the Hanoverian Bench, Convocation might have simply renewed and protracted the quarrels between the two Houses, which make the Convocational Records of Queen Anne's reign such dreary reading. It is possible that along with noisy disputes such a deadlock in all practical action might have existed, as would even further lower the public estimation of the Church. Still when we find amongst the Bishops such names as those of Wake, and Gibson, and Potter, and Butler, and Secker, it cannot be doubted that if they had been permitted to consult together, instead of being obliged to act alone in cases of unparalleled difficulty, some means would have been devised for stemming the irreligion and infidelity of the times; and instead of discountenancing enthusiasm they would have solved amongst themselves the important question as to how such zealous workmen as the Wesleys and Whitefield might be utilized to the benefit of the Church. "The Church in danger" was a frequent cry in the eighteenth century; and the danger was real and imminent when the Church, having first been bound hand and foot, was afterwards gagged by the State. The State did its best to destroy the Church; its short-sighted policy rebounded on its own head.

From Walpole's time to the first Reform Bill Bishoprics were generally given to ensure Parliamentary support, and ministers made no scruple of confessing that they bestowed the highest offices in the Church to gain political adherents. This period is marked by great nepotism on the part of Bishops and cringing to ministers of the day. In the appointment of Bishops learning and piety were secondary considerations, and frequently no considerations at all. Mr. Grenville said he considered Bishoprics to be of two kinds, bishoprics of business for men of learning, and bishoprics of ease for men of family; amongst the former he reckoned Canterbury, York, London, and (on account of its nearness to Cambridge) Ely; amongst the latter, Durham, Winchester, Salisbury, and Worcester[m]. Most of the Bishops were men of aristocratic connection; and if some of them were men of learning also, yet their time was so much occupied in writing controversial books in defence of the outposts of Christianity, and they so often, in consequence of the poorness of their Sees, held other preferments *in commendam*, and were consequently absentees, that efficient Diocesans they were not.

There were, indeed, many excellent Bishops[n], but

---

[m] Bishop Newton's Autobiography.

[n] Their paucity, however, will be apparent if we compare the

The Decline of the Church. 293

of these the greater number owed their advancement not to their Churchmanship, but because it was expected that they would be useful to the government, and that they would become Latitudinarians. Wake and Gibson had greatly aided the government by their writings; Secker had been a Presbyterian; Butler a Dissenter, known to Clarke. Lord Shelburne bestowed the See of Llandaff on Dr. Watson, hoping, says the Bishop, "I was a warm and universal partisan; and he told the Duke of Grafton he hoped I might occasionally write a pamphlet for the administration[o]." Those were the days in which the custom of visiting a Diocese once during his Episcopate was established by a Bishop of Winchester; of confirming once in his Episcopate by the Metropolitan of York; of never residing in his Diocese by the Bishop of Llandaff[p]. Bishops were to be seen in the House of Lords, at the levees of

---

number of eminent Bishops in the single reign of Charles II. with those from George I. to the accession of Queen Victoria. In the reign of Charles II. (not including the survivors of Charles I.'s reign): Morley, Sanderson, Cosin, Walton, Hacket, Barrow, Sparrow, Wilkins, Gunning, Pearson, Fell, Sancroft, Lake, Ken, Sheldon, Turner. Total, 16 in 25 years.—From reign of George I. to William IV.: Potter, Gibson, Chandler, Kennet, Secker, Butler, Pearse, Warburton, Louth, Barrington, Hurd, Porteus, Horsley, Horne, Marsh, Van Mildert, Kaye, Blomfield, Bagot, Phillpotts, Denison. Total, 21 in 123 years.

[o] Anecdotes of the Life of R. Watson, i. 157.
[p] Quarterly Review, CXIV. 543.

Ministers, in the palace of the King, but rarely, where they ought to be, in their Dioceses.

Bishop Watson's self-applauding estimate of his episcopal life (1782—1816) which he spent at Calgarth Park, in Westmoreland, affords too sad a picture of the times not to be mentioned. "I have now," he says, "spent almost twenty years in this delightful country, but my time has not been spent in county bickerings, in indolence, or intemperance. No! it has been spent partly in supporting the religion and constitutions of the country; by seasonable publications, and principally in building farm-houses, blasting rocks, enclosing wastes, in making bad land good, in planting larches, and implanting in the hearts of my children principles of piety and self-government." His income was made up to £2,000 by the emoluments arising from sixteen Livings, on nine of which he kept a resident curate. It scarcely seems to have occurred to him that the office of a Bishop involved any episcopal responsibilities.

Lambeth Palace, during the Primacy (1768—1783) of Archbishop Cornwallis, created much scandal through the balls given there, and the splendour of its festivities. The Countess of Huntingdon, the famous Selina, was bold enough to upbraid the Archbishop's wife for her share in the business; she might as well have attacked a lioness in her den; and being assailed with the titles of "Methodist" and "hypocrite," she determined to seek an interview with the King, who wrote the following letter to the Archbishop:—"My good Lord Primate, I could not delay giving you the mortification of the grief and concern with which my breast was afflicted at receiving authentic information that routs had made their way into your palace. At the same time, I must signify to you my sentiments on this subject, which hold those levities and vain dissipations as utterly inexpedient, if not unlawful, to pass in a residence for many centuries devoted to divine studies, religious retirement, and the extensive exercise of charity and benevolence; I add, in a place where so many of your predecessors have led their lives in such sanctity as has thrown lustre on the pure religion they professed and adorned. From the dissatisfaction with which you must perceive me to behold these improprieties, not to speak in harsher terms, and on still more pious principles, I trust you will suppress them immediately; so that I may not have occasion to shew any further marks of my displeasure, or to interfere in a different manner. May God take your Grace into His Almighty protection. I remain, My Lord Primate, your gracious friend, G. R."

The following letter, written in 1791 by a member of the same family, Dr. James Cornwallis, Bishop of Lichfield and Coventry, to William Pitt, gives a specimen of the manner in which Bishoprics were negotiated:—"After the various instances of neglect and contempt which Lord Cornwallis[q] and I have experienced, not only in violation of repeated assurances, but of the strongest ties, it is impossible I should not feel the late disappointment very deeply. With respect to the proposal concerning Salisbury, I have no hesitation in saying that the See of Salisbury cannot in any respect be an object to me. The only arrangement which promises an accommodation in my favour is the promotion of the Bishop of Lincoln to Salisbury, which would enable you to confer the Deanery of St. Paul's upon me." Mr. Pitt made an indignant reply, and the Bishop a humble apology; but the latter knew well what he was about, and received a few days afterwards the promise from the Prime Minister: "I can only say that I have no reason to believe that the Bishop of Lincoln would wish to remove to Salisbury; but if he were, I should have no hesitation in recommending your Lordship for the Deanery of St. Paul's[r]."

And if the Bishops were remiss in their duties, not less so were the Cathedral dignitaries. It was no uncommon thing for a Bishop to hold with his Bishopric a Deanery also. Herring (afterwards Archbishop of Canterbury) held the Deanery of Rochester with the Bishopric of Bangor. The Bishopric of Rochester and the Deanery of Westminster were nearly always held together. When Dr. Zachary

---

[q] The Bishop's brother.
[r] Stanhope's Life of P. H., ii. 129.

The Decline of the Church. 297

Pearse, Bishop of Rochester, thought of resigning the Deanery of Westminster which he had hitherto held with it, Bishop Newton tells us how he used "all the arguments he could to dissuade the Bishop from his purpose of separating the two preferments, which had been united for near a century, and lay so convenient to each other that *neither of them would be of the same value if separated;* and if once separated, they might perhaps never be united again, and his successors would have reason to reproach and condemn his memory."

This same Bishop Newton[s], the author of the "Dissertation on the Prophecies," tells us with regard to the Chapter of his own Cathedral that "the Bishop has several times been there for months together without seeing the face of Dean, or Prebendary, or anything better than a Minor Canon." Zachary Pearse, Bishop of Rochester, 1756—1774, asked one of his Prebendaries, "Pray, Dr. S., what is your time of residence at Rochester?... The Prebendary told him he resided there the *better* time of the year; but the Doctor meant that he *only resided there during the week of audit*[t]."

The position of the Clergy in the eighteenth century was very different from what it had been before the Reformation. The abolition of the monasteries, and the confiscation of their revenues by the Crown,

---

[s] Bishop of Bristol, 1761—1782.
[t] Autobiography of Bishop Newton, i. 127.

had left the Church in a very impoverished condition. Burnet tells us that in his day hundreds of cures were worth only £20, thousands only £50 a year, and Dean Swift says there were at least ten Bishoprics, the income of which did not exceed £600 a year. Stackhouse (1680—1752), the well-known author of the "History of the Bible," himself a clergyman, in his book the "Miseries and great Hardships of the Inferior Clergy in and about London," draws a sad picture of the Curates, and says they were "objects of extreme wretchedness." Their salary was frequently nearer £20 than £50: less than the Sexton's, and not so punctually paid. The common fee for a sermon was a shilling and a dinner; for reading prayers, two-pence and a cup of coffee. They lived in garrets, appearing in the streets in tattered cassocks [u].

Adam Smith, in his "Wealth of Nations" (1776), says that £40 a year, the pay of journeymen shoemakers in London, was considered very good pay for a Curate; whilst many Clergymen received less than £20, a smaller sum than was earned by industrious workmen of all trades in the metropolis.

---

[u] At what period in the eighteenth century the wearing of the cassock in the streets was discontinued, or when the Bishop's cassock degenerated into the unmeaning apron, and the Bishops acquired the name (not altogether unsuitable at that time) of "old women in aprons," the author has not been able to discover.

There were many rich prizes to be gained, and there were many of the Clergy well-fitted by their abilities and learning to hold the highest stations in the Church; who were able to command respect in (as the English Court under the first two Georges was) the most dissolute Court in Europe; or to maintain the cause of Christianity against sceptics and infidels. Whatever faults the Clergy of the eighteenth century had, there is no reason to doubt what Lord Stanhope says, "the lives of the Clergy were, as a rule, pure." The public are plentifully informed of the bad deeds of those times, as well as of those Clergymen who went about preaching and speaking in public. But how many Clergymen must there have been who went on quietly and unostentatiously in their daily duties, without their good deeds being known or published! This we are not told. It was not the fault of the Clergy generally that the Bishops and other Dignitaries made large fortunes, and used their patronage for private purposes. It was not the fault of the Clergy that their own incomes were so small; that there were hundreds of Livings without Parsonages, and that the Church fabrics were falling into decay. Who knows the number of the poorer, unobtrusive Parish Priests who did their work, under increasing difficulties, quietly and laboriously in their country parishes, known amongst the cottages rather than in the dwellings of the rich, or in the fashionable churches, or in Town Halls and newspapers?

Still there is no doubt that the general standard of the Clergy was low. Many of the Parochial Clergy never went near their parishes from Sunday to Sunday; many even of the better sort of Clergymen, who did not spend their time in field-sports, were to be seen lounging at the fashionable watering-places, or at the levees of the great people of the day. From this class the high stations of the Church—the Bishoprics and Deaneries—were filled; the one end and aim of this superior grade of beneficed Clergy seemed to be to obtain some higher post, and so equal the status of those with whom they were accustomed to associate. This class of Clergy were probably absentees, and paid a Curate to perform their duties for them. But the general run of Incumbents were even worse than this. If they lived on their glebe they often led the lives of ecclesiastical squires; they hunted, shot, drank the squire's port, and joined the friendly rubber. They performed their Sunday duties with easy and decorous regularity; they read the prayers with emphasis, and their sermons in monotone. No music varied the dulness of the services except one, or at the most two Metrical Psalms, taken, when the Old Version of Sternhold and Hopkins could be tolerated no longer, from the scarcely better New Version of Tate and Brady, accompanied by the squeaking of a cracked flageolet, or the growling of a bass-viol. The favourite sermons were those of Tillotson and Blair. If they preached their own sermons, it was necessary for the Clergy to be very careful about the language they used; Charles Wesley was charged before the Somersetshire magistrates with swearing, because he quoted the text "he that believeth not shall be damned;" and again, before the Yorkshire magistrates, for favouring the Pretender, because he prayed God to "bring back His banished ones[x]."

Many of the Clergy had to serve two or more churches on the same Sunday, in which case, after finishing the service in one church they would gallop off as quickly as possible to another; the church was then shut up till the following Sunday. If called upon for some extra duty, they would hurry over the burial or marriage-service, vested in a surplice not unfrequently thrown over the hunting-coat and top-boots. But with all their faults they were generally beloved by the poor; if they had the means, they were liberal in their charities; if they were sent for to attend the sick or dying, they were ready to give their services; they knew how to say the kind word, or point out the right way; but they did not set the example, there was no zeal, no enthusiasm.

---

[x] Paley recommended the Clergy to write one sermon and steal five. That model Landlord, Sir Roger de Coverley, gave his excellent Chaplain a volume from which to preach, and if he asked him who was going to preach on the following Sunday, the answer would be, "the Bishop of St. Asaph in the Morning, and Dr. South in the Afternoon."—Spectator, No. 106.

As most of the Clergy were University men, a few words must be said as to the state of the two Universities. Dr. Johnson, who was for some time an undergraduate at Pembroke College, Oxford, tells us his Tutor was "very worthy, but very ignorant," and on one occasion he complained to this Tutor, " Sir, you have sconced me two-pence for non-attendance at a lecture not worth a penny." Adam Smith, who went as an undergraduate to Balliol in 1740, says: " In the University of Oxford the greater part of the Professors have for many years given up the pretence of teaching. The discipline is in general contrived not for the benefit of the students, but for the interest, or more properly speaking, the ease of the masters." Gibbon, at one time an undergraduate at Magdalen, Oxford, speaks of one of the Tutors who " remembered that he had a salary to receive, but forgot that he had a duty to perform;" and that the fourteen months he spent at Magdalen were "the most unprofitable of his life." He complained that no instruction in religion was ever given him; that the juniors suffered from associating with the Fellows in the Common Room, whose "dull deep potations excused the brisk intemperance of youth."

In 1748 Lord Chesterfield writes to his son: " What do you think of being Greek Professor at one of the Universities ? It is a very pretty sinecure, and requires very little knowledge, much less than I hope you have already of that language." About 1750

The Decline of the Church. 303

Thurlow, afterwards Lord Chancellor, himself remarkable for his knowledge of Greek and Latin, was obliged to take his name off the books of Caius College, Cambridge, for hinting in public what every body knew but dared not say, that the Dean of his College was ignorant of Greek. Lord Eldon, who took his B.A. Degree at Oxford in 1770, said "An examination for a degree at Oxford was a farce in my time. I was examined in Hebrew and History: 'What is the Hebrew for the Place of a Skull?' said the Examiner. 'Golgotha,' I replied. 'Who founded University College?' I answered, 'King Alfred.' 'Very well, Sir,' said the Examiner, 'then you are competent for your degree.'" Dr. Vicesimus Knox, Head Master of Tunbridge School, gives a further insight into an Oxford Examination [r]. Every candidate for the B.A. Degree was required to be examined by three Masters of Arts of his own choosing, the examination taking place between 9 and 11 A.M.; and it was considered a piece of good management to procure three pleasant, good-tempered examiners, and to ply them well with wine in the previous night. A frequent subject of examination was the last drinking-bout, or the pedigree of horses, and to while away the time till the clock pointed at eleven, a newspaper or a novel was read; when the expected hour arrived the much-desired "Testamur" was signed by the

---

[r] Essay 77.

three Masters. We will cite one instance more of the manner of life at the Universities as recorded by William Wilberforce. " I was introduced," he says, speaking of Cambridge, "on the first day of my arrival to as licentious a set of men as can well be conceived. They drank hard, and their conversation was even worse .... often indeed I was horrorstruck at their conduct, and after the first year I shook off my connection with them." Nor were the Fellows of his College (St. John's) much better : " The Fellows of the College did not act towards me the part of Christians, or even honest men. Their object seemed to make me idle. If I ever appeared studious they would say to me, ' Why in the world should a man of your fortune trouble himself with fagging?" We need not be surprised with the description which Scott the commentator gives of his fellow-candidates for Ordination; that they were mostly " Oxonian and Cambridgian bucks, who knew more of the wine and girls of their respective neighbourhoods, and of setting-dogs, race-horses, and guns in the country, than of Latin, and Greek, and Divinity[z]."

The natural result of such a state of things was, as has been already related, a general relaxation of morals throughout the nation. It was an age of irreligion and of immorality following as a consequence

---

[z] Life, p. 36.

upon it. Gambling[a], drinking[b], the violation of the marriage vow[c]; these, beginning at an early part of it, were carried on through the century to an extent which we in the present day can scarcely imagine.

It does not come within the scope of a work like this to give a minute description of the vices which brought this realm of England to the brink of ruin. We will sum up what other writers said at various times of the century, in the description of murders and robberies (often in open daylight and frequented streets) which Horace Walpole gives in 1782: "We are in a state of war at home which is shocking."

---

[a] Of Charles James Fox, Horace Walpole wrote in February, 1770, he "shines equally at the hazard table and in the House of Commons;" in November, 1770, he writes again, "Lord Holland is dying, and paying Charles Fox's debts, or most of them, for they amount to £130,000." The Duke of Grafton, who was once Prime Minister, lost, in gambling, his seat of Euston Hall in one night to the Duke of Cumberland.—Wright's England, ii. 6.

[b] In 1736, on account of the great increase of drunkenness, a Gin Act was passed; it was stated that "the constant and excessive use of Geneva had already destroyed thousands of his Majesty's subjects . . . destroying at the same time their morals and driving them into all manner of vice and wickedness." Notwithstanding the difference of population, the consumption, says Mr. Massey (History, ii. 82), was equal to what it is now.

[c] In 1779 Shute Barrington, Bishop of Llandaff, said in the House of Lords that as many divorces had occurred during the first seventeen years of George III. as were recorded in the whole previous history of the country. And yet this was little compared to the state in Paris.

And he—a man who is not generally given to moralizing—assigns the reason: "No wonder—how should the morals of the people be purified, when such frantic dissipation reigns above them? Contagion does not mount, but descends."

Bishop Newton, writing in the same year (1782), speaks of the perils which threatened the country; he says that the gross immorality of the people, masquerades, and other popular amusements, as well as gaming, adultery, and all kinds of vice, led to attention being paid to private and to the neglect of public interests; to a want of spirit and irresolution in the councils of the nation; and that generals and admirals thought so little of the interests of the country, that foreign enemies who were threatening the coasts of England were not so bad as enemies at home [d].

The best Bishops of the century deplored, but they could not remedy, the prevailing evils. Secker, Bishop of Oxford (afterwards Archbishop of Canterbury), thus (as early as 1738) charges his candidates for Holy Orders: "You cannot but see in what a profane and corrupt age this stewardship is committed to you; how grievously religion and its ministers are hated and despised." Gibson, Bishop of London, complains, in 1741, that the gangrene had penetrated the middle classes, generally the last to

---

[d] Bishop Newton's Autobiography, i. 178.

be infected by immoral contagion. Butler, Bishop first of Bristol (1738—1750), and afterwards of Durham (1750—1752), tells us that he lived at a time "when the licentiousness of the upper class, combined with the irreligion industriously propagated against the lower," was producing total "profligacy;" and in a charge to the Clergy of Durham in 1751, he spoke of the "avowed scorn of religion in some, and a growing of it in the generality;" and this same Prelate refused the Primacy in 1747, on the ground that "it was too late for him to try to support a falling Church."

One charge, and that the most important, which the Liberationists in the present day make against the Church is, that she has failed in her mission. We grant that during the eighteenth century she did fail. But whose fault was it? There is only one answer— The State's. The Church was never more active, never stood higher, than during the first fifteen years of the eighteenth century ; the State did all it could to weaken it, and it succeeded. And what is the lesson that Englishmen, of all political parties, of all religious denominations, should learn from that disastrous period? The very opposite, we imagine, to that which the Liberationists suggest. If the Church of England had not been divinely instituted, she never could have weathered the storm, she could not have regained the position that she held before. Yet she has done so, and her having done so is the clearest proof that she is the instrument in God's hand to the English nation. She outnumbers all the Dissenting brethren, she possesses by far the greatest share in the wealth and the learning of the country; of all Communions she is the most liberal, the most comprehensive; above all things, she is the friend of the poor, such as, if the decrees for disestablishment and disendowment went forth, could never be replaced. Englishmen know what the Church has done for them in the past. Will they barter their birthright for a mess of pottage? throw away a certainty for an idea? It is well to learn a lesson from the sad experience of our forefathers in the eighteenth century; to learn into what a depth of degradation not only the Church but the State also may fall, when the Church is silenced and rendered powerless. What happened once may happen again, if ever the influence of the Church is lowered and weakened by the State.

CHAPTER II.

THE SILENCING OF CONVOCATION.

GEORGE I. was crowned in Westminster Abbey on October 20, 1714; in the following January Parliament was dissolved; and when the new Parliament met on March 17, there was found to be a large preponderance of Whig members. The King in his speech thanked his faithful and loving subjects for the zeal they had shewn in defence of the Protestant succession, and he declared that the established constitution in Church and State should be the rule of his government, and the happiness and prosperity of his people the chief care of his life.

Although the King manifested strong prepossessions for the Whigs, the Tories did not give way without a struggle. Religion was mixed up with the political disputes. The cry of "the Church in danger" was revived; the party-cry was "Down with the Whigs; Sacheverell for ever." In several towns the meeting-houses of the Dissenters were destroyed, and the health of King James openly drunk in the streets [a].

---

[a] The Tories, however, did not have it all on their side; the "Freeholder," No. 411, states that all the churches in London

The impeachment by the Whig government of the former ministers only added fuel to the flames. Lords Oxford, Bolingbroke, and Ormond were accused of high treason. Bolingbroke and Ormond fled to France, but Oxford stood his ground; they were all three impeached, and bills of attainder were passed against Bolingbroke and Ormond. Oxford was sent to the Tower, where he was kept a prisoner for two years; in 1717 he was brought to trial and acquitted. Bolingbroke for a time openly joined the Pretender, but soon gave up his cause as hopeless, and was allowed to return to England in 1723. Ormond died abroad in 1745.

Troubles also arose from another quarter. The Jacobites considered that the time was favourable for an insurrection and invasion of the country, and there were risings in favour of the Pretender both in Scotland and England. But the Pretender lacked the courage and energy that was required; the rebellion was easily suppressed, and Jacobitism discouraged. These risings were followed by an important change in the law. The national discontent still continued, and the ministry, fearing the results of a fresh election, devised a plan for establishing their own administration: the Triennial Act was repealed, and a Bill passed for allowing the same Parliament to continue for seven years, by which the then existing Parlia-

---

were kept shut, and that if a Clergyman appeared in the streets, ten to one he was knocked down.

ment was enabled to continue in power till 1722. Under such circumstances the Septennial Act which is still in force was passed in 1716.

The King received several addresses of congratulation on the suppression of the rebellion and on his return from Hanover. One was from the Dissenting ministers, another from the University of Cambridge; but Oxford was not so lavish of her compliments. A spirit far from loyal to the Hanoverian succession prevailed in that University. The Duke of Ormond had been their Chancellor, and his brother, Lord Arran, was chosen in his place; whilst the conduct of the undergraduates was so opposed to the new government, that it was thought necessary to send a military force to Oxford to keep them in subjection. So when it was proposed at a meeting of the Vice-Chancellor and Heads of Colleges to vote an address to the King, Dr. Smalridge, Bishop of Bristol, observed that the rebellion had been long suppressed; that there would be no end to addresses if one was to be presented to the King every time he returned from his German dominions; and that any favour the University might have received was more than counterbalanced by a whole regiment being quartered on them. At Cambridge a similar feeling had at first manifested itself. On the night of King George's birthday in 1715, an anti-Hanoverian feeling manifested itself amongst the undergraduates, at which Dr. Sherlock, the Vice-Chancellor, was accused at conniving. But Mr. Waterland, who succeeded him as Vice-Chancellor, and who was a stedfast supporter of the Hanoverian succession, managed to allay these animosities. On the day after Dr. Waterland's election (November 5, 1715), Dr. Bentley, the Master of Trinity, preached a celebrated sermon against Popery at St. Mary's; and the government was pacified [b], and by way of marking its approval Dr. Waterland was made a Royal Chaplain, and the King made to the University a present of the noble library which he had purchased from the late Bishop More of Ely, containing more than 30,000 volumes [c].

The different conduct of the two Universities, and the different treatment they received, gave rise to the following squibs. The first is by an Oxford man:—

"King George, observing with judicious eyes
The state of both his Universities,
To Oxford sent a troop of horse; and why?
That learned body wanted loyalty.
To Cambridge books he sent, as well discerning
How much that loyal body wanted learning."

The rejoinder, which was scarcely so happy, was from the pen of Sir William Browne, a Cambridge man [d]:—

---

[b] Van Mildert's Life of Waterland, p. 13.

[c] Waterland was, at any rate at first, one of the few friends of Bentley. In 1717 the latter was elected Regius Professor of Divinity, because Waterland, who was generally thought to be the fittest person, refused to stand against him.—Biog. Britannia, article "Waterland."

[d] Founder of the Prizes for Odes and Epigrams.

The Silencing of Convocation. 313

> "The King to Oxford sent a troop of horse,
> For Tories own no argument but force;
> With equal skill to Cambridge books he sent,
> For Whigs admit no force but argument."

The appointment of several Bishops soon fell to the King. Dr. More, Bishop of Ely, died the day before, and Dr. Fowler, Bishop of Gloucester, on the same day as Queen Anne. "Many received it," says Calamy[e], "a happiness that these Bishops lived so long, because by that means their vacated Bishoprics were filled up by King George." To the Sees thus vacated Dr. Fleetwood and Dr. Willis were appointed; the former being translated from St. Asaph to Ely, and Dr. Willis becoming Bishop of Gloucester[f], whilst Dr. Wynne was appointed Bishop of St. Asaph[g].

On March 17, 1715, died, in his seventy-second year, Gilbert Burnet, Bishop of Sarum. Shortly after his death a letter appeared in the "Gentleman's Magazine," which must be taken as a proof of his unpopularity: "Last Tuesday night (March 22, 1714-15) the body of that great and good man, the late Dr. Burnet, Bishop of Sarum, was interred near the Communion Table in Clerkenwell Church. As the corpse was conveying to the church, the rabble (that shows no distinction to men of great parts and learning, when once they conceive an ill opinion of them) flung

---

[e] Own Life, ii. 306.
[f] Bishop of Sarum, 1721; of Winchester, 1723; died, 1743.
[g] Bishop of Bath and Wells, 1727; died, 1743.

dirt and stones at the hearse, and broke the glasses of the coach that immediately followed it." (Vol. lviii. 952.) Burnet was succeeded at Salisbury by Talbot, Bishop of Oxford [h], father of the Lord Chancellor; Potter, Canon of Christ Church, and Regius Professor of Divinity, succeeding him at Oxford [i].

On December 14, 1714, Dr. Tenison, Archbishop of Canterbury, died. Thomas Tenison (1636—1714), having graduated at Corpus Christi College, Cambridge (of which he became a Fellow in 1662), was privately ordained in 1659 by Bryan Duppa, ejected Bishop of Salisbury; after holding a curacy at Cambridge, and some small preferments, he was, in 1680, made a Royal Chaplain, and appointed to the vicarage of St. Martin's-in-the-Fields, London. Though never a great theologian, yet as a parish priest, both in preaching and in working, he was most successful; he was one of the promoters of the charity-schools and the libraries of Dr. Bray; he was one of the London Clergy who resisted the unconstitutional measures of King James, and though a firm opponent to Romanism, he showed so much tact and discretion as to gain the esteem of that monarch. When William came to the throne his strong Whig principles and Latitudinarian opinions at once marked him out for High Church preferment. After being, in 1689, Archdeacon of London, and having acted as

---

[h] Bishop of Durham, 1721.
[i] Dr. Potter, Archbishop of Canterbury, 1737.

one of the Commissioners (of whom he was amongst the most active) for the review of the Prayer-Book, he was, in 1691, removed from a sphere for which he was well adapted to the Bishopric of Lincoln, in which position he was active and popular, and was soon afterwards offered, but refused, the Archbishopric of Dublin. In 1694, on political rather than on spiritual grounds, he was raised to the Primacy of all England, for which he was, especially at such a time, ill-fitted, for being a Whig and a Latitudinarian, he was little likely to assert the rights of the Church over the claims of the government. On the death of Queen Mary he was appointed one of the Commissioners for Ecclesiastical Preferments, who being mostly men like-minded with himself, promoted Latitudinarians to the high places in the Church. He had as strong a dislike as Tillotson to Convocation; hence arose the Controversy respecting the rights and privileges of Convocation, after which Tenison was obliged to yield to public opinion and to convene one. But his Latitudinarian views, which were shared by many of the most prominent Bishops, caused a wide divergence between the two Houses. Faults there were, no doubt, on both sides; the Clergy, in learning often the superiors of the Bishops, thought the object of the Bishops was to make the Church a mere political machine, and Tenison, firm as a rock (as he has been described), was too unbending and too unconciliatory to pour oil upon the troubled waters. His Primacy was the reverse of successful; but he was, according to his lights, a conscientious, as he was certainly a munificent, Prelate; amongst other legacies in his will he founded a charity-school at Lambeth for the education of twelve poor girls, and another school at Croydon; he left £1,000 for two Bishoprics to be founded, one on the Continent, the other in one of the Isles of North America; £1,000 to Queen Anne's Bounty for the augmentation of small Livings in Kent; £500 to the Corporation for the Relief of Clergymen's Widows and Children; and £100 to the French Protestant refugees.

On the death of Archbishop Tenison the Primacy was offered to Dr. Hough, Bishop of Lichfield[j], who declined it, as we are told, from modesty[k]; it was then accepted by Dr. Wake, Bishop of Lincoln, who was succeeded at Lincoln by Dr. Gibson[l]. In this same year the notorious Hoadly was appointed Bishop of Bangor. In 1717 Dr. Offspring Blackall, Bishop of Exeter, died, and was succeeded by Launcelot Blackburn[m]. In the same year Lloyd, Bishop of Worcester, who was one of the seven Bishops

---

[j] Dr. Hough was the President of Magdalen College, Oxford, who was elected against James II.[nd]'s nominee.

[k] Worcester Diocesan Hist., p. 334. Lord Lyttelton styles Hough "the good Bishop," and describes him as an "ideal" Bishop.   [l] Bishop of London, 1723.

[m] Archbishop of York, 1724.

The Silencing of Convocation.

committed to the Tower, died at the age of ninety, and was succeeded by Hough, Bishop of Lichfield, who had refused the Primacy, Dr. Chandler being appointed to Lichfield [n]. In 1718 Samuel Bradford was consecrated Bishop of Carlisle [o], and White Kennet, Dean of Peterborough, a violent partisan of the Low Church party, and the vigorous opponent of Atterbury in the Convocation Controversy, was appointed Bishop of that See [p].

Ths appointment to a Bishopric of such a man as Hoadly was a disgraceful and tyrannical act on the part of the government; hostile governments have at times done much to weaken the Church, but nothing was so bad as this : it was an appointment that every one knew must bring, not only the Church but religion generally into contempt, for Hoadly's principles were opposed both to Christianity and to those mutual relations between Church and State on which the government of England is founded. Hoadly was little, if at all, short of a Socinian ; some idea of the character of the man may be found in the fact that for the six years during which he held the See of Bangor, he never (as far as is known) put his foot in the Diocese, but employed his time in writing pamphlets against that Church which it

---

[n] Bishop of Durham, 1730. [o] Bishop of Rochester, 1723.
[p] White Kennet (1660—1728) in 1693 was appointed to the Rectory of Shottisbrooke by Mr. Cherry, the patron of the Nonjurors.

was his duty to defend. It was not long before troubles broke out.

But we must give some account of the previous history of this troubler of Israel in the eighteenth century. Benjamin Hoadly (1676—1761), born at Westerham, in Kent, was educated under his father, who was Master of Norwich Grammar School. He had two brothers, Samuel, who died at University College, Oxford, at the age of seventeen years, and John (1678—1746), who attained even higher preferment in the Church than his more famous brother Benjamin [q]. Benjamin—after graduating at St. Katharine's Hall, Cambridge, where he was cotemporary with his after-opponent, Bishop Sherlock [r] — was in 1701 appointed Lecturer of St. Mildred's in the Poultry, where he was unsuccessful, for according to his own showing he "preached the Lectureship down to £30 per annum [s]." In 1704 he was appointed

---

[q] Bishop Burnet made him his Chancellor, Canon Residentiary, and Archdeacon of Sarum, as well as Rector of St. Edmund's. His brother Benjamin made him a Canon of Hereford. In 1727 he was consecrated Bishop of the united Sees of Leighton and Ferns, in Ireland, in 1730 Archbishop of Dublin, and in 1742 Archbishop of Armagh.

[r] A little preliminary skirmishing seems to have taken place between them even at Cambridge. Coming out of lecture one day, Hoadly said to Sherlock, "Well, Sherlock, you came out fairly to-day, by help of a translation." "No," replied Sherlock, "I tried all I could to get one, and could hear of only one copy, and that you had secured."

[s] "He preached it down to £30 a year, as he pleasantly ob-

Rector of St. Peter-le-Poer, London [t], and in 1710 to the Rectory of Streatham [u].

Hoadly was one of those men who are never happy unless they are in hot water. In 1703, at which period of his life he was comparatively orthodox [v], he published a Treatise on "The reasonableness of Conformity to the Church of England," which involved him in a controversy with the Nonconformist Calamy, who had written the "Abridgement of the Life of Baxter," to which the Treatise of Hoadly was an answer.

But, to omit the many attacks he made upon the Church, in September, 1705, he preached before the Lord Mayor of London a sermon which brought down upon him the censure first of Compton, Bishop of London, and then of the Lower House of Convocation. But so well did Hoadly play his part, that in 1710 he gained the favour of the Whigs, who were in power: they determined that he had often strenu-

---

served, and then thought it high time to quit it."—Works, I. viii.

[t] Owing in a great measure to the recommendation of Dr. William Sherlock, Dean of St. Paul's, and father to the future Bishop, to the Chapter.

[u] The former Living he held till he was translated to Hereford, and the latter until his translation to Salisbury.

[v] It is only justice to state what he said of himself: "I can myself with a pure conscience conform;" and that when he was a parish priest, "he never omitted the Athanasian Creed when it was ordered to be read in church."—Nichols' Lit. An., ii. 747.

ously supported the principles on which the nation proceeded in the late happy Revolution, and "that an humble address be presented to her Majesty that she would be graciously pleased to bestow some dignity of the Church on Mr. Hoadly for his eminent services both in Church and State." The Queen answered, "That she would take a proper opportunity to comply with their desires,"—"which, however, she never did [x]."

In 1716 some posthumous papers of Dr. Hickes the Nonjuror were published, which set forth "the constitution of the Catholic Church, and the nature and consequences of schism." In reply to the statements made in these papers, which were considered highly offensive to the government, Hoadly, soon after he was made a Bishop, published "A Preservative against the Principles and Practices of the Nonjurors both in Church and State; or, An Appeal to the Consciences and Common Sense of the Christian Laity," in which he denied the necessity of Communion with any visible Church, and maintained that nothing but sincerity was required of a Christian. The challenge thrown down in the Preservative was repeated the following year in a sermon which he preached on March 31 before the King in the Chapel Royal of St. James's, on St. John xviii. 36, "Jesus answered, My kingdom is not of this world," in

---

[x] Hoadly's Works, ix.

which he maintained that Christ never intended to found such a Visible Church as the Church of England, and impugned all tests of Orthodoxy and all Ecclesiastical government. The Sermon and the Preservative, both of which were founded on the same principles, were obnoxious not only to the Nonjurors, but also to all honest members of the Church, even those who were well disposed to the Hanoverian Government.

Before proceeding further with the career of Hoadly, we must resume the account of the proceedings of Convocation since the accession of George I. At the commencement of his reign Convocation was allowed to assemble together with the Parliament on March 17, 1715. On April 7, the two Houses presented a joint address to the King, in his reply to which he said, "I thank you for your very dutiful and loyal address. . . . You may be assured I will always support and defend the Church of England as by law established, and make it my particular care to encourage the Clergy." The licence which the King sent to the two Houses contained certain points on which they were to deliberate similar to those submitted to them in the late Session. As this was the last Convocation which was allowed to sit for the transaction of business for more than 150 years, it may be interesting to state the subjects committed to it; they were comprised under the following heads:—

The regulating the proceedings in excommunication and commutation of Penances.

The making provision and transmitting more exact terriers, and accounts of glebes, tithes, and other possessions and profits belonging to benefices.

The regulating the licences for matrimony according to the canon, in order to the more effectual prevention of clandestine marriages.

The preparing a form for consecrating churches and chapels.

The better settling the qualifications, titles, and testimonials of persons who offer themselves for Holy Orders.

The making the seventy-fifth Canon, relating to the sober conversation required in ministering, more effectual.

The making the forty-seventh Canon, which provides for curates, where ministers are lawfully absent from their benefices, more effectual; as likewise the forty-eighth Canon, touching the licensing such Curates.

Rules for better instructing and preparing young persons for Confirmation, required by the sixty-first Canon, and for more orderly performing of that office.

The Bishops undertook to prepare the third, fourth, fifth, and eighth heads of business, and referred the others to the Lower House. Some progress was made by each House; a form for consecrating churches

The Silencing of Convocation. 323

and chapels[7] was drawn up by the Bishops, to which several amendments were carried in the Lower House, but first the death of Archbishop Tenison, and afterwards the troubles which Hoadly caused, prevented its receiving synodical authority.

The Commissioners appointed for building the fifty new churches authorised in the reign of Queen Anne having addressed the King as to the difficulty of procuring a fitting maintenance for the ministers who should be appointed to them, and praying him to recommend it to the care and wisdom of Parliament, his Majesty heartily recommended the matter to the House of Commons "for the honour of the Church of England and the advancement of our holy religion." In answer to this message the House unanimously resolved: "That this House will effectually enable him to pursue and perfect so pious and so glorious a work." The two Houses of Convocation united in an address of thanks to the King, stating that the message "so piously intended and so well received cannot fail of its desired effect, to the honour of the Church of England, and the advancement of our holy religion," and they expressed a hope that "after all the declarations your Majesty has been pleased to make in favour of our Established Church, and the real proofs you have given for its interests, none will be found so unjust as to

---

[7] A larger form had been adopted by Convocation and approved by Queen Anne in 1712, but never came into use.

doubt of your affection to it;" and they spoke of "the many blessings we enjoy under your Majesty's most auspicious government," and of "the returns of honour and obedience due to so good and gracious a sovereign."

We must now return to Hoadly's business, and that which sprang from it, the Bangorian Controversy.

In consequence of the betrayal of the Church by one of its Bishops, a Committee of the Lower House of Convocation[z] drew up a report reflecting on the teaching of Hoadly, and "a Representation about the Bishop of Bangor's Sermon of the Kingdom of Christ" to the Upper House was prepared on May 3, 1717. The tendency of Hoadly's two works was represented to be, "Firstly, to subvert all government and discipline in the Church of Christ, and to reduce His kingdom to a state of anarchy and confusion. Secondly, to impugn and impeach the regal supremacy in causes ecclesiastical, and the authority of the legislature to enforce obedience in matters of religion by civil sanctions." Passages were adduced from the Preservative and the Sermon in proof of these two propositions, and the Archbishop and Bishops were requested to interpose their authority. Wake had now succeeded Tenison as Archbishop; Burnet, the great opponent of Convocation, was dead;

---

[z] The Committee consisted of Dr. Thomas Sherlock, Dean of Chichester, Mosse, Blisse, Friend, Cannon, Dawson, Davis, Sprat, Barrett.

Atterbury, its strong advocate and supporter, had become a member of the Upper House; and there is little doubt that the Representation would have received the almost unanimous assent of the Bishops. But the leaders of the Whig government knew that the Lower House of Convocation was not well affected towards them; they were afraid of the unanimity of Convocation; and even before the Representation was presented to the Upper House they interposed; Convocation was prorogued by special order of the King, and was never permitted until very recent times to meet again for the transaction of business.

Out of Hoadly's case arose the Bangorian Controversy, which continued, for a long time after Convocation was suppressed, outside the walls of the Jerusalem Chamber. The Controversy was begun by Dr. Snape, Provost of Eton and Canon of Windsor[a], in a "Letter to the Bishop of Bangor," which was so popular that it ran through seventeen editions in one year. Soon afterwards appeared Dr. Thomas Sherlock, Master of St. Catharine's Hall, Cambridge, who, next to Law, was Hoadly's most powerful antagonist; he published several pamphlets on the subject, the most important of which was "A Vindication of the Corporation and Test Acts, in answer to the Bishop of Bangor's reasons for a Repeal of

---

[a] Appointed in 1719 Provost of King's College, Cambridge.

them, 1718[b]." A clergyman of a different stamp appeared in the person of Dr. Hare, Dean of Salisbury[c], who published several pieces during the Controversy. Hare was himself a Latitudinarian, although of a less pronounced type than Hoadly; he was the Author of "A Letter on the Difficulties and Discouragements which attend the study of the Scriptures in the way of private judgment," a work which had been censured by Convocation as tending to Scepticism. But Hoadly's most formidable opponent was William Law, the Nonjuror; his "Three Letters to the Bishop of Bangor" were the most powerful work produced by the Bangorian Controversy, and are amongst the finest specimens of controversial writing in our language. Law's Letters Hoadly never answered, for the plain reason (as was supposed) that they were *unanswerable*[d].

The Controversy, which is chiefly important in

---

[b] Dr. Sherlock, Bishop of Bangor, 1728; of Sarum, 1734; of London, 1748.

[c] In 1726 Dean of St. Paul's, the next year Bishop of St. Asaph, in 1731 Bishop of Chichester; he was the ancestor of the two brothers Augustus and Julius Hare, the latter of whom inherited from him the Living of Hurstmonceux.

[d] Dean Sherlock said "he knew but one reason why his Lordship did not answer him," meaning that they could not be answered; and Jones of Nayland characterized them as "incomparable for truth of argument, brightness of wit, and purity of English."—The Scholar Armed, as quoted in Overton's Life of Law, p. 20.

connection with the silencing of Convocation, was carried on for several years with great ability, and not a little acrimony; there was scarcely a Clergyman of any eminence at the time who did not write on one side or the other; several hundred pamphlets, many of a very violent nature, were published, and personalities even between Bishops were imported into it in a manner far from creditable to either side.

Hoadly, however, basked in the Royal favour; four of the King's chaplains—Snape, Sherlock, Hare, and Mosse—were removed from their posts, whilst he himself, as a reward for never visiting his Diocese for the six years during which he held it, was in 1721 translated to the See of Hereford.

The suppression of Convocation in 1717, at the very time when it was most needed, when Diocesan and Ruri-decanal Synods had no existence, was nothing short of a national calamity. By the suppression of Convocation a strong barrier against licentiousness and the pestilential publications which swarmed in the eighteenth century was thrown down; at a time when the State expected the Church to help it, the State had deprived it of its armour, and the Church was helpless. What would the Dissenters say if the State deprived them of the means of supporting their doctrine and discipline? What would the Presbyterians say if their General Assemblies were forbidden by the State? or the Independents, if their Congregational

Union ? or the Wesleyans, if their Conferences were forbidden them ? " Shall the Presbyterian Kirk of Scotland," asked Dr. Johnson, in 1763, "have its General Assembly and the Church of England be denied its Convocation ? " How was it possible during those critical times of the eighteenth century that the Church could be properly governed and do its duty to the country, except through its deliberative Assembly ? Its Convocation is the very life of the Church of England. " The Convocation or Ecclesiastical Synod of England," observes Blackstone[e], "differs considerably in its Constitution from the Synods of other Christian kingdoms, those consisting wholly of Bishops, whereas with us the Convocation is a miniature of a Parliament, wherein the Bishop presides in legal state ; the Upper House of the Bishops represents the House of Lords, and the Lower House, composed of the representatives of the several Dioceses at large, and of each particular Chapter therein, resembles the House of Commons with the Knights of the Shire and the Burgesses." The rights of Convocation by the laws of England, and the powers of the Lower House as claimed by Atterbury and the majority of the Clergy, were doubtless exaggerated, yet they were greater than those enjoyed by the Presbyters in other Episcopal bodies ; and it was certainly beneficial that the Lower House should

---

[e] Comment., i. 280.

exercise the veto which was permitted to them when the Latitudinarian Bishops were attempting to tamper with the Prayer-Book. The Bench of Bishops, thanks to the Revolutionary Government, was occupied by a set of men who were unbelievers in the Divine right of their Order, and cared only to magnify their secular, at the expense of their spiritual, authority; they were men who would have been the foremost to exclaim against the nation being governed without a Parliament, and yet they saw no harm in the Church, that part of the Constitution which they were specially called upon to defend, being governed without a Convocation. The Clergy of the Lower House valued the Church on its Ecclesiastical at least as much as on its Parliamentary side, and they felt that they were the true representatives alike of the doctrines of the Church and the wishes of the people.

But what was there in the constitution of Convocation which could give offence either to the State or to the Latitudinarian Bishops? The Powers of Convocation had been abridged and defined by the memorable Act of Submission in the reign of Henry VIII. Previously to that Act the Archbishop could assemble the Clergy of his Province in Convocation, and could dissolve or continue and arrange its sittings for the business of the Crown or for other business at his pleasure. But by the Act of Submission four points were established: (1) That Convocation can only be assembled by the King's writ;

(2) That when assembled it cannot constitute Canons without the King's Licence; (3) That when it agrees on Canons agreeably with the Royal Licence, it cannot enforce them without the Royal Assent; (4) That even then the Canons can only be executed with four limitations: (*a*) that they are not against the King's Prerogative; nor (*b*) against the Common Law; nor (*c*) against the Statute Law; nor (*d*) against the laws and customs of the land.

So long as Convocation was necessary to the Crown, that is to say, so long as it had the power of taxing the Clergy, and the House of Commons had not that power, so long it secured the right of meeting together with every Parliament, and this right of meeting involved the right of petitioning and, within certain limits, of legislating for the Church[f]. But by a verbal agreement made in 1664, between Lord Chancellor Clarendon and Archbishop Sheldon (an arrangement supposed to be favourable to the Clergy who always paid more than a fair proportion of taxes), the privilege of taxing themselves was bartered away, and henceforward the Clergy were included in the taxes proposed by the House of Commons[g]. Convocation was thus rendered less necessary to the Crown, and a succession of prorogations, which before Charles II.nd's time was impossible, was re-

---

[f] Stubbs' Constit. Hist.

[g] "The greatest alteration," says Bishop Gibson, "ever made in the Constitution without an express law."

sorted to so frequently as to lead for a time to the virtual extinction of Convocation [h]. In consequence of these interruptions in its proceedings, to which must be added the fact that many of the books which contained its memoranda, especially those of the Upper House, were destroyed in the fire of London, great ignorance as to the usages and prerogatives of the two Houses prevailed amongst the members of Convocation, and when they again met, quarrels as to their respective rights and privileges took place between them. So that when after long abeyance the two Houses met it was under exceptional circumstances, very different from those which exist, or are likely to exist, now.

It is necessary to bear these facts in mind. When people in the present day read of the disputes between the Bishops and the Clergy in Convocation nearly two hundred years ago, they sometimes talk of the insubordination of the Clergy, and forget that there is no connection between the state of things that existed then and that exists now. The unhappy feuds which then took place between the two Houses not only created a feeling lasting to the present day against Convocation, but also a fixed conviction that

---

[h] "Ever since 1662," writes Burnet (O. T., iii. 45), "the Convocation had indeed continued to sit, but to do no business; so that they were kept at no small charge in Town, but only to meet and read the Latin Liturgy, and consequently it was an ease to be freed from such attendance to no purpose."

no change of circumstances could justify its revival. The Anglican Church has always held the Episcopate in high respect. But Bishops are not infallible; they may do wrong, and they have done wrong: and we should ask ourselves this question, What should we do in the present day if the State puts itself, as it did through the eighteenth century, in open antagonism to the Church? if the door of promotion was shut against the orthodox, and opened only to Latitudinarians and Freethinkers? That was what really happened at the beginning of the last century. And through the action of the State, the State no less than the Church was brought to the very verge of ruin; and that England was saved from the horrors of the French Revolution is due to the fact that the Church, though thwarted and weakened in every conceivable way, was still alive; and that it awoke out of sleep at the very time when the greatest danger was threatening the country.

When a controversy extends over several years, it nearly always happens that both parties, if not equally, yet in some degree, are in fault. It was so in the Convocation disputes of the last century. In those disputes it happened more than once that the Lower Clergy, even when they were right, acted with so much warmth as to put themselves in the wrong; whilst the Upper House, with few exceptions, acted with such calmness as to make themselves, even when they were wrong, appear to be right. Yet of

The Silencing of Convocation. 333

one thing we may be certain. Had the Clergy of the Lower House been men like-minded with Tillotson, or Tenison, or Burnet, we should not in the present day have enjoyed our Prayer-Book unmutilated, or the ceremonies and discipline of our Church unimpaired; and the fact that the Lower House, by its opposition to the heretical Bishop Hoadly, was the cause of the suppression of Convocation is an ever-abiding memorial of the benefit which that venerable body has conferred on the Church.

The new Archbishop (Wake) was a man of greater learning and of a more Catholic spirit than his predecessor, Tenison; and gave hopes of better things for the Church, had it only been allowed the same liberty, we might say the same toleration, which we shall find was permitted to the Dissenting bodies throughout the eighteenth century. The year 1717, the same year that Convocation was silenced, witnessed an interesting and, for such a time, a remarkable movement, which, although it led to no practical result, deserves recording: viz. an attempt at promoting a union between the Anglican and Gallican Churches. We must, however, give a short account of the Catholic-minded Archbishop, the author of the movement.

William Wake (1657—1737), after graduating as Student at Christ Church, Oxford, went, soon after his ordination, to Paris, as Chaplain to Lord Preston, Envoy Extraordinary at that Court. Whilst he was in Paris he met with a copy of "The Exposition of the Doctrine of the Catholic Church," written in 1671 by the famous Bossuet [j], one of the most skilful controversialists of that or any other age [k]: a work in which the author extenuated certain doctrines of the Roman Catholic Church, with the design of removing the objections to it held by Protestants. The book appeared to be intended rather to smooth away difficulties than to put forth the Roman doctrines fairly, and so, although it was marked with the approval of the Archbishop of Rheims, and nine other Bishops, Pope Clement X. refused to sanction it, and it was formally condemned by the University of Louvain as well as the Doctors of the Sorbonne. Thereupon, according to Wake's statement, the whole edition was at once suppressed, and another, with the objectionable parts omitted, speedily sent to the Press, and put forth just as if no previous edition had been published. But the original edition fell into Wake's hands, and called from him a work, in which he put Bossuet in this awkward dilemma: "It is not impossible for a Bishop of the Church of Rome either not to be sufficiently instructed in his religion to know what is the doctrine of it, or not sufficiently

---

[j] "The eagle of Meaux," as Hallam calls him, "lordly of form, fierce of eye, and terrible in his beak and claws."

[k] Bossuet (1627—1704), Bishop of Condom in 1669, which he resigned on being appointed Tutor to the Dauphin; in 1681 Bishop of Meaux.

sincere as to represent it without disguise." The controversy which followed between the two does not fall within the scope of this work; the above incident is only related to show how Wake, when he was only thirty years of age, won his spurs against the greatest controversialist of the day.

In 1693 Wake published "An English version of the Genuine Epistles of the Apostolical Fathers, with a preliminary discourse concerning the use of those Fathers," a work of great importance at a time when, under the Latitudinarian Bishops, a theological apathy had set in, and the Patristic writings were neglected and unread, or if read, subjected only to disparagement. In that work he advocates the study of the early Fathers of the Church on the ground "that they were cotemporary with the Apostles and instructed by them; that they were men of an eminent character in the Church, and therefore could not be ignorant of what was taught in it; that they were careful to preserve the doctrine of Christ in its purity and to oppose such as went about to corrupt it; . . . that they were endued with a large portion of the Holy Spirit, and as such could hardly err in what they delivered as the Gospel of Christ; and that their writings were approved by the Church of those days which could not be mistaken in its approbation of them." In the same year Wake was appointed to the Rectory of St. James's, Westminster. In the Convocation Controversy (his part in which has been already narrated) the chief work was Wake's; "The state of the Church and Clergy of England in their Councils, Synods, Convocations, Conventions, and other public Assemblies, historically deduced, from the Conversion of the Saxons to the present time, 1703," which was decisive of the Controversy in general. In 1701 Wake was appointed Dean of Exeter, in 1705 Bishop of Lincoln, in 1716 Archbishop of Canterbury.

At the time that Wake became Archbishop, France was much agitated by the Bull "Unigenitus[1]," which, dated September 8, 1713, was issued by Pope Clement XI., and condemned one hundred and one propositions extracted from Pasquier Quesnel's " Le Nouveau Testament en Francois." Quesnel's book, which was written by him with the view of propagating Jansenism, was published with the approval of Noailles, Bishop of Chalons[m], and had an immense sale, and made many converts. The Bull, which Clement was induced to issue by Louis XIV. and the Jesuits, occasioned great commotion in France. Noailles and many other Prelates and eminent people in that country refused to receive it, and appealed from the papal authority to that of a general Council[n].

At this time, and under such circumstances, an

---

[1] From its first words, "Unigenitus Dei Filius."
[m] Afterwards Archbishop of Paris.
[n] At a later period, however, Noailles accepted the Bull.

attempt, conducted on one side by Dr. Wake, Archbishop of Canterbury, and on the other by Du Pin, Head of the Theological College of the Sorbonne, was made to unite the Anglican and Gallican Churches. Du Pin, encouraged by some letters which had passed between Dr. Wake and Mr. Beauvoir, Chaplain to the British Embassy at Paris, expressed a desire for a union between the two Churches, for that "the differences between them on most points were not so great as to render a reconciliation impracticable," and the large-hearted Archbishop willingly entered into a correspondence with Du Pin for that object[o]. From first to last Wake insisted on the orthodoxy of the English Church, and exhorted Du Pin to maintain, if not to enlarge, the rights of the Gallican Church, and he thought such a reformation might be effected that not only the most rational Protestants, but many Roman Catholics also, might be induced to join the Church of England. In March, 1718, Dr. Patrick Piers de Girardin, one of the Doctors of the Sorbonne, in a discourse delivered before that Society, exhorted the Doctors to revise the doctrines and rules of the Gallican Church, in order to show that they did not hold every ultramontane

---

[o] The Author of the "Confessional" says, "this pretended Champion of the Protestant Religion had set on foot a project for union with a Popish Church, and that with concessions in favour of the grossest superstitions and idolatry." This is the very thing Wake did *not* do.

doctrine, and thus to render a reconciliation with the English Church more feasible than one with the Greek Church could ever be. At the request of Wake, Dr. Du Pin drew up, with the sanction of the Sorbonne, his "Commonitorium," which took a review of the XXXIX. Articles, to the greater part of which it offered no objection;—it allowed the Celebration of the Holy Eucharist in both Kinds; the performance of Divine Service in the vulgar tongue, and the marriage of the Clergy; whilst as to the ultimate settlement of the doctrine concerning Purgatory, Indulgences, the veneration of Saints, relics or images, he thought there would be no difficulty. To this "Commonitorium" the Archbishop declined to bind himself; he refused to allow the Pope a primacy of jurisdiction by divine right, but was willing to concede him a primacy of rank and honour as being the Bishop of what once had been the Imperial City;—on no other terms could a union be effected. The principle from which Wake started was the Independence of every National Church; he advocated an agreement between the Anglican and Gallican Churches on points of doctrine; "in other matters a difference should be allowed until God should bring them to a union in them also." It was simply a proposal for a union between the Anglican and Gallican Churches; there was no question of a general reunion of the divided Churches of Western Christendom. It is very questionable whether even such a union as Wake advocated would ever have been sanctioned under George I. and the Latitudinarian Bishops; the correspondence, however, was suddenly cut short, for when Wake's Letters, dated May 1, 1719, reached Paris, Du Pin was dead. The Jesuits were furious at what had taken place between the two Churches; the Abbé Dubois interfered, and Dr. de Girardin was threatened with the Bastile; Pope Clement XI. expressed his admiration for Wake, and declared it was a pity he was not a member of the Roman Catholic Church.

Still the Catholicity of the English Church made its mark upon its Gallican neighbour, and in 1723 Dr. Courayer, a Member of the Order of St. Benedict, and Canon and Librarian of the Abbey of St. Geneviéve at Paris, published a work which was translated into English under the title of "A Dissertation on the Validity of the Ordination of the English, and of the succession of the Bishops of the Anglican Church." The value of this work is that Courayer was himself a Roman Catholic, and a man of learning and eminence, and that he did not write for the purpose of defending the English Church; on the contrary, as to our separation from Rome at the Reformation, he was against us; but as to our Ordinations he says: "The validity of the English Ordinations stands upon the strongest evidence, has the most authenticated acts, the most express testimonies, the most uncontested facts to oppose to fable and forgery, to mistaken reasonings, and unauthenticated deductions;" that the Roman custom of reordaining English Priests is "contrary to all the received maxims of the Church in the matter of reordination, and that it is founded upon opinions that are abandoned, and upon doubts that have no foundation [p]." On August 27, 1727, the University of Oxford conferred upon Courayer the Degree of D.C.L.; but Cardinal Noailles, the Bishop of Marseilles, and other Gallican Bishops siding against him, he thought it the safer plan to leave France, and in 1728 took refuge in England; he was received here with the greatest kindness from Archbishop Wake, Bishops Sherlock and Hare, and many of the Aristocracy; a pension of £100 a year, which Queen Caroline doubled, was settled upon him; and he died a Roman Catholic on October 17, 1776, at the age of 95 years, and was buried in the cloisters of Westminster Abbey.

---

[p] In allusion to the fiction of the "Nag's Head."

CHAPTER III.

THE NONJURING SCHISM.

WE have in a former chapter[a] given an account of the secession from the Church of the Nonjurors who refused to take the oaths to William and Mary; we must now carry on their history to the time when, whatever their position may have been at first, they lapsed into formal schism.

For some time before and after the suspension of the Bishops, meetings, which their enemies stigmatized as the "Lambeth Club," or the "Holy Jacobite Club," attended by the Bishops of Norwich, Ely, Bath and Wells, and Peterborough, were held, under the Presidency of Sancroft, at Lambeth Palace, to deliberate on the affairs of the Church. On February 9, 1692, Sancroft executed a deed through which he delegated his Archiepiscopal functions to Lloyd, Bishop of Norwich[b]. He styles himself "a humble Minister of the Metropolitan Church of Canterbury," and dates it from "my poor cottage which is not

---

[a] Part I. chap. iv.
[b] "Te vicarium meum ad præmissa, rerumque mearum ac negotiorum actorem, factorem, et nuntium generalem, vigore harum Literarum, eligo, facio, et constituo."

yet made a sufficient covering for me in this sharp winter, here in Friesingfield[c], at this time even very hard frozen, situated within the bounds of your Diocese," whither, he says in an earlier part of the same document, he had retired, " seeking where in my old age I may rest my weary head[d]."

In May, 1693, Hickes, the deprived Dean of Worcester, was (by the wish as it was said of King James) despatched to St. Germains, with a request that the deposed monarch would, agreeably to the Statute of Henry VIII., nominate two out of the number of the Nonjurors (a list of whom Hickes took with him) as Suffragan Bishops. James accordingly, after first consulting the Pope, the Archbishop of Paris, and Bossuet, Bishop of Meaux, nominated Hickes and Wagstaffe, who in November, 1694 (and consequently after Sancroft was dead), were consecrated by Bishops Lloyd, Turner, and White, in the presence, as was said, of the Earl of Clarendon, Hickes as Suffragan Bishop of Thetford, and Wagstaffe of Ipswich. Efforts were made, but in vain, to obtain Ken's approval to this proceeding.

The first generation of Nonjurors[e], as they differed on the grounds on which they refused to take the oath, differed also in their attitude to the Church. Some did not go so far as others. Bishop Frampton, for instance, attended the services of his parish church,

---

[c] " In campo gelido."   [d] " Ubi fessus senio requiescerem."
[e] Part I. chap. iv.

The Nonjuring Schism. 343

and frequently catechized the children in the afternoon, and expounded to them the sermon which they had heard. Nelson was in the habit of expressing his dissent when the Royal Titles were given to the King and Queen. Mr. Cherry used to rise from his knees when the names of the King and Queen were introduced, and to stand facing the congregation. Dodwell was firm in his adherence to those whom he called the "invalidly deprived Fathers," and used to lull his conscience by sliding off his knees and sitting on his hassock. Other Jacobite worshippers satisfied themselves, to the great amusement of their neighbours, by turning over the leaves of their Prayer-Books with unnecessary vehemence so as to avoid hearing the unpalatable names.

The Nonjurors differed also in their opinions as to the duration of their separation from the Church. Ken and Frampton thought that the question as to the oaths only affected those who, having already taken them to James, were afterwards in the lifetime of that King required to take them afresh to William and Mary. At an early period of the separation, after the death of Bishop White in 1698, and of Turner in 1700, when Ken, Lloyd, and Frampton were the survivors of the deprived Bishops, Ken wrote to Hickes (whose answer has not been preserved), expressing an opinion that the time had arrived for their return to the Church.

When King James died in 1701, it might have been hoped that the breach would have been healed; but unfortunately the Oath of Abjuration which required all Clergymen, Fellows of Colleges, and Schoolmasters, to acknowledge William not only (as before) *de facto*, but also *de jure*, King, embittered the feelings of the Nonjurors, and widened the breach by adding to their number new converts.

During the reign of Queen Anne, who was probably in heart no enemy to their Jacobite feelings, the Nonjurors were allowed to rest in peace and tranquillity, and had her reign been prolonged, probably most of them would have returned to the Church; her early death, however, put an end to all their hopes, and to the restoration of the Pretender. At the time of the Rebellion of 1715, the Nonjurors and Jacobites naturally fell under suspicion; they were in consequence subjected to much harsh treatment, and the Oath of Abjuration was tendered to all suspected persons. It was at that time that William Law, the successful opponent of Hoadly in the Bangorian Controversy, refused to take the oath, and was deprived of his Fellowship at Emmanuel College, Cambridge.

But in 1710, on the death of Lloyd, who, with the exception of Ken himself, was the last of the Nonjuring Bishops, Nelson and Dodwell wrote to Ken asking if he had any longer any claim upon their allegiance, and they received from him the answer that "he was always against that practice which he saw would perpetuate the schism.... He apprehended it was the judgment of his brethren, that the death of the canonical Bishops would render the invaders canonical, in regard the schism is not to last always [f]." Queen Anne, as already stated, offered to reinstate Ken in his bishopric; Ken, therefore, might, after that offer was made and refused, be considered to have willingly vacated his See. So Nelson and Dodwell and many of the more moderate Nonjurors returned to the Church; Nelson being received back by his friend Dr. Sharp, Archbishop of York, in the church of St. Mildred's, Poultry, where he received the Holy Communion for the first time since the Revolution [g]. Dodwell living, as he did, in the Diocese of Burnet, who of all the Bishops was the most obnoxious to the Nonjurors, bravely tendered his obedience to his Diocesan; but he went out of his way to speak of the "loose Latitudinarian principles of the day." In his answer to Dodwell Burnet styled him "one of the most conceited men of the age." Dodwell, however, had only one year to live, and had seen enough and suffered enough in his time from quarrels and controversies; so he

---

[f] Dodwell wrote a Treatise, "The Case in View," as to what the duties of the Nonjurors would be when the Nonjuring Bishops should die; and when the Nonjuring Sees were canonically vacated he wrote another Treatise, "The Case in Fact."

Life of Sharp, by his Son, ii. 31.

bore the reproof and returned a humble answer. Burnet, who was never a hard or unforgiving opponent, was softened, and wrote on April 24, 1711, a kindly reply, in which he said, "I send two of my Expositions of the Church Catechism to your children; I pray God to bless you and them [h]."

When Ken died in 1711, all the first generation of Nonjuring Bishops were dead, and Wagstaffe died in 1712. As Hickes' Diocesan (Lloyd) had died in 1710, there can be no question that Hickes' Commission as Suffragan was dissolved; when therefore (as we shall presently see) he ordained other Priests as Bishops, he was formally guilty of schism, and the Scotch Bishops whom he summoned to assist him were acting beyond their jurisdiction in consecrating Bishops within the Province of Canterbury.

Hickes was now the Leader of the Nonjuring Community. George Hickes (1642—1715) educated at St. John's and Magdalen Colleges, Oxford, and afterwards a Fellow of Lincoln, was one of the most learned Anglo-Saxon Scholars of the day. In 1680 he was made a Prebendary of Worcester, and in the same year was appointed by Archbishop Sancroft to the Vicarage of All-Hallows, Barking. In the following year he became Chaplain in Ordinary to the King, in 1683 Dean of Worcester, and when the Bishopric of Bristol fell vacant in the following year

---

[h] Secretan's Nelson, p. 76.

the King is reported to have said he could not offer him so poor a Bishopric, but that if he would accept it, he might hold the Deanery of Worcester *in commendam*. What Hickes' answer was does not appear; but, as he was a High Churchman, all hopes of preferment under James II. vanished. He refused to take the oaths to William and Mary, and was deprived of his Deanery; but on reading in the Gazette the appointment of Mr. Talbot[1] to his Deanery, he affixed the following Protest to the door of Worcester Cathedral: "Whereas the office, place, and dignity of Dean of this Cathedral Church of Worcester was given and presented unto me for a freehold during my natural life by Letters Patent under the Broad Seal of King Charles II. ... whereas I am given to understand that my right to the said office and dignity has of late been called in question, and that one Mr. Talbot, M.A., prefers a title to the same.... I do hereby publicly protest and declare that I do claim a legal right and title to the said office and dignity of Dean against the said Mr. Talbot and all other persons pretending title to the same.... I do hereby dissent as of no force against this my declared right to the office, place, and dignity of Dean of this Cathedral Church." By this protest Hickes exposed himself to danger, and expecting the resentment of the government, he was

---

[1] Afterwards Bishop successively of Oxford, Salisbury, and Durham.

obliged for several years to live hidden in the house of White Kennet (a man of very different Church principles to himself), and was accustomed to wear a layman's dress in order to escape notice. The part he took in continuing the Nonjuring Schism we shall notice presently.

William Law (1686—1761) became a Fellow of Emmanuel College, Cambridge, in 1711. He was not in the number of those who refused to take the oaths to William and Mary, and it was not until he was called upon to take the oath of Abjuration unto George I. that he became a Nonjuror, whereupon he was deprived of his Fellowship, and became one of the saintliest and one of the most learned of their number. Following the example of many Nonjurors who took tutorships in the families of noblemen and gentlemen, he became Tutor, about 1727, at Putney, to Edward Gibbon, the father of the Historian, where he resided as "the most honoured friend and spiritual adviser of the whole family[k]," and where he left in the memory of the family the character "of a worthy and pious man, who believed all that he professed, and professed all that he believed." The reputation he gained as a Controversial writer from his "Three Letters to Hoadly" has been already noticed, but his fame chiefly rests on his "Treatise on Christian Perfection," and "The

---

[k] Gibbon's "Memoirs of my Life and Writings."

Serious Call to a Devout and Holy Life adapted to the state and condition of all orders of Christians." His "Serious Call," written in 1726, probably made an impression greater than was produced by any religious book of the eighteenth century. To it John Wesley attributed the religious movement which bears his name. Bishop Warburton, who was not generally very delicate in his sentiments, said (although in very different language) the same thing: "Mr. William Law begat Methodism, and Count Zinzendorf rocked the cradle[1]." Thus it appears from Wesley's own statement that a High Churchman and a Nonjuror was the originator of Methodism. Dr. Johnson said indeed that Law was no reasoner; but what he meant by that saying it is difficult to understand, for Law's "Three Letters to Hoadly" are a masterpiece of close and sound reasoning. But it is more pleasant and more satisfactory to learn that to the "Serious Call" Dr. Johnson attributes his first religious impressions. He tells us he had been a "lax talker against religion;" that when he went to Oxford he took up the "Serious Call," expecting to find it a dull book, and perhaps to laugh at it; but he says, "I found Law an overmatch for me; and that was the first occasion of my thinking in earnest about religion, after I became capable of rational enquiry." Similarly, to the "Seri-

---

[1] In another place he said, "The Devil acted as midwife to Mr. Wesley's new-born babes."

ous Call," Charles Wesley, George Whitfield, Henry Venn, and Scott the Commentator confess their acknowledgments for religious impressions: but with the later Evangelical development Law had little to do; he was too sound a Churchman for them, and not a sufficiently violent opponent of Rome to please them; he, like many others who are not violent Protestants, was charged with Romanism; the Evangelicals complained (and this charge was not altogether groundless) that there was too little gospel teaching in it, and transferred their affections to a work (which in no other respect except with regard to their narrow views could be compared to it), Hervey's "Theron and Aspasio [m]."

In his early life Law had been deeply impressed with the writings of the Christian Mystics, but it was not until 1734 that he embraced the views of Jacob Behmer, whom he pronounces to be "the strongest, the plainest, the most open, intelligible, awaking, and convincing writer that ever was." But to the very end of his life, although he was frequently regarded as a *mere mystic* and hopeless enthusiast, Law never left hold of the Catholic doctrines of the Church to which he had adhered through life.

After the death of Wagstaffe in 1712, Hickes (as has been said before) was the only Nonjuring Bishop left, and he determined to continue the Nonjuring Epis-

---

[m] See Overton's Life of Law.

copate. But as three Bishops are required for a canonical consecration of a Bishop, he had recourse to the Bishops of Scotland, and by the aid of the Scottish Bishops, Campbell and Gadderer, he consecrated, in 1713, Jeremy Collier, the Ecclesiastical Historian[n], Samuel Hawes, and Nathaniel Spinckes as Bishops; and when Hickes died in 1715, these three, in 1716, consecrated two more Bishops, Gandy and Brett.

At this period in the history of the Nonjurors an extremely interesting, although fruitless, correspondence commenced between the Nonjuring Bishops and the Patriarchs of the Oriental Church, of which we have an account drawn up by Brett soon after the scheme failed [o].

When Arsenius, Archbishop of Thebais, was, in 1716, on a visit to London for the purpose of soliciting assistance for his afflicted brethren in Alexandria, "A Proposal for a Concordate between the Orthodox and *Catholic Remnant of the British Churches* and the Catholic and Apostolic Oriental Church" was drawn up by the Nonjuring Bishops, and translated into Greek by Spinckes. This document Arsenius carried with him to Moscow, where the Czar was so interested in, and so highly approved of, the movement,

---

[n] The first volume of his "Ecclesiastical History" was published in 1708, the second in 1714.

[o] The account of the correspondence drawn up by Brett is preserved in Bishop Jolly's MSS., and will be found in Lathbury's *Nonjurors*, p. 310.

that he sent it by the Proto-Syncellus to the Patriarch of Alexandria, to be communicated by him to the other Patriarchs. The principal heads of the Nonjuring proposal were: that whilst the Canonical rights of the Patriarchs of Antioch, Alexandria, and Constantinople were recognised, and an equality of honour with the Bishop of Rome given to the Patriarch of Constantinople, a principality of Order be allowed to the See of Jerusalem as the true mother Church and principal of Ecclesiastical unity, whence all other Churches have been derived. That the Catholic Remnant of the British Churches be reciprocally acknowledged as part of the Catholic Church. "In order to establish such a Concordate, until a firm and perfect union can be fixed, *the suffering Catholic Bishops of the old constitution of Great Britain*" next mention some points in which they agree and other points of disagreement with the Eastern Church. They agree—that the Holy Ghost is Consubstantial with the Father and the Son, and they explain the Procession of the Holy Ghost to mean nothing more than that He is sent forth by the Son from the Father; that the Holy Communion ought to be received in both Kinds, and that in this respect the Latin Church is in error; that there is an intermediate state in which those departed this life wait in hope and join in the worship of the Church Militant, but that there is no Purgatorial fire and no redemption of souls out of the fire of Purgatory by the suffrages of the living. The points in which they disagreed were :—with regard to General Councils having the same authority as the Bible; as to the honours due to the Mother of our Lord; to the Invocation of Saints; Transubstantiation; and the worship of Images.

The answer of the Eastern Patriarchs to these proposals was dated from St. Petersburgh, August 21, 1721, and was entitled "The Answer from the Orthodox of the East to the proposals sent from Britain for a union and agreement with the Oriental Church."

The Patriarchs refused to make any concessions, and they gave their reasons at length :—The "Oriental Church, the Immaculate Bride of the Lord, has never at any time admitted any novelty, nor will at all allow of any. And why should they have the preference given to Jerusalem? .... The Holy Church of Christ with us consists of four pillars, namely, the four Patriarchs, and continues firm and immovable. The first in order is the Patriarch of Constantinople; the second the Pope of Alexandria; the third of Antioch; the fourth of Jerusalem." Still, "if those who are called the remains of the primitive orthodoxy" have any particular preference to the Apostolical throne of Jerusalem, "we grant and allow it, only let them not despise the ancient order, nor accuse it of error, nor reject it." But on this point they add: "It is necessary also that he (the Patriarch of Jerusalem) either immediately or by deputation, consecrate the British Bishops by the Grace of the Holy Spirit, no other Patriarch, but that of Jerusalem, daring to ordain in Britain, or to enter upon his jurisdiction." If things to be revived needed a Synodical examination, they promise to submit them "to a Council of the Universal Church."

As to the Liturgy:—"The remnant of primitive piety," if united to them, should make use of the Liturgy of the Oriental Orthodox Church, that, viz., which was written by St. James, the brother of God, but abbreviated by St. Basil, and again epitomized by St. Chrysostom. As to the English Liturgy, they had neither seen nor read it, but they were suspicious of it, because that many various heresies, and schisms, and sects have arisen in those parts. As to the other points of agreement, they generally concur, but they state their belief in Seven Sacraments, although "two only exceed in necessity, and are such as no one can be saved without them."

Then as to the points of disagreement: "This," they say, "is not to be wondered at, for being born and educated in the principles of the Lutheran Calvinists, and possessed with their prejudices, they tenaciously adhere to them, like ivy to a tree, and are hardly drawn off." The proposition relating to the Eucharist the Patriarchs consider to be blasphemous, and they express their belief in Transubstantiation; as to Images, to honour the Saints by pictures is an ancient piece of devotion which they daily practise.

In their reply to the Eastern Patriarchs, after thanking them for their answers, the Nonjurors express confidence in an appeal to Scripture and to the Primitive Church, which determining rule is common to both Churches. In the claims of the Patriarchs they generally concur, but they conceive that the British Bishops may remain independent of all Patriarchs. As to the charge of Lutheran Calvinism, they declare that none of its distinguishing features can be charged against them. But as to the claim of the Patriarchs for seven General Councils as of equal authority to the Holy Scriptures, although they accept the first six General Councils, yet they could not advance so far as to believe the Fathers of those Councils to be assisted with an equal degree of Inspiration with the Prophets, Evangelists, and Apostles; and with regard to the Seventh Council assembled at Nice they could not assent to the giving even the worship "*Dulia* to angels or departed Saints." With regard to Transubstantiation, they could not accept it, for it had no foundation in Scripture, and was " plainly denied by the most celebrated Fathers of the Primitive Church."

The Nonjurors conclude : " Having represented the difference between us, we are now to suggest a temper and a compromise between us." They observe, that if liberty should be accorded on the points of disagreement; if their Patriarchal Lordships would remember that Christianity is no gradual religion, but was left entire by the Evangelists and Apostles; if they would be governed not by the precedents of later times, but by the first four centuries (not excluding the fifth), and not hold themselves unalterably bound by the decisions of the East in the eighth century, which was even then opposed by an equal authority in the West; then they were not without hope that " the Orthodox Oriental Church and the Catholic Remnant in Britain may at last join in the solemnities of Religion, and be much more intimately one fold under one Shepherd, Jesus Christ."

This reply, dated May 29, 1722, was delivered to some Greeks in London, to be by them transmitted to the four Eastern patriarchs. A Letter was also addressed to Arsenius signed by—

Archibaldus (Campbell) Scoto-Britanniæ Episcopus.

Jacobus (Gadderer) Scoto-Britanniæ Episcopus.

Jeremias (Collier) Primus Anglo-Britanniæ Episcopus.

Thomas (Brett) Anglo-Britanniæ Episcopus.

In a letter written in 1722 to the Nonjurors from Moscow, Arsenius stated that it was the wish of the Emperor that two of the party should proceed to Russia for the purpose of mutual conference. The same proposal was made in a letter dated August

25th, 1723, from the Russian Governing Synod, who in the next year also forwarded another letter to the Nonjuring Bishops. This document is addressed, " To the most Reverend the Bishops of the Catholic Church of Great Britain, our dearest brothers." A synod had been assembled to consider the answer of the Nonjuring Bishops, and that answer was now transmitted to England. It is called "The Orthodox Confession of the Apostolical, Catholic, and Oriental Church of Christ." They state that "it is neither lawful to add anything to their doctrines nor to take anything from them; and that those who are disposed to agree with us in the divine doctrines of the Orthodox Faith must necessarily follow and submit to what has been defined and determined by ancient Fathers and the holy Œcumenical Synods from the time of the Apostles and their holy successors, the Fathers of our Church, to this time. We say they must submit to them with sincerity and obedience, and without any scruple or dispute. And this is a sufficient answer to what you have written."

To send deputies to Russia, as the Czar proposed, would have sorely taxed the resources of the Nonjurors. Shortly afterwards, however, the Czar, who had befriended the movement, died, and thus the matter was dropped. The indiscretion also of the Patriarch of Jerusalem in sending copies of the proposal to Archbishop Wake, knocked the scheme on the head; Wake, who probably thought the whole affair unworthy of notice, let the matter rest; he did not wish to expose the papers and to subject the Nonjurors to ridicule and misrepresentation [p].

Meanwhile, and shortly after the proposal to the Greek Church was made by the Nonjurors, a breach of communion—a schism within a schism—sprang up in their ranks, and the Nonjurors became split up into two parties, with respect to what were called "the Usages." Collier, the Historian, who, since the death of Hickes, had been their leader, together with Brett and Campbell, the Scottish Bishop, advocated a return to the usages sanctioned under the first Prayer-Book of King Edward VI., and in 1717 published a reprint of the First Communion Book. On the other hand Spinckes, Hawes, and Gandy wished to adhere to the Prayer-Book of 1662 [q]. In 1718 the two parties separated from each other, and each, by the aid of the Scottish Bishops, consecrated Bishops for their own party. Thus (on the side of the Non-usagers) Bedford and Tayler were in 1721 consecrated by Hawes, Spinckes, and Gandy; in 1724 Whelton and Talbot by Tayler; in 1725 Black-

---

[p] Lathbury's Nonjurors, p. 357.

[q] The *usages* as proposed were four in number: (1) The Mixed Chalice; (2) Prayer for, instead of mere commemoration of, the departed; (3) The Invocation of the Holy Ghost upon the Bread and Wine; (4) The Oblatory Prayer after the Prayer of Consecration.

bourn and Hall by Spinckes, Gandy, and Doughty; in 1728 Rawlinson by Gandy, Doughty, and Blackbourn; and Smith by Gandy, Blackbourn, and Robinson. On the side of the Usagers, in 1722 Griffin was consecrated by Collier, Campbell, and Brett; in 1727 Thomas Brett, jun., by Brett, Griffin, and Campbell. After the death of the two principals (that of Collier in 1726 and of Spinckes in 1727) the separation ended, and a reunion was for a time effected, and from that time forward the Usages were adopted by the whole body; in 1731 Mawman was consecrated by Brett, T. Brett, jun., and Smith; and in 1741 Gordon, by Brett, Smith, and Mawman. Gordon was the last of the *regular* Nonjurors. But there was an irregular offshoot, which the regular body refused to recognise, on the ground that their first consecrations were irregular; thus, Lawrence[r] was consecrated by the Scottish Bishop, Campbell, acting on his own authority; Deacon was consecrated by Campbell and Lawrence; and Brown (whose real name is supposed to have been Johnston, a brother of the Marquis of Annandale) was consecrated by Deacon alone; Price and Cartwright were consecrated by Deacon, Garnet and Boothe by Cartwright. Differences arose between the two parties, Brett being the head of the regular party, Campbell and Lawrence of the Separatists, the only bond of union

---

[r] Author of "Lay Baptism Invalid."

between them being enmity to the Church of England; the failure of the Rebellion of 1745 enfeebled the party; the firm establishment of the House of Hanover on the accession of George III. completed its ruin; their numbers dwindled away; Cartwright formally renounced the schism before the end of the century, and on the death of Boothe in 1805 the Nonjurors became extinct.

The above account, we are aware, does not afford to most readers an interesting study, but, however, the history of the Nonjurors, whether the earlier or later generation, and of their position with regard to the Church in the eighteenth century, could not be altogether omitted. And before parting with them we must notice one or two matters connected with the Nonjurors which have at present been omitted. In 1696, at the execution, for their complicity in a plot against William III., of Sir John Friend and Sir William Perkins, Collier, with two other clergymen, Cook and Snatt, got into trouble by giving them public absolution on the scaffold. Collier defended himself; Sir William Perkins (he asserted) had *desired* that absolution should be pronounced on the day of execution, but Collier was refused admittance to the prison, and therefore was obliged to give him absolution at the place of execution *by the imposition of hands*, using the Form in the *Visitation of the Sick*. Some "animadversions" on Collier's "Defence" were published by command of Archbishop

Tenison by Hody[s], in which he stated that no form or ceremony ought to be used by any clergyman which was not positively enjoined by the Church. In reply to this, Collier instanced the case of Bishop Sanderson, who "about a day before his death desired his chaplain, Mr. Pullen, to give him absolution; and at his performing that office, he pulled off his cap that Mr. Pullen might lay his hand upon his bare head." Cook and Snatt were committed to prison on a charge of High Treason; Collier absconded, and was outlawed in consequence, although he was afterwards allowed to return and to pursue his literary pursuits in peace.

Of Jeremy Collier (1650—1726) Lord Macaulay says[t]: "We shall not be suspected of regarding the Politics or Theology of Collier with partiality; but we believe him to have been as honest and courageous a man as ever lived[u]." At the end of the seventeenth

---

[s] Humphrey Hody (1659—1706), elected in 1684 a Fellow of Wadham; in 1698 appointed Professor of Greek; in 1704 Archdeacon of Oxford; in 1701 he bore an important part in the Convocation Controversy, and published "A History of English Councils and Convocations," and dying in 1706 was buried in the chapel of Wadham College, to which he was a liberal benefactor.

[t] Essays, ii. 172.

[u] Lord Macaulay seems to have taken a particular fancy to Collier. In his History he says of him, "He was, in the full force of the words, a good man. He was also a man of eminent abilities, a great master of sarcasm, a great master of rhetoric.

century the stage was disgraced with the worst form of ribaldry and obscenity, the principal play-writers vieing with each other in producing the most licentious comedies. In 1698 Collier published his "Short view of the Profaneness and Immorality of the English Stage," in which he exposed the plays of Dryden, Vanbrugh, Wycherley, and Congreve. The success of the *Short View* was immense, and by order of the King, the Master of the Revels (as the officer was called who presided over those amusements) was authorized not to license any plays which contained irreligious or immoral expressions; a speedy reform in the lighter literature of the day was the result, and this improvement was due to Collier.

In 1717 Lawrence Howell, who had in 1712 been ordained Priest by Hickes, was committed to Newgate for writing a Pamphlet, "The case of Schism in the Church of England truly stated," in which he argued that the Clergy who took the oath were schismatics. He was further sentenced to pay a fine of £500, to three years' imprisonment, and to find four securities till the fine was paid, in £500 each, himself to give security for £1,000, and to be twice whipped. He asked, "Who will whip a clergyman?" The Court told him it did not recognise him as a clergyman, because his ordination by a Nonjuror was illegal; he was then ordered to be stripped of his

His ready though undigested learning was of immense extent."
—Hist., iii. 459.

gown in Court. The corporal part of the punishment was remitted, but he died a prisoner in Newgate in 1720.

That the Nonjurors were sometimes far from delicate in manifesting their animosity to the Church appears in the case of Whelton. White Kennet, Dean of Peterborough, had rendered himself so obnoxious to the Nonjurors, that Whelton, who was at the time Rector of Whitechapel, caused his portrait to be introduced into an Altar-piece in that church in the character of Judas Iscariot. That prominent place had been intended for Burnet, but the plan was changed, and it was assigned to Kennet instead. Kennet, whilst shooting in 1689, had been wounded by the explosion of his gun, and always afterwards wore a velvet patch on his forehead, so that his portrait was easily recognised by every one. The people went in crowds to the church to see this indecent exhibition, and the portrait had to be removed by order of the Bishop of London. In 1710 Whelton was, on account of a sermon which he had preached, deprived of his Living by the government, and joined the Nonjurors. After his consecration as a Nonjuring Bishop (although on account of its uncanonical character he was never recognised as such by the Nonjuring body generally) he, together with Talbot, who was the oldest Missionary of the S.P.G., went to America, where he exercised his Episcopal functions in confirming, and probably in some cases ordaining also. He was, however, ordered on his allegiance to return to England, and Talbot was deprived of his office of Missionary by the Society[x].

There was no doubt much to blame in the conduct of the Nonjurors, but they have had a hard measure meted out to them by our popular historians. If we form our estimate from Macaulay, or Hallam, or Buckle, or Stanhope, or Green, or (that "fons et origo mali") Bishop Burnet, we should be judging the Nonjurors on the testimony of men who were utterly out of sympathy with them in principles and temperament[y]. Our popular historians are obviously biassed in their judgment. The leader of the Nonjurors was certainly Archbishop Sancroft; and it is not easy to find one contemporary writer, except Burnet, who does not speak of him with the highest praise; and Burnet's charges were soon completely refuted[z]. Of both generations of Nonjurors alike it may be said that they were the salt of the Church in those days, and that their loss at such a time was irreparable. They were the legitimate successors, although perhaps not the equals, of Andrewes, and Hammond, and Jeremy Taylor, and of that noble galaxy of Divines of the seventeenth century, of whom it was said "Clerus Anglicanus stupor mundi." With such names as

---

[x] Wilberforce's Hist. of the American Church, p. 161.
[y] Ch. Quar., July, 1885.
[z] Dean Swift branded Burnet's charge against Sancroft as "false as hell."

Bentley, and Berkeley, and Waterland, and Butler, and Warburton, besides those of Bingham, Wall, Prideaux, and many others, it cannot be said that during the eighteenth century there was any lack of champions of the Faith who could meet assailants with whom no arguments from Scripture and the Fathers availed, with weapons taken from their own armoury; yet the learning which the Nonjurors took out with them—the knowledge of the Fathers, and ancient Liturgies, and Primitive Ritual and Discipline— was that very kind of learning which was most needed to counteract the new School of Theology which was coming to the front. And although the Nonjuring theology (as a whole) stands on a lower level, and has in it a larger negative and Protestant element, than that of the great Caroline Divines of the seventeenth century—a fact obviously due to the circumstance that whilst Puritanism was the formidable enemy in the earlier period, Romanism had taken its place after the accession of James II.—yet the Nonjurors hold an important place in the Theology of the last and of the present centuries. Dodwell in ancient history, Collier and Carte in modern history, Parker as a commentator, Baker and Hickes as antiquaries, Howell as a canonist, Hickes and Brett in theology, Kettlewell, Nelson, Law, Spinckes, and Deacon in devotional theology, Leslie as a Polemic—these are names surpassed by none except those of Bull and Butler; and when we think of these and other such names we shall understand how disastrous to the Church the reign of William III. was. The deprivation of the Nonjurors might have been a necessity; but it was a very disastrous necessity; doubly disastrous at a time when Latitudinarians were appointed to high places in the Church in the place of those very persons who were most needed to compensate the defects which Latitudinarian theology introduced into the Church.

CHAPTER IV.

THE DEISTICAL CONTROVERSY.

WE have already described the early phases of the Trinitarian Controversy, in which first Sherlock and South, and afterwards Whiston and Clarke, were the principal actors. The same soil which was congenial to heresy was congenial also to infidelity; and Anti-Trinitarianism, if it rejected Atheism and Polytheism, was certainly favourable to Deism. There can be little doubt that to the exaggerated principles of Toleration, and the prevalent Latitudinarianism of the day, the scepticism and infidelity, which raged since the beginning of the eighteenth century, were mainly attributable. Following the path mapped out by the Latitudinarian Bishops people began to ask—What is truth? How is truth to be found? So long as the Church was acknowledged to be the centre of unity, and Catholicity the test of orthodoxy, the standpoint of Christianity was clear enough; but, contended the Rationalist, the authority of the Church has now been invaded and denied, and the supremacy of private judgment established by Bishops of the Church.

The aphorism of Chillingworth, " The Bible and the Bible only, the religion of Protestants," as advocated by Archbishops Tillotson and Tenison[a], led other people into a different interpretation of the Bible from that of which they approved themselves[b]. Chillingworth discarded everything as inferior to Reason. Reason gives knowledge; Faith gives only belief, which is part of, and therefore inferior to, Reason; by Reason, therefore, we must distinguish between truth and falsehood. Hooker, no less than Chillingworth, advocated the jurisdiction of Reason, but it was its use, not its abuse, which he advocated; for he added, as the safeguard to Reason, the judgment of the individual ought to bow to the judgment of the Church, as laid down by the General Councils and the voice of Ecclesiastical tradition.

But when once this supremacy of "Reason" was established, and people claimed, each one for himself, to put his own interpretation on the Bible, next came the question, What is the Bible? and then next, Who is this Christ of whom the Bible speaks?

It was thus that the Deists, a race of Freethinkers, scarcely numerous or uniform enough in their teach-

---

[a] The question does not appear to have occurred to them, Who determined what the Bible is? Why are there so many and no more Canonical Books of the Old and New Testament? The answer of course is, The Church; notably the Council of Carthage, A.D. 395.

[b] Collins, the Deist, actually speaks of Archbishop Tillotson as "one whom all English Freethinkers own as their head." Whitfield said of him that "he knew no more of Christianity than Mahomet."

ing to be called a Sect (having a common rendezvous at the Grecian Coffee House near Temple Bar) arose; who rejected all revealed religion, attacked the authority of the Bible, and endeavoured to establish a system utterly subversive of every moral principle; a system under which a person might lead a life of unreserved sensuality under the delusion that "death is an eternal sleep."

Such a system had, although in a mitigated form, been at an earlier period advocated by Lord Herbert of Cherbury (1581—1648), the brother of the saintly George Herbert, who lived during the troublous times of Charles I. He asserted the perfection of Natural Religion, and discarded all extraordinary revelation as unnecessary. Natural Religion he summarized under five heads :—(1) There is a Supreme God; (2) He is to be worshipped; (3) Piety and virtue are the necessary requirements for that worship; (4) Men must forsake their sins and God will pardon them; (5) There are rewards and punishments for good and bad, or, as he sometimes terms it, here and hereafter.

This system was carried much further by Hobbes (1588—1679) the Patriarch, as he has been called, of Freethinkers. A considerable impulse was given to Freethinking by John Locke (1632—1704), the tendency of whose teaching, though he was no Deist himself, and though he wrote without reference to Theology, and probably without thinking of the logical result of his teaching, was to make Reason the measure and judge of truth, so that the Deists were able to borrow their weapons from his armoury. Locke was no Deist, but those who flooded England with their infidel writings in the eighteenth century only went one step further than Locke, when, in the exercise of their reason, they asserted the supremacy of Natural, and rejected all Revealed Religion.

The Deist, as the name, in contradistinction to the Atheist, implies, believed in some sense in a God. Neither the name nor the opinions of Deism were new. Its name, as applied to the opponents of religion generally, existed in Switzerland in the middle of the sixteenth century, and was thence imported into England; Viret, the contemporary and friend of Calvin, speaks in his *Instruction Chrétienne* (published in 1563) of persons who called themselves Deists.

But the parent of English Deism was René Descartes (1596—1650), who first formulated the principle that nothing is true save what is evident to the reason, and that *evidence* is the test of truth. Born at La Haye in Touraine, he was educated at the Jesuit College of La Flèche, and on the philosophical teaching of the Jesuits he grounded his own plans of philosophy. He was certain of his own existence, because he was certain that he felt and thought. The relation between thought and existence he expressed in the words "Cogito, ergo sum," and on this he grounded his philosophy, that whatever is *clearly and distinctly thought must be true.* The truth of the existence of a Supreme Being he established on the idea of inferiority and omnipotence evolved in us by the consciousness of our own limitations apart from any revelation. We must now turn to the English Deists.

The most famous Deists of the eighteenth century were Toland, Lord Shaftesbury, Collins, Woolston, Tindal, Morgan, Chubb, and Lord Bolingbroke.

In 1696 Toland (1671—1722), an Irishman who had left the Roman Catholic Church and become a Dissenter, put forth the most important Deistical work which had as yet appeared, " Christianity not Mysterious [e]." His object was to make Reason the sole standard of Revelation, and to show that the Gospel contains nothing mysterious nor above reason. He styles himself a Christian, but he asserts that " faith is far from being an implicit assent to anything above reason ; that such a notion directly contradicts the ends of Religion, the nature of man, and the wisdom and goodness of God." He draws a parallel between the ancient heathen and (as he calls them) the *new-coined* Christian mysteries, and says, " I could draw out this parallel much further, but here is enough to show how Christianity became mysterious, and how so divine an institution did, through the craft and

---

[e] Or, "A Discourse showing that there is nothing in the Gospel contrary to Reason, nor above it, and that no Christian Doctrine can be properly called a Mystery."

ambition of Priests and philosophers, degenerate into mere Paganism." The work was censured in England by the Lower House of Convocation, and condemned by a committee of religion in the Irish Parliament, which ordered the book to be burnt by the common hangman, one member proposing that Toland himself should be burnt; but further proceedings against him were prevented by his flight from the country.

In 1694 he published the "Amyntor [d]," which contained "A Catalogue of Books attributed in the primitive times to Jesus Christ, the Apostles and other eminent persons, with several important observations relating to the Canon of Scripture." He advocated the addition of the Epistles of Clement, Ignatius, Polycarp, and the Shepherd of Hermas to the Canonical books. He raked together spurious gospels and pretended sacred books to a number exceeding eighty, books which bore on them the plainest marks of forgery and imposture, and these he represented as having an equal authority with the four Gospels and the other sacred books of the New Testament. His object was to show that the New Testament deserves no greater credit and is not more reliable than books which are admitted to be forgeries. The principal answers to Toland proceeded from Dr. Stillingfleet in his "Vindication of the Trinity," in which he animadverted on Locke's Essay

---

[d] Or, a defence of his previous publication, "The Life of Milton."

on the Human Understanding, from Dr. Clarke[e], and Dr. Lardner[f].

Lord Shaftesbury (1671—1713, the grandson of the infamous member of the Cabal Ministry), whom Voltaire termed "the boldest of the English Deists," was the author of various works, the principal of which was his "Characteristics of Men, Manners, Opinions, and Times," published in 1711. Lord Shaftesbury wrote for the sake of applause, and in a tone of polished irony, rather than from a love of truth. Though more than once in his writings he expresses sentiments favourable to Christianity, he denounced the doctrine of future rewards and punishments as unphilosophical and of a demoralizing tendency. "It has," he says (to quote one out of many similar passages), "a tendency to create a stricter attention to self-good and private interest, and must insensibly diminish the affection towards public good or the interest of society, and introduces a certain narrowness of spirit, which is observable in devout persons of almost all religions and persuasions." He follows Hobbes in making the civil magistrate the sole judge of religious truth and orthodoxy, and resolves doctrines and opinions in religion, and the authority of what

---

[e] "Some Reflexions on that part of the book called Amyntor, which relates to the writings of the Primitive Fathers and the Canon of the New Testament."
[f] "The Credibility of the Gospel History."

shall be accounted Holy Writ, into the appointment of the State, and talks of the Sovereign answering for us in matters of religion [g]. Like the Deists generally, he intimates that the Gospel is only a scheme propounded by the Clergy for aggrandizing their own power; and says that "the holy Records themselves were no other than the pure invention and artificial compliment of an interested party in behalf of the richest corporation and most profitable monopoly which could be erected in the world [h]." He tells us that the sacred writers "had recourse to humour and diversion as the proper means to promote religion, and strengthen the established faith;" that our Saviour's discourses were sharp, witty, and humourous; and that His miracles were done with a certain air of festivity, and in such a manner that it is impossible not to be moved pleasantly at their recital. He represents Christianity as in the main "a witty, good-natured religion;" he speaks of a "burlesque religion;" and insinuates that there is an artful pretence to cover a deep design, and a scheme laid out for worldly ambition and power. But his works are altogether so mixed up with levity and ridicule, that it is impossible to pronounce when he is jesting and when in earnest. He advocates ridicule as the test of religious truth, there being no mode of ascertaining

---

[g] Characteristics, ii. 353. [h] Ibid., p. 336.

what is really serious and what ridiculous but "by applying ridicule to see if it will bear," since "nothing is ridiculed but what is deformed, and nothing proof against ridicule but what is handsome and just [i]." This position that ridicule is a test of truth, Warburton, in his "Dedication to the Freethinkers," published in 1738, denied. Shaftesbury's works attracted but little criticism, although they were not unnoticed by Berkeley and Warburton, and by Balguy in his "Letter to a Deist [k]."

Anthony Collins (1676—1729, whose works were the text-book of the French Encyclopædists) was educated at Eton and King's College, Cambridge, and was once an intimate friend of Locke, who declared "he had as much love for truth for truth's sake as ever he had met in anybody," but this was before he was the determined foe that he afterwards became to Christianity. Locke, had he lived, would certainly have withdrawn the compliment. In 1709 Collins published "Priestcraft in Perfection," and the controversy which it caused induced him to publish his "Historical and Critical Essay" on the

---

[i] Essays on Enthusiasm and Wit and Humour.

[k] "Concerning the Beauty and Excellency of Moral Virtue, and the support and improvement which it receives from the Christian Religion." John Balguy (1686—1748) took the part of Hoadly in the Bangorian Controversy; he was father of Thomas Balguy (1716—1795), appointed Archdeacon of Winchester by Hoadly, who in 1781 was offered but refused the See of Gloucester.

XXXIX. Articles, in which he attacked the genuineness of the first clause of the XXth. Article[1], as having authority neither from Convocation nor Parliament. In 1713 he published his principal work, "A Discourse of Freethinking [m]," in which he inveighed violently against the Clergy, and spoke of the "pious frauds" of ancient Fathers and modern Clergy, of their forgeries and misstatements, and the narrowness of the clerical mind. He gives a long list of Freethinkers, amongst whom he places Solomon. This work soon after it appeared was answered by Hoadly, who exposed the dishonest insinuations, false reasonings, and pernicious tendency of the treatise; but Collins was completely pulverised by Bentley, at the time Master of Trinity College, Cambridge, who, writing under the pseudonym of Phileleutherus Lipsiensis, exposed his blunders, his frequent mistranslations, his wilful perversions and misrepresentations of the authors whom he quoted; a work for which Bentley received the thanks of the Cambridge Senate, Dr. Sherlock being then Vice-Chancellor of the University.

Bentley's work might have been thought sufficient to silence Collins for the future, but in 1724 he published "A Discourse on the grounds and reasons

---

[1] "The Church hath power to decree Rites and Ceremonies," &c.

[m] "A Discourse of Freethinking, occasioned by the Rise and Growth of a Sect called Freethinkers."

of the Christian Religion." In this work he maintained that our Saviour and His Apostles placed the whole proofs of Christianity upon the prophecies of the Old Testament; those prophecies, as cited in the New Testament as proofs of Christianity, he maintained to be allegorical, and therefore no proofs at all. Collins' book called forth no fewer than thirty-five answers, the principal ones proceeding from Dr. Chandler, Bishop of Lichfield and Coventry, and Chandler the Presbyterian, Berkeley, Sherlock, Bullock, Sykes, and Whiston. In answer to his opponents, especially Bishop Chandler, Collins, in 1727, published a defence, entitled " The Scheme of Literal Prophecy considered," in which he attacked the antiquity and authority of the Book of Daniel and the prophecies contained in it. This work again called forth several answers and produced one advantage, viz. that it gave occasion to a full examination of the nature and design of the Old Testament prophecies, and placed some difficult passages in a clearer light [n].

Woolston (1669—1731), who had been a Fellow of Sidney Sussex College, Cambridge, and had taken Orders, but had been deprived of his Fellowship, was probably a madman, indeed he seems to have thought so himself. It was Woolston's object to allegorise away the miracles, as Collins had the prophecies, of

---

[n] Leland's View, p. 65.

our Saviour. His first work was published in 1705, entitled "The old Apology for the Truths of the Christian Religion against the Jews and Gentiles revived," in which he maintained that Moses was an allegorical person, and the miracles of the Pentateuch were also only allegories. He professed himself to be a moderator between Collins and his opponents, with which view he, 1721, published "The Moderator between an Infidel and an Apostate," in dialogues tending to show that the Gospel miracles of themselves could not prove Christ to be the Messiah; and this opinion he afterwards carried much further in "Six Discourses on the Miracles of our Saviour," which appeared in 1727, 1728, and 1729. The design of these Discourses was to show that the great facts related in the Gospels are to be wholly understood in a mystical and allegorical sense, and that taken in their literal sense they are absurd and false; that if our Saviour's miracles, literally understood, will not abide the test of reason, they must be rejected, and with them our Saviour's authority must be rejected also. The curing the blind man with clay and spittle was, he contends, no miracle at all, but a pretence under which a sovereign balsam was applied to a slight disorder of the eyes, which were wearing away with age. When our Saviour discovered to the woman of Samaria the secrets of her past life, He exercised the trick of a fortune-teller. The three miracles recorded of raising the dead to life, viz. those of Jairus' daughter, of the widow's son, and of Lazarus, he attributes either to a natural course or to imposture. Jairus' daughter was only in a fit; the case of the widow's son was a mere contrivance between Jesus and the young man; the resurrection of Lazarus, to which he objects as being mentioned by only one out of the four Evangelists, was such a contexture of folly and fraud as is not equalled in romantic history: his being buried and lying four days in the grave was a concerted plan, in order that Jesus might have the honour of appearing to raise him from the dead: and the fact that the Jews went about to kill Him, and that Jesus withdrew from them, is a proof that they knew He was guilty of a fraud, and that He Himself also was conscious of it.

There still remains our Lord's own Resurrection; how could he overthrow that? He condemns it as a complication of absurdities, incoherences, and contradictions. He insinuates that the guards set by the Roman Governor at the request of the Chief Priests over the body of Jesus suffered themselves to be bribed and intoxicated by His disciples. But what he lays especial stress upon is a supposed covenant between the Chief Priests and the Saviour's disciples, that the seal with which the door of the sepulchre was secured should not be broken till the three days were entirely past; and that therefore the rolling away the stone from the sepulchre before that time was a breach of the covenant and a proof of imposture. And a strong proof of the imposture of the Resurrection lies in the fact that Jesus did not afterwards show Himself to the Chief Priests and rulers of the Jews.

Woolston, who was, as has been mentioned, considered a madman, seemed at first scarcely to deserve notice. But eventually no fewer than sixty answers to his Discourses were produced, the most important writers being Bishop Gibson, Nathaniel Lardner (a Presbyterian Minister, who defended the miracles in "A Vindication of our Lord's Miracles"), Dr. Zachary Pearce of St. Martin's, London [o], and Dr. Smallbrook, Bishop of St. David's; but the most remarkable work of all was, "The Trial of the Witnesses of the Resurrection of Jesus Christ," published in 1729, by Dr. Sherlock, who the year before had been appointed to the Bishopric of Bangor. Woolston, mad as other people considered him, had no mean idea of his own abilities; he says he would "cut out such a piece of work for the Boylean Lectures as shall hold them tug so long as the ministry of the letter and a hireling Priesthood shall last [p]." In answer to

---

[o] Afterwards Bishop of Rochester.

[p] The Boyle Lectures had been founded for the very purpose of counteracting (amongst other heretics) the Deists; for a Course of Eight Sermons preached annually, to defend the Christian Religion against Atheists, Deists, Pagans, Jews, and Mahomedans.

the Bishop of London and the Bishop of St. David's, Woolston published two pamphlets, the first in 1729, and the second in 1730, entitled "A Defence of his Discourses on the Miracles of our Saviour against the Bishops of London and St. David's and his other Adversaries." He was indicted for his blasphemous writings, and being found guilty he was sentenced to a year's imprisonment, to pay a fine of £100, and to find securities to the amount of £2,000 not to repeat the offence; he died in the King's Bench in 1731 [q].

Matthew Tindal (1656—1733), educated at Lincoln College, Oxford, and afterwards a Fellow of All Souls, seceded to Rome, but reverted, we will not say to the Church, but to Rationalism. He was a man of scandalous life, but, from the constructive character of his writings, was called "The Christian Deist." Collins had attacked the Prophecies, Woolston the Miracles. Such open attacks upon the Bible and the character of our Saviour, calculated as they were to prejudice the ignorant and vicious, were little able to affect people of taste and refinement. It was therefore necessary that Christianity should be attacked in a manner more calculated to influence people of refined and philosophical minds. With this object in view, Tindal, in 1730, published his work, "Christianity as old as the Creation, or the

---

[q] "I have read Woolston," wrote the venerable Dr. Cutler, of New England, to Dr. Zachary Grey, "with horror; but think the Devil has lent him a great deal of his wickedness, but none of his wit."—Nich. Lit. An., i. 481.

Gospel a republication of the Law of Nature." This work was henceforward considered the standard work of Deism, and more than any other work called forth Butler's Analogy. The original Law of Nature, Tindal contended, is so perfect that nothing could subsequently be added to or taken from it. Revelation is superfluous; mysteries are accretions introduced by the Clergy for their own purposes; Christianity, except in name, is nothing new, and nothing more than the development of the Law of Nature; the Scriptures, so far from being serviceable to direct men in faith and practice, are only suited to perplex them; they give very wrong and unworthy impressions of the Deity; there is an opposition between the Old and New Testaments; the Prophecies of the Old Testament are involved in hopeless confusion, and on those of the New no reliance can be placed, because even the Apostles were deceived in believing that the end of the world would come in their generation. All who were opposed to him, and favoured positive precepts in religion, he terms Demonists, and the Clergy of all times he stigmatises as *for the most part mortal enemies to the exercise of Reason, and even below brutes.* Many answers appeared to this work of Tindal's, the chief of which were A Pastoral Letter from Gibson, Bishop of London, Dr. Waterland's "Scripture Vindicated," Law's "Case of Reason[r]," and Balguy's "Second Letter to a Deist;" whilst

---

[r] "Or, Natural Religion fairly and fully stated, in answer to a Book entitled 'Christianity as old as the Creation.'"

fuller answers were made, in 1732, by Dr. Conybeare, Rector of Exeter College, Oxford, in "A Defence of Revealed Religion against the Exception of a late writer, in his Book entitled Christianity as old as the Creation," which reply Warburton designated as " one of the best reasoned books in the world [s]."

Dr. Morgan, who, like Tindal, called himself a Christian Deist, was once a Dissenting Minister, but had been expelled from the communion of his sect for Arianism. In 1737 he published "The Moral Philosopher, in a Dialogue between Philalethes, a Christian Deist, and Theophanes, a Christian Jew." Morgan advanced little beyond what had already been put forth by other Deists. Christianity, according to him, was only a republication of Natural Religion. He thoroughly rejects the Old Testament. The Law of Moses he represents as "having neither truth nor goodness in it, and as a wretched scheme of superstition, blindness, and slavery, contrary to all reason and common sense, set up under the specious popular pretence of a divine instruction and revelation from God." As to our Saviour, although he professes great veneration for Him, yet he attributes to Him motives altogether contradictory to such a feeling. Our Saviour pretended to be the Messiah foretold by the Prophets, yet He knew well that those prophets spoke only of a Jewish Prince who

---

[s] Dr. Conybeare was in the same year appointed Dean of Christ Church, and in 1750 Bishop of Bristol.

was to be a temporal King in Judæa. He did not renounce this character till His death, when he absolutely disclaimed His being the Messiah predicted by the Prophets, and died upon that renunciation. The Apostles preached different and antagonistic gospels; as to miracles, prophecies, and extraordinary gifts of the Holy Ghost, Morgan disbelieves them all. He speaks with respect of St. Paul, who, he says, was a Freethinker and opposed to the Law, and of the Gospels he accepts only that of St. Luke, the companion of St. Paul. Like Dr. Colenso of recent years, he makes Samuel to be the author of the Book of Genesis, and it was his contention that the omission of the doctrine of a future state in the Mosaic institution was a proof against the truth of that doctrine; which called forth from Warburton "The Divine Legation of Moses[t]." Warburton fought Morgan on his own ground and defeated him. He admitted Morgan's propositions as to the omission of the doctrine of a future state in the Pentateuch in their fullest extent, and proceeded to demonstrate from that very omission that a system which could dispense with a doctrine, which is the very bond of human society, must have come from God Himself. The ground chosen by

---

[t] Dr. Morgan afterwards published a second volume of the "Moral Philosopher, or a further Defence of Moral Truth and Reason," and in 1740 a third volume of the "Moral Philosopher, or Superstition and Tyranny inconsistent with Theocracy."

Warburton, although suited to his adventurous spirit, was new and bold, and caused great alarm to the friends of Revelation. His book offended many, even of the Warburtonians, especially that passage in the Divine Legation, which spoke of Moses using a *pious fraud* by mentioning in his description of the Fall, not the agent of the Fall, the Devil, but his *instrument*, the Serpent. Warburton does not seem to have prided himself on his orthodoxy, for on April 29, 1741, he wrote to Dr. Middleton, "We shall neither of us be esteemed orthodox writers [u]." But this matter of the "pious fraud" seems to have offended even Middleton, for in a letter to Dr. Doddridge, dated August 5, 1741, Warburton says, "I understand by a common friend that I have disgusted Dr. Middleton in what I have said of Moses' fraud, the Serpent, and the Papists borrowing of the Pagans."

Chubb (1679—1746) was a tallow-chandler at Salisbury, and a man of no education, who embraced the views of Whiston, and wrote a number of tracts on Arianism. He professed to be a friend of Christianity, but it is not difficult to see that his object was to overthrow it. Chubb rejects the Jewish Revelation entirely, and contends that SS. Peter and Paul condemn it as unworthy of the Deity. As to the Christian Revelation, he pretends to think favourably of Christ's Divine Mission; he admits that

---

[u] Watson's Life of Warburton.

Christ lived and died as the Bible declares, but our future hopes by no means depend on His sufferings; the highest character he attributes to Christ is that He was "the Founder of the Christian Sect," and "that He laid the foundation of a new sect amongst the Jews;" but the opening of St. John's Gospel is only the private opinion of the writer. "It is probable," Chubb says, "that Christ's mission was divine; at least it appears so to me, from the light or information I have received concerning it." He, however, does all in his power to invalidate it, especially the prophecies and miracles, and represents the Resurrection of Christ as an absurd and incredible theory. He supposes that Christianity (although the statements are somewhat contradictory) was originally only designed to be supplementary to Judaism, that the Mosaical dispensation was always to continue in full force, that the Gospel was to be preached to the Jews only and not to the Gentiles at all, though the Apostles deviated from the rule. Of Mahometanism he speaks favourably. "It cannot surely be true that the great prevalence of Mahometanism was owing to its being propagated by the sword . . . . and whether the Mahometan Revelation be of divine origin or not, there seems to be a plausible pretence, arising from the circumstances of things, for stamping a divine character upon it [x]."

---

[x] Posthumous Works, ii. 30.

Henry St. John (1678—1751), created in 1712 Viscount Bolingbroke, was Secretary of State for War in 1704, and for Foreign Affairs in 1710, in which capacity he concluded the Peace of Utrecht in 1713. But the accession of George I. to the throne gave their death-blow to the Tories, and Bolingbroke's political hopes expired, and being compelled to fly from England, he accepted the post of Seeretary of State under the Pretender, which, however, after the failure of the Rebellion of 1715 he was compelled to resign. During his residence in France he made the acquaintance of Voltaire and Montesquieu; and in 1723, through the influence of the Duchess of Kendal, he was allowed to return to England, where, however, finding his chances of political success hopeless, he returned to France in 1735, from which country he wrote those "Letters on the Study of History," in which he violently attacked Christianity. Bolingbroke, a brilliant man of the world himself, was the Apostle of Freethinking to the upper, as Chubb was to the lower, classes. He would adapt religion to sinners of rank and fashion; and would impose no restraints on what he termed "gentlemanly" vices. The Church had greatly erred in condemning polygamy, which he maintained (contrary to all fact) was necessary for the development of the population; and monogamy he condemned as an "absurd, unnatural, and cruel imposition." After his death, in 1751, his philosophical works were, agreeably to his instructions, given to the world in March, 1754, by David Mallet, a Scotchman, which brought down upon Bolingbroke the just indignation of Dr. Johnson. " Sir," said he, " he was a coward and a scoundrel ; a scoundrel for charging a blunderbuss against religion and morality, and a coward because he had no resolution to fire it off himself, but left half-a-crown to a beggarly Scotchman to draw the trigger after his death y."

But Bolingbroke appeared on the scene after Butler's Analogy was published, after which time, although a herd of noisy followers joined in the Deistical controversy, the career of Deism was practically ended, and the victory for the Church gained [z]. Suffice it to say that Bolingbroke abuses everybody and everything. He does not argue, he sneers, against Moses and the Prophets, against Jews and Christians, against religion and the Clergy. On the Clergy he made a general onslaught as " fools, knaves, cheats, madmen, imposters, and blasphemers.' Moses must be regarded with contempt as a philosopher, with horror as a divine; St. Paul was a fanatic ; the writings of all the Fathers of the Church consist of nothing but nonsense and artifice. Against Warburton he is particularly bitter, and inveighs against him as a " scribbler " and " a stupid fellow,"

---

[y] Boswell's Life of Johnson, ch. xi.

[z] Hume's " Treatise on Human Nature" was published in 1739, three years after Butler's Analogy appeared.

and it is only just to state that Warburton's attack on him after his death, in "A View of Lord Bolingbroke's Philosophy, in four Letters to a Friend," was written in language not less vulgar and offensive than Bolingbroke's. When expostulated with on language so unbecoming a clergyman and a gentleman, Warburton said that in combating Bolingbroke's "red-hot impiety" he had put himself in the "place of a scavenger, who ought not to be blamed for the stench from the dirt he was endeavouring to remove[a]."

It is difficult to determine in which class, whether amongst the Infidels or Deists, to place Middleton. Archbishop Potter considered him a Deist. Middleton and Dr. Nicholas Mann were, in 1737, candidates for the Mastership of the Charterhouse, a much coveted position. Bishop Sherlock spoke in his own name and that of the other Bishops to Walpole against Middleton, and Mann was elected. "I suppose you know you have chosen an Arian?" said Middleton to Archbishop Potter. "An Arian," replied the Archbishop, "is better than a *Deist*."

Conyers Middleton (1683—1750), educated at Trinity

---

[a] Watson's Life of Warburton, 420. Another Deist, Peter Anet, appeared at the beginning of George III.'s reign. In a work entitled "The Free Enquirer," he made a violent attack on Christianity, and in 1762 he was, by order of the Court of King's Bench, committed to Newgate for a month, and was ordered to stand in the pillory twice, and afterwards to be kept to hard labour in Bridewell for a year.—Ann. Reg. 1762, p. 113.

College, Cambridge, where he gained a Fellowship in 1706, which he soon resigned on making an advantageous marriage, was in 1731 elected Woodwardian Professor, and in 1734 Librarian to the University, and was honourably known for his "Life of Cicero;" but it is difficult to go further without pronouncing him either an infidel, or something very near it, in the guise of a Clergyman. His life was one series of bitter and disreputable controversies. In 1708 he joined the Fellows of his College in a petition to the Bishop of Ely against Bentley, the pugnacious Master of the College, a man as quarrelsome as himself; he thenceforward became Bentley's bitter enemy, and all that can be said in his favour is that one came out of the quarrel as badly as the other. In 1717 a dispute with Bentley, who was at the time Regius Professor of Divinity, with regard to an extortionate demand on Middleton when he took his D.D. degree, called forth several pamphlets, and amongst them Middleton's first considerable work, entitled "Remarks and Further Remarks on Proposals for a new Edition of the Greek Testament[b]." Middleton paid, under protest, the money demanded of him by Bentley, but afterwards sued him in the Vice-Chancellor's Court, and Bentley, refusing to acknowledge the jurisdiction of the Court, was, in 1718, deprived of all his degrees.

---

[b] Edited by Bentley. Bentley said of these works of Middleton, "I scorn to read what the rascal has written."

In 1724 Middleton lost his first wife, and travelled on the Continent, spending some time at Rome, whence in 1729 he wrote "A Letter from Rome showing an exact conformity between Popery and Paganism; or the Religion of the present Romans derived from that of their heathen ancestors." This work, in which he endeavoured to show that the rites and ceremonies of the Roman Catholic Church are taken from the Pagans, passed through four editions in the author's lifetime. But the book gave clear indications of the bias of the author's intellect; a suspicion was raised that he cared as little for the miracles of the Apostles as for the Romish Church, and this suspicion paved the way for the storm that broke out on his next publication in 1731. In a letter to Dr. Waterland, which he at first published anonymously, but which was soon known to be his, containing some remarks on the latter's reply to Tindal's "Christianity as old as the Creation," Middleton took a line which exposed him to the reproach of infidelity[c]. He gave up the literal truths of the Mosaic narratives, and while proposing to indicate a ready method for confuting Tindal, he in reality abandoned everything for which Waterland contended. Middleton advocated amongst other

---

[c] His dislike to Waterland probably arose from Waterland's being one of Bentley's few friends. Bentley used to sneer at Middleton as "fiddling Conyers," from his love for music.

things a partial, instead of a plenary, inspiration of Scripture—a distinction which he held to be "necessary to a Rational Defence of Religion"—by which any person would be able to get rid of any part of the Bible which did not approve itself to his judgment; and whilst he acknowledged *a general belief* in the divine origin and inspiration of the Books of the Old and New Testament, he asserted that "*we are under no obligation of Reason or Religion* to believe that the Scriptures are of *absolute and universal inspiration.*"

This work, which was answered by Pearce, Bishop of Rochester, created general indignation, and he barely escaped being deprived of his degrees and offices at Cambridge. The feeling was intensified in 1748 by his " Free Enquiry into the Miraculous Powers which are supposed to have subsisted in the Church from the earliest ages[d] through successive Centuries," &c., to which he had written an Introduction in the previous year. This work was refuted by (amongst others) Dodwell and Church, on whom the University of Oxford conferred the degree of D.D., and against whom Middleton was preparing a reply when he died. At his death he left behind him a Tract on " The Insufficiency and Inability of

---

[d] On his marrying a third wife in his old age, Bishop Gooch congratulated her: "he was glad she did not dislike the *ancients* as much as her husband did."

Prayer," which his wife wisely kept in MS. during her lifetime, and after her death Dr. Heberden, to whom she bequeathed her papers, put it into the fire[e].

Perhaps we should be right in considering Middleton as a Deist. Like his friend Dr. Gooch, Bishop of Ely, he was at first a strong Tory, and like him he turned a zealous Whig; probably disappointed ambition caused his hostility to the Church[f]. Like the Deists he maintained that there were contradictions in the four Evangelists; he accused St. Matthew of "wilfully suppressing or negligently omitting three successive descents from father to son in the first chapter of his Gospel;" he asserted that the Apostles were sometimes mistaken in applying the Prophecies of our Saviour, and he considered the fall of man an allegory.

To sum up. The common object of Deism was to assert the supremacy of Reason. It insisted on the sufficiency of natural, as opposed to revealed Religion: the improbability of any other than a natural religion being made to only one, and that an obscure, people like the Jews; on the moral and textual difficulties of the Bible; on the immorality of a system of rewards and punishments as the in-

---

[e] Bishop Newton's Life, p. 25.
[f] A friend once lamented to him that he had not been made a Bishop; Middleton answered, "Then, Sir, as they have not thought fit to trust me I am at liberty to speak my mind."

centive to a holy life; it tolerated nothing supernatural [g], no miracles, no prophecies; it would eliminate from religion all dogmatic teaching which could not be verified by reason, and would thus eliminate Christianity altogether.

The development of Deism was gradual, passing through three different phases. The first phase may be regarded as "No Dogmatic Theology," as taught by Toland; the second as "No Historical Christianity," as taught by Chubb; the third as "No Christianity at all," as taught by Bolingbroke. Toland commenced with the denial of miracles, which was followed in a coarser strain by Collins. From mysteries in doctrine the attack advanced to the supernatural in fact, by Collins on prophecies, by Woolston on the miracles. And then, when everything above reason was eradicated from the Christian belief, next the authority of the teachers fell with the belief, and Christianity became in the hands of Tindal and Morgan a scheme without any authority of its own, only to be accepted on account of doctrines discernible by the light of Nature [h].

Yet so far from considering themselves the enemies of religion, the Deists threw that stigma upon the Clergy, and professed that they themselves acted only in the interests of religion, which they disencumbered

---

[g] Hence by the Germans Rationalism is not unfrequently termed *Naturalism*.

[h] Q. R., cxv. 80.

from the accretions of ages. Thus Tindal, in "Christianity as old as the Creation," thinks that he has "laid down such plain and evident rules as may enable men of the meanest capacity to distinguish between religion and superstition; and has represented the former in every part so beautiful, so amiable, and so strongly affecting, that they who in the least reflect must be highly in love with it." So Chubb says that "he has rendered the Gospel of Christ defendable upon rational principles." And again the same writer says, "Where's the sense and reason of imposing parochial priests upon the people to take care of their souls, more than parochial lawyers to look to their estates, or parochial physicians to attend to their bodies, or parochial tinkers to mend their kettles?"

When we consider the great popularity that attended their writings, we may form some idea of the mischief which Deism must have spread through the country. Woolston's Discourses are said to have sold to the number of thirty thousand, and to have called forth in a short time sixty replies. Against Collins' "Discourses of Freethinking" thirty-four works are said to have been published in England alone, and the number in foreign languages to have amounted in all to seventy-nine; whilst Tindal's "Christianity as old as the Creation" called forth no fewer than one hundred and fifteen replies. The poison penetrated to the Universities. In 1729 the Heads of Colleges at Oxford complained of the prevalence of

Deism amongst the Undergraduates, and in 1730 three students were expelled on this charge; and in 1739 several Cambridge Undergraduates were found to be inoculated with the same opinions [1].

During the reign of Deism, the Church did its duty well and effectually. Of the numerous Church works published in defence of Christianity, the principal were Sherlock's "Trial of the Witnesses of the Resurrection of Jesus," Conybeare's "Defence of Revealed Religion," Berkeley's "Minute Philosopher," and Warburton's "Divine Legation of Moses;" whilst amongst lesser luminaries must be mentioned Leslie, Sykes, Stebbing, and Balguy. But far surpassing all was the immortal Analogy of Butler, a work published in 1736, the result of twenty years' hard thinking, those years spent at the very time when Deism was at its height, and which struck at the very root of infidelity. Thanks to these champions of the Faith, Deism was vanquished, but not before it had left its mark in a two-fold manner on the Church of the eighteenth century; first, by drawing to itself the most able intellects of the day, and forcing the highest and most learned part of the Clergy, instead of attending to the extension of practical religion, to occupy themselves in defending the outposts of Christianity; and secondly, [because the fashionable society of the day was often inclined to

---

[1] Monk's Life of Bentley, ii. 391.

form their lives according to the creed of Deism, and to live as men only can live when the restraints of the Christian religion are removed.

The tide of Deism was, however, stemmed rather than Deism itself eradicated; or perhaps it may be said that Deism itself was smothered in the deadness of the eighteenth century, when little interest was taken in theological questions. Owing to the patronage which it received from the State, it lingered on for a time; it revived in the scepticism of Hume and the sneers of Gibbon, both of whom received lucrative appointments under government. Paine's " Age of Reason" widely diffused its poison through the lower classes, and it was not finally driven from the country till the Evangelical movement, which arose towards the end of the century. "We, too, in England," says Burke, " have had writers who made some noise in their day, but they now repose in oblivion. Who, born in the last fifty years, has read one word of Collins, Toland, Tindal, or Morgan, who called themselves Freethinkers?"

CHAPTER V.

THE GROWTH OF TOLERATION (1714—1784).

GEORGE I., on the assembling of his first Privy Council, declared: "Having been willing to omit no opportunity of giving all possible assurances to a people who have already deserved so well of me, I take this occasion also to express to you my firm purpose, to do all that is in my power for the supporting and maintaining the Churches of England and Scotland, as they are severally by law established, which I am of opinion may be efficiently done without the least compromise; in *the toleration allowed by law to Protestant Dissenters*, so agreeable to Christian charity, and so *necessary to the trade and riches* of this great kingdom."

The Church had been left by Anne, not only unfriendly to the Hanoverian family, but far too powerful to suit the purposes of the Government; to weaken the Church, therefore, was its chief endeavour. We have seen how Convocation was suppressed. But before the suppression of Convocation was effected, the Government, in 1714, during the primacy of Tenison, issued *Directions* to the Clergy against intermeddling with affairs of State in their sermons or lectures; "Whereas unusual liberties have been taken by several of the said Clergy in intermeddling with the affairs of State and Government and the Constitution of the Realm, which may be of very dangerous consequence if not timely prevented, we direct that none of the Clergy, in their sermons or lectures, presume to intermeddle in any affairs of State or Government, or the Constitution of the Realm, save only on such special feasts and fasts as are or shall be appointed by public authority, and then no further than the occasion of such days shall strictly require."

The abortive insurrection of 1715 on behalf of the Pretender was easily suppressed; Jacobitism was discouraged, and the Hanoverian interests strengthened. The same feeling which biassed the government against the Church led it to favour Dissent. As early as 1715 the Dsssenters began to urge their claims upon the new government for a greater Toleration, and demanded (as they said), in the interest both of themselves and of the House of Hanover, the repeal of the Test and Corporation Acts, as well as of the Occasional Conformity and Schism Acts [a]. By the commencement of 1717 the agitation had assumed a more systematic form; the Dissenters, encouraged by marks of royal favour, and feeling that the sun was rising on them "after a night of tempest and horror," moved the King for

---

[a] Calamy, ii. 344.

a redress of their grievances; and meetings to promote the object which they had in view, were held in various parts of the country. On December 13, 1718, Lord Stanhope, who had become Principal Secretary of State, brought forward in the House of Lords, under the title of "An Act for strengthening the Protestant interests in these kingdoms," a Bill for the relief of Protestant Dissenters, which proposed the repeal, not only of the Occasional Conformity and Schism Acts, but also of some clauses in the Test and Corporation Acts. The Bill was opposed not only by High Churchmen and Tories, but that part relating to the Test and Corporation Acts by the Whigs also. Wake, Archbishop of Canterbury, declared that these Acts were "the main bulwarks and supporters of the Established Church;" he expressed great tenderness for the Dissenters, although he thought at the same time that, by the practice of Occasional Conformity, they made a wrong use of the Toleration granted them at the Revolution. Dawes, Archbishop of York, followed on the same side. Hoadly, then Bishop of Bangor, maintained that all religious tests were an invasion of the natural rights of man, an injury to the State, and a scandal to religion; he contended that the Occasional Conformity and Schism Acts were in effect persecuting laws, and that if they could be defended, then that all the persecutions of Christians, and even the Inquisition itself, could be defended also. Hoadly was

The Growth of Toleration.

ably answered by Smalridge, Bishop of Bristol: but the Bill was advocated by Gibson, Bishop of Lincoln, and Willis of Gloucester, who were on the road to preferment, Gibson to London and Willis to Winchester, and by White Kennet, Bishop of Peterborough. In vain Robinson, Bishop of London, contended that "all places of trust are in the hands of those of the National Church." In vain Atterbury remarked on the mischief which the Dissenters were bringing on the Church; the Bill, but not till the clauses relating to the Test and Corporation Acts had been withdrawn in Committee, passed the House of Lords by 53 to 33 votes, and the Commons by 243 to 202, the majority in the latter House being chiefly due to the Scotch members [b]. Stanhope promised the Dissenters that the full measure was only deferred to a more convenient season; his premature death occurred soon afterwards; the convenient season did not arrive for 109 years, although we shall see that nearly every year from the accession of George II. an Indemnity Act was passed, which enabled Dissenters to hold office just as if there had been no law against it. So that the Dissenters thenceforward enjoyed the privilege of joining in the highest offices of the Church

---

[b] A clause, however, was inserted in the Act that no Mayor, nor Bailiff, nor other Magistrate, should attend any conventicle with the ensigns of his office, under pain of being disqualified from holding any public post.

for one hour, and the liberty of endeavouring to undermine it for the rest of the year.

In 1721 the Quakers presented a petition to Walpole, imploring relief from certain disabilities under which they fancied that they laboured on account of the form in which they made their affirmations[c]. Walpole had especial reasons for favouring the Quakers. A large body of them was established in Norfolk, and especially in Norwich, who had always voted for his candidates at the elections[d]. A Bill was accordingly brought into the Commons in December, 1721, and had an easy passage through that House. But the London Clergy were strongly opposed to the relief; they presented a petition against it on the ground that "an oath was instituted by God Himself as the surest bond of fidelity amongst men." It expressed their " serious concern lest the minds of good men should be grieved and wounded, and the enemies of Christianity triumph, when they shall see such condescensions made by a Christian Legislature to a set of men who renounce the divine institutions of Christ, particularly that by which the faithful are initiated into His Religion and denominated Christians, and who, on that account, according to the uniform judgment of the Catholic Church,

---

[c] The form imposed by the Statute of William III. contained the words "In the presence of Almighty God," which the Quakers objected to as equivalent to an oath.

[d] Coxe's Life of Walpole, i. 478.

cannot be deemed worthy of that sacred name." The petition, although presented by Dr. Dawes, Archbishop of York, was voted to be a libel, and ordered not to be received. Atterbury spoke in the House of Lords against indulgences being accorded to a set of people who were barely Christians. The Quakers' Affirmation Bill, however, passed (in 1722) by a large majority, Archbishop Wake, and Potter, Bishop of Oxford (afterwards Archbishop of Canterbury), joining in a protest against it [e].

The great champion of the Church, and on that account the most formidable opponent to the Hanoverian Government, was Atterbury, Bishop of Rochester; so Walpole's next step was to get rid of him. In 1720 the prospects of the Jacobites seemed to brighten with the birth of a son to the Pretender; and the suppression of Convocation, and the evident hostility of the government to the Church and favour shown to the Dissenters, had caused a wide-spread disaffection, which seemed to favour the cause of the Stuarts. In 1721, therefore, the Pretender, greatly exaggerating the state of affairs, and misunderstanding the feelings of the country, issued an absurd manifesto, in which he proposed that King George should give up England to him, whilst he

---

[e] There was at the time a deep-rooted antipathy to Quakers; they were called (for what reason is not clear) Aminadabs, and were represented as hypocrites, cheats, liars, and immoral livers.—Ashton's Queen Anne, i. 137.

on his part promised to procure for the King the title of King of Hanover. A conspiracy was set on foot to proclaim James III. King of England [f], and in this conspiracy Atterbury was accused of being implicated. But, before narrating the troubles that came upon him, we must give a sketch of the previous life of this great, if somewhat indiscreet, man, then the most prominent of all the Bishops, the most eloquent defender of the Church, whose loss was the greatest blow that could have befallen it at such a time.

Francis Atterbury (1662—1731) was the younger son of the Rev. Lewis Atterbury, who became in 1649 a Student of Christ Church, and grandson of the Rev. Francis Atterbury, who in 1648 subscribed the "Solemn League and Covenant [g]." Atterbury's elder brother, Lewis, was, like himself, educated at Westminster under the famous Dr. Busby, and at Christ Church, Oxford; and in 1680 Francis Atterbury left Westminster at the head of those (amongst whom was Gastrell [h]) who were elected Students to

---

[f] The government turned this conspiracy to account; and an Act of Parliament was passed imposing a fine of £100,000 on the real or personal estates of all Roman Catholics in the kingdom, to defray the expenses necessitated by the conspiracy, and by a subsequent motion the tax was extended to the Nonjurors.

[g] Wood's Athen. Oxon.

[h] Bishop of Chester, 1714.

Christ Church¹. After taking his degree he remained up at Christ Church as Tutor till 1691. In May, 1687, Obadiah Walker, the Romanist Master whom James II. had obtruded on University College, under the assumed name of Abraham Woodhead published a Pamphlet entitled " Some considerations on the spirit of Martin Luther and the original of the Reformation ;" and the same year Atterbury published his "Answer" to the book, in which he made a spirited defence of Luther, which Burnet pronounces to be one of the ablest of the many vindications of the Church of England ᵏ. In 1698 he became Preacher at the Rolls. In 1700 he entered on the Convocation controversy (of which an account has been already given); it is now generally admitted that the victory rested with his opponent Wake, but Atterbury was then and afterwards regarded as the champion of the Church against Erastianism¹; and as a reward he received the thanks of the Lower House of Convocation, and the degree of D.D. from the University of Oxford. In 1701 he was appointed Archdeacon of Totnes by Bishop Trelawney, and on

---

¹ Aldrich, an old Westminster boy, also became a Canon of Christ Church in 1681, in 1689 Dean of Christ Church, and was one of Atterbury's greatest friends.

ᵏ Dict. of Nat. Biog., Article, Atterbury.

¹ Warburton, who was no friend to Convocation, wrote to Hurd : "Atterbury goes upon principles; all that Wake and Kennet could possibly oppose are precedents."—Ibid.

the accession of Queen Anne one of her Chaplains, and in 1704 Dean of Carlisle. Two years previously, Dr. Nicholson, who had been appointed in 1682 Archdeacon of Carlisle, was raised to the Bishopric of that diocese [m], and to him Atterbury applied for institution: but as the Letters Patent appointing Atterbury to the Deanery were dated July 15, and the late Dean Grahme did not resign until August 5, the Bishop at first refused to institute him [n]. A quarrel followed, which turned upon a series of quibbles. Nicholson had published an English Historical Library, a somewhat inaccurate work, which Atterbury, at the time Preacher at the Rolls, attacked in his book on " The Rights, Powers, and Privileges of an English Convocation ;" to which Nicholson replied in " A Letter to the Rev. White Kennet against the unmannerly and slanderous objections of *Mr.* Francis Atterbury, Preacher at the Rolls." But the University of Oxford had, as above stated, created Atterbury a D.D., and was indignant, and refused to confer a Doctor's Degree on Nicholson, on account of the "seeming contempt" cast on the University by his pamphlet, which called a person *Mr.* when the University had made him a D.D., and for "a severe and indecent reflexion upon the proceedings

---

[m] Nicholson graduated at Queen's College, Oxford; he became Bishop of Derry 1718, and in 1727 Archbishop of Cashel, but he died five days afterwards.

[n] Nicholson's Life, p. 10.

of the University º." Against this charge Nicholson defended himself by saying that when he published his pamphlet Atterbury was only Mr.; and in turn he reflected upon Atterbury for calling him *Mr.* when he was really *Bishop Elect*.

So that when Atterbury was appointed to the Deanery of Carlisle, the Bishop and the Dean met on far from amicable terms. In 1707 the Bishop determined (according to the power given him by the Statute of Henry VIII.) to visit the Chapter, and to enquire into some disputes which had taken place amongst its members. Dr. Todd, however, one of the Prebendaries, instigated, it was said, by Atterbury, contended that the Queen, and not the Bishop, was the local Visitor, and the Bishop in consequence suspended and afterwards excommunicated Dr. Todd. Dr. Todd obtained a prohibition against the Bishop from the Court of Common Pleas; the whole of the Episcopate became alarmed, and Archbishop Tenison wrote a letter to his Suffragans, recommending the case of the Bishop as their common cause; soon afterwards an Act of Parliament was passed which removed all doubt for the future, and established the validity of the local statutes given by Henry VIII. to his New Foundations ᴾ.

º The words objected to were his calling Atterbury "an ambitious wretch in his insolent attempts against our ancient and Apostolical Church government."

ᴾ "An Act to impower his Majesty to amend, alter, and

The Tory Reaction of 1710 brought Atterbury to the front, and he was chosen Prolocutor of Convocation against his former antagonist, White Kennet, and for the last four years of Queen Anne's reign he was the stedfast opponent of the Latitudinarian party and the most prominent member in the Lower House of Convocation.

In 1711 he was transferred from the Deanery of Carlisle to that of Christ Church, and in 1713 promoted to the See of Rochester, holding with it, through the objectionable custom usual at that time, the Deanery of Westminster. He fell into an Episcopal hornet's nest. He had, as we have seen, published (when only in his twenty-fourth year) a work in vindication of Martin Luther; he was also an admirer of Milton, the enemy of the Stuarts, a thing which in the eyes of many Tories was no less than a crime [q]; nevertheless he was disliked by the Latitudinarian Bishops for the strong line he had taken in defence of the Church; and he found on the Episcopal Bench his old opponents, Burnet, Nicholson, and Wake, to whom were soon added Gibson, in 1716 Hoadly, and in 1718 White Kennet.

Had Queen Anne not died so prematurely, Atterbury, on the death of Tenison, would probably have been raised to the Primacy, no Bishop equalling him

---

improve the Local Statutes and Ordinances of Cathedral and Collegiate Churches."

[q] Macaulay's Biog.

in Parliamentary talents; with a fine person and a graceful delivery he ranked amongst the first preachers of the day; but the same powers which recommended him in the late reign made him an object of suspicion to the Hanoverian government. He, together with Bishop Smalridge [r], refused to sign a " Declaration of Confidence " drawn up by the Bishops after the Rebellion of 1715, because he considered that it reflected on the Church party, and by degrees he became more and more alienated from the ruling powers. The government thought that something must be done with him; the Whig party knew that his loss would be the greatest that could befall their opponents, for there was no one to take his place; either he must be gained over to their side, or he must be got out of the way. It was confidently asserted that Walpole made him the prospective offer of the See of Winchester when it should become vacant, until which time he offered him a pension of £5,000 a year, if he

---

[r] George Smalridge (1663—1719), educated at Westminster, and Student of Christ Church; in 1704, during Jane's illness, he filled his place as Regius Professor of Divinity, and was disappointed at not succeeding him. He succeeded Atterbury both as Dean of Carlisle and Dean of Christ Church, and was commonly said to carry the buckets to extinguish the fire which Atterbury had kindled (Nich. Lit. Hist., iii. 231); in 1714 appointed Bishop of Bristol. Whiston in his Memoirs includes him as an Arian, but Smalridge met the charge in a Letter to Trelawney, Bishop of Winchester.

would only discontinue his attendance in the House of Lords. Atterbury of course refused, and his fate was sealed. For now, on August 24, 1722, he was apprehended under suspicion of holding a correspondence with the Stuarts, and committed to the Tower. That Atterbury was innocent of the charge brought against him is probable, but that he had been dabbling in politics in a manner calculated to lay him open to suspicion there can be little doubt; but as to the degree of his guilt it is impossible to form an opinion; it was believed by one party, and discredited by the other. The fact that in his banishment he espoused the cause of the Stuarts proves nothing; there were many in England who were contented to live quietly under the Hanoverian government, and yet would have hailed with joy the return of the Stuarts. After he had been two months in the Tower, during which time he met with very cruel treatment, his daughter, Mrs. Morris, presented a petition to the Court of the Old Bailey, that, in consideration of his weak state of health, he might either be bailed or at once brought to trial. Both requests were overruled. Nothing can excuse the unnecessary cruelty with which Atterbury was treated. Everything taken to him in the Tower, even some pigeon-pies, were carefully examined [s]. The Clergy stood

---

[s] "It is the first time," wrote Pope to Gray, "dead pigeons have been suspected of carrying intelligence."

by him, and he was publicly prayed for, under the pretext of being in bad health, as "one afflicted with the gout," in many of the London churches[t].

His supposed conspiracy was not sufficient to produce a conviction in a Court of Law: so he could only be reached by a Bill of Pains and Penalties before the House of Commons. He refused, however, to acknowledge any jurisdiction but that of his peers, and was accordingly, on May 6, summoned to the bar of the House of Lords, where he made in his own defence one of the most touching and eloquent speeches on record. The Bishops took a prominent part against him; Gastrell, Bishop of Chester, who had been educated with him at Westminster School, was the only Bishop who spoke in his favour; Willis, Bishop of Gloucester, made a violent speech against him and had his reward, for he was soon afterwards promoted to Winchester, the See that Walpole had intended for Atterbury; and Bishop Wynne, of St. Asaph, gave evidence against him, which was proved to be unfounded. The evidence for the prosecution was inconclusive, but he was found guilty by 83 to 43 votes, and was sentenced to deprivation and banishment for life.

---

[t] A print was circulated representing him looking through the bars of his prison, with the portrait of Laud in his hand, on which were inscribed the words—
"A second Laud,
Whose Christian courage nothing feared but God."

The crowd that attended him from the Tower to the ship which was to convey him to his exile brought back to remembrance the scene exhibited at the Trial of the Seven Bishops; on June 16, 1723, he left England never to return. In the sixth year of his banishment he was attacked by a severe illness, and his daughter, having obtained the necessary permission from the English government (for Parliament had forbidden any British subject to hold intercourse with him), resolved to see him. But it was at the risk of her own life. In vain the doctors warned her of the peril which she incurred; she had only one wish—to see him and to die. In spite of his illness the Bishop travelled to Toulon to meet her; they met; the daughter received from him the Holy Eucharist; and that night she died.

The Bishop died in Paris on February 15, 1731, in the 69th year of his age; his body was brought to England, and on May 12 he was buried in Westminster Abbey; but even then the government continued their suspicions, and ordered the coffin to be searched, for fear it might contain some Jacobite papers.

Nothing more plainly shows the rapid decay that had overtaken the Church since the Hanoverian succession than the different treatment that was meted out to Sacheverell and to Bishop Atterbury. In 1710 Sacheverell, who had nothing but his High Church views to recommend him, was made the idol

The Growth of Toleration. 413

of the populace, and was rewarded by the government; only thirteen years later, Bishop Atterbury, the champion of the High Church party, was banished from the kingdom as a formidable opponent to the dynasty.

We must now go back a little to see how matters fared with the Dissenters, and we shall find the government not only favouring the consciences of Dissenters, but their pockets also. In 1721 Dr. Calamy, a Presbyterian Minister, published a volume of sermons preached by him in Salter's Hall, which he not only dedicated to the King, whom he compared, as Defender of the Faith, to Charlemagne, but of which he also personally presented a copy to his Majesty. The King was pleased to tell Calamy that he took the Dissenters as his hearty friends, and at the same time gave him a quiet hint, "to let him know that in the approaching elections of Members of Parliament he depended on them to use their influence, wherever they had any interest, in favour of such as were heartily in favour of him and of his family." This, taken with what follows, looks to us in the present day very much like bribery and corruption, especially when we bear in mind that the King could not speak a word of English, and consequently that Walpole could not have been a stranger to the proceeding.

A few days afterwards Calamy presented another copy of his sermons to "the three young Princesses who stood in a row before him," and who said, " Sir, we hope these good prayers will be continued, for which we shall be very thankful." This must have been a very pretty scene, but its effect is somewhat marred by what followed. A reward soon came. First, a message was sent to Calamy from the Treasury with an enclosure of £50. Next, in 1723, followed a grant from the Royal bounty of £500 " for the use and behalf of the poor widows of Dissenting ministers." This grant was soon increased to £1,000 a year, and £500 was to be paid every half year for assisting "either ministers or their widows." But the matter was to be kept secret, and even the Dissenting historians relate that this incident about the secrecy " cast an unpleasant suspicion over the whole business," and "some people persisted in looking at it as a bribe to secure Dissenters' votes [u]." Such is the history of the "Regium Domum" in the reign of George I.[x]

On June 3, 1727, King George left England for Hanover; on his journey he was seized with a para-

---

[u] Skeats, 319; Stoughton, i. 118.

[x] The "Regium Domum" to Dissenters began in 1672 at £600; William III. raised it to £1,200; how it was increased in 1723 is related here; in 1784 it was raised to £2,200; in 1792 to £5,000; in 1863, when it was abolished, it had reached £39,746. This does not exhaust the catalogue of State donations to the Dissenters, but surely this was Endowment of Dissent by the State!

lytic stroke, and on June 11 he died at Osnaburg, in the 68th year of his age, and was succeeded by his son, George II.

Of Church History, apart from that of the Dissenters, during the reign of George II. there is little or none, so we must now carry on the progress of Dissent till the end of the reign of the second King of the House of Hanover.

In the first year of the new reign an Act of Indemnity was passed in Parliament, which, with the exception of six years, was renewed every year until 1828, when the Act was passed, relieving Protestant Dissenters from the operation of the Corporation and Test Acts, and enabling them to hold offices just as if they had qualified under those Acts.

George II., when Prince of Wales, hated Walpole, whom he called a "rogue" and a "rascal;" but shortly after he became King he altered his mind, and found that he could not do without him.

The first Parliament of the new reign met in January, 1728. The Whigs, under the leadership of Walpole, possessed a large majority in the new House of Commons, and the Dissenters, who had given them valuable assistance, thinking they had a strong claim on Walpole's gratitude, commenced, in 1730, an agitation for the repeal of the Test and Corporation Acts. Walpole was in a dilemma; he did not wish to offend the Dissenters, and his personal feelings were in favour of a repeal: but his motto was "to let well alone" ("quieta non movere"), and having once burnt his fingers in the Sacheverell business, he did not wish to do so again, or to risk a recurrence of the Sacheverell demonstrations. Still he considered himself bound to the Dissenters, who he felt had a strong claim upon him; and another general election was not far distant, in which, if the wishes of the Dissenters were complied with, the Queen and Walpole knew the High Church party would to a man vote against him. The government wished the Repeal question to be deferred. But how was it to be managed? There was one person, and one person only, who could extricate them from the difficulty, and that person was Hoadly, who stood well with the Dissenters and the Low Church party. But Hoadly was in by no means an angelic temper: the valuable Bishopric of Durham had lately been conferred on Dr. Chandler, and he expected that it would have been conferred on himself. Both the Queen and Walpole hated Hoadly, as did also the King; but for that matter the King hated all Bishops generally, but Hoadly in particular. It was with the greatest difficulty that the Queen succeeded in persuading him to use his influence with Dissenters. Hoadly after a time consented to do so, and with the result usual in such cases (to use a common expression) of falling between two stools; the Dissenters thought he had used his influence too strongly against them, whilst the Court party thought he had not gone far enough in their interests.

But Hoadly was not the man to sell his services cheaply, and as he had lately been disappointed with respect to Durham, he took care to make sure of Winchester. Walpole accordingly promised him, "If any vacancy should occur, you are as sure of succeeding as if you were now in possession." So when Willis, Bishop of Winchester, was lying at the point of death, Lord Hervey, who had the peculiar taste (which was shared by few) of liking Hoadly, wrote to him to come immediately from Salisbury to urge his claims. "You know the King's two ears," he said (meaning the Queen and Walpole), "apply to them both." He did so, but he was only just in time, for Walpole, having forgotten Hoadly, was on the point of offering the vacant see to Potter, Bishop of Oxford; but being reminded by Hoadly of his claim, Walpole told the Queen that it would be scandalous to break the promises made to him[y]. Thus was Hoadly raised in 1734 to the See of Winchester, and when he arrived at that ecclesiastical pinnacle, and knew that he had nothing further to expect, his Latitudinarian principles grew stronger than ever.

Again, at the General Election of 1734, at which the Whigs obtained another, although smaller, majority than in the last Parliament, the Dissenters gave Wal-

---

[y] Herv. Mem., ii. 445.

pole their cordial support, and in return they in 1736 urged their claims for the abolition of the Test Act. Walpole had often promised them that a good time would come, so Dr. Chandler, the Nonconformist Minister, asked him when that good time, which he was so fond of talking about, would come. Walpole was taken off his guard and answered him, "If you require a specific answer, I will give it in one word—Never[2];" and when on March 12, 1736, leave was asked to bring in a Bill for the repeal of the Corporation and Test Acts, Walpole opposed the motion, and it was lost by 251 to 125 votes; and again in March, 1739, a similar motion was again opposed by the government and lost by 188 to 89 votes.

Still, when he could safely do so without losing Parliamentary support, Walpole was very scrupulous to gratify the wishes of the Dissenters. The Act of Toleration had especially favoured the Quakers, but there was one clause in the Act which seemed to them to affect their conscientious scruples. It provided that "nothing in the Act should be construed to exempt any of the persons aforesaid (the Quakers) from paying of tithes and other parochial duties to the Church or Minister, nor from any prosecution in any Ecclesiastical Court or elsewhere for the same." In the month of March, 1736, a

---

[2] Coxe's Walpole.

petition was presented by the Quakers for relief from the vexatious and expensive operation of the Tithe Laws; they represented that though from motives of conscience they refused to pay tithes, Church-rates, and other Ecclesiastical duties, they were exposed to grievous sufferings by prosecution in the exchequer, ecclesiastical, and other courts, to the imprisonment of their persons, and the ruin of their families. The petition was not against the payment of tithes (for these they knew they *must* pay), but since they could only conscientiously pay them *by compulsion*, that compulsion might be enforced as easily and inexpensively to them as possible. This, therefore, was a mere sentimental grievance, yet the "Quakers' Relief Bill" found favour with Walpole, and passed the House of Commons by 164 to 48 votes, but only to be rejected in the Lords, although by a small majority of 54 to 35 votes, fifteen Bishops voting against it. The mortification of Walpole and of the Queen was extreme. The Bishops as a body offended the King, the Queen, and the Government. Not only had they voted against the Bill, but they had stirred up the country against it. Sherlock wrote against it; Gibson urged the Clergy by the cry of "the Church in danger" to exert their influence against it. Walpole pronounced the Bishops to be one as bad as the other. The King denounced them as "a parcel of black, canting, hypocritical knaves." The Queen, with still greater indelicacy, asked Sherlock if he was "not ashamed to be overruled a second time by the Bishop of London (Gibson), and, after all she had said to him, in following the Bishop of London in Rundle's affair, how could he be blind and weak enough to be running his nose——" but here her language is really too gross to be quoted [a]. But Walpole never forgave Gibson, who, through his vote on this occasion, lost the friendship of Walpole, and (it is supposed) the Primacy also.

The Parliamentary Session of 1753 was marked by two Acts of Parliament, one entitled "An Act to permit persons professing the Jewish religion to be naturalized by Parliament, and for other purposes therein mentioned;" the other for the better preventing of clandestine marriages.

The first of these Bills was introduced in the House of Lords, through which it had an easy stage, and met with no opposition from the Bishops. In the House of Commons it was violently opposed. Petitions against the Bill flowed in from all sides. Adversaries to the Bill said:—"If the Jews should come to be possessed of a large share of the land of the kingdom, how are we sure that Christianity will continue to be the fashionable religion?" "To naturalize the Jews," said others, "was to rob Christians of their birthright;" "it was to give a lie,"

---

[a] Herv. Mem., ii. 93.

The Growth of Toleration. 421

said a third party, "to all the prophecies of the Bible which said they are to remain without any fixed habitation till the coming of the Messiah." The Bill, however, passed by a majority of forty-one votes, and received the royal sanction.

The government supported the Bill because they thought they saw in the naturalization of the Jews a great accession to the monied interest of the country, and an increase of their own influence amongst the members of that community; but they did not reckon on the reception it met with in the country. The Act became the subject of national horror and execration. Every part of the kingdom resounded with the reproach of the ministry who had enforced such an odious measure, and of the Bishops who had let it pass unopposed by them [b]. So universal was the indignation, that in the November Session of the same year, on the very first day, Ministers, in fear of an approaching election, brought in and carried a Bill for its repeal [c]. The Jewish religion continued *not* to be tolerated; and for a series of years Lord Chancellors, beginning with Lord Hardwicke and ending with Lord Eldon, held that a bequest for the maintenance of a Synagogue was void, because the Jewish religion was not toler-

---

[b] The Bishop of Norwich, who voted for the Bill, was insulted during his Confirmation tour, and a mob of boys pursued him crying out, "Come and circumcise us."

[c] Smollett ii. 97 and 130.

ated in England. Such was the condition of a sect which was not *established*.

The second of the two measures referred to above was Lord Hardwicke's Marriage Act of 1753. Between the law of the Church and the law of the land, with regard to marriages, a wide difference prevailed, for, whilst the Canons required that marriages should be solemnized in the parish churches at stated hours, an equally valid union for all civil purposes might be effected in a private house or a tavern, as in a church. It is true, by Acts of Parliament passed in the reign of William III., and still later in that of Anne, Clergymen who performed marriages without banns or licence were subjected to a fine of £100. But there were some Clergymen against whom Episcopal censures and suspension "ab officio et beneficio" were of no avail, for they had no money and no preferments to lose, and as to character, they were so sunk in vice and degradation as to be strangers to it. Especially was this the case with regard to a set of men known as the "Fleet Clergy." Clergymen, as well as laymen, confined for debt, could, by payment of money and finding security, live in certain streets outside the walls, but within the "rules" or "liberties" of the prison; a privilege which it was the interest of the Warden to encourage; and so lax was the discipline on the part of this official, that prisoners were allowed to attend balls at the West End of London, and to frequent

The Growth of Toleration. 423

the fashionable watering-places [d]. Some of these Fleet Clergy were kept in the payment of the tavern-keepers of the neighbourhood (board and lodging with a salary of £25 a year being considered an adequate remuneration), whilst the landlord fitted up a chapel in his tavern, where he himself acted as clerk, and pocketed the fees. Sometimes Fleet Clergymen who considered themselves of a higher stamp celebrated marriages in their own lodgings, and kept touters of both sexes, many of whom were skilful pickpockets, and became the pest of the neighbourhood, who advertised the aristocratic connection of their clients, their degrees at Oxford or Cambridge; that they were no common Fleet Parsons, but "regular-bred clergymen," "above committing those little mean actions that some men impose upon people." This state of the Marriage Laws created not only much scandal, but great misery also. Young men of noble families were forcibly dragged into these houses and married to women of bad character, a brass curtain-ring being substituted for the usual ring of gold [e]. Innocent young girls from the country

---

[d] The Commissioners appointed at the beginning of the reign of George II. to enquire into the state of the gaols considered that the net profits of the Warden of the Fleet prison exceeded £5,000 a year.

[e] Swinburne writes in Charles II.'s time: "it skilleth not at this day what metal the ring be." The Sarum Manual assumes that it would be *silver*. The Duke of Hamilton's run-away match with Miss Gunning was performed with a brass curtain-

became the dupes of the gamblers and led-captains who haunted fashionable assemblies under disguise, and awoke to their shame only to find themselves bound for life to some ruined spendthrift.

The immediate cause of Lord Hardwicke's Act arose out of the Law of *precontract* which existed in Scotland. A husband who had lived happily with his wife for thirty years was claimed as her husband by another woman to whom he had been *contracted* in early life. The opposition to Lord Hardwicke's Act was immense, and even riots ensued. Outside the walls of Parliament Roman Catholics and Protestant Dissenters saw that the Act would compel them to be married in the parish churches, and complained that they would thus be placed under the Clergy of the Church. Inside Parliament there was a fierce opposition from members, who either themselves or whose friends had been clandestinely married[f]. An amendment, exempting Scotland from its operation, in the hope that it would be fatal to

---

ring; whilst some marriages were performed with the ring of the church key or a strip cut from the bride's glove.—Jefferson's Brides and Bridals, i. 139.

[f] Amongst these was Henry Fox, afterwards Lord Holland, and Horace Walpole, the former of whom had in 1744 run away with the daughter of the Duke of Richmond; whilst two members of the family of the latter, viz. his great-uncle, Sir Edward Walpole, had married without banns or licence the daughter of the Duke of Leeds, and his sister-in-law, Lady Orford, had married, in May-Fair Chapel, a son of Earl Ferrers.

the Bill, was brought forward and passed the House of Commons; but rather than risk the loss of the Bill, Lord Hardwicke accepted the amendment, and a proviso was added that "nothing in the Act should extend to that part of Great Britain called Scotland." But from this proviso a great evil arose. Run-away matches were afterwards performed first in the Isle of Man; this, however, was stopped by a Statute of the Island in 1757. Guernsey and Jersey were next tried, but the long sea-voyage proved an objection. The fashion then veered round to Scotland, where marriages were performed by footmen, lawyers' clerks, and hotel waiters, wholly devoid of Orders. But the long and tedious journey, often accompanied by danger where pursuit was dreaded, was a drawback to this plan; so Gretna, as the nearest point to England, was selected, where marriages were for many years conducted by a mock-parson in gown, bands, and an orthodox three-cornered hat[g]. Another drawback to the Act was that the Royal Family were exempted from its operation[h].

---

[g] This proceeding lasted till 1856, when it was stopped by an Act, 19 and 20 Victoria, by which no marriage in Scotland is valid unless one of the parties had at the date thereof his or her usual place of residence there, or had lived in Scotland for twenty-one days next preceding the marriage.

[h] This defect was met by the Royal Marriage Act, 12 George III.; this Act was passed in consequence of the clandestine marriages of the King's brothers, the Duke of Gloucester, who

Lord Hardwicke's Act decided that all marriages should be celebrated after banns published on three successive Sundays, in the parish church, and suits in the Ecclesiastical Courts by reason of *precontract* were put a stop to[i]. It required that in the marriages of minors the consent of the parents or guardians should be first obtained; that all marriages should be entered in a book kept for that purpose, stating whether the marriage was celebrated after banns or by licence, and whether either of the contracting parties was under age; it decreed capital punishment on any one who should wilfully destroy or falsify the parish registers; and no marriage, except those of Jews or Quakers, should be solemnized except by Clergymen according to the English Prayer-Book[k].

---

in 1766 was secretly married in a drawing-room in Pall Mall to the Countess of Waldegrave, niece of Horace Walpole, and the Duke of Cumberland, who was privately married in 1771 to the Hon. Ann Horton; which marriages a Commission consisting of the Archbishop of Canterbury, the Lord Chancellor, and the Bishop of London, pronounced to be valid.

[i] When redress could no longer be obtained in the Ecclesiastical Courts, proceedings in the Civil Courts, known as actions for "Breach of promise," came into vogue.—Jefferson's Brides and Bridals, i. 129.

[k] In the same year a Bill was prepared for keeping an Annual Register of Births, Marriages, and Deaths, but it was thrown out for one (amongst others) curious reason, that it would furnish the enemies of England with the means of knowing the strength of the country. In 1836 the necessity of Dissenters being married in the parish church was removed.

In 1751 a change in the Calendar was made by an "Act for regulating the commencement of the year and for correcting the Calendar," so as to assimilate the style in Great Britain and Ireland to that used in other countries of Europe. In order to effect this purpose, it was now enacted that the eleven days between the 2nd and 14th of September should be omitted, so that the next day in 1752 to the 2nd of September should be the 14th; and the year, instead of commencing, as it did before, on March 25, for the future should commence on January 1. It was necessary also to make a change in the Calendar with regard to Easter. This change, however, in the Calendar (which remedied a great inconvenience) was received with much opposition. On one side people declaimed it as a Popish innovation[1]; other people spoke of the profaneness of changing the Saints' Days, and altering the time of immoveable Feasts; whilst others had a vague idea that their lives would be shortened by eleven days[m].

George II. died on October 25, 1760, and was succeeded by his grandson, George III., the first of his race who could boast that he had "been born and

---

[1] The plan adopted was that appoined by Pope Gregory XIII. in 1582.

[m] Coxe's Pelham. Hogarth has immortalized this opposition in his picture of the Election Feast, in which the Whig Candidate, to flatter the vulgar prejudice, inscribed on his banner " Give us back our ten days."

bred a Briton." It was a gain to the Church that the new King was at least a moral and religious man. It is pleasant to dwell on the simple and pure life of the King, on his many good qualities, which contrasted so strongly with the character of his two predecessors. It is pleasant to read how at his Coronation he took off his Crown before receiving the Holy Eucharist. "The King," says Archbishop Secker[n], "asked me if he should not take off his Crown; I said the office did not mention it; he asked me if it would not be suitable to such an act of religion. I said, Yes. But the Queen's Crown would not come off so easily[o]."

Again, when Dr. Wilson, one of his chaplains, flattered him in a sermon which he preached in the Chapel Royal, the King, instead of being pleased, wrote him a serious reprimand, and reminded him that "he went to Church to hear God praised, not himself."

His father having died when he was only twelve years of age, the education of the future King of England was left entirely to his mother, a woman who was strict in the observance of her religious duties. She allowed him to mix little with the world, thinking, and not without reason, that the young men of the period were so vicious that they

---

[n] Dr. Secker baptized, confirmed, married, and crowned George III.

[o] Stanley's Memorials of Westminster Abbey.

might contaminate her son; so he grew up from youth to manhood innocent of evil, and unsophisticated by the vices of the Court [p].

He took to himself a wife—a Royal Lady, it is true, from one of the petty principalities of Germany —a homely little woman with a narrow understanding, but virtuous and pious, and who contributed much towards the amendment of morals in the highest classes of society during this reign.

George III. had by nature a fair, but moderate, understanding, which was not improved by education; he was ignorant and narrow-minded; and though strictly religious, his character is represented as not open nor generous, but sullen and resentful. The same narrowness and limited understanding which characterized his whole public life; which made him oppose American freedom and Roman Catholic Emancipation; which, at a time when the penal code was so barbarous [q] that juries refused to convict and judges to condemn the prisoners, suggested as the only remedy, to "hang more thieves," affected also his conduct to the Church. The Queen

---

[p] "No boys," said the Duke of Gloucester to Hannah More, "were brought up in a greater ignorance of evil than the King and myself."—Hannah More's Life and Correspondence.

[q] Blackstone (1723—1780) mentions 160 offences, some of them of the most trifling kind, which were punishable with death. On one day, September 22, 1783, no fewer than fifty-eight persons received sentence of death. — Phillimore's George III., i. 50.

continued a Lutheran to her dying day; the King, though professing to be a Churchman, could no more shake off his "Germanical[r]" nature than "the Ethiopian could change his skin, or the leopard his spots," and was no Churchman at all; he did not like the Athanasian Creed, and always avoided repeating it; he was fond of Protestant Dissenters, but was always exclaiming that he "hated all Roman Catholics;" he was stubborn and determined (although the Bishops tried to dissuade him) in keeping the Sunday Bands at Kensington and on the Esplanade at Weymouth.

During the first ten years of his reign he managed to reduce government to a shadow, and before twenty years had passed he forced the American Colonies into revolt, and as it then appeared, brought England to the very verge of ruin. In vain, with regard to Roman Catholic Emancipation, Pitt told him[s] that "the measure would be attended with no danger to the Established Church or to the Protestant interest in Great Britain or Ireland;" that "the political circumstances under which the exclusive laws originated, arising either from the conflicting power of hostile and nearly balanced sects, from the apprehension of a Popish Queen or successor, and a foreign Pretender, and a division in Europe between

---

[r] This was the term by which Archbishop Parker described the refugees from Germany in the reign of Elizabeth.

[s] Letter to the King, Jan. 31, 1801.

the Catholic and Protestant powers, were no longer applicable to the present state of things." In vain Lord Melville showed him the absurdity of supposing that the Coronation Oath could absolve him from doing his duty to his country, under the sanction of Parliament; the only answer he could get from the King was, "None of your Scotch metaphysics." Lord Eldon once quoted, with respect to his "unflinching firmness" in the matter of Roman Catholic Emancipation, the King's since-memorable words: "I can give up my Crown and retire from power; I can quit my palace and live in a cottage; I can lay my head on a block and lose my life; but I cannot break my Coronation Oath;"—words no doubt indicative of inflexible goodness of heart, but certainly proofs of a defective education and narrow judgment. George III. could not lay claim to the Divine Right, but in other respects his mind equalled in obstinacy that of James II., and had he reigned in 1688, instead of at the end of the eighteenth and in the early years of the nineteenth centuries, it is only too probable that he would have shared the fate of that monarch.

The King soon showed himself sensible of the prevalent vice and immorality of the times, and in the first year of his reign he issued a Proclamation for the better observance of the Lord's Day[1], against

---

[1] Against "playing on the Lord's Day at Dice, Cards, or any other game whatever, either in public or private houses."

excessive drinking and profane swearing, and against public-houses being kept open during the hours of Divine Service, and other dissolute and immoral practices.

The condition of the State at the accession of George III. was particularly favourable to the cause of religious toleration. There was no longer any danger from the exiled Stuarts; their last battle had been fought and lost in 1745; no one cared any longer to drink the health of "Charlie over the water," for the young Pretender had sunk into a hopeless voluptuary. Jacobitism had died out; the Tories ceased to correspond with the exiled family, and were freed from the taint of the Jacobite heresy which had so long excluded them from the government. There was therefore no longer any reason why the Whigs should possess the exclusive favour of Royalty. Both parties in the state vied with each other in attachment to the throne. The Church, under the stimulus of the Wesleyan movement, was beginning, although very slowly, to recover from that period of religious apathy which had so long prevailed. Dissent, too, began to show signs of returning life and increased activity. And with returning life Dissent soon began to renew its claims; a feeling of the rights of the Dissenters to religious toleration gained ground and found response in Parliament; so that the history of the Church of England from 1760 to 1830 is little more than the history of the progress of Dissent. But before resuming the subject of Dissent we must mention one or two circumstances more directly concerned with the history of the Church.

On January 30, 1772, the anniversary of the Martyrdom of King Charles I., an absurd sermon, containing sentiments opposed to the Revolution, was preached before the House of Commons by Dr. Nowell, Principal of St. Mary Hall, Oxford. Only the Speaker and four Members of the House of Commons having been present at the sermon, the usual vote of thanks was made to the preacher; but when the sermon was printed, and the obnoxious sentiments were read, a motion was made and carried in the House of Commons that the vote of thanks should be cancelled, whilst by another motion the sermon was condemned to be burnt by the common hangman. A motion that the Service for King Charles I.'s Day, as being blasphemous and containing a parallel between the martyred King and the Saviour, should be expunged from the Prayer-Book, was opposed by Sir Roger Newdigate, Member for the University of Oxford, and was defeated by 125 to 97 votes.

On February 17 of the same year Mr. Seymour, whose family estates consisted of confiscated abbey lands, moved in the House of Commons for leave to bring in a Bill to secure the possession of such estates against dormant claims of the Church. As the civil "Nullum tempus Bill[u]" had made concessions in one direction, it was contended that a like reason prevailed why a similar limit should be placed on ecclesiastical claims also. The opponents of the measure objected that it was necessary for the Church to retain the power of reviving its claims in order to protect it from encroachments; that whilst in the case of the Crown the power might be made an instrument in the hands of the strong to oppose the weak, in the case of the Church it was a protection to the weak against the strong. The motion was defeated by 141 to 117 votes.

We now come to the progress of Dissent. The first step to a more complete toleration of Dissenters was taken on April 3, 1772, when Sir Henry Hoghton brought in a Bill for relieving Dissenting ministers and schoolmasters from the subscription, as required by the Act of Toleration, to the XXXIX. Articles. He was, however, opposed by the Tories, who contended that as the laws were never enforced, the grievance was imaginary rather than real; whilst by others it was contended in favour of the Bill that whilst such subscriptions operated against the conscientious, they were disregarded by the profligate. But as the government was desirous of uniting with the Protestant against the Roman Catholic Nonconformists, the Bill met with little opposition in the

---

[u] So called from the maxim "Nullum tempus occurrit regi" ("No length of time is a bar to the claims of the King).''

House of Commons, where the second reading was carried by 70 to 9 votes. The King, however, was opposed to it; in the House of Lords, where it was advocated by Lord Chatham and Lord Mansfield, it was vigorously opposed by the Episcopal Bench, particularly by the Archbishop of York, the Bishops of London, Oxford, Peterborough, and Llandaff[x], the last of whom cited passages from the writings of Dr. Priestley which excited the horror of Churchmen; one Bishop, however, Dr. Green, of Lincoln, voted for it[y], and the Bill was defeated by a large majority[z]. On March 2 in the following year another Bill with the same object in view was brought in by Sir Henry Hoghton, only to meet a similar fate. The Dissenters were themselves opposed to the Bill from a fear that Socinianism might profit if it passed, and declared themselves contented with the toleration already afforded them.

On January 30, 1779, Dr. John Ross, who had in the previous year been appointed to the See of Exeter, in a sermon preached before the House of Lords advocated an extension of toleration to Dis-

---

[x] Dr. Shute Barrington.

[y] The King could not understand a Bishop voting according to his conscience: "Green, Green," he exclaimed, "he shall never be promoted."

[z] It was in one of the debates on this subject that Lord Chatham is reported to have described the Church of England as Popish in her Liturgy, Calvinistic in her Articles, and Arminian in her Clergy.—Stanhope, v. 459.

senters, and as in 1778 certain concessions had been made in favour of the Roman Catholics, Sir H. Hoghton succeeded in carrying his Bill to a successful issue. Dissenting ministers and schoolmasters were thenceforward admitted to the benefits of the Toleration Act without signing any of the XXXIX. Articles; the sole requirement being a declaration from them that they were Christian and Protestant Dissenters, and took the Scriptures for their rule of faith and practice [a].

In the previous year the Penal Laws against the Roman Catholics had been brought under review [b]. A loyal address had been made to the King by members of that Church expressing attachment to his person and to the civil constitution of the country, their exclusion from the benefits of which did not diminish their loyalty, whilst they received thankfully the relaxations already granted them, waiting patiently, without presuming to suggest either the time or the measure, any further indulgence that might be granted them. They dissented, they said, from the Established Church on purely conscientious grounds;

---

[a] May's Constitut. Hist. "This was the first step in the direction of an enlarged Toleration for 90 years."—Skeats, 465.

[b] The principal Penal Laws since the Revolution against the Roman Catholics were: 1 Will. and Mary c. 9, 15, 26; 9 and 10 Will. III. c. 32; the Act of 1700; another Act in 1711; 1 George I. c. 55, after the Rebellion of 1715; another in 1722; and again after the Rebellion of 1745.

they held no opinions inconsistent with the duties of good citizens; they referred to their irreproachable conduct for many years; to their unalterable attachment to their country; to their detestation of the designs of any foreign power against the Crown, or the safety and tranquillity of the subject.

On May 14 Sir George Saville moved for leave to bring in a Bill for the repeal of certain penalties and disabilities provided in the Act of 10 and 11 William III., entitled "An Act to prevent the further growth of Popery." The motion was seconded by Mr. Dunning, who stated the great and grievous penalties under which Roman Catholics suffered; the perpetual imprisonment as felons and traitors of Popish Priests and Jesuits for celebrating Mass; the forfeiture of the estates of Roman Catholics, who had been educated in foreign countries, in favour of the next Protestant heir, so that a son, if a Protestant, could deprive a Roman Catholic father of his estate; and the deprivation of Roman Catholics of the power of acquiring estates by purchase.

The Bill passed the House of Commons without a dissentient voice, and with but slight opposition the House of Lords also, Dr. Hinchcliffe of Peterborough being the only Bishop who opposed it. Thenceforward all that was required of a Roman Catholic was to subscribe an oath of allegiance to the King, and to disclaim the Pope's authority over this kingdom, or his power to absolve the people in England from obedience to the government as by law established.

Some of the laws against the Roman Catholics had, as stated in the House of Commons, ceased to be necessary, others were at all times a disgrace to humanity. The Bill extended only to England, but when the Lord Advocate proposed to introduce a similar Bill for Scotland, a country which had nothing to fear from Roman Catholics, a storm of fanatical fury broke forth in that country. In Edinburgh and Glasgow the chapels of Roman Catholics were destroyed, their property demolished, and their lives threatened. From Scotland this miserable bigotry passed into England, where the "No Popery" cry was raised; the people formed themselves into "Protestant Associations," and broke out into open rebellion under the presidency of the half-witted Lord George Gordon; London was pillaged for three days; the houses of Roman Catholics were destroyed, the prisons were broken into and set on fire, and the prisoners released, many of them to perish in the flames [c]. The Protestant feeling was particularly excited against Sir George Saville and Lord Mansfield, the latter of whom had lately screened a Roman Catholic Priest from persecution in a Court of Justice [d]. His house was set on fire; not only his books

---

[c] The King himself was accused of Popery, and placards with the inscription, "A great man at his devotions," were posted about, exhibiting him in the dress of a monk kneeling at a Roman Catholic Altar on which stood a Crucifix.

[d] The plaintiff had accused the defendant of being a Roman Catholic Priest. "And what reason have you, Mr. Payne," said

but his valuable manuscripts, which were beyond
price, were burnt; he himself was seized by the mob,
and his life was endangered, when he was with
difficulty rescued by Archbishop Markham of York,
who ran from the House of Lords to his assistance,
and whose lawn sleeves were torn off and thrown
in his face. Dr. Thurlow, Bishop of Lincoln, and
brother of the Lord Chancellor, was obliged to seek
refuge from the mob in a house from which he escaped
along the tiles dressed in a woman's garment. The
tumult was at last put down by the military, after
many lives were lost and money to the value of
£180,000 expended; twenty-one of the rioters were
executed; the wretched fanatic who had caused all
the misery escaped: instead of being thrown into
a common gaol, he was treated as a state prisoner,
and dignified by imprisonment in the Tower, and
acquitted on the charge of High Treason [e]. A strong
Protestant feeling pervaded the nation; advertise-
ments appeared in the newspapers stating that his

---

the Judge, "to believe that? Were you ever in Rome? or did
you see him ordained?" "No," replied Payne, "but I heard
him say *Dominus Vobiscum*, and preach in a Popish Conventicle." "And pray, Mr. Payne, may not you and I say
Dominus Vobiscum, or pray in Latin, or pretend to preach?
Yet I am of opinion there is not one in this court who takes
us for Roman Catholic Priests."—Adolphus's Hist. of England, ii. 557.

[e] He afterwards renounced Christianity and embraced Judaism, and in 1793 died in Newgate of the gaol fever.

Majesty's hosier was one of the staunchest Protestants in the kingdom, and that his Majesty's wine-merchants were also Protestants[f].

After the riots were quelled, the Protestant Associations continued to press their bigotry on the Legislature, and a Bill was passed in the House of Commons depriving Roman Catholics of the right of keeping schools where Protestants were taught; the Lords, however, rejected it as passed under fear of popular outrage, and therefore derogatory to the dignity and independence of Parliament. The miserable riots, however, had the effect of postponing for years any further attempt to obtain relief for Roman Catholics.

---

[f] Lord Mahon's Hist., vii. 36.

CHAPTER VI.

LEADING CHURCHMEN OF THE PERIOD.

AT no period of its history have more conspicuous names at one and the same time adorned the English Church than during that part of the eighteenth century with which we are now concerned. When we mention such names—amongst the Archbishops and Bishops, as those of Wake, Potter, Secker, Atterbury, Gibson, Berkeley, Sherlock, Butler, Wilson, Conybeare, Warburton, Louth, and Horne; amongst Priests, those of Bentley, Bingham, Prideaux, Waterland, and Wall—it will be readily imagined that the difficulty of enumerating the leading divines of the day proceeds rather from the abundance than the dearth of material. We shall endeavour in this chapter to give a short account of some of the leading Anglican Archbishops, Bishops, and Priests, as are not mentioned in other parts of this work.

And first as to the Archbishops. Archbishop Wake died in January, 1737. Towards the close of his life he had become so weighed down with infirmities both of mind and body that the principal care of the Church had devolved upon Dr. Gibson, Bishop of

London, and the Archbishop died at the age of fourscore years, leaving his valuable manuscripts, valued at £10,000, to Christ Church, Oxford. He was succeeded at Canterbury by Dr. Potter, translated from the See of Oxford.

John Potter (1674—1747), born at Wakefield, where his father was a Draper, and educated at Wakefield School [a], entered University College, Oxford, at the age of fourteen. In 1694 he was elected a Fellow of Lincoln, and in 1697, when only twenty-three years of age, he edited Plutarch, Basil, and Lycophron, and published the first volume of his Antiquities of Greece, the second volume appearing the next year. In 1704 he became Chaplain to Archbishop Tenison, who collated him to several preferments; in 1706 he was appointed Chaplain to Queen Anne; in the following year he published his great work, the "Discourse of Church Government," with the design of vindicating the Church of England from the charge of Erastian principles. In 1708, through the interest of the Duke of Marlborough, he succeeded Dr. Jane as Regius Professor of Divinity and Canon of Christ Church, and in 1715, shortly after having published the works of Clemens Alexandrinus, he was promoted to the See of Oxford, holding with it the Regius Professorship of Divinity. In a charge to his

---

[a] This school is celebrated for having as its scholars, Potter, Bentley, Bingham, and Dr. Radcliffe, founder of the Radcliffe Library at Oxford.

Clergy of that diocese, Dr. Potter warned them against the opinions of Hoadly, at that time Bishop of Bangor. A short controversy ensued between the two prelates. In vindicating himself against Hoadly's reply, Bishop Potter stated that he had been accused, whilst upholding Protestant principles for decency's sake, not only of favouring Popery, but of being a Papist in disguise, because he had in his charge referred his Clergy to the practice and writers of the primitive times, and to the next ages after the Apostles. "I am not," he said, "the least apprehensive of my being suspected as a favourer of popery by any man who knows the true meaning of popery; but sure it is such a compliment to the Popish religion as no Protestant would have made, who understands his own principles, to date its rise from the time of Constantine; the claim of infallibility, and of the Papal supremacy, as now exercised, the doctrine of Transubstantiation, Invocation of Saints, Image worship, prayers in an unknown tongue, forbidding laymen to read the Scriptures, to say nothing of other peculiar tenets of the Church of Rome, having never been heard of during the reign of this great Emperor, or for a long time after, as a very little insight into the Popish controversies or Ecclesiastical historians would have shown the author." On the accession of George II. Bishop Potter was chosen to preach the Coronation Sermon on October 11, 1727. When the See of Canterbury became vacant on the death of

Wake, Queen Caroline was desirous of appointing Gibson, Bishop of London, to succeed him; he was so confessedly the first Bishop of the day that he was commonly styled the "heir apparent of Canterbury." But Gibson had offended Walpole by his opposition to the "Quakers' Relief Bill," and the same objection lay against Sherlock. Walpole wished to appoint Hare, Bishop of Chichester, but Lord Hervey strongly supported Potter. "Why cannot you," he said, "appoint some Greek blockhead that has learning enough to justify the appointment, and not sense enough to make you repent it?" He strongly insisted upon Potter's appointment: "The Queen loves him; his character will support you for sending him to Lambeth; his capacity is not so good, nor his temper so bad, as to make you apprehend any great danger from his being there." It was strange that such a Churchman as Potter should be a friend of the Queen. But Potter was a man of learning, which she valued somewhat, and a Whig, which she valued more, and she could rely upon his adherence to Walpole and the Whig government. Being a High Churchman, he did good service to the Church in those perilous times when Latitudinarianism was rampant; he was orthodox, even if his orthodoxy was somewhat cold and dry, and a zealous supporter of the Church's interests [b].

---

[b] Though a draper's son, he is said to have been very haughty. He died immensely rich, and disinherited his eldest

Leading Churchmen of the Period. 445

After Dr. Potter came two Archbishops whom nature meant to be nobodies, but whom good fortune and their Latitudinarian views raised to the See of Canterbury—Dr. Herring, and Dr. Hutton.

Thomas Herring (1691—1757) was educated at Jesus College, and became a Fellow and Tutor of Corpus Christi, Cambridge. He held at different times various Church appointments; at Cambridge he was incumbent of Trinity Church[c]; in 1722 he became Chaplain to Dr. Fleetwood, Bishop of Ely; in 1726 Precentor at Lincoln's Inn, and Chaplain to the King; in 1731 Dean of Rochester; in 1737 Bishop of Bangor, holding the Deanery of Rochester *in commendam*, and in 1742 he was translated to York. When the rebellion of 1745 broke out, it was Archbishop Herring who first gave the alarm, and aroused the nation from its lethargy, and also raised £40,000 for the defence of the kingdom; for this valuable service to the House of Hanover, and without any special qualifications for the post, he was, in 1747, on the death of Archbishop Potter, raised to the Primacy[d]. A controversy took place in 1749, between

---

son for marrying against his wishes, but obtained for him Church appointments to the value of £2,000 a year (Nich. Lit. An., i. 178), and left the whole of his fortune, valued at £90,000, to his second son, who was a disgrace to society.

[c] The church of Simeon in later days.

[d] Dean Hook, in his Ecclesiastical Biography, says that from his zeal for the Hanoverian family he was nicknamed the *Red Herring*.

the Archbishop and Sherlock, Bishop of London, as to the right of the former to an option [e]. The Archbishop made his option of St. George's, Hanover Square, to which the Bishop of London objected; eventually a compromise was effected, and the Archbishop accepted St. Anne's, Soho [f].

Archbishop Herring held the Primacy for ten years; but an illness which he contracted in 1753 so shattered his constitution, that for the last four years of his life he lived in privacy at Croydon, where he died in 1757.

His successor, Dr. Hutton (1693—1758), was even less distinguished than Dr. Herring. Educated at Jesus College, Cambridge, he was made Prebendary of York by Archbishop Blackburne, in 1745 he followed Dr. Herring as Bishop of Bangor, as he followed him again in 1747 to York, and again in 1757 to Canterbury. He died, however, within a year of his attaining the Primacy, and of him little can be learnt, and that little not to his praise, viz. that he was a Latitudinarian, and a patron and admirer of Archdeacon Blackburne [g].

---

[e] An Archbishop had formerly the choice (which was called the option) of any one dignity or benefice in the gift of any Bishop consecrated by him. This privilege has been abandoned by English Archbishops since 1845.

[f] For an account of Dr. Herring's Arian opinions, see Part II. chap. vii.

[g] Horace Walpole, however, speaks of him as a "well-bred man and devoted to the ministry."

At York Dr. Hutton was succeeded by Dr. Gilbert. Of Dr. Gilbert Bishop Newton relates, with all seriousness, an anecdote which, as showing a ritual practice approved at that time, deserves to be recounted [h]. He invented a mode of conferring Confirmation which, says the Bishop, *had a wonderful effect*. The practice had, it appears, prevailed of a Bishop laying hands on two or four persons, and saying the form of prayer over them; but Archbishop Gilbert went the whole length of the Table, silently laid his hands on each, and then, drawing back to the Communion Table, pronounced the prayers over all at once.

In 1758 an Archbishop of a very different type, Dr. Secker, translated from the See of Oxford, succeeded to the Primacy. Thomas Secker (1693—1768) was, like Bishop Butler, born of Dissenting parents, and together with him was educated at a Dissenting school at Tewkesbury, being intended by his parents for the ministry. But not satisfied with the principles of the Dissenters, he was disinclined to enter their ministry, although at the same time he did not see clearly what doctrines or what Church he should embrace; he therefore, at the end of 1716, applied himself to the study of physic, which he pursued both in London and Paris. In the meantime his schoolfellow, Joseph Butler, had, on conviction, changed

---

[h] Autobiography of Bishop Newton, i. 77.

from Dissent to the Church, and in 1714 entered at Oriel College, Oxford. A correspondence was kept up between the two friends, the one writing from Paris, the other from Oxford, and when Butler became Preacher at the Rolls he induced Secker to conform to the Church of England. Secker having taken, in 1721, a medical degree at Leyden, entered the same year as a gentleman commoner at Exeter College, Oxford, and having received, after one year's residence, a degree by diploma from the University, was, in 1722, ordained Deacon by Dr. Talbot, Bishop of Durham. A short digression may perhaps be allowed, that a few words may be said of Dr. Talbot, who obtained such high preferments in the Church.

He does not appear to have been a very estimable Bishop; he was a great admirer of the Arian, Clarke, and lamented that he was prevented, by Clarke's unwillingness to sign the XXXIX. Articles, from advancing him to the highest preferments in his diocese [1]. Dr. Talbot owed his rapid promotion in the Church to his kinsman, Lord Shrewsbury. In 1691 he succeeded the Nonjuror, Dr. Hickes, as Dean of Worcester; in 1699 he succeeded Dr. Fell as Bishop of Oxford, holding the Deanery of Worcester *in commendam*. On the accession of George I. he was appointed Dean of the Chapel Royal; in 1715 he succeeded Burnet as Bishop of Salisbury, and

---

[1] Nich. Lit. Hist., i. 419.

in 1721, on the death of Lord Crewe, he was translated to Durham [k]. He was noted for his avarice, and notwithstanding his large income was constantly in debt, from which his eldest son, Lord Chancellor Talbot, had to extricate him. The Bishop's second son, Edward Talbot, was elected a Fellow of Oriel in 1712, where he became the friend of Butler, and through Butler of Secker, both of whom he recommended to his father the Bishop [l].

Having been ordained Deacon by Dr. Talbot, Secker's rise was rapid. Bishop Talbot made him his Chaplain, and soon gave him the living of Houghton-le-Spring (which he exchanged in 1727 for that of Ryton), and a prebend at Durham; in 1732, through the influence of Bishop Sherlock, he was made one of the King's Chaplains, and in the following year Rector of St. James's, Piccadilly. There he obtained the reputation of being one of the first preachers of the day, and having gained the high opinion of Queen Caroline, he was, in 1735, appointed Bishop of Bristol, whence he was, in 1737,

---

[k] It was hinted that he did not obtain the opulent See of Durham without disgorging a *douceur* of six or seven thousand pounds.—Hutchinson's Hist. of Durham, i. 573.

[l] The Church owes a debt of gratitude to Bishop Talbot, who was the friend and patron of three of the best Bishops of the eighteenth century,—Dr. Benson, Bishop of Gloucester, Bishop Butler, of Bristol and Durham, and Dr. Secker, Bishop of Bristol, Oxford, and Archbishop of Canterbury.

translated to Oxford. In 1750 he gave up the rectory of St. James's and his prebend at Durham, and became Dean of St. Paul's ; in 1758 he was promoted to the Primacy.

Bishop Secker, in a charge to his Clergy in 1750, gives a sad account of the churches in the diocese: "Some have scarce been kept in necessary repair, and others by no means duly cleaned from annoyances, which must gradually bring them to decay: water undermining and rotting the foundations, earth heaped up against the outside, weeds and shrubs growing upon them ; too frequently the floors are meanly paved, or the walls dirty or patched, or the windows ill-glazed, and it may be in part stopped up, or they are damp, offensive, and unwholesome."

After he was made Archbishop, he became a liberal benefactor to Church objects. He was a promoter of religious institutions, of the maintenance of schools for the poor, the rebuilding or repairing parsonages and churches; he gave £600 towards building a chapel in the parish of Lambeth, and a liberal benefaction to the S.P.G. and S.P.C.K.[m] Archbishop Secker lived eight years into the reign of George III., dying in 1768. Bishop Newton tells us that he was too considerable a man to live without enemies. Whether from misrepresentations

---

[m] His endeavours for a Colonial Episcopate will be related in the chapter on the American Church.

Leading Churchmen of the Period. 451

from those who were opposed to him, or from a certain coldness of manner which was habitual to him, Secker was not a favourite with George III., and so in his Archiepiscopate a different mode of making Church appointments was begun [n]. In former reigns the Archbishop had the principal direction of ecclesiastical preferments, or, at any rate, nothing of importance was done without his being consulted. Henceforward the ministers engrossed all the powers into their own hands; the Bishops were "little more than cyphers even in their own churches, unless the preferments happened to be in their own gift, and then perhaps the ministers were troublesome by their solicitation [o]."

On the death of Archbishop Secker the Primacy was offered to the King's former tutor, Dr. Thomas, Bishop of Sarum, and on his refusing it, the King wished it to be offered to Dr. Terrick, Bishop of London; but Dr. Frederick Cornwallis, Bishop of Lichfield and Dean of St. Paul's, younger son of the fourth Baron Cornwallis, was a personal friend of the Duke of Grafton, the Prime Minister, and was through his favour appointed.

We have already noticed [p] the severe letter of remonstrance which the King wrote to this Archbishop, on the representation of the Countess of Hunting-

---

[n] Bishop Newton, i. 119.   [o] Ibid.
[p] Page 295.

don, as to unseemly festivities which occurred at Lambeth Palace. That incident Bishop Newton charitably ascribes to an excess of good-nature or hospitality on the part of the Archbishop; "he kept an elegant table," he says; "has not a grain of pride in his composition; is easy of access; receives every one with affability and good-nature; is courteous, obliging, and condescending, and as a proof of it, he has not often been made the subject of censure even in this censorious age."

In justice to Archbishop Cornwallis, it must be stated that in 1777 he, together with Dr. Porteus (who had that year been raised to the See of Chester), incurred much abuse, and was met with "No Popery" cries, because he advocated the decent observance of Good Friday, which at that time had almost become obsolete. The angry mob exclaimed that "his arrogance" in advocating the closing of the shops on that day would soon be followed by "the elevation of the Host and Crucifix to prostrate crowds in dirty streets." For many weeks together the Presbyterian newspapers were full of abuse towards Archbishop Cornwallis and his family. The London "Evening Post" of May 29, 1777, spoke of the young prelate Porteus as with a "sort of outlandish name," and complained of his "shutting up the city shops on Good Friday, which as a sanctified, hypocritical triumph over both reason and Scripture—the civil and religious right of Englishmen—could not

Leading Churchmen of the Period. 453

but be highly acceptable to tyrant and hypocrite of every denomination, particularly at Court ^q."

Another point must be added in Archbishop Cornwallis's favour. Whereas his predecessors either had not the spirit or the generosity to place the portrait of Archbishop Sancroft amongst those of the other Archbishops in Lambeth Palace, Dr. Cornwallis obtained leave from the Master of Emmanuel College, Cambridge, to have a copy taken from the portrait in the Hall of that College, and thus added the portrait of Sancroft to the portraits of the other Archbishops of Canterbury ^r.

From the Archbishops we pass to the Bishops of London. And first to Bishop Gibson, who, after having held the See of Lincoln from 1716 to 1723, was in the latter year translated to London. Edmund Gibson (1669—1748) was educated at Queen's College, Oxford, and at an early period of his life came under public notice through various publications, which shewed his knowledge of the Classics, and his accurate acquaintance with the Northern languages, as well as with Roman and Saxon antiquities and British topography. Archbishop Tenison made him his librarian at Lambeth, and his private chaplain; and through the Archbishop's interest he became Precentor and Residentiary at Chichester, Rector of

---

^q See Church Quarterly Review, ix. 196.
^r D'Oyly's Life of Sancroft, 77, n.

Lambeth, and Archdeacon of Surrey. The part he took in the Convocation controversy led him to a course of study which resulted in the publication, in 1713, of his famous "Codex Juris Ecclesiastici Anglicani," the learned and comprehensive work on the legal rights of the Clergy, and of the Constitution, Canons, and Articles of the English Church, which is the established repertory of our statutes and usages. Being a friend of the Hanoverian succession, he was, in 1716, appointed to the See of Lincoln, and having refused the See of Winchester, was in 1723, on the recommendation of Dr. Wake, appointed to that of London; during the long illness of Archbishop Wake he was virtually Primate of England, and he was so confessedly the first Bishop of the day that it was commonly thought he would be Wake's successor. He was Walpole's chief adviser in ecclesiastical matters, and Walpole was represented as leaning too much upon him and making him a Pope[s]. Nevertheless, Gibson was too conscientious to be popular with the King or government; he offended the King by opposing and procuring from the Bishops an address against masquerades, to which the King was much attached; he offended the government by his opposition to the appointment of Rundle to the See of Gloucester; and he offended Walpole in particular by the part

---

[s] And "a very good Pope he is," replied Walpole.

Leading Churchmen of the Period. 455

he took in the "Quakers' Relief Bill;" so he was passed over, and Dr. Potter appointed instead to Canterbury. Whilst Gibson was Bishop of London he procured an endowment from the Crown for a course of sermons to be preached in the Chapel Royal of Whitehall, by twelve clergymen selected in equal numbers from Oxford and from Cambridge. His literary pursuits did not hinder him from the proper discharge of the higher duties of a Bishop; his Pastoral Letters were those of an earnest and profoundly religious prelate; and few tracts stated so fairly, or so vigorously refuted, the aggressions of the Deistical writers, at that time so dangerous to the State [t].

Dr. Gibson was succeeded in 1745 by Dr. Sherlock. Thomas Sherlock (1678—1762), son of the Dr. William Sherlock who, having first joined the Nonjurors, recanted, and was appointed to the Deanery of St. Paul's in 1691. He was educated at Eton, and graduated at Catharine's Hall, Cambridge, being a contemporary and a member of the same Hall with Hoadly, whose vigorous opponent he afterwards became. In 1704 he succeeded his father at the Temple, and at once became known as one of the rising Clergymen of the day [u]; in 1714 he was elected Master of Catharine

---

[t] Milman's St. Paul's, 457.
[u] The following squib prophesied his career :—
"As Sherlock at Temple was taking a boat,
The waterman asked him which way he would float;

Hall. For some time he was almost as unpopular as his father had been. Like his father, he at first scrupled about taking the oaths, but on the Sunday after the battle of Preston he preached a sermon in favour of the House of Hanover, which people were unkind enough to say, ought to have been preached the Sunday before, and the next year (1716) he was appointed to the Deanery of Chichester[x].

In the Bangorian Controversy, in which he was one of Hoadly's most formidable opponents, he published a number of pamphlets, the principal one being entitled "A Vindication of the Corporation and Test Acts in answer to the Bishop of Bangor's Reasons for the Repeal of them," and for the part which he took in the controversy he was deprived by the government of his post as King's Chaplain. In 1725 he attacked Collins's "Discourse of the grounds and reasons of the Christian Religion," in six discourses, preached at the Temple, and published

---

  'Which way?' says the Doctor; 'why, fool, with the
    stream ;—
  To Paul's or to Lambeth was all one to him.'"
He became Bishop of London and so gained St. Paul's, but refused Lambeth.

  [x] With regard to the part taken by the two Sherlocks the following lines, which pretend to be poetry, were written :—
   "As Sherlock the elder, with his *jure* divine,
    Did not comply till the Battle of Boyne ;
    So Sherlock the younger still made it a question
    Which side he should take till the Battle of Preston."

under the title of "The use and intent of Prophecy in the several ages of the Church." In 1728 he was appointed to the See of Bangor, which had been held by his antagonist Hoadly. In 1729 he published against the Deist Woolston "The Trial of the Witnesses of the Resurrection of Jesus," a work which went through fourteen editions, and which Leland described as being "universally admired for the polite and uncommon turn, as well as the judicious manner of treating the matter." In 1734 he succeeded Hoadly as Bishop of Salisbury; in 1747 he refused, on account of illness, the Primacy, to which Dr. Herring was appointed, but on his recovery from illness he accepted in the following year the See of London. As Bishop of London—when the Londoners were frightened out of their senses by the earthquake of 1750, when a more religious spirit was for a time prevalent amongst the people, when the churches were crowded with penitent sinners, and the hand of charity was liberally opened—Bishop Sherlock sought to improve the occasion, and addressed a "Pastoral Letter to the Clergy and Inhabitants of London and Westminster, on occasion of the late Earthquakes." Within a month more than 100,000 copies of this letter were sold; but (it must be added) when the fears of the people vanished, they were soon reconciled to their old vices, which they seemed to resume with redoubled affection.

Bishop Sherlock died on July 18, 1761, leaving

behind him several volumes of sermons, which were supposed to be a model of pulpit eloquence[y]. To him succeeded as Bishops of London a number of decent mediocrities: Dr. Thomas Hayter, translated from Norwich in 1761, Dr. Richard Osbaldeston, 1762, and Dr. Richard Terrick, 1764. One notable feature in the episcopacy of Dr. Osbaldeston and Dr. Terrick was their stern and uncompromising Protestantism. When the former was Bishop of London, Archbishop Secker thought that foreign Churches had an advantage over the Church of England in possessing monuments, and wished to introduce them into St. Paul's; the Bishop, however, was inflexible; there had been no monuments before, and there should be none in his time. Again, when Bishop Newton was Dean of St. Paul's, it was observed to him that all churches had at the east end one monument, that on which were inscribed the Ten Commandments[z]. In 1773 Sir Joshua Reynolds conveyed to the Dean an offer that the Royal Society should, at its own expense, decorate the interior of St. Paul's with pic-

---

[y] Bishop Sherlock died worth £150,000. Chandler, Bishop of Durham, Willis, Bishop of Winchester, Potter, Archbishop of Canterbury, Gibson and Sherlock, Bishops of London, "all died shamefully rich, some of them worth more than £100,000, and to these must be added Dr. Gilbert, of York."—King's Anecdotes, p. 184.

[z] The Bishop gives us the lines:—
"Moses and Aaron upon a church wall,
  Holding up the Commandments for fear they should fall."

tures; Sir Joshua Reynolds himself, Angelica Kauffman, Mr. West, and Mr. Barry were to be the artists, and the pictures were to be submitted for approval of the Dean and Chapter. The Dean and Chapter were much pleased with the idea, but Archbishop Cornwallis and Bishop Terrick were unbending in their Protestantism, and would not listen to the idea, since people might regard it as an artful introduction of Popery[a].

Dr. Lowth, translated from Oxford to London in 1777, was a prelate equalled by few and surpassed by none of his time. Robert Lowth (1710—1787), educated at Winchester and New College, was, in 1741, elected Professor of Poetry at Oxford, in which capacity he delivered the Lectures afterwards published in 1753 under the title of "Prælectiones Academicæ de sacrâ Poesi Hebræorum," in which he dealt with the difficult subject of Hebrew versification. Those Lectures brought him into a controversy with Warburton, into which it is not our purpose to enter further than to say that Lowth had advanced positions about the Book of Job and the Mosaic cosmogony, which Warburton considered to be levelled against his own personal views. The controversy was carried on in a manner which reflected little credit on either side, but in defence of

---

[a] Newton's Autobiography, i. 145. No doubt St. Paul's was happily saved, but the reasons assigned are instructive.

Dr. Lowth it must be remembered if, in the heat of argument, he was led to use language at variance with the usual gentleness of his character, that Warburton was his antagonist, a man pachydermatous above all others, on whom nothing but the strongest language could have the least effect. In 1766 Lowth was appointed to the See of St. David's, a few months afterwards he was translated to Oxford, from whence, in 1777, he was appointed to the See of London [b]. In 1778 he published the last and the greatest of his literary works, his translation of the Book of Isaiah, with the design not only of giving an exact representation of the meaning and words of the Prophet, but also to "imitate the air and manner of the author, to express the form and fashion of the composition, and to give the English reader some notion of the peculiar turn and cast of the original." In 1783, on the death of Archbishop Cornwallis, the Primacy was offered to Bishop Lowth, but, on account of his infirmities and family bereavements, refused by him.

During the episcopate of Bishop Lowth an im-

---

[b] At this point of his life a pleasing story is related of Bishop Lowth. He and John Wesley met at dinner in 1771, and the Bishop refused to sit above him at the table: "Mr. Wesley," he said, "may I be found sitting at your feet in another world;" and when Wesley refused, the Bishop requested him to take the upper seat, as he was deaf, and did not wish to lose a word of his conversation.

portant decision with regard to Bonds of Resignation was given in the Law Courts. A simoniacal practice had long existed under which patrons of Livings bound the Clergymen whom they presented to resign their Livings when called upon to do so. Towards the end of 1781 a case of this nature arose between Bishop Lowth and Mr. Disney Fitche, with regard to which Lord Loughborough decided that bonds of resignation were good in law. But in 1783 an appeal was made from this decision to the House of Lords, when the judgment of the lower Court was reversed; general bonds of resignation were declared to be illegal, and all presentations thus procured to be simoniacal and void. Bishop Lowth died at Fulham in 1787 [c].

A greater than any of his contemporary Bishops was Butler, Bishop successively of Bristol and Durham. Joseph Butler (1692—1752) was born at Wantage in Berkshire; his father, a shopkeeper in that town, being a Presbyterian, and designing his son for the Presbyterian Ministry, Joseph Butler was sent to a Dissenting Academy at Gloucester (which was afterwards removed to Tewkesbury), where he contracted a life-long friendship with Secker, afterwards Archbishop of Canterbury, who, like him, was at the time a Dissenter. Whilst at Tewkesbury, Butler, then only in his twenty-second

---

[c] Porteus's Life, p. 84.

year, first gave proof of those great metaphysical powers for which he has since been distinguished, by a correspondence with the Arian, Clarke, on the publication by the latter of "The Demonstration of the Being and Attributes of God." In his last letter Dr. Clarke pays Butler a well-deserved compliment: "We seem to have pushed the matter in question between us as far as it will go; and, upon the whole, I cannot but take notice, I have very seldom met with persons so reasonable and unprejudiced as yourself in such debates as these."

Being dissatisfied with the principles of Nonconformity, Butler resolved to take Orders in the Church, and was entered, in 1714, although reluctantly, by his father at Oriel College, where he made the acquaintance of Mr. Edward Talbot, a Fellow of that College[d], on whose recommendation he was, shortly after his Ordination, appointed to the preachership at the Rolls Chapel[e]. In 1726 he was appointed by Dr. Talbot, at that time Bishop of Durham, to the valuable Living of Stanhope. His friends, and particularly Dr. Secker, who was then one of the King's Chaplains, were desirous of bringing him out of that seclusion, and to Queen Caroline the Church owes a debt of gratitude for

---

[d] Son of Dr. Talbot, successively Bishop of Oxford, Salisbury, and Durham. See page 449.

[e] In 1726 he published his famous "Fifteen Sermons," preached in that chapel.

seconding their wishes. The Queen, who had doubtless heard of Butler's sermons, asked Dr. Blackburne, Archbishop of York, whether the excellent Dr. Butler was dead. "No, Madam," was the Archbishop's reply, "but he is buried." Mr. Butler was drawn out from his retirement, and his friend Secker obtained for him from Lord Chancellor Talbot the appointment as his Chaplain. In 1736 Butler was appointed Clerk of the Closet to Queen Caroline, and at her request he used to attend, between seven and nine o'clock in the evening, her meetings, where he would find the curious medley of Berkeley, Clarke, Hoadly, Sherlock, and Secker, to converse with her on theological and philosophical subjects. In the same year in which he was appointed Clerk of the Closet to the Queen, before the work was given to the public, he presented her with a copy of his Analogy[f].

It would be as presumptuous as it is impossible within the limits of such a work as this, to analyse this, the most profound work of philosophical theology extant in any language. It was a work written against the Deists with the object, as Butler states himself, of answering "as he went along, every possible objection that might arise to any one against any position" of his, and it thoroughly effected the immediate end it had in view; but it can scarcely be denied that the style is obscure, and that the work as a system of practical theology is useless. Nor

---

[f] "The Analogy of Religion, Natural and Revealed, to the Constitution and Causes of Nature."

is this to be wondered at, when we bear in mind that it is the result of twenty years' hard thinking; a work which might have been extended into folios contracted into one small volume. As an exercise of the reasoning faculties it is beyond doubt excellent, but it could not have been sufficiently read, and if read, not sufficiently studied, to effect to any great extent a change in the public mind. It wanted some one to explain it, and such it found in Archbishop Secker: "Dr. Secker's chief merit," says Bishop Hurd, "and surely it was a very great one, lay in explaining clearly and popularly in his sermons the principles delivered by his friend Dr. Butler in his famous book, the Analogy, and showing the important use of them in religion [g]."

The Queen recommended Butler for a Bishopric, but did not live long enough to see her wishes fulfilled; she died in 1737; but the year after her death the King, mindful of her wishes, preferred him to the See of Bristol [h], to which, in 1750, was joined the Deanery of St. Paul's.

On the death of Archbishop Potter in 1747 the Primacy of all England was offered to, but refused by, Butler, on the ground, it was said, that the state

---

[g] Warburton's Works, i. 69. We hope, however, that its readers would be more appreciative of it than his eccentric nephew, John Butler, to whom he gave a copy, but who exchanged it for an iron vice, which he coveted, in the possession of a neighbour.

[h] We find from his Memoranda that Butler privately administered the Holy Eucharist to the Queen before her death.

of the Church of England was beyond remedy. "He lived[i]," he said, at a time when the "licentiousness of the upper classes combined with the irreligion industriously propagated amongst the lower was tending to produce total profligacy;" when there existed a "levelling spirit upon Atheistical principles;" when "religion was become so very *reasonable* as to have nothing to do with the hearts and affections;" when "in every view of things and upon all accounts irreligion was the chief danger; when to preach love to our enemies was called rant;" when "there was a general decay of religion in the nation observed by every one." But though he refused Canterbury[k], he accepted in 1750, although not unconditionally, the See of Durham. The Lord Lieutenancy had hitherto, inappropriate as it may seem, been held by the occupants of the Palatine See, and these two appointments the Duke of Newcastle now thought of separating. Dr. Butler did not want to go to Durham; he did not seek translation; but if he did accept the See, he said he would not consent that it should be shorn of its honours during his occupancy. The Lord Lieutenancy was not for the time withdrawn from it, and so he accepted the See.

---

[i] Sermons, vol. i.

[k] The nephew alluded to above immediately hastened to London, and offered him £20,000 if he would accept the Primacy.—Bartlett's Memoirs of Butler, p. 98.

Dr. Butler lived to deliver only one Charge (in 1751) to the Clergy of his new Diocese; and at a time when public worship and the outward forms of religion were suffering under a general decay, the Bishop not unreasonably tried to stem the evil by calling their attention to the "importance of external religion." When any evil has to be removed, greater energy displayed, and any path out of the beaten track pursued, the clergyman who tried to find the remedy was then, as now, sure to be accused of Romanism. So it was with the saintly Bishop Wilson; and simply because Butler recommended to his Clergy the use of outward observances to promote piety, a long series of attacks was made upon him as "addicted to superstition and inclined to Popery." The first was made soon after the charge was delivered, in a pamphlet entitled "A serious enquiry into the use and importance of External Religion;" it was published anonymously, but the author was brought to light by Archbishop Secker, and discovered to be the notorious Archdeacon Blackburne.

Bishop Butler died in 1752. In 1767, that is to say fifteen years after his death, the rumour was, for the first time, circulated that he died " in communion with the Church of Rome," a Church "which makes use of Saints, Saints' Days, and all the trumpery of Saint-worship[1]." Archbishop Secker, Bishop Butler's inti-

---

[1] "The Root of Protestant Errors Examined," 1767.

mate friend, well knew the falseness of the accusation, and writing under the name of "Misopseudes," called upon the writer to produce his authority for the "gross and scandalous falsehood [m]." His opponent, writing under the *nom de plume* of "Phileleutherus," supported the charge on the general ground that "there was nothing improbable in it, when it is considered that the same Prelate put up the Popish insignia of the Cross in his Chapel when at Bristol, and in his last Episcopal Charge *has squinted much* towards that superstition." Archbishop Secker thought fit to answer this paper in a second letter, subscribed again "Misopseudes," in which he again defended his friend, if defence was necessary; the Archbishop, however, somewhat irrelevantly and weakly stated his opinion, that in putting up the cross in Bristol the Bishop "did amiss," he himself wishes he had not done it; and then the Archbishop cuts away the ground from under his own feet, and remarks, "Most of our churches have crosses upon them; are they therefore Popish churches? The Lutherans have more than crosses in theirs; are the Lutherans therefore Papists?" The story is instructive in the present day; and the sequel is not less instructive.

[m] Other enemies of Butler wrote under the pseudonyms of "Old Martin," "Latimer," "An Impartial Protestant"—N.B. a person writing under this title is sure to be found the most bigoted and partial of all opponents—"Paulinus," "Misonothus."

Dr. Halifax, Bishop of Gloucester (1781—1789), presumed to take Butler's part, and in consequence he in turn was subjected to the same accusation.

Bishop Butler held views as to the revenues of his See very different from those in vogue at his time. He looked upon himself as a mere trustee for the Church, bound to expend the whole in the maintenance of a *decent figure* suitable to his station, in hospitality and acts of charity. There is a tradition at Bristol that he spent the whole, and more than the whole, of his income on that See[n]: and at Durham he made an equally good use of his money: "Three days a week he entertained the principal gentry in the county and neighbourhood, and the Clergy were always welcome guests at the Palace. When on one occasion a gentleman called upon him for some charitable object, the Bishop asked his steward how much money there was in the house. 'Five hundred pounds, my Lord,' was the answer. 'Five hundred pounds!' exclaimed the Bishop, 'what a shame for a Bishop to have so much money; give it away, give it all to this gentleman for his charitable plan[o].'" No wonder that such a man hated nepotism and regarded only merit; so particular was he in this respect that

---

[n] The sums expended by him at Bristol are estimated at £4,000 and £5,000; and when his friends remonstrated with him he said, "The Deanery of St. Paul's pays for it."

[o] Bartlett's Mem., 197.

one of his nephews, who was considered a *superior* man, but whom the Bishop does not seem to have thought so, said on one occasion to him, " Methinks, my Lord, it is a misfortune to be related to you."

A writer second only to Butler, but inferior to him in every respect as a Bishop, was Warburton. William Warburton (1698—1779) was in 1714 articled to an attorney, but his love of books determined him to seek ordination ; he never went to the University, but was ordained Deacon in 1723 by Archbishop Dawes, although not ordained Priest until 1727, and then by Bishop Gibson of London. Through the interest of Sir Robert Sutton, Warburton obtained first the living of Griesley, afterwards that of Brand-Broughton, and on the occasion of the King's visit to Cambridge in 1728 he obtained an M.A. degree. In 1736 he published his great work, " The Alliance between Church and State [p]," in which he places the Church of England upon a completely different basis from Hooker's, and asserts a position which none but an Erastian would adopt [q]. He speaks of Church

---

[p] Or, "The necessity and equity of an established religion and a test-law demonstrated from the essence and end of civil society upon the fundamental principles of the law of nature and nations."

[q] Even the Dissenting Historian, Dr. Stoughton, says, i. 276, "Nobody, however Erastian, would seriously adopt Warburton's line of argument."

and State as two sovereign and independent powers, which, as they are concerned in contrary provinces, can never meet to clash; both Church and State are benefited by the alliance between them, the Church *receiving an endowment for its ministers*, whilst it exerts its influence for the benefit of the State by promoting virtue and good order. It is, he maintains, the duty of the State to select the strongest as the Established Religion, and as soon as that superiority ceases, then to choose some other sect which is more popular. All sects should have perfect toleration, but not so as to injure the established religion; but Dissenters should not object to "Tests," nor to support the established Church, because the Church is not maintained to teach any particular religious opinions, but for the benefit of the State of which they, as well as Churchmen, are members. This is about the lowest theory of an established Church and of the connection between Church and State which can be well devised; it degrades the Church into a State machine, and lowers the Clergy to the rank of an ecclesiastical police. But this view, having no other authority to rest on, is only valuable as Warburton's opinion. Warburton was a man who had an ingrained love of paradox, and a deep-rooted antipathy to the opinion of others; the authority of the Church he would think only on a par with his own; every one who differed from him was "a fool" or "an ass;" John Wesley was "a hypocrite;" Whitfield was "mad." Warburton was an almost universal reader [r], but perhaps what the great Bentley said of him was true, that "he had a voracious appetite for knowledge, but he doubted whether he had a good digestion [s];" he had the *cacoëthes scribendi*, and would rush into print before he had digested his subject; and there was something which he courted more than utility or truth, viz. fortunate boldness or ingenious error [t]. In 1737 Queen Caroline asked Hare, Bishop of Chichester, to recommend her some one of learning and ability to entertain her with his conversation, and he recommended to her the author of the "Alliance between Church and State." This recommendation was gladly received by the Queen, and she determined to obtain for Warburton a Bishopric, but she died in the following November, and her desire was for the time frustrated.

In 1738 he published against the Deist, Morgan, the first volume of his great work, "The Divine Legation of Moses demonstrated on the principles of a Religious Deist [u]." The omission in the Books of Moses of a future state of reward and punishment had been urged by the Deist, Morgan, as an argument against the truth of Moses's mission. Warburton

---

[r] He took the trouble to learn the Spanish language, in order that he might read Don Quixote in the original.
[s] Cumberland's Mem., i. 40.
[t] Q. R., vii. p. 400.
[u] The second volume appeared in 1741.

admitted the premises and denied the conclusion; he fought Morgan on his own ground, and argued that a system which could dispense with such a doctrine, which was the very cement of human society, must necessarily have come from God. The work caused great alarm, not only on account of the novelty of the hypothesis, but also for an *obiter dictum* which Warburton had made concerning the origin of the book of Job. It was attacked as fiercely (to use his own words) as if it had been "the Divine Legation of Mahomet," and in less than two months he was obliged to publish "A Vindication." But the work as a literary performance has rendered his name immortal, and has placed him at the head, not of "English theology only, but almost of English literature. To the composition of this prodigious performance, Hooker and Stillingfleet could have contributed the erudition, Chillingworth and Locke the acuteness, Taylor an imagination even more wild and copious, Swift, and perhaps Eachard, the sarcastic vein of wit; but what power of understanding, except that of Warburton, could have amassed all these materials, and then compacted them into a bulky and elaborate work so consistent and harmonious[x]?"

---

[x] Quarter. Review. After the appearance of the Divine Legation, Mr. Weston, who had been Head Master of Oakham school, where Warburton was educated, expressed his surprise, for he "had considered that young Warburton at school was the dullest of all dull people."

In 1738 Warburton was appointed Chaplain to the Prince of Wales. When, in 1741 (the year in which he published his second volume of the Divine Legation), he was on a visit to Dr. Conybeare, Dean of Christ Church, it was proposed to confer upon him a D.D. degree; but the degree was refused by Convocation, a slur which Warburton never forgot. In 1746 he was chosen Preacher of Lincoln's Inn; in 1753 Prebendary of Gloucester, in 1754 Chaplain in Ordinary to the King, when, thinking that this new dignity demanded a D.D. degree, he sought and obtained the degree, which had been refused him at Oxford, from Dr. Herring, Archbishop of Canterbury. In 1755 he became a Prebendary of Durham, and in 1757 was appointed to the Deanery of Bristol[y], and on January 20, 1760, he was consecrated Bishop of Gloucester. In 1768 he founded the Lecture, called after him the Warburtonian Lecture, at Lincoln's Inn, to prove the truth of revealed religion in general and of the Christian religion in particular: and he died at Gloucester in 1779, in the eighty-first year of his age.

Dr. Warburton, though a learned, was far from being a model, prelate. He had followers who after

---

[y] In reading himself in, it was observed that Warburton omitted the Athanasian Creed appointed for the day, and although he read it on the following Sunday, when it was not appointed to be read, it was questioned whether he was ever, in legal strictness, Dean of Bristol.—Nich. Lit. An., v. 609.

him were called Warburtonians: but if he had a friend at all it was Bishop Hurd, whose admiration of him was excessive. Warburton never got over the defects of his early life, and the very thing he needed was a University education. His sense of humour was strong but coarse; he did not care how he wounded people, if only he could get his point; his taste seems to have been neither just nor delicate; he and Dr. Lavington, Bishop of Exeter, attacked the Methodists in language which offended every serious mind; Warburton, however, surpasses his brother Bishop in brutality of invective, not to mention his using Scripture with an irreverence approaching to profaneness[2]. Even his biographer, Bishop Hurd, admits that, as a Diocesan, "he did nothing," and for the singular reason that "he knew that nothing was to be done." He resembled in many respects, and was almost as quarrelsome as, the great Bentley, of whom we will presently give a sketch.

We must not forget to say a few words of Warburton's biographer, and the editor of his works, Bishop Hurd. Richard Hurd (1720—1808), whom George III. called "the most naturally polite man he ever knew," the son of a farmer in Staffordshire, graduated at Emmanuel College, Cambridge, of which he became a Fellow. Through a compliment which he paid in his Commentary on the *Ars Poetica*

---

[2] Q. R., vii. 407.

of Horace to Warburton, he laid the foundation of a life-long friendship with him; and in 1750 he was, on Warburton's recommendation, appointed Whitehall Preacher by Bishop Secker. After holding the livings of Thurcaston and Folkton, Hurd was, in 1765, appointed Preacher at Lincoln's Inn; in 1767, Archdeacon of Gloucester by Warburton, and in 1768 Preacher of the first course of the Warburtonian Lectures. In 1775 he was advanced to the See of Lichfield and Coventry, and in the following year he succeeded Dr. Markham as tutor to the Prince of Wales and the Duke of York. In 1781, on the death of Dr. Thomas, and the translation of Dr. Brownlow North to the See of Winchester, Dr. Hurd succeeded the latter as Bishop of Worcester, and was appointed Clerk of the Closet to George III. In 1783, on the death of Archbishop Cornwallis, he was offered, but refused, the Primacy of Canterbury, which was then conferred on Dr. Moore[a].

We learn from the life of Bishop Hurd an account as to how the Church services were at that time performed in the army, from which it appears that the Church in the army laboured under the general apathy of religion. Bishop Hurd asked an officer who was staying at his Palace: "Pray tell me how Divine Service was performed during the siege,

---

[a] Dr. Johnson, who saw the cloven foot in every political opponent, said of him, "I am glad he did not go to Lambeth, for after all I think he is a Whig at heart."

and how many chaplains had you?" "I told him," said the officer, "there was only one, and he was the deputy to the Chaplain of a Scotch Regiment, the 73rd; that he did the duty at seven in the morning to the English regiments according to the Established Church, and afterwards to the 73rd after the Church of Scotland, *to which he belonged*, and that both services were performed off the drum head."

With Hurd everything was Warburton and himself; William Warburton was the first divine, first philosopher, first critic of the day, and Richard Hurd was the second. As an author Hurd was "feebly elegant and coldly panegyrical," even when, as in the case of Warburton, his admiration was excessive. When he tried to commend, as in the case of Secker, the friend of his hero, he could give little more than a damning praise; of Bishop Lowth, the opponent of Warburton, he could speak in terms of measured approbation and comparative, though disguised, contempt: "Dr. Lowth was a man of learning and ingenuity, and of many virtues, but his friends did his character no service by affecting to bring his merits, *whatever they were*, into competition with those of the Bishop of Gloucester (Warburton). His reputation as a writer was raised chiefly in his Hebrew literature, as displayed in two works, his Latin Lectures on Hebrew Poetry, and his English Version of the Prophet Isaiah: the former is well and elegantly composed, but in a vein of criticism not above the common: the latter, I think, is chiefly valuable, as it shows how little is to be expected from Dr. Kennicott's work." On the other hand, Hurd wanted nothing of that spitefulness which is common to the disciples of the Warburtonian school, of that cruel and anatomical malignity, which in dissecting the character of an antagonist can lay bare with "indifference, the quivering fibres of an agonized victim[b]." Though only the son of a farmer, he had a great idea of his own dignity: we are told how when he travelled from Worcester to Bristol hot baths, he went attended by twelve servants; and though the parish church was only a quarter of a mile from Hartlebury Castle, he used to go there in his carriage with his servants in full livery[c]. This, however, could not have been always the case, for an old tradition in Hartlebury still records the good old Bishop walking every Sunday at the head of his household, like a Patriarch of old, to the parish church[d]. And we read how, when he received at his castle his mother, the farmer's wife, he would with "stately courtesy" lead her to the head of the table.

Dr. Zachary Pearce (1690—1774) affords an instance of a Priest who was made a Bishop, and was

---

[b] Dr. Johnson called Hurd, on account of his cold precision, a "word-picker," whilst others for the same reason called him "an old maid in petticoats."
[c] Kilvert's Life of Hurd, p. 200.
[d] Worcester Dioc. Hist., p. 339.

obliged to continue a Bishop, in spite of himself. Educated at the Charterhouse, he graduated at Trinity College, Cambridge, of which he was elected a Fellow, through the interest used with Dr. Bentley by Lord Chief Justice Parker, afterwards Lord Chancellor Macclesfield [e]. In 1720 he was promoted by the Lord Chancellor to the Rectory of St. Bartholomew, near the Exchange; and in 1723 (also by the Chancellor) to St. Martin's-in-the-Fields. Being one of Queen Caroline's favourites, he was recommended by her to Walpole, and was in 1739 (after her death) appointed to the Deanery of Winchester, holding with it the Vicarage of St. Martin's [f]. In 1744 he was appointed Prolocutor of the Lower House of Convocation.

Dr. Pearce was a man who could from his heart cry "Nolo Episcopari," and yet he could not keep out of a Bishopric. Archbishop Potter, in 1746, sounded him upon the subject, and all his Grace could get out of him was, "I will tell your Grace very frankly that I have no thoughts of any Bishopric." Accordingly, when the See of Bangor fell

---

[e] When Pearce went to thank Lord Macclesfield for giving him the living of St. Bartholomew, Exchange, his Lordship said, "You need not thank me, but Dr. Bentley." "How is that, my Lord?" "Why, when I asked Dr. Bentley to make you a Fellow, he consented to do so on the condition that I would promise to *unmake* you as soon as it lay in my power."

[f] The Deanery was worth £600 and St. Martin's £500 a year.

Leading Churchmen of the Period. 479

vacant in 1748, and the Duke of Newcastle offered it to him, he refused it. Thereupon Lord Chancellor Hardwicke thought fit to remonstrate with him: "If Clergymen of learning and merit," he said, "will not accept of Bishoprics, how can the ministers of State be blamed if they are found to fill them with others less deserving?" Pearce saw the force of this reasoning, and consented to accept the See of Bangor.

When Bishop Wilcocks was dying in 1755, Archbishop Herring asked Dr. Pearce if he would accept the See of Rochester, with the Deanery of Westminster, as usual, *in commendam*. He replied, that so far from desiring another Bishopric, he intended to ask the King's leave to resign Bangor; his father, he said, had lately died, and he, as eldest son, had succeeded to his property. Dr. Herring tried to persuade him a second and a third time, but in vain; at length, however, he was induced by the Duke of Newcastle to consent, and accepted the See of Rochester. On the death of Bishop Sherlock in 1761, and again on the death of Bishop Osbaldeston in 1764, he was offered, but refused, the See of London, on the ground that he had always resolved never to accept Canterbury or London, but, on the contrary, he desired to resign the See which he held.

And here comes in a remarkable instance of the great disadvantage to the Church of the then existing relations between Church and State. Being 73 years of age, Bishop Pearce felt he could no longer properly perform his episcopal duties, and requested the King that he might be allowed to resign. He told the King of various instances in which Bishops had resigned their Sees; so the King consulted Lords Mansfield and Northington, who were of opinion that the request might be granted. "Am I then, Sir, to suppose," said the Bishop, "that I have your Majesty's consent?" "Yes," replied the King; and the King held out his hand and the Bishop kissed it as the token of consent.

State reasons, however, against the arrangement soon cropped up; the ministry objected, and the King retracted his promise: the Bishop was obliged to remain Bishop; in 1768, however, he resigned the Deanery, which was double the value of his See, but the Bishopric he was obliged to retain, and he died Bishop of Rochester in 1774[g].

Dr. Horne, Bishop of Norwich, belongs to a later period than that with which we are now engaged, but as he was the advocate and defender of a system of theology which was much in vogue during the earlier period, it seems not unfitting to include him in this chapter. But we must first say a few words

---

[g] Bishop Pearce was principally known as an author from his editions of Longinus and Cicero, and he gave Dr. Johnson considerable help in his Dictionary. Amongst numerous charities he left £5,000 to the College for Clergymen's widows at Bromley.

Leading Churchmen of the Period. 481

as to the "Hutchinsonian" system to which we refer.

John Hutchinson (1674—1737) published in 1724 (with reference to Newton's *Principia*) the first part of *Moses' Principia*, in which he defended the Mosaic cosmogony, and devised a system of physical science utterly at variance with Newton's theory of gravitation. The leading principle of what is called the Hutchinsonian system is that the Hebrew language is not only the primitive language of the human race, but that it was expressly revealed from heaven, and that its *construction* and *radical terms* contain certain hidden truths which are the elements, not only of true religion, but of all rational philosophy. Thus, by a careful study of the language, this philological school thought that it had discovered in the Hebrew roots an important meaning which ran through all the derivative forms, and was the key to the interpretation of Scripture. These crude ideas were (owing to the devout manner in which Hutchinson handled Scripture) for a time so successful as to commend themselves to some pious people, especially at Oxford, who had taken alarm at the atheistical conclusions which they thought to be deducible from the Newtonian doctrines, and who, although they did not necessarily agree in his peculiar etymological views, were strong admirers of Hutchinson's reverential treatment of the Bible.

Such was George Horne (1730—1792), and such

his biographer, William Jones (1726—1800[h]). George Horne[i], born at Otham near Maidstone, where his father was Rector, was at the age of fifteen years elected to a Scholarship at University College, Oxford ; in 1749 he became Fellow, and in 1768 President, of Magdalen. In 1753 he published a spirited defence of the Hutchinsonians in " A .fair, candid, and impartial state of the case between Sir Isaac Newton and Mr. Hutchinson," and thenceforward the charge of being a Hutchinsonian was invidiously applied to him. He remarked in answer to the charge, that it was a hard measure that such names should be applied to Clergymen, "who only preach the doctrines and enforce the duties of Christianity from the Scriptures..." There are many names of this kind now in vogue. If a man preaches Christ, that He is the end of the Law and the fulness of the Gospel, "You need not mind him, he is a Hutchinsonian!" If he mentions the assistance and direction of the Holy Spirit with the necessity of prayer, mortification, and the taking up of the Cross, "O, he is a Methodist!" If he talks of the Divine right of Episcopacy, without a word concerning the danger

---

[h] Commonly known as Jones of Nayland. Educated at the Charterhouse, and University College, Oxford; the author, in 1753, of a "Full Answer to Bishop Clayton's Essay on Spirit ;" and the originator of the " British Critic."

[i] Afterwards "without exception the best preacher in England."—Horne's Life by Jones.

of schism, "Just going over to Popery!" In 1766 Dr. Horne published his principal work, "A Commentary on the Book of Psalms," which speedily gained an immense popularity. His sermons, differing as they did from the cold, undogmatic type then in vogue, and being practical and devotional, marked him out as "the best preacher in England." His rise to the highest posts in the Church was now secured. In 1781 he was appointed Dean of Canterbury, when he wished to resign the Presidency of Magdalen, but the College could not be induced to part with him; and in 1790 Bishop of Norwich. "Report says," wrote a Clergyman at the time, "that the Dean of Canterbury is to be our Bishop." "Yes," was the answer, "so I hear, and I am glad of it, for he will make a truly Christian Bishop." "Indeed," was the rejoinder; "well, I do not know him myself, being a Cambridge man, but it is currently reported at Norwich that he is a Methodist [j]." But Dr. Horne was sixty years of age, and survived his appointment to the Bishopric only two years. "Alas," he exclaimed, as he entered the Episcopal Palace, "I have come to these steps at a time of life when I can neither go up them nor down them with safety." He died in 1792, in his sixty-second year.

---

[j] Stoughton, vol. ii. 63. The epithet "Methodistical" applied to earnest men was at that time a characteristic of the Church of England; in our days the fashion has veered round again, and an earnest Clergyman is a "Papist."

We must now leave such gentle and amiable prelates as Dr. Zachary Pearce and Dr. George Horne, and turn to that turbulent and bellicose priest, Dr. Bentley[k]. Richard Bentley (1662—1742), after being educated at Wakefield school[l], was admitted at the age of fourteen a subsizar at St. John's College, Cambridge, at that time presided over by Dr. Francis Turner, one of the immortal " Seven Bishops." He was afterwards elected a Scholar, but in consequence of a statute limiting the number of Fellows from each county to two, he was ineligible to a Fellowship at that College. After having taken his degree he, together with Hody, became tutor to the son of Stillingfleet, Dean of St. Paul's, whom he accompanied to Oxford, making choice of that University in preference to Cambridge, in order that he might have the benefit of the Bodleian; and it was no doubt through his intercourse with Stillingfleet, with whom he lived from 1683 to 1689, that he was led to devote much of his time to the study of Theology. It does not come within our province to accompany Bentley in his philological pursuits; it must suffice to say that

---

[k] The "Jubar Anglicanum," "Lux Britanniæ," and "Sidus Britannicum," as he was called by foreign scholars.—Scott's Mem. of Jonathan Swift, i. 15.

[l] Bentley established his character as a scholar at Cambridge; during his residence at Oxford, he attracted the attention of the scholars of Europe as an author; under Stillingfleet he became a Theologian.

he soon obtained the reputation of being the first of living English scholars, in fact one of the first Classical scholars in Europe, of that or any other age; but he bore also a prominent place in the theological literature of the eighteenth century. When the Hon. Robert Boyle founded the Lectureship which bears his name, Bentley, at that time only a deacon, but chaplain to Bishop Stillingfleet, was chosen to preach the first course of Lectures for 1692. He took as his subject the "Confutation of Atheism;" and he so successfully applied the discoveries revealed in Sir Isaac Newton's "Principia" to the confirmation of Natural Theology, and to demonstrate the existence of an intelligent and omnipotent Creator, that Atheism was regarded as untenable, or, as Bentley himself not very humbly expresses it, "Atheism henceforward sheltered itself under Deism [m]." Bentley, says Bishop Monk, was the first to explain the irresistible force of these discoveries in the proof of a Deity.

Bentley's success was acknowledged on all sides; the reason why he was not elected to preach the second course of Boyle Lectures is unknown; for some reason or another Kidder, Bishop of Bath and

---

[m] Humility was not Bentley's forte. A nobleman having once remarked to Bishop Stillingfleet, "That Chaplain of yours is a very extraordinary man:" "Yes," was the reply, "if he only had the gift of humility, he would be the most extraordinary man in Europe."

Wells, was the Lecturer in 1693; Bentley, however, was again elected Lecturer for 1694; and so great was his success that the Boyle Lectureship was for a third time offered to, but refused by, him [n].

In 1692 he was preferred by Bishop Stillingfleet to a stall in Worcester Cathedral, and the next year to the keepership of the Royal Library at St. James's. At this period took place the celebrated Boyle controversy between Bentley and the Hon. Charles Boyle, afterwards Earl of Orrery, as to the genuineness of the Epistles of Phalaris: Bentley exposed their spuriousness, Boyle defended them; the victory is now awarded to Bentley, but Boyle, assisted, as was supposed, by Atterbury, conducted his case with so much wit and humour, that the public were for a time biassed in his favour; but Bentley's Dissertation on Phalaris, a work of profound learning [o], cut away the ground from under his opponent's feet.

In 1699 Dr. Montague, the Master of Trinity College, Cambridge, having been appointed by the Crown to the Deanery of Durham, Bentley, though a member of St. John's College, was nominated by the Commissioners whom King William, on the death of Mary, had appointed for ecclesiastical appointments,

---

[n] Monk's Bentley.

[o] Of this work Professor Porson spoke as "that immortal Dissertation."

to succeed him as Master. Trinity had at that time fallen from its high estate, not more, perhaps, than other colleges—for the memories of Barrow, Pearson, and Newton were still fresh upon it—yet because its height had been greater than others its fall seemed more apparent. As thoughts were entertained of sending the young Duke of Gloucester to Trinity, Bentley was selected as a suitable Master; but not long after his election troubles broke out, and for thirty-eight years the college became a scene of turbulence and litigation; Bentley's life was an almost incessant course of quarrels, in which he was always wrong, yet always came off victorious. In 1714 the college, in hopes of getting rid of him, had recourse to the last resort, an appeal to Dr. More, Bishop of Ely, as Visitor of the college: Bentley refused to recognise the Bishop's authority, and alleged that the Crown was the Visitor; the Crown lawyers, after a trial which lasted six weeks, decided against Bentley, and in favour of the Bishop's jurisdiction; the Bishop prepared a sentence of ejectment against him, but before it was executed the Bishop died [p].

But this was only the commencement of quarrels; Dr. Bentley still continued to rule the college with despotic although contested authority. In 1718 he

---

[p] After his death his written judgment was found, "We remove Richard Bentley from his office of Master of the College."

was deprived of his degrees by the University for having failed to appear, in obedience to a decree, before the Vice-Chancellor's Court at the suit of Conyers Middleton; but in 1724 the University was compelled, by a legal process, to restore to him his degrees. In 1733 he was again brought to trial at Ely House, before Dr. Greene, Bishop of Ely, and sentenced to be deprived of the Mastership; but again there was a hitch; again Bentley got off; the victory ultimately rested with him, and in 1742 he died Master of Trinity in the eighty-first year of his age.

Dr. Bentley was Archdeacon of Ely [q], and Regius Professor of Divinity at Cambridge, and the Church had a narrow escape of having him for a Bishop. On the vacancy of Chichester in 1709, before the quarrels at Trinity, although they were on the eve of commencing, had actually begun, strong influence, supported especially by Dr. More, Bishop of Ely, in favour of Bentley was brought to bear, but happily without success, on the Queen herself. When Bristol was vacant in the following year, Bentley was spoken of for that See, but whether Bentley considered (as it was said) the stipend insufficient to support the dignity of a Bishop, or in consequence of the great agitation which was just commencing, the See was not filled up till the great revolution that fol-

---

[q] Appointed in 1701.

lowed the Sacheverell business, and then it was conferred on Dr. Robinson.

Time would fail us to make more than a passing mention of such names as those of Bishop John Conybeare (1692—1755), elected in 1730 Rector of Exeter College, Oxford, in 1732 Dean of Christ Church, in 1750 Bishop of Bristol; who wrote, in 1732, against Tindal's "Christianity as old as the Creation" his "Defence of Revealed Religion," one of the ablest vindications of Revealed Religion which the Church has ever produced;—of Dr. William Wall (1646—1728), who wrote, in 1707, the famous "History of Infant Baptism;" of Dean Humphrey Prideaux (1648—1724), the author of the "Connexion of the History of the Old and New Testaments," who, in 1702, was appointed Dean of Norwich. Enough has been written to show that during the period with which we are now concerned there was a number of divines possessed of intellect and learning rarely equalled, never surpassed, in the Church of England, and more than a match for the most formidable assailants of Christianity.

For the last, but not the lowest, place, as holding a different position from other Bishops in the Church, we have reserved the model Bishop of that or any other period, him whom men of all schools of thought agree to honour as "the good" Bishop Wilson.

Thomas Wilson (1663—1756), born at Burton, in the County Palatine of Chester, on December 20,

1663, was educated at Trinity College, Dublin (which at that time was much patronized by families from Lancashire and Cheshire), on an allowance of £20 a year. In 1686 he was ordained Deacon, and appointed to the curacy of Winwick in Lancashire, of which his maternal uncle, Dr. Sherlock, was the Rector. Having thus received the small addition to his income of £50 a year, he determined to increase his charities. " I have hitherto," he says, in a memorandum, "given but one-tenth of my income to the poor; I do purpose, and I thank God for putting it into my heart, that all the profits which it shall please God to give me, and which shall become due to me after the 6th August next (after which time I hope to have paid my small debts), I do purpose to separate the fifth part of all my incomes, as I shall receive them, for pious purposes, and particularly for the poor."

In 1692 the Earl of Derby appointed him his domestic chaplain and tutor to his only son, Lord Strange, with whom he travelled abroad for three years [r]. The See of Sodor and Man had been vacant for four years, ever since the death of the late Bishop, Dr. Baptist Levinz; and at last Archbishop Sharp, in whose province the See was, complained to

---

[r] An anecdote is related stating how, when his pupil was about to sign a paper which he had not read, the tutor dropped some burning sealing-wax on his finger as a lesson to him never to act so incautiously.

the King; the King insisted that Lord Derby, in whom the appointment lay, should at once fill up the See, or that he would himself appoint the Bishop. Lord Derby accordingly offered it to Mr. Wilson; in fact (to use his own expression), he "was forced into the Bishopric," and was consecrated a Bishop on January 16, 1697, at the Savoy Church, by Archbishop Sharp and the Bishops of Chester and Norwich. On his arrival in his new diocese he found the palace, which had not been inhabited for eight years, in a state of ruin, which put him to the expense of £1,400; in order to enable him to meet which expense Lord Derby offered him the Living of Battesworth; but although his Bishopric was only worth £300 a year, and it had been the custom of his predecessors to hold with it a Living *in commendam*, he resolved never to hold two preferments with cure of souls. In 1698 he married.

Dr. Wilson now thoroughly entered on the duties of his diocese with that patriarchal simplicity which distinguished the whole of his episcopate. He was distressed that the expenses he had incurred compelled him for a time to diminish his charities, but he always considered that the money he derived from the Church belonged to the Church, of which he was only the steward. Much poverty at the time prevailed in the Island, to relieve which he always kept what he called "the poor's drawer," in which was deposited at first a tenth, then a fifth, then a third, and at last half his income. He also kept a "poor's chest" for corn and meal, which he often inspected to see that it was filled to the brim, for the poor and needy; and when it was meted out he gave instructions to his steward "not to stroke it, but give full measure." He personally enquired into the circumstances and wants of his people; he even kept a stock of spectacles for the aged poor that they might be able to read their Bibles: people, it was said, sometimes outwitted the Bishop, but he was wont to say, "I would rather give to ten unworthy, than one deserving object should go away without relief."

He was particularly careful in his dealings with the Clergy. He watched their conduct and directed their studies previous to their ordination, and afterwards he would keep them a whole year in his house in order to train and advise them for their work; he held frequent Synods, and addressed to his Clergy Pastoral Letters of advice.

With the assistance of Dr. Bray he established parochial libraries in the Island; in 1699 he issued a tract on the "Principles and Duties of Christianity," the first work ever printed in the Manx language; in the same year he published in that language the Church Catechism; and in February, 1703, he, together with the Archdeacon, Vicars General, and Clergy, drew up those Ecclesiastical Constitutions which made his diocese the model diocese of the day. We must give one of these Constitutions at length, in order to show the method he adopted (the nearest approach in modern times to primitive discipline) for the suppression of vice:—" For the more effectual discouragement of vice, if any person shall incur the censures of the Church, and having done penance shall afterwards incur the same censures, he shall not be admitted to do penance again (as has been formerly accustomed) until the Church be fully satisfied of his sincere repentance; during which time he shall not presume to come within the church, but be obliged to stand, in a decent manner, at the church-door, every Sunday and Holyday, the whole time of morning and evening service, until, by his penitent behaviour and other instances of sober living, he deserve and procure a certificate from the Minister, Churchwarden, and some of the soberest men of the parish, to the satisfaction of the Ordinary; which if he do not so deserve and procure within three months, the Church shall proceed to excommunication; and that during these proceedings the governor shall be applied to not to permit him to leave the island. . . . And whenever any daring offender shall be, and continue, so obstinate as to incur excommunication, the pastor shall affectionately exhort his parishioners not to converse with him, upon peril of being partakers with him in his sin and punishment."

The effect of these constitutions was that for twenty

years the spiritual condition of the diocese sensibly improved: the number of the Clergy increased, new churches and new schools were built, the laity were impressed with the duties of their faith, so that Lord Chancellor King said, "If the ancient discipline of the Church were lost, it might be found in all its purity in the Isle of Man."

But another Earl of Derby arose, who not only appointed another governor (Captain Horne) and another Archdeacon (Horrobin), with the express purpose of counteracting the work of the good Bishop, but also caused several pernicious works, notably one styled the "Independent Whig," to be circulated in the Island, "ridiculing the Clergy of all religions, the Sacraments, the Holy Scriptures, and all God's Ordinances[1]." Captain Horne did all he could to oppose the Bishop, and to impede that ecclesiastical discipline which would have been so useful in checking the spread of these objectionable publications. A personal grievance was not long wanting to the governor.

In 1719 the governor's wife having been found guilty of slandering a widow of good character living in the Island, the Bishop ordered that she should be refused the Holy Communion until she had asked forgiveness for the great wrong she had done. The Archdeacon, however, in order to please the

---

[1] Keble's Life of Wilson, p. 500.

governor and to oppose the Bishop, admitted her to Communion, and was in consequence suspended by the Bishop *ab officio et beneficio*. The Archdeacon, instead of appealing to the Metropolitan, applied to the Civil power; and the governor subjected the Bishop and the Vicars General to a trial, "during which they were treated in the most contemptuous manner imaginable, and for several hours were made to stand like criminals at the bar." The result was that the Bishop was fined £50 and his two Vicars General £20 each; and when they refused to pay this "arbitrary and unjust imposition [t]," they were, on St. Peter's Day, 1722, conveyed to Castle Rushin, where they were confined for nine weeks in a damp and unwholesome cell, in which the Bishop contracted a disorder which deprived him ever afterwards of the free use of his right hand, and no one was allowed to visit them. But "the concern of the people was so great that they assembled in crowds, and it was with difficulty they were restrained from pulling down the governor's house by the mild behaviour and persuasion of the Bishop, who was permitted to speak to them only through a grated window, or address them from the walls of the prison, whence he blessed and exhorted hundreds of them daily [u]."

---

[t] Cruttwell's Life of Wilson, p. 117.
[u] The Bishop used to tell his friends afterwards that he

After he had been kept nine weeks in prison, the proceedings of the governor were reversed, as arbitrary and unjust, by the King in Council; and the Bishop's memorandum of August 31 contains the words, "Discharged out of prison." "The day of his release was a day of general jubilee throughout the Island. Persons from all parts of the country assembled to welcome back their revered Pastor, once more restored to the light of day.... Old and young, rich and poor, broke forth into acclamations of joy, and formed such a procession as had never before been witnessed. The populace wished to spread their clothes under the Bishop's feet when he came out of the Castle [x]."

But the costs of the proceedings entailed upon the Bishop expenses which he could ill afford. In vain he was advised to prosecute the governor to recover damages; in vain the King, in order to reimburse him, offered him the See of Exeter, vacated by the translation of Bishop Blackburne to York. The good Bishop would not desert his flock; but determined, though persecuted, to stand by his diocese; it appears that the appointment of his successor would not, as in ordinary cases, rest with the Crown, and he

---

"never governed the diocese so well as in the time of his imprisonment." It was during his imprisonment that he formed the plan of translating the Scriptures into the Manx language.

[x] Stowell, p. 177.

feared the kind of successor which would be sent from Knowsley. When he refused the See of Exeter, the King promised to defray his expenses out of the Privy purse; but "the King going soon afterwards to Hanover, and dying before his return, this promise never was fulfilled [y]." The only recompense he received was a sum of £300, not a sixth part of his expenses, through a subscription raised by the Archbishop of York.

Bishop Wilson, restored from prison to his diocese, never relaxed his discipline. Church discipline had indeed, through the opposition of the civil authorities, received a rude shock; evil doers are naturally not indisposed to shake off the shackles which the censures of the Church impose upon them. So in the Isle of Man "offenders appear ofttimes to have braved out this sentence; the awful name of excommunication appears more frequently, but with less effect." Still, "from 1720 to 1736, the number of persons dealt with as subjects of the Manx Church criminal discipline, mostly in the Chapter and Consistory Courts, appears to be not less than 1450:" gradually the causes that required the discipline grew less frequent; so that from 1736 to 1755 the number of names is only about 68 [z].

On May 25, 1727, Archdeacon Horrobin resigned his Living in the Isle of Man, and found a patron in

---

[y] Cruttwell's Life of Wilson. [z] Keble, 690 and 816.

Bishop Hoadly, by whom he was collated to a Living in the diocese of Salisbury [a].

In 1735 Bishop Wilson paid his last visit to England, where his name and reputation gained him honour from all quarters. Wherever he went the people knelt and asked his blessing. He appeared at Court in his usual simple dress, and with a small skull-cap on his head, his shoes fastened with leather thongs instead of buckles, his silvery hair flowing down upon his shoulders; the King (George II.) was so struck with his venerable appearance, that he rose to meet him, and taking him by the hand requested him, "My Lord, I ask your prayers." The Queen turned to several Bishops who were present at the levee, and said, "See here, my Lords, is a Bishop who does not come for translation [b];" she desired, but in vain, to keep him in England; no prospect of a Bishopric, no increase of income, could induce him to forsake his diocese.

Bishop Wilson had intended to translate the Scriptures into the Manx language, but he lived to complete only the Gospel of St. Matthew. On the death of the Earl of Derby [c], the Lordship of the Isle of Man passed into the family of the Duke of Athol. The

---

[a] Keble, p. 664.   [b] Stowell's Life of Wilson.
[c] In 1765, in consequence of illicit practices which were carried on there, the Island passed by Act of Parliament to the Crown of England.

good Bishop Wilson died on March 7, 1756, and Mark Hildesley (1698—1772)[d], a man like-minded, and who made it his endeavour to follow in the steps of his predecessor (although, as he lamented, "haud passibus æquis"), was selected by the Duke of Athol to succeed him. He at once set himself, with the help of the Society for Promoting Christian Knowledge, to carry out the arduous work commenced by Bishop Wilson, of translating the Bible into the Manx language. His one wish was to live long enough to see the completion of the work. On November 28, 1772, he received the last part of the translation, and sung "Nunc, Domine, dimittis;" two days afterwards he was seized with a stroke of apoplexy, and died on December 7.

Bishop Wilson, after having held the See of Sodor and Man for fifty-eight years, died in the ninety-third year of his age. But the memory of the "good" Bishop has never died; his "Sacra Privata" is a book which bears the impress of his piety; for years afterwards his name was held in the greatest veneration, and the aged Clergy of the diocese would, with tears of affection in their eyes, recount his many virtues. A High Churchman, he was broad in his sympathy and love. Everybody loved Bishop Wilson. Churchmen were proud of him; Dissenters, Quakers, even

---

[d] Educated at the Charterhouse, afterwards Fellow of Trinity College, Cambridge.

Roman Catholics, often attended Church to hear him preach. Wherever he went, people would flock around him to ask his blessing. Nor was the feeling confined to his diocese, or to England. Cardinal Fleury said he believed that he and Bishop Wilson were the two poorest Bishops in Europe; he came over from France to visit him, and asked the Bishop to visit him in return in France: in such esteem did he hold him, that he obtained an order from his government that no French privateers should ravage the coasts of the Isle of Man[e].

---

[e] Cruttwell, Stowell, Keble.

END OF VOL. I.

Printed by Parker and Co., Crown Yard, Oxford.

www.ingramcontent.com/pod-product-compliance
Lightning Source LLC
Chambersburg PA
CBHW051158300426
44116CB00006B/352